Common Interests, Uncommon Goals

Histories of the World Council of
Comparative Education Societies
and its Members

CERC Studies in Comparative Education

21. Vandra Masemann, Mark Bray & Maria Manzon (eds.) (2007): *Common Interests, Uncommon Goals: Histories of the World Council of Comparative Education Societies and its Members*. ISBN 13: 978-962-8093-10-6. 384pp. HK$250/US$38.

20. Peter D. Hershock, Mark Mason & John N. Hawkins (eds.) (2007): *Changing Education: Leadership, Innovation and Development in a Globalizing Asia Pacific*. ISBN 13: 978-962-8093-54-0. 348pp. HK$200/US$32.

19. Mark Bray, Bob Adamson & Mark Mason (eds.) (2007): *Comparative Education Research: Approaches and Methods*. ISBN 10: 962-8093-53-3; ISBN 13: 978-962-8093-53-3. 444pp. HK$250/US$38.

18. Aaron Benavot & Cecilia Braslavsky (eds.) (2006): *School Knowledge in Comparative and Historical Perspective: Changing Curricula in Primary and Secondary Education*. ISBN 10: 962-8093-52-5; ISBN 13: 978-962-8093-52-6. 315pp. HK$200/US$32.

17. Ruth Hayhoe (2006): *Portraits of Influential Chinese Educators*. ISBN 10: 962-8093-40-1; ISBN 13: 978-962-8093-40-3. 398pp. HK$250/US$38.

16. Peter Ninnes & Meeri Hellstén (eds.) (2005): *Internationalizing Higher Education: Critical Explorations of Pedagogy and Policy*. ISBN 962-8093-37-1. 231pp. HK$200/US$32.

15. Alan Rogers (2004): *Non-Formal Education: Flexible Schooling or Participatory Education?* ISBN 962-8093-30-4. 316pp. HK$200/US$32.

14. W.O. Lee, David L. Grossman, Kerry J. Kennedy & Gregory P. Fairbrother (eds.) (2004): *Citizenship Education in Asia and the Pacific: Concepts and Issues*. ISBN 962-8093-59-2. 313pp. HK$200/US$32.

13. Mok Ka-Ho (ed.) (2003): *Centralization and Decentralization: Educational Reforms and Changing Governance in Chinese Societies*. ISBN 962-8093-58-4. 230pp. HK$200/US$32.

12. Robert A. LeVine (2003): *Childhood Socialization: Comparative Studies of Parenting, Learning and Educational Change*. ISBN 962-8093-61-4. 299pp. HK$200/US$32.

11. Ruth Hayhoe & Julia Pan (eds.) (2001): *Knowledge Across Cultures: A Contribution to Dialogue Among Civilizations*. ISBN 962-8093-73-8. 391pp. HK$250/US$38.

10. William K. Cummings, Maria Teresa Tatto & John Hawkins (eds.) (2001): *Values Education for Dynamic Societies: Individualism or Collectivism*. ISBN 962-8093-71-1. 312pp. HK$200/US$32.

9. Gu Mingyuan (2001): *Education in China and Abroad: Perspectives from a Lifetime in Comparative Education*. ISBN 962-8093-70-3. 252pp. HK$200/US$32.

8. Thomas Clayton (2000): *Education and the Politics of Language: Hegemony and Pragmatism in Cambodia, 1979-1989*. ISBN 962-8093-83-5. 243pp. HK$200/US$32.

7. Mark Bray & Ramsey Koo (eds.) (2004): *Education and Society in Hong Kong and Macao: Comparative Perspectives on Continuity and Change*. Second edition. ISBN 962-8093-34-7. 323pp. HK$200/US$32.

6. T. Neville Postlethwaite (1999): *International Studies of Educational Achievement: Methodological Issues*. ISBN 962-8093-86-X. 86pp. HK$100/US$20.

5. Harold Noah & Max A. Eckstein (1998): *Doing Comparative Education: Three Decades of Collaboration*. ISBN 962-8093-87-8. 356pp. HK$250/US$38.

4. Zhang Weiyuan (1998): *Young People and Careers: A Comparative Study of Careers Guidance in Hong Kong, Shanghai and Edinburgh*. ISBN 962-8093-89-4. 160pp. HK$180/US$30.

3. Philip G. Altbach (1998): *Comparative Higher Education: Knowledge, the University, and Development*. ISBN 962-8093-88-6. 312pp. HK$180/US$30.

2. Mark Bray & W.O. Lee (eds.) (1997): *Education and Political Transition: Implications of Hong Kong's Change of Sovereignty*. ISBN 962-8093-90-8. 169pp. [Out of print]

1. Mark Bray & W.O. Lee (eds.) (2001): *Education and Political Transition: Themes and Experiences in East Asia*. Second edition. ISBN 962-8093-84-3. 228pp. HK$200/US$32.

Order through bookstores or from:

Comparative Education Research Centre
Faculty of Education, The University of Hong Kong, Pokfulam Road, Hong Kong, China.
Fax: (852) 2517 4737; E-mail: cerc@hkusub.hku.hk; Website: www.hku.hk/cerc

The list prices above are applicable for order from CERC, and include sea mail postage. For air mail postage costs, please contact CERC.

No. 7 in the series and Nos. 13-15 are co-published with Kluwer Academic Publishers and the Comparative Education Research Centre of the University of Hong Kong. Books from No. 16 onwards are co-published with Springer. Springer publishes hardback versions.

CERC Studies in Comparative Education 21

Common Interests, Uncommon Goals

Histories of the World Council of Comparative Education Societies and its Members

Edited by
Vandra Masemann, Mark Bray & Maria Manzon

Springer   **Comparative Education Research Centre**
The University of Hong Kong

Comparative Education Research Centre
Faculty of Education, The University of Hong Kong
Pokfulam Road, Hong Kong, China

Cover design by Vincent Lee.
Type-setting, layout and index by Emily Mang.

Contents

III: Lessons from the Histories

List of Tables

List of Figures

Abbreviations

AACTE	American Association of Colleges of Teacher Education
AAEC	Asociación Argentina de Educación Comparada
ACER	Australian Council for Educational Research
ACES	Australian Comparative Education Society
ACIES	Australian Comparative and International Education Society
ADEA	Association for the Development of Education in Africa
ADECE	Association pour le développement des échanges et de la comparaison en éducation
AERA	American Education Research Association
AESA	American Educational Studies Association
AFDECE	Association française pour le développement de l'éducation comparée et des échanges
AFEC	Association francophone d'éducation comparée
AICES	Australian and International Comparative Education Society
AIF	Agence intergouvernementale de la francophonie
AISEC	Asociación Iberoamericana de Sociedades de Educación Comparada
ANPAE	Associação Nacional de Política e Administração da Educação
ANZCIES	Australian and New Zealand Comparative and International Education Society
ANZHES	Australian and New Zealand History of Education Society
APC	Asociación de Pedagogos de Cuba
APC-SEC	Asociación de Pedagogos de Cuba (Sección de Educación Comparada)
BAICE	British Association for International and Comparative Education
BALID	British Association for Literacy in Development
BATROE	British Association of Teachers and Researchers in Overseas Education
BCES	Bulgarian Comparative Education Society
BCES	British Comparative Education Society (1979-83)
BCIES	British Comparative and International Education Society
BEd	Bachelor of Education
BERA	British Educational Research Association
BNU	Beijing Normal University
CCEK	Council on Comparative Education of Kazakhstan
CCES	Chinese Comparative Education Society
CCES-T	Chinese Comparative Education Society-Taipei
CEDE	Centro Europeo dell'Educazione
CER	*Comparative Education Review*

CERC	Comparative Education Research Centre, The University of Hong Kong
CERN	Citizenship Education Research Network
CES	Comparative Education Society
CES	Comparative Education Section (of a larger society)
CESA	Comparative Education Society of Asia
CES-CPS	Comparative Education Section - Czech Pedagogical Society
CES-CSPS	Comparative Education Section - Czechoslovak Pedagogical Society
CESE	Comparative Education Society in Europe
CESHK	Comparative Education Society of Hong Kong
CESI	Comparative Education Society of India
CESP	Comparative Education Society of the Philippines
CIDA	Canadian International Development Agency
CIDEC	Comparative, International and Development Education Centre
CIE	*Canadian and International Education*
CIEP	Centre international d'études pédagogiques
CIES	Comparative and International Education Society
CIESC	Comparative and International Education Society of Canada
CIS	Commonwealth of Independent States
CMAEC	Conseil mondial des associations d'éducation comparée
CMSEC	Conseil mondial des sociétés d'éducation comparée
CNIER	China National Institute of Educational Research
CONICYT	Council for the Advancement of Science and Technology
CPC	Communist Party of China
CPS	Czech Pedagogical Society
CRHES	Collectif de recherche sur les situations de handicap, l'éducation et les sociétés
CSE	Chinese Society of Education
CSPS	Czechoslovak Pedagogical Society
CSSAE	Canadian Society for Studies in Adult Education
CSSE	Canadian Society for the Study of Education
CSSHE	Canadian Society for the Study of Higher Education
CUHK	Chinese University of Hong Kong
CYC	Company of Young Canadians
CUSO	Canadian University Service Overseas
DFID	Department for International Development (UK)
DGfE	Deutsche Gesellschaft für Erziehungswissenschaft
EASA	Education Association of South Africa
ECEEAS	Egyptian Comparative Education and Educational Administration Society
ECNU	East China Normal University

EGCE	Egyptian Group of Comparative Education
EPICE	Institut européen pour la promotion et l'innovation de la culture dans l'éducation
EU	European Union
GCES	Greek Comparative Education Society
GDR	German Democratic Republic
HES	History of Education Society
HKERA	Hong Kong Educational Research Association
HKU	The University of Hong Kong
HKUST	Hong Kong University of Science and Technology
HPS	Hungarian Pedagogical Society
HPS-CES	Hungarian Pedagogical Society (Comparative Education Section)
HU	Hebei University
IAER	Israeli Association for Educational Research
IAIE	International Association for Intercultural Education
IBE	UNESCO International Bureau of Education
ICCE	International Committee of Comparative Education
ICE	Instituto de Ciencias de la Educación
ICES	Israel Comparative Education Society
ICT	Information and Communications Technologies
IDRC	International Development Research Centre
IEA	International Association for the Evaluation of Educational Achievement
IEEPS	Institut européen d'éducation et de politique sociale
IEPR	Institute for Educational and Psychological Research
IERD	Institute for Educational Research and Development
IEY	International Education Year
ILO	International Labour Organisation
IRE	*International Review of Education*
ISCAE	International Society of Comparative Adult Education
ISCPES	International Society for Comparative Physical Education and Sport
JCES	Japan Comparative Education Society
JDS	John Dewey Society
JICA	Japan International Cooperation Agency
KATEE	Centres of Advanced Technical and Vocational Education
KCES	Korean Comparative Education Society
KEA	Kenton Education Association
KNUE	Korea National University of Education
KPC	Katholiek Pedagogisch Centrum
KSSE	Korean Society for the Study of Education
KVEDGE	Kommission für Vergleichende Erziehungswissenschaft in der Deutschen Gesellschaft für Erziehungswissenschaft

LACE	London Association of Comparative Educationists
MA	Master of Arts
MESCE	Mediterranean Society of Comparative Education
NCATE	National Council for Accreditation of Teacher Education
NENU	Northeast Normal University
NGO	Non-governmental Organisation
NGVO	Nederlandstalig Genootschap voor Vergelijkende Studie van Opvoeding en Onderwijs
NIER	National Institute for Educational Research (Japan)
NOCIES	Nordic Comparative and International Education Society
NSCTE	National Society of College Teachers of Education
ODM	Overseas Development Ministry (UK)
OECD	Organisation for Economic Co-operation and Development
OEI	Organización de Estados Iberoamericanos
OIF	Organisation internationale de la francophonie
OISE	Ontario Institute for Studies in Education
OPIET	Operational Program for Initial Education and Training
PCES	Polish Comparative Education Society
PES	Philosophy of Education Society
PESA	Philosophy of Education Society of Australia
PIRLS	Progress in Reading Literacy Study
PISA	Programme of International Student Assessment
PRC	People's Republic of China
RAE	Russian Academy of Education
RCCE	Russian Council of Comparative Education
RCCP	Russian Council of Comparative Pedagogics
REDCOM	Réseau européen de dissémination en éducation comparée
REEC	*Revista Española de Educación Comparada*
RICE	Research Information for International and Comparative Education
ROC	Republic of China
SAANZ	Sociology Association of Australia and New Zealand
SACHES	Southern African Comparative and History of Education Society
SAECE	Sociedad Argentina de Estudios Comparados en Educación
SASE	Southern African Society of Education
SBEC	Sociedade Brasileira de Educação Comparada
SCCE	Soviet Council of Comparative Education
SCCP	Scientific Council on Comparative Pedagogics
SCNU	South China Normal University
SEEC	Sociedad Española de Educación Comparada
SEPC	Sociedad Española de Pedagogía Comparada
SICESE	Sezione Italiana della CESE
SIG	Special Interest Group

SIIVE	Section for International and Intercultural Comparative Education
SIIVEDGE	Sektion International und Interkulturell Vergleichende Erziehungswissenschaft in der Deutschen Gesellschaft für Erziehungswissenschaft
SOMEC	Sociedad Mexicana de Educación Comparada
SPE	Society of Professors of Education
SPS	Slovak Pedagogical Society
SRAPS	SACHES Research and Publications Scheme
SSHRC	Social Sciences and Humanities Research Council
TCES	Turkish Comparative Education Society
TCIES	Thailand Comparative and International Education Society
TIMMS	Third International Mathematics and Science Study
TVET	Technical and Vocational Education and Training
UAT	Universidad Autónoma de Tamaulipas
UCLA	University of California at Los Angeles
UDEM	Universidad de Monterrey
UGC	University Grants Committee
UIE	UNESCO Institute for Education
UK	United Kingdom
UKFIET	United Kingdom Forum for International Education and Training
UN	United Nations
UNE	University of New England
UNED	Universidad Nacional de Educación a Distancia
UNESCO	United Nations Educational, Scientific and Cultural Organization
UNEVOC	UNESCO International Centre for Technical and Vocational Education and Training
UREAG	Under-Represented Ethnic and Ability Groups
US	United States
USA	United States of America
USSR	Union of Soviet Socialist Republics
VSO	Voluntary Service Overseas
WCCES	World Council of Comparative Education Societies
WCEFA	World Conference on Education for All
WTO	World Trade Organisation

Acknowledgements

This book of histories has its own history, in which many people took part either wittingly or unwittingly. We wish first to thank those who originally had the idea for this book and tried to get it underway. They include Namgi Park, who first suggested it in a 1997 meeting of the WCCES Executive Committee; Raymond Ryba, who had intended to undertake the project and who kept meticulous archival files which helped us to do it; Nikolay Popov, who gave enthusiastic encouragement and who was the first to finish his society's chapter; and David Wilson, who in 1999 invited the WCCES Executive Committee to adopt the idea, who persuaded Edmund King to head the project until he was no longer able to do so, and who himself spearheaded the project for several years and wrote several papers on the history of the field. We also thank Annemarie Ryba for assiduously sorting and packing Raymond's files after his death, and for sending them to Toronto where David Wilson and Vandra Masemann used them when writing their chapters.

Kent State University, USA, where Gerald Read spent most of his professional career, is home to the official WCCES archives. The opportunity to keep the archives at Kent State University Library arose from the initiative of Kim Sebaly. We thank the two Heads of its Department of Special Collections and Archives, Nancy Birk and Cara Gilgenbach, who have cared for these archives and made them available for perusal. We also thank Erwin H. Epstein of Loyola University, USA, for his interest, his careful attention to matters of constitutional history, and his encouragement for us to finish the book.

For the individual chapters, we are very grateful to all the authors and their colleagues for finding and organising their files and for researching the histories of their WCCES Presidencies or their societies. We appreciate their patience and forbearance in the long editorial process. We also thank Anne Hamori, the first Secretary General of the officially-constituted WCCES, for granting us a personal interview and giving us her recollections of the early history of the WCCES.

At the University of Hong Kong (HKU) many people, particularly in the Comparative Education Research Centre (CERC), worked in various ways to bring this work to fruition. Mark Mason, the CERC Director, provided constant encouragement and included the book in the series 'CERC Studies in Comparative Education'; the HKU Strategic Research Theme funded Vandra Masemann's visit to Hong Kong in 2005 to meet with Mark Bray and Maria Manzon for work on the book; and the Sik Sik Yuen Education Research Fund financed interviews conducted by Maria Manzon for this project. We also thank Wu Shuchen, Mitsuko Maeda and Andrey Uroda who assisted with bibliographic references in German, Japanese and Russian. We thank Vincent Lee for his work on the cover; and, perhaps most of all, we thank Emily Mang for her technical expertise, the index, and her constant cheerful support.

Specific acknowledgements are due to individuals who shared from their personal collections the photographs in Chapter 30. They are Anne Hamori (Picture 1), Japan Comparative Education Society (Picture 2), Vandra Masemann (Pictures 3, 4, 6 and 9), Erwin H. Epstein (Picture 5), Anne Hickling-Hudson (Picture 7), Hu Jingfei (Picture 8), and Emily Mang (Picture 10).

We are filled with a great sense of appreciation for the contributions of many scholars, named and unnamed in this book, who have made comparative education such a rewarding field of study and practice. We dedicate this book to all of those who came before us and to all of those who will succeed us in the field.

Series Editor's Foreword

It is with great pleasure that I welcome this book as a significant addition to the *CERC Studies in Comparative Education* Series. The book is both about the field of comparative education, and at the same time explicitly comparative itself. In the editors' words, it "compares the comparers": it shows ways in which the field of comparative education has varied in different parts of the world, and it portrays instructive changes over time. The book offers an illuminating account of the factors that have influenced the shape of the field of comparative education in different locations, cultures and language groups, and thus has broad significance for the field.

The Comparative Education Research Centre (CERC) at the University of Hong Kong has had a special relationship with the World Council of Comparative Education Societies (WCCES). CERC began to play a role when its then Director, Mark Bray, was Assistant Secretary General of the WCCES in the second half of the 1990s. CERC set up the WCCES website at that time, and assisted with various organisational matters. Then, during the period 2000 to 2005, CERC hosted the WCCES Secretariat, becoming a hub for WCCES operation, with Emily Mang providing excellent support. Bob Adamson, my immediate predecessor as CERC Director, was among the people who worked actively in the Secretariat. He held the formal position of WCCES Assistant Secretary General (2002-05), and was followed by Maria Manzon (2005). Close links between CERC and the WCCES continued after 2005, including the hosting in early 2007 of a meeting of the WCCES Executive Committee in conjunction with the annual conference of the Comparative Education Society of Hong Kong (CESHK) and the biennial conference of the Comparative Education Society of Asia (CESA).

I am also proud to introduce this book in my capacity as President of the CESHK, which is one of the WCCES member societies. The WCCES has given the CESHK a global voice and a network of related societies. The CESHK is a small society, but has received significant encouragement from the WCCES and is glad to have been able to contribute to its affairs.

Finally, CERC has played a major role in the production of this book. Vandra Masemann came to Hong Kong in November 2005 to work with Mark Bray and Maria Manzon, and was supported in this by the Comparative Education Strategic Research Theme of the University of Hong Kong. Vandra Masemann is a distinguished figure in the field of comparative education, who has been both President and Secretary General of the WCCES, and also President of both the US-based Comparative and International Education Society (CIES) and the Comparative and International Education Society of Canada (CIESC). Mark Bray has likewise been both President and Secretary General of the WCCES, as well as one of my predecessors as President of the CESHK. Maria Manzon was a distinction Masters student at the University of Hong Kong, who then proceeded to her doctoral studies under the supervision of Mark Bray and myself. Her doctoral research field is closely linked to the subject of this book.

The book also benefits greatly from the distinguished authorship of the individual chapters. The section on the WCCES itself has been written by former Presidents, some of whom have also had links with the University of Hong Kong either as visitors or, in one case (Anne Hickling-Hudson), as a Commonwealth Scholar. Most of the chapters on the individual societies have been written by Past Presidents of those societies, all distinguished figures in the field themselves.

The book shows that it is possible to talk of a global field of comparative education, of which one manifestation is the WCCES itself. At the same time, the emphases of the field are very different in, say, China, South Africa and France. These are among the factors that make the field so interesting and productive. CERC is proud to make its own contribution to the field in multiple ways, including through the publication of this book.

Mark Mason

Editor
CERC Studies in Comparative Education Series

Director
Comparative Education Research Centre
The University of Hong Kong

Introduction

Mark BRAY, Maria MANZON & Vandra MASEMANN

This book contains a set of institutional histories, each of which is set within a wider context. The specific field on which the book focuses is that of comparative education. More broadly, the book can be taken as an illustration of the ways in which professional organisations may be established and operated, and how domains of study may evolve over time.

The book has been created as a project of the World Council of Comparative Education Societies (WCCES). This is an umbrella body which brings together a number of national, sub-national, regional and language-based comparative education societies. Part I of the book focuses on the history and development of the WCCES. Part II contains a set of histories of WCCES member societies. In each case, the authors explain the contexts in which the society was created and the ways in which the society developed. Part III is an analysis of the patterns and themes addressed in the book. Remarking on the forces which have shaped both the global body and the member societies, the writers comment on variations and commonalities in different parts of the world. They also identify significant changes over time.

This Introduction begins with an explanation of what the WCCES and the member societies are, and what they do. It then indicates the process through which the book was assembled, and remarks on the orientations which the various authors have taken. The Introduction also situates the book within the broader literature on comparative education and the social sciences.

The WCCES: What It Is, and What It Does

The WCCES was founded in 1970 in Ottawa, Canada. It evolved from an International Committee of Comparative Education which had been convened in 1968 by Joseph Katz, of Canada's University of British Columbia, and brought together the four national societies and one regional society for comparative education then existing. Over the decades, additional societies joined, and by 2007 the WCCES had 36 member societies.

In the preface to the Proceedings of the 1st World Congress of Comparative Education Societies, at which the WCCES was formed, Katz (1970, p.5) wrote that:

> The Congress itself is evidence that people will work together to achieve not only common but uncommon goals as well.

The title for the present book is partly taken from this sentence. Chapter 1 explains in more detail the characteristics of the individuals and bodies that came together to form the WCCES, and the book as a whole shows the extent to which scholars, practitioners and societies in the field of comparative education have common interests.

Their goals are uncommon in the sense that they have a distinctiveness arising from a special mission. In addition to considering the administrative and juridical aspects of creating a Council and a continuing Congress, the 1970 event focused on two major themes: the place of comparative and international education in the education of teachers, and the role and rationale for educational aid to developing countries. Katz (1970, p.4) wrote that these themes were:

> of special significance in today's world, a world that is divided between the haves and the have-nots; between the developed and the developing; between the nationally and internationally inclined; between the industrial and the agricultural; and between those who suffer an annual average income of $50.00 and those who also enjoy $4500.00. For comparative educators interested in examining the similarities and differences in the educative process of various groups the examination of the educational relationships obtaining between the overdeveloped and the underdeveloped areas of the world constitute a very special challenge.

Not all members of the comparative education societies that constituted the World Council even at that time were equally concerned with such issues. Thus, both then and since, many scholars and practitioners in the field have focused exclusively on industrialised countries and on theoretical, methodological and other issues. However, from the start the World Council did have this particular emphasis, which also underpins the work of the United Nations Educational, Scientific and Cultural Organization (UNESCO). Financial and administrative support for the 1970 Congress was contributed by UNESCO, and one of the seven Congress resolutions was that the newly-formed World Council should seek consultative status with UNESCO.

These origins shaped the documents which in due course became the WCCES administrative instruments. The Statutes evolved over time, but the version approved in 1996 remained current at the time of writing this book. They stated (WCCES 1996, Section 2) that the broad goals of the Council were:

- to advance education for international understanding in the interests of peace, intercultural co-operation, mutual respect among peoples and observance of human rights; and
- to improve education systems so that the right of all to education may be more fully realised.

The Statutes then specified two professional aims, namely:

- to promote the study of comparative and international education throughout the world and enhance the academic status of this field;
- to bring comparative education to bear on the major educational problems of the day by fostering cooperative action by specialists from dif-

ferent parts of the world.

Then the Statutes indicated that to achieve these aims, the WCCES would:

- encourage the teaching of, and research in, comparative education;
- promote interdisciplinary collaboration in the development of comparative approaches to the study of educational problems;
- facilitate cooperation between comparative educationists of different countries and regions, and foster the establishment of professional associations and groups of comparative educationists;
- support international programs in education and the agencies responsible for them, by focusing the attention of comparative research workers on the major problems encountered in these programmes;
- organise research projects for which there is a particular need; and
- improve the exchange of information about research and methodological developments in comparative education.

Table 0.1: World Congresses of Comparative Education Societies

No.	Year	Place	Theme
1.	1970	Ottawa, Canada	Education and the Formation of the Teaching Profession; Educational Aid to Developing Countries
2.	1974	Geneva, Switzerland	Efficiencies and Inefficiencies in Secondary Schools
3.	1977	London, United Kingdom	Unity and Diversity in Education
4.	1980	Tokyo, Japan	Tradition and Innovation in Education
5.	1984	Paris, France	Dependence and Interdependence in Education: The Role of Comparative Education
6.	1987	Rio de Janeiro, Brazil	Education, Crisis and Change
7.	1989	Montreal, Canada	Development, Communication and Language
8.	1992	Prague, Czechoslovakia	Education and Democracy
9.	1996	Sydney, Australia	Tradition, Modernity and Postmodernity
10.	1998	Cape Town, South Africa	Education, Equity and Transformation
11.	2001	Chungbuk, Republic of Korea	New Challenges, New Paradigms: Moving Education into the 21st Century
12.	2004	Havana, Cuba	Education and Social Justice
13.	2007	Sarajevo, Bosnia and Herzegovina	Living Together: Education and Intercultural Dialogue

Over the decades, the WCCES has achieved these aims in multiple ways. During the early years the Council had a regular Bulletin and Newsletter, which in due course were replaced by a website. The WCCES has encouraged research through grants and organisation of professional meetings, and it has sponsored publication of various books. Most prominent among its activities has been the organisation of World Congresses, which in each case have been hosted by a WCCES constituent society. Table 0.1 lists the Congresses and their themes between 1970 and 2007. Various chapters in this book contain comments on the challenges of identifying appropriate hosts and locations for the Congresses. The authors also remark on the impact of the Congresses in the regions in which they have been held, and on the importance of the Congresses being held in different parts of the world.

At each World Congress, a General Assembly has brought together individual members of WCCES constituent societies. On each occasion WCCES officers have reported on the work of the WCCES during the years since the previous Assembly, and decisions have been taken if necessary on constitutional and other matters.

Between Assemblies, the WCCES has been managed by an Executive Committee comprising the Officers (President, two Vice-Presidents, Secretary General, and Treasurer), which has met at least once a year. During the early years, the WCCES Presidency was linked to plans for forthcoming Congresses. Since approval of the 1996 Statutes, Presidents have been elected from among nominees identified by search committees. Since that time, the WCCES has also had two Vice-Presidents, one being a nominee of the society which hosted the last Congress and the other being a nominee of the society due to host the next Congress. The Executive Committee has brought together the Presidents or other representatives of all the member societies. By custom, the Chairpersons of the standing committees have also been invited to Executive Committee meetings. In 2007, the standing committees were responsible for admissions and new societies; congresses; finance and fund-raising; publications; research; and special projects.

The WCCES Member Societies: What They Are and What They Do

The five societies that came together to form the Council in 1970 were the:

- Comparative and International Education Society (CIES) of the USA,
- Comparative Education Society in Europe (CESE),
- Japan Comparative Education Society (JCES),
- Comparative and International Education Society of Canada (CIESC), and
- Korean Comparative Education Society (KCES).

This list contains four national societies (for the USA, Japan, Canada and Korea), and one regional society (for Europe). Over the decades additional societies joined, and Table 0.2 lists the 36 societies which were members in February 2007.

Table 0.2: Member Societies of the WCCES

Asociación de Pedagogos de Cuba (Sección de Educación Comparada) (APC-SEC)
Association française pour le développement de l'éducation comparée et des échanges (AFDECE)
Association francophone d'éducation comparée (AFEC)
Australian and New Zealand Comparative and International Education Society (ANZCIES)
British Association for International and Comparative Education (BAICE)
Bulgarian Comparative Education Society (BCES)
Chinese Comparative Education Society (CCES)
Chinese Comparative Education Society-Taipei (CCES-T)
Comparative Education Section of the Czech Pedagogical Society (CES-CPS)
Comparative Education Society of Asia (CESA)
Comparative Education Society in Europe (CESE)
Comparative Education Society of Hong Kong (CESHK)
Comparative Education Society of India (CESI)
Comparative Education Society of the Philippines (CESP)
Comparative and International Education Society (CIES)
Comparative and International Education Society of Canada (CIESC)
Council on Comparative Education of Kazakhstan (CCEK)
Egyptian Comparative Education and Educational Administration Society (ECEEAS)
Greek Comparative Education Society (GCES)
Hungarian Pedagogical Society (Comparative Education Section) (HPS-CES)
Israel Comparative Education Society (ICES)
Japan Comparative Education Society (JCES)
Korean Comparative Education Society (KCES)
Mediterranean Society of Comparative Education (MESCE)
Nederlandstalig Genootschap voor Vergelijkende Studie van Opvoeding en Onderwijs (NGVO)
Nordic Comparative and International Education Society (NOCIES)
Polish Comparative Education Society (PCES)
Russian Council of Comparative Education (RCCE)
Sektion International und Interkulturell Vergleichende Erziehungswissenschaft in der Deutschen Gesellschaft für Erziehungswissenschaft (SIIVEDGE)
Sezione Italiana della CESE (SICESE)
Sociedad Argentina de Estudios Comparados en Educación (SAECE)
Sociedad Española de Educación Comparada (SEEC)
Sociedad Mexicana de Educación Comparada (SOMEC)
Sociedade Brasileira de Educação Comparada (SBEC)
Southern African Comparative and History of Education Society (SACHES)
Turkish Comparative Education Society (TCES)

The broad objectives of each of these societies resemble those for the WCCES. The societies exist to promote research in the field of comparative education, and to encourage dialogue among scholars in different parts of the world. As explained in various chapters in this book, some societies have additional objectives, such as contribution to policy making and to advocacy. Some societies are small, with less than a few dozen members; but others have memberships that reach into the thousands. While most WCCES members are independent societies, some are specialised sections within broader professional societies. Several societies run journals, and most organise periodic conferences. All have Comparative Education in their names, but six include the related field of International Education. One links educational administration with comparative education, another links history of education with comparative education, and a third includes intercultural education with comparative and international education.

In addition to the societies listed in Table 0.2, some bodies were created and joined the WCCES between 1970 and 2007 but subsequently ceased to function. The demise of comparative education societies is important to note alongside the birth of societies. Table 0.3 gives a chronological account of the birth (and demise) of the societies that have been members of the WCCES.

Table 0.3: Chronology of WCCES Member Societies

1950-60	1960-70	1970-80	1980-90	1990-00	2000-07
Established:					
USA	Europe	Hungary	Brazil	Bulgaria	Philippines
	Czechoslova-	Australia	Italy	Southern	Argentina[2]
	kia	Francophone	Soviet	Africa	Mexico
	Japan	Dutch-	Hong Kong	Greece	Mediterranean
	West	speaking	Egypt[1]	Poland	Kazakhstan
	Germany	Chinese-Taipei	Colombia	Egypt[2]	Turkey
	UK	Spain	Nigeria	Nordic	
	Canada	China	Israel	Cuba	
	South Korea	India	Czech	Russia	
		London (LACE)		Asia	
	WCCES (1970)	Argentina[1]		France	
				(AFDECE)	
				Portugal	
				Ukraine	
Ceased activities:					
	Czechoslova-		London	Colombia	Ukraine
	kia		(LACE)	Nigeria	Portugal
			Soviet	Egypt[1]	
				Argentina[1]	
Cumulative total (net)	7	17	24	32	36
Other societies that expressed interest in joining WCCES but did not do so					
			Venezuela	Romania	Arab World
				Albania	
				Panafrica	

Note: The table is based on the year of foundation of societies, not of their joining the WCCES. Two national societies appeared to have become defunct, and were de-listed from the WCCES, but were replaced by new societies that were subsequently admitted. These are denoted with a numerical superscript, e.g. Argentina[1]. LACE = London Association of Comparative Educationists.

Table 0.4 further classifies the 36 member societies existing at the beginning of 2007 by type and geographic coverage. Twenty eight were national (for example for China and Poland) or sub-national (for example for Hong Kong). Six were regional (for example for Asia, Europe and the Mediterranean), and two were language-based (for speakers of French and Dutch). Classifying the societies by geography (and placing the language-based societies in the regions from which the societies were administered), the largest groups were in Europe and Asia. One society served Australia and New Zealand, but no society explicitly served other parts of the South Pacific. Africa was also poorly served, and only three societies served South America and the Caribbean. Comments on this geographic coverage are presented at various points in this book. The geographic emphases are allied with linguistic and cultural emphases, and have implications for the nature of the global field.

Table 0.4: WCCES Member Societies by Region and Type

Nature	No.	%	Region	No.	%
National &			Europe	16	44%
sub-national	28	78%	Asia	11	31%
Regional	6	17%	North America	3	8%
Language-based	2	5%	South America &	3	8%
Total	36	100%	Caribbean		
			Africa	2	6%
			Australasia	1	3%
			Total	36	100%

Note: This table shows the membership as of January 2007.

The Process of Preparing this Book

The project which led to this book originated in the late 1990s. The idea was first raised formally in 1997 during the 25th meeting of the WCCES Executive Committee in Mexico City. Namgi Park, Chairperson of the Publications Standing Committee, suggested that a useful project for the World Council, especially to benefit its newer members, would be the preparation of a history. Two years later, Nikolay Popov of the Bulgarian Comparative Education Society (BCES) suggested that each member society should prepare an institutional history, and that these histories could be assembled into an edited volume. This project was accepted by the WCCES Executive Committee in 1999 during its 27th meeting in Toronto, Canada. David Wilson, then WCCES President, issued a general call for manuscripts. He received some response, but it was not strong enough to allow him to proceed with the project.

The idea was taken up again in March 2004, when the Executive Committee resolved to make the endeavour an official WCCES project and to give it a stronger impulse by using the forthcoming 12th World Congress in Cuba to stimulate discussion and analysis. Subsequently, David Wilson handed over the project to the leadership of Vandra Masemann, Mark Bray and Maria Manzon. A strong response was received to the proposal for a set of panels during the 12th World Congress, and several follow-up panels were organised in the meetings of member societies, both for the intrinsic interest of these panels and as a way to substantiate some of the facts presented in draft chapters.

For reasons of space, it was not possible in this book to include full chapters on all 36 member societies in addition to the chapters on the WCCES itself. One of the challenges, therefore, was to decide which member societies should have full chapters and which, by corollary, should not. The decision was made to focus on the societies which had longer histories, in preference to ones which had been founded only after 1995. Further decisions were in effect made by the societies themselves, since not all responded to the invitation to prepare chapters. Nevertheless, to ensure recognition of all societies, the book does present key facts on societies which do not have full chapters (see Chapter 30). The ordering of societies in Part II is by date of foundation. Thus, it starts with the CIES, which was founded in 1956 and is the oldest in the field. It then moves to CESE, which was founded in 1961 and is the second-oldest, and so on.

The chapters have been prepared in different ways, according to the preferences of their authors and the societies on which they are reporting. The chapters on the WCCES are all written by former Presidents, and to some extent take the form of memoirs. Table 0.5 lists the Presidents between 1970 and 2007. Three of them (Joseph Katz, Brian Holmes and Masunori Hiratsuka) had already died before the project commenced, and chapters on their periods therefore had to be written by their successors. One President, David Wilson, died in 2006 after writing his chapter but before publication of the book. The loss of these pioneers underlined for the editors the urgency of recording histories while the remaining actors were still able to recount their perspectives and experiences.

Table 0.5 also lists the Secretaries General, who have commonly provided continuity and institutional memory. Particularly to be noted in this respect is Raymond Ryba, who was Secretary General from 1983 to 1996. Following his death in 1999, Ryba's papers were transported to Toronto, Canada, where they were consulted by David Wilson and Vandra Masemann in preparation for this book. The papers were then sent to the WCCES archives at Kent State University, Ohio, USA, where they joined other documentation which was examined during the preparation of the book.

Table 0.5: WCCES Presidents and Secretaries General

Presidents		Secretaries General	
Joseph Katz	1970-1974	Arthur Godbout	1970-1972
Brian Holmes	1974-1977	Anne Hamori	1972-1978
Masunori Hiratsuka	1977-1980	Leo Fernig	1978-1982
Erwin H. Epstein	1980-1983	Raymond Ryba	1983-1996
Michel Debeauvais	1983-1987	Vandra Masemann	1996-2000
Vandra Masemann	1987-1991	Mark Bray	2000-2005
Wolfgang Mitter	1991-1996	Christine Fox	2005-
David N. Wilson	1996-2001		
Anne Hickling-Hudson	2001-2004		
Mark Bray	2004-2007		

The chapters for the member societies have been written by persons designated by those societies. In most cases, this has been one or more Past Presidents. Some chapters were written largely from memory with the assistance of correspondence and personal files available to the authors, while others have resulted from interviews and circulation of drafts. The CIES has an official Historian, and over the decades has taken care to deposit records in an archive at Kent State University. Other societies have dispersed or almost no archives and fading memories, and one of the side-products from this project has been strengthened awareness of the need both to record history and to maintain archives.

In all cases, the histories are of course accounts written by individuals who have viewed their materials through the lenses that those individuals have chosen to employ. As such, they should not be considered definitive histories which remove the need for further research and interpretation. Indeed rather to the contrary, the editors of this volume and the WCCES Executive Committee will be glad if the various chapters serve as a starting point for further investigation and for reinterpretation with different perspectives. The chapters contain varying amounts of detail, and many are the first to be written on the periods covered for the societies in question.

A Broader Framework

No existing work closely resembles the present book, but some previous reviews of the field are related and should be noted (e.g. Masemann 1994). Several of the chapters refer to existing histories of the field in particular geographic locations, many of which refer to the activities of individual societies (e.g. McDade 1982; Leclerq 1998; Sutherland 2004; García Garrido 2005); and many books contain outlines of historical developments (e.g. Jones 1971; Van daele 1993; Wang 1999; Ferrer 2002; Bray et al. 2007).

Perhaps the most relevant precursor is the book edited by Halls (1990), Part II of which was entitled 'Comparative Education Around the World' and contained chapters on:

- Western Europe (Brian Holmes),
- The Socialist Countries (H.G. Hofmann and Zia Malkova),
- North America (Robert F. Lawson),
- Latin America (A. Oliveros),
- Asia and the Pacific
  - China, India, Japan and Korea (Tetsuya Kobayashi),
  - Australia and New Zealand (Robin Burns),
- Africa (A.B. Fafunwa), and
- The Arab States (Khemais Benhamida).

The unit of analysis was clearly one of political geography rather than of professional society for comparative education, as in the present volume; but several chapters did mention professional societies. Moreover, the concluding chapter by Cowen (1990) focused explicitly on comparative education infrastructures. It began (p.321) by observing that "[as] comparative educationists, we do not know very much about ourselves", and proceeded by asking:

> What are the social structures of our professional lives and how do they act upon us? Is there one comparative education world-wide, or are there different national views of what comparative education is? What is the interplay of comparative education at the national and the international levels through the infrastructures of comparative education: the centres of comparative and international education studies, the international, regional and national professional societies of comparative educationists, and the specialized journals associated with comparative education?

The chapter explicitly mentioned the WCCES (p.323), together with CESE, the Dutch-speaking Comparative Education Society and the British, Chinese and Spanish societies, and it elaborated on the existence of comparative educations (in the plural) according to the perspectives of scholars working in different language groups and academic traditions. This notion was developed subsequently in other publications (e.g. Cowen 2000), and is clearly relevant to the present work. Comparative education can be seen as a global field, but the work conducted in and through the different societies may have different emphases which arise from the specifics of culture and social priorities in, say, Greece, India and South Africa. The book goes further than the Halls volume, presents materials from years that have passed since the appearance of that book, and is organised within a framework that focuses specifically on the professional societies.

Thus, the rationale for this project has been three-fold. First, it has had an anthropological and sociological justification, examining the cultural traditions of the societies and the ways in which new generations have been socialised into the work that their forefathers and foremothers started. The second justification has been reflective and reflexive. Universities and other institutions commonly teach teachers and researchers that their thinking can be improved by interacting with one another, by synthesising their classroom experiences, and by combining theory and practice. This project has allowed comparative educationists to undertake such tasks in their own field. The third rationale has been narrative. The project has opened the possibilities for participants to have a long and intense conversation, to retread their steps, and to try to see the road ahead. The editors urged participants not to just write their individual memoirs but also to discuss their ideas and to make their contributions multi-faceted and cooperative.

With a yet wider lens, the book may be viewed in the context of literature on the construction of fields and disciplines, particularly in the social sciences. Becher and Trowler (2001) focused on the nature of academic "tribes and territories", examining ways in which disciplinary boundaries are drawn and evolve over time. Game and Metcalfe (1996) appositely suggested that debates about the scope and nature of academic fields should be thought of as stories or narratives, because this process allows for more open accounts than an unreflexive approach.

Of particular relevance to the reading of the histories in this book is the work of Graham et al. (1983), who highlighted the legitimating function of disciplinary histories and distinguished between the users and the producers. The two most common audiences of disciplinary histories are external supporters of the field such as governments and the lay public, and the internal disciplinary community. With the former group the authors of histories usually wish to stress the field's utility and/or cultural value. By contrast, a common internal function is to legitimate political interests within the field. This can be achieved by extending "the present (or what is to become the future) as far as possible into the past, thereby constructing an image of continuity, consistency and determinacy" (Graham et al. 1983, p.xvii).

The main producers of disciplinary histories include both professional historians and amateurs. The latter are usually practitioners of the field who write and rewrite their field's history for strategic purposes. In contrast, the professional historians write for the members of the academic community of historians, and usually endeavour to give objective historical accounts as scientifically as possible. Many of the chapters in this book are written by people who would in this sense be described as amateurs. However, some of the authors do have training in history, and all have training in some academic field of enquiry and in accompanying skills of research and analysis. Such matters would be useful for readers to bear in mind as they go through the book. Discussion will return to these considerations in the final chapter.

References

Becher, Tony & Trowler, Paul R. (2001): *Academic Tribes and Territories: Intellectual Enquiry and the Culture of Disciplines*. 2nd edition, Buckingham: The Society for Research into Higher Education and Open University Press.

Bray, Mark; Adamson, Bob & Mason, Mark (eds.) (2007): *Comparative Education Research: Approaches and Methods*. CERC Studies in Comparative Education 19, Hong Kong: Comparative Education Research Centre, The University of Hong Kong, and Dordrecht: Springer.

Cowen, Robert (1990): 'The National and International Impact of Comparative Education Infrastructures', in Halls, W.D. (ed.), *Comparative Education: Contemporary Issues and Trends*. Paris: UNESCO, and London: Jessica Kingsley, pp.321-352.

Cowen, Robert (2000): 'Comparing Futures or Comparing Pasts?'. *Comparative Education*, Vol.36, No.3, pp.333-342.

Ferrer, Ferran (2002): *La Educación Comparada Actual*. Barcelona: Ariel Educación.

Game, Ann & Metcalfe, Andrew (1996): *Passionate Sociology*. London: Sage Publications.

García Garrido, José Luis (2005): 'Diez Años de Educación Comparada en España'. *Revista Española de Educación Comparada*, Vol.11, pp.15-36.

Graham, L., Lepenies, W. & Weingart, P. (1983): *Functions and Uses of Disciplinary Histories*. Dordrecht: D. Reidel Publishing Company.

Halls, W.D. (ed.) (1990): *Comparative Education: Contemporary Issues and Trends*. Paris: UNESCO, and London: Jessica Kingsley.

Jones, Phillip E. (1971): *Comparative Education: Purpose and Method*. St. Lucia:

Queensland University Press.

Katz, Joseph (1970): 'The Purpose, Plan and Program for the World Congress of Comparative Education Societies', in *Proceedings of the First World Congress of Comparative Education Societies*, Vol.2. Ottawa: Secretariat, World Council for Comparative Education, pp.4-5.

Leclerq, Jean-Michel (1998): *L'éducation comparée: mondialisation et spécificités francophones*. Actes du congrès international sur «L'histoire et l'avenir de l'éducation comparée en langue française». Paris: Association francophone d'éducation comparée.

Masemann, Vandra (1994): 'Comparative Education Societies', in Husén, Torsten & Postlethwaite, T. Neville (eds.), *The International Encyclopedia of Education*. 2nd. Oxford: Pergamon Press, pp.942-948.

McDade, Daniel F. (1982): 'The Things that Interest Mankind: A Commentary on 30 Years of Comparative Education'. *British Journal of Educational Studies*, Vol.30, No.1, pp.72-84.

Sutherland, Margaret B. (2004): 'The Rise and Fall of Comparative Education in Scotland'. *Scottish Educational Review*, Vol.36, No.2, pp.219-226.

Van daele, Henk (1993): *L'éducation comparée*. Paris: Presses Universitaires de France.

Wang, Rujer (1999): *Comparative Education*. Taipei: Wunan Publishing House. [in Chinese]

WCCES (1996): 'Statutes'. World Council of Comparative Education Societies.

1

The World Council from 1970 to 1979

Vandra MASEMANN & Erwin H. EPSTEIN

The major impetus for the founding of the World Council of Comparative Education Societies (WCCES) came from a Canadian, Joseph Katz of the University of British Columbia. The first World Congress was held in Ottawa, Canada, in August 1970 during the UNESCO-designated International Education Year (IEY). Edmund King later described the way in which the idea took form (Letter to Raymond Ryba, 12 March 1998):

> I was there at the time, when [Joseph] Lauwerys and Leo Fernig (often in London) and Joe Katz were laying the groundwork for the WCCES. Katz spent a year in London on sabbatical, and during that time he and Lauwerys were often together.... Lauwerys [was] the European founding partner in the nascent WCCES ... [and] above all else, Lauwerys insisted that the administration and official centre of the WCCES should be housed in London. Joe Katz was, so to speak, an equal but distant partner 'in partibus infidelium'.

Other important players included Antanas Paplauskas-Ramunas of the University of Ottawa; William Brickman, founder of the Comparative Education Society (CES) in the United States; Brian Holmes, one of the founders of the Comparative Education Society in Europe (CESE); Gerald Read of Kent State University in the United States; Masunori Hiratsuka, founder of the Japan Comparative Education Society (JCES); and Leo Fernig from the United Nations Educational, Scientific and Cultural Organization (UNESCO), who gave considerable support and assistance to the idea.

Pre-history

Katz (1978) stated that he first had the idea for an International Education Year, during which he wished to hold a world educational Congress, as early as 1960, and that the idea was approved in principle by the CES of the United States in 1961. The concept was discussed at the Meeting of Experts convened at the UNESCO Institute for Education (UIE) in Hamburg, Germany, courtesy of Saul B. Robinsohn the UIE Director, in 1963. It was then presented to the Canadian National Commission for UNESCO and to the Phi Delta Kappa Commission on

International Relations in Education, and approved in 1964 by Phi Delta Kappa International. In 1964, the concept of an International Education Year was also approved by the Educational Research Councils (or their equivalents) of India, Australia, New Zealand, Canada and others. The idea was presented to a section meeting of the American Educational Research Association in Chicago in 1965.

Katz, who chaired the International Relations Commission of Phi Delta Kappa, met in 1966 with members of the US Bureau of Education and the Cultural Affairs and Planning staff of the US Department of State to discuss the proposal. In 1967 the Williamsburg Conference on the World Crisis in Education gave further support for the International Education Year as presented by US President Lyndon Johnson. Also in 1967, the same year that the Comparative and International Education Society of Canada (CIESC) was formed, UNESCO declared that 1970 would be designated the International Education Year.

Katz's Plan for the World Council

In a note written in 1975, Joseph Katz listed the events that led to the first World Congress and the World Council's early years (Katz 1975). He viewed the Council's initial history as composed of four stages: the Congress (1961-64), the Conception (1965-70), the Council (1971-74), and the Commitment (1975-85). The 'Congress' seems to refer to the initial discussions that he had had with others in that period about the idea of holding an international conference to get the newly created comparative education societies together. By the Conception, he clearly had the World Council in mind. In the late 1960s, there were only five widely-recognised comparative education societies: those of the USA, Europe, Japan, Korea and Canada. During this time a committee was formed, consisting of representatives of these organisations, to explore the formation of a World Council.

The Council in Katz's note referred to the period when the WCCES was established, acquired its Secretariat at the UNESCO International Bureau of Education (IBE) in Geneva, Switzerland, held its second World Congress, and started issuing its Newsletters and fostering communication among the member comparative education societies. Katz viewed the Council developing in the third period largely as a series of national/regional society meetings in Ottawa, Calgary and Vancouver in Canada; Hamburg, Germany; Paris, France; Frascati, Italy; San Diego, USA; and Sydney, Australia. He noted that the World Council operated with no fees or subsidies.

The Commitment in Katz's note referred to an era when the Council would grow in numbers. Indeed, the Council held three more World Congresses during that period, and it seemed as if it would become a permanent organisation. By Commitment, Katz meant that the Council would pursue three overriding objectives entitled:

- Internationalization of Man,
- Cooperation of Cultures, and
- Rationalization of Societies.

By the first of these, he meant reduction of the extremes of nationalism and the social, economic, political, spiritual, and technological development of individuals. He referred to 'Cooperation of Cultures' as individual and institutional value systems, natural and human resources, and the cultural as well as intellectual base of societies. 'Rationalization of Societies' was to come about through cooperation with such organisations as the UIE, IBE, other parts of UNESCO, and the Organisation for Economic Co-operation and Development (OECD). Through such cooperation, the World Council was expected to establish a research and development baseline and 'common goals for mankind'.

By the time Katz wrote his two-page outline in 1975, the original five constituent societies of the World Council had grown to nine. According to Katz's outline, these included the US-based Comparative and International Education Society (CIES), the regional society – CESE, national societies in Japan, South Korea, Canada, Australia, and Spain, and two language-based societies representing the Francophone and Dutch-speaking communities of comparativists. Katz reported on bodies in Great Britain and Germany which were subgroups of CESE. He identified a need for the World Council to expand its focus and membership in Africa, South America and Asia.

Events Leading up to the 1st World Congress

In 1968, a group of scholars formed the first International Committee of Comparative Education (ICCE). Its members were Joseph Katz (Canada), Masunori Hiratsuka, (Japan), Stewart Fraser and Gerald Read (USA), Sun Ho Kim (South Korea), and Joseph Lauwerys (CESE – Europe). In 1969, this Committee met in Calgary, Canada, with representatives from the University of Ottawa. It accepted the invitation of Lionel Desjarlais, Dean of the Faculty of Education in Ottawa, to host the 1st World Congress. According to Gerald Read, the members of the Committee in 1969 were Masunori Hiratsuka, Stewart Fraser, Gerald Read, Sun Ho Kim, and Joseph Lauwerys (Read 1985, p.2).

The Committee met again in January 1970 at the Comparative Education Centre at the University of Ottawa to draw up plans for the World Congress. The meeting was chaired by Joseph Katz and hosted by Antanas Paplauskas-Ramunas, Director of the Centre. Additional members, according to Gerald Read, were Philip Idenburg, president of CESE, and four representatives from Canada: Robert Lawson, Fred Whitworth, Antanas Paplauskas-Ramunas, and Andrew F. Skinner (Read 1985, p.2). The participants discussed the three subjects to be addressed in the Congress, namely "The administrative and juridical aspects of creating a council; the place of comparative education in teacher training; and the role and rationale for educational aid in developing countries" (Godbout, Minutes, 17-18 January 1970, p.1). They also discussed the allocated budget (Cdn.$26,000), and arranged the lists of invited speakers and discussants. They established a Secretariat in Ottawa to handle Congress arrangements, which was voted a budget of Cdn.$4,500 to begin its work. It was then officially given the name World Congress of Comparative Education Societies Secretariat, to be headed by the Secretary General of the Comparative Education Centre at the University of Ottawa and assisted by the Dean, Director, and Assistant Directors of the Centre (Godbout, Minutes, 17-18 January 1970, p.2). Katz noted that funding was provided for the Congress primarily by the Canadian International Development Agency (CIDA), with supplementary assistance from the International Bureau of Education, the Canadian Commission for UNESCO, and Gerald Read from Kent State University, USA (Katz 1978, p.8; see also Read 1985, p.2). In the Congress Proceedings, additional thanks were given to UNESCO Headquarters in Paris (France), the University of British Columbia (Canada), the Governments of Quebec and Ontario (Canada), the Comparative Education Societies, and the University of Ottawa and its Comparative Education Centre (Katz 1970, p.2).

Several policy items decided upon at that meeting in January 1970 are still in effect today. The Congress was to be an open event, with invitations sent to comparative education societies throughout the world. A fee would be charged for registration, with an additional fee for "wives [sic] of members attending" (Godbout, Minutes, 17-18 January 1970, p.3), and a reduced fee for students. Sums were to be allocated for travel expenses, but the recipients of these allocations were not specified. Simultaneous translation in English and French was to be provided.

The First World Congress

The Congress took place from 17 to 21 August 1970, and had two themes:

- The Place of Comparative and International Education in the Education of Teachers, and
- The Role and Rationale for Educational Aid to Developing Countries.

Joseph Katz opened the Congress by outlining its rationale during the International Education Year: "We meet, in short, to help people everywhere through education to substitute the civilized minds of men for the uncivilized instincts of nature" (Katz 1970, p.1). He went on to say that the participants at the Congress shared common interests but were pursuing uncommon goals. In doing so, he was highlighting a continuing theme in comparative education about similarities and differences, which has been usually taken to refer to the objects of comparative study itself. In this case, he was referring to comparative education societies, which shared a common interest in comparative and international education, but whose members were trying to exceed the goals of those who had gone before by creating an international meeting place to share ideas and contribute to the 'Internationalization of Man' by reducing the extremes of nationalism and encouraging the social, economic, political, spiritual and technological development of societies (Katz 1975).

Although no archival evidence is available of an election, it is clear that Joseph Katz was elected the first President of the World Council at this Congress (Katz 1978, p.9). Participants at the event drafted a constitution for discussion, and approved a recommendation that the International Committee become the World Council for Comparative Education, with its Secretariat at the University of Ottawa. Gerald Read indicated (1985, p.2) that there were some 300 educators from 30 countries at the Congress. Of the 150 registrants listed in the Proceedings, about one third were Canadians from educational and governmental posts. The students present, who were over 50 in number, were mostly from Canada and the United States. Speakers were from Canada, the USA, West Germany, Australia, Israel, England, Sweden, South Africa, Cuba, Northern Ireland, Romania, Turkey, Japan, Nigeria, Ceylon, Uganda, Korea, France, New Zealand, Jamaica, Tanzania, Cameroon and El Salvador. Among the many Canadians present, those who were later active in or presidents of the CIESC included Lionel Desjarlais (University of Ottawa), Daniel Dorotich (University of Saskatchewan), Richard Heyman (University of Calgary), Shiu Kong (University of Toronto), Ralph Miller (then at CIDA), Andrew Skinner (University of Toronto), David Wilson (Ontario Institute for Studies in Education, University of Toronto) and Mathew Zachariah (University of Calgary). The first World Congress definitely had a long-term effect on the comparativists in the host country, a pattern which was to be seen after subsequent World Congresses.

The Period from 1971 to 1979

Organisational Developments
The WCCES Presidents following Joseph Katz during this period were Brian Holmes from the United Kingdom (1974-77) and Masunori Hiratsuka from Japan (1977-80). It was decided that the major financial support for hosting a World Congress would come from the host society, and that the Chairman [later designated President] of the World Council would be named by the host institution or society responsible for the Congress (Read 1985, p.3). This pattern was adhered to during the 1970s and 1980s, but external political events altered the pattern in the 1990s.

The 1971 meeting in Hamburg, Germany reviewed the work and began planning for the next World Congress. The World Council for Comparative Education (WCCE) was renamed the World Council of Comparative Education Societies (WCCES). Arthur Godbout, who was the Secretary General of the Comparative Education Centre (1969-73) at the University of Ottawa, and the first ICCE Secretary, was described in the biographical note on the website that introduces his archives at the University of Ottawa (www.crccf.uottawa.ca/fonds/ P122.html) as the head of the Secretariat ("chef du secretariat") of the Conseil mondial d'éducation comparée – that being the French-language version of the WCCE name. The biographical note describes him as holding the post from 1970 to 1973. However, although the University of Ottawa was willing to host the World Council Secretariat, "no supporting funds were forthcoming to maintain the Secretariat" (Read 1985, p.3). Leo Fernig, then IBE Director, offered to house the Secretariat at the IBE in Geneva, Switzerland. Accommodation at the IBE required the World Council to be registered as an international non-governmental organisation with UNESCO. In June 1972 the World Council accepted Fernig's offer, and the WCCES Secretariat was housed in the Palais Wilson office of the IBE. Fernig invited Anne Hamori, a long-time employee of the IBE (then aged 60), to work in the Secretariat on a supernumerary arrangement (Hamori 2004). She thus became the Secretary General of the World Council after it was officially constituted, a post which she held from 1972 to 1978. According to Hamori, the World Council was registered with the Geneva Bureau of Commerce in 1972 (Hamori 2004). The World Council's application for consultative status with UNESCO as a non-governmental organisation (Category C) was approved in 1972 (Katz 1978, p.9).

The Newsletters produced by Anne Hamori during this period were comprehensive and voluminous (up to 95 pages). The first volume was issued in 1973. They were mimeographed, and later printed, on white paper with a bright blue band for the masthead – the same colour that was later chosen for the logo and displayed on the front of this book. The Newsletters contained detailed information on upcoming Congress programmes and travel arrangements, news from the constituent societies, news from UNESCO, articles of interest from the IBE and other organisations, and a bibliography of recent publications. The Newsletters were completely bilingual in French and English.

In 1977, Leo Fernig was replaced as IBE Director. By January 1978, the IBE, which had funded Hamori's office, gave notice that her salary would be terminated as of June of that year (though it was extended to July with World Council funds). The Japan society agreed to take over the Secretariat from Hamori only for a brief period until the 4th Congress in July 1980 (WCCES, Minutes, 7 July 1980, Saitama).

World Congresses: 1974-1980

As mentioned in the Introduction to this book, the most prominent the activities of the World Council have been the World Congresses. The 2nd World Congress of Comparative Education Societies was held in Geneva, Switzerland in 1974, the 3rd in London, UK in 1977, and the 4th in Tokyo, Japan in 1980 with a Pre-Congress in Seoul, South Korea (see Table 0.1 in the Introduction).

In 1973, the World Council met in Frascati, Italy to review plans for the 2nd World Congress. Anne Hamori, recalling her organisation of the 2nd World Congress in 1974, noted that the Congress was not hosted by a member society as such, and that most of the event was in the building of the World Council of Churches in Geneva. Those premises were not available on the first day of the meeting, and Anne Hamori was able to secure use of the United Nations facilities (Hamori 2004). The papers kept quite closely to the Congress theme on 'Efficiencies and Inefficiencies in Secondary Schools', which had been selected with a view to promoting an IBE international conference. Indeed, from that period onwards, the WCCES was invited to send observers to major IBE conferences (Katz 1978, p.10). The event was more modest in scope than the 1st World Congress had been. It set a pattern for future Congresses in having five working groups, all within the conference theme, which reported back to the final plenary session.

The World Council Executive Committee had agreed at its 1974 meeting in Geneva to extend an invitation to the Japan society to hold the 4th World Congress in 1980. The Japan society accepted the invitation. In 1975, the WCCES met in Sèvres, France and approved the theme 'Unity and Diversity in Education' for the 3rd World Congress in London, UK. The 3rd World Congress was held in conjunction with the CESE meeting in 1977 at the Institute of Education at the University of London. Anne Hamori recalled that the WCCES presence was rather humble. Initially, the WCCES had been allocated a table in the corner, along with the British Section of CESE, and Anne Hamori felt that she had to push for greater visibility. The Congress attracted 350 participants from 40 countries (Katz 1980, p.2), and incorporated meetings both of the sections of CESE that dealt with various aspects of the main theme and parallel sessions of the World Congress. There were no Research Commissions as such, although Brian Holmes was active later in the one on research methodology in comparative education. The final plenary session dealt with the reports on the three approaches to diversity and unity – European, Third World, and the World as a whole. At these two Congresses, there was as yet no General Assembly for the participants to air their general questions or for the WCCES to report to the individuals from member societies. However, there was a session at the 1977 Congress called the General Business Meeting. At this meeting, the JCES was officially designated the host for the 4th World Congress. Thus, the JCES President, Masunori Hiratsuka, was named the incoming President of the World Council. The Council agreed also to accept an invitation from the Korean society to hold a 1980 pre-Congress event.

Moving into the 1980s
The pre-Congress in Seoul, South Korea was held from 3-5 July 1980, just before the 4th World Congress in Japan. The Tokyo Congress was very successful, having the largest number of participants to date – approximately 450 individuals from 35 countries – and admitting four new members (India, Britain, the Federal Republic of Germany, and Argentina), bringing the total membership in the Council to 13. Erwin H. Epstein was named as incoming President, as the CIES proposal to mount the 5th World Congress in Monterrey, Mexico had been accepted. The Council expected him to build on this success and bring the world organisation to a new level of prominence.

References
Godbout, Arthur (1970): Minutes of the Meeting of the International Committee of Comparative Education held at the Comparative Education Centre of the Faculty of Education of the University of Ottawa, Ontario, January 17 and 18. Mimeographed, 3pp.

Hamori, Anne (2004). Interview by Mark Bray, in collaboration with Charles Magnin and Astrid Thomann, 9 September. Geneva, Switzerland.

Katz, Joseph (1970): 'The Purpose, Plan and Program for the World Congress of Comparative Education Societies', in *Proceedings of the First World Congress of Comparative Education Societies*, Vol.1. Ottawa: Secretariat, World Council for Comparative Education, pp.1-2.

Katz, Joseph (1975): Typescript on WCCES history. 2pp.

Katz, Joseph (1978): 'Chronology of the International Education Year and the World Council of Comparative Education Societies'. *World Council of Comparative Education Societies Newsletter/Conseil mondial des sociétés d'éducation comparée bulletin*, Vol.VI, No.1, pp.6-11.

Read, Gerald (1985): 'The World Congress of Comparative Education Societies'. Mimeographed, 6pp.

2

The World Council at the Turn of the Turbulent 80s

Erwin H. EPSTEIN

This is a personal memoir of my presidency of the World Council of Comparative Education Societies (WCCES). My term as President began at the 4th World Congress in Tokyo in July 1980 and ended in April 1983. The first two years of that period coincided, with only a few months' variation, with my position as President-elect and President of the US-based Comparative and International Education Society (CIES). Those years thus marked a time when I was President of both the World Council and of the CIES, the first and largest national comparative education society.

The Second Decade Begins: The Early 1980s

The way my World Council presidency began is plausibly the most interesting and important aspect of my term in office. As background to that period, it is important to know the context of my election, especially as it relates to my position in the CIES.

Preparing a Proposal for a World Congress in 1983

I was notified of my nomination to run for Vice-President of the CIES by a phone call from then President-elect Thomas La Belle in spring 1979, and was elected in March 1980. At the time La Belle called, I was professor of sociology and chair of the social sciences division at the University of Missouri-Rolla in the USA, but scheduled to spend a year's leave of absence at the Universidad de Monterrey (UDEM) in Mexico, beginning in August 1979. La Belle insisted in his call that if I were elected, my leave in Mexico would not present a problem to the Board of Directors and the membership, and with that assurance I accepted the nomination.

Around the time of my nomination and election, the CIES decided to change its constitution to include a Vice Presidential term prior to President-elect. The revised CIES protocol dictated that the Vice-President would succeed automatically after one year to President-elect, and then to President after another year. Prior to the change, individuals became President-elect and then President, with no provision for Vice President prior to President-elect. Under the previous constitution, the President was responsible for planning the national CIES meeting, but under the changed constitution, that responsibility was given to the President-elect. Hence, I was elected as President-elect in March 1980 and succeeded to the presidency of CIES in March 1981. Effectively, this meant that I would become the first and only CIES President who would not have to plan a national meeting.

The combination of constitutional changes which freed me from the most onerous responsibility of the CIES presidency cycle, being at a Mexican university during my election to high office in the CIES, and being delegated the responsibility of representing the CIES at the 1980 pre-Congress and World Congress in Seoul and Tokyo respectively, caused me to think hard about the convergence of these events. I began discussing with José Luis Quintero, the former rector and at that time director of the Division of Educational Sciences at UDEM, about the possibility of a World Congress in Monterrey. Such a conference, I argued, would stimulate widespread interest in comparative education throughout Latin America. The World Council had been stalled since 1975 with only nine constituent societies, and was eager to expand, especially in the developing world. Although in 1980 the Asociación Argentina de Educación Comparada (AAEC) was admitted at the Tokyo Congress, it afterward became defunct and was delisted from the WCCES membership list. Thus, outside the USA and Canada, there were no members from the Western Hemisphere. I felt that a proposal for a Congress in Mexico would be of keen interest to the World Council as a means of spreading the field beyond Europe, Asia, and North America.

A key issue in such a proposal related to sponsorship. Quintero and I believed that UDEM would be well-positioned as a host, and that the thriving city of Monterrey would be an ideal venue. However, Mexico neither had nor expected to have a comparative education society. Clearly, the only prospect for success would be if the US society were to be the host. A World Congress had not been held in the US, and the prospect for one hosted by the US society in the US was unlikely. Moreover, a World Congress in Mexico without the direct involvement of the US society would compete with the national CIES meeting, coming only a few months apart. I considered that the only alternative for a successful proposal for a conference in Mexico would be a combined CIES national meeting and World Congress. Such a combined conference would virtually guarantee participation of CIES members, who had not attended previous World Congresses in significant numbers. For the first time, I felt, the largest comparative education society might be directly and substantially involved in a World Congress.

At Quintero's urging, I gave a proposal to UDEM's rector, Iván Espinosa, who presented it to the university's Board of Trustees. The proposal envisaged that:

- the 5th World Congress would take place in Monterrey in July 1983 and last for about five days;
- the number of participants would be approximately 500-800;
- the CIES would have the major responsibility for the academic pro-

gramme;
- UDEM would have the major responsibility for on-location organisation;
- UDEM would guarantee adequate financial support; and
- in all other respects, UDEM would collaborate with the CIES.

Rector Espinosa, in a letter to me as President-elect of the CIES, wrote (23 May 1980): "I am pleased to report that the Board of Trustees of this university has approved of your proposal and I am in a position to guarantee the support that you seek for a collaborative effort between UDEM and the CIES for sponsorship of the World Congress". The unconditional support by the UDEM Board of Trustees to the Congress included a subvention of US$100,000 (over and above receipts from registration revenue), funded by a grant secured by UDEM from the Acción Cultural y Asistencial, a philanthropic foundation (letter from G.V. de Palacios to Quintero, 15 July 1981). This was a major commitment, and virtually guaranteed a successful combined World Congress and CIES meeting.

There were, however, several obstacles. First, I had to convince the CIES Board of Directors to accept the proposal. This was no small matter. For one thing, this would be a CIES meeting combined with a World Congress held outside the US. To be sure, the venue would not be unprecedented. The March 1980 CIES meeting at which the proposal would be discussed was itself being held outside the US – in Vancouver, Canada – and it would not be for the first time. Besides having had a previous CIES meeting in Canada, the CIES had held a national meeting in Mexico City in 1978. However, although the CIES meeting in Mexico was a programmatic success, the CIES lost a significant amount of money. More importantly, under the new CIES Constitution, I no longer had the responsibility to plan a CIES meeting. A requirement of the Board's approval would be the willingness not of my immediate successor, but of my successor's successor. Since neither my successor nor that person's successor had yet been elected to office, the matter was complicated.

Fortunately, in view of UDEM's substantial material and moral commitment, the Board at its Vancouver meeting in March 1980 approved my proposal with the understanding that if the proposal were not accepted by the World Council, the responsibility for planning the 1983 CIES meeting would revert to the Vice-President to be elected in 1981. There were, however, other obstacles. At its June 1979 meeting in Valencia, Spain, the WCCES Executive Committee agreed to extend a formal invitation to the Comparative Education Society of India (CESI), which had not yet been formally admitted to the Council, to host the 5th World Congress. The Executive Committee added that the CIES would be approached about holding the Congress if the Indian society declined (Minutes, Valencia, 26 June 1979). Moreover, the CIES, with the exception of Gerald Read's work in the earliest years, had contributed very little to World Council activities, and I knew that more was expected of the world's largest comparative education society. The negligible support of the CIES would put me in a defensive position. In this regard, I was animated by CIES President La Belle's letter appointing me representative to the World Congress. The letter stressed the importance that the CIES attached to its involvement in the WCCES, and encouraged me to pursue my proposal aggressively at the Tokyo Congress in July 1980.

Confronting Ignominy: Withdrawing and Reinstating the World Congress Proposal

I did not go to the Tokyo Congress with closed eyes. The WCCES Executive Committee had agreed at its 1974 meeting in Geneva to extend an invitation to the Japan Comparative Education Society (JCES) to hold the 4th World Congress in 1980. The Japan society accepted the invitation, and, at the 3rd World Congress in 1977 in London, the Council agreed to accept an invitation from the Korean Comparative Education Society (KCES) to hold a 1980 pre-Congress (Minutes of the General Assembly, London, 1 July 1977). The pre-Congress in Seoul, South Korea, was held from 3-5 July 1980, just before the World Congress in Japan. I viewed the pre-Congress as an opportunity to gauge the feelings of participants to the idea of a US-sponsored Congress in Mexico.

However, before I had a chance to survey participants at the pre-Congress, a chance encounter with a Taiwanese professor impelled me to reverse course and withdraw my proposal to hold the 5th World Congress in Mexico, despite all the effort that had gone into the proposal and the hard-won support of both the CIES and UDEM. That encounter was with Cheng Chungshin, professor of education and philosophy at the National Taiwan Normal University in Taipei.

Cheng informed me that because of a protocol of the Japanese Commission to the United Nations (UN), which was providing much of the funding for the Tokyo Congress, scholars from South Africa and the Republic of China (Taiwan), including Cheng, were to be excluded from formal participation in the Congress programme. I was profoundly disturbed by Cheng's remarks, because I viewed the UN protocol, if indeed it existed, as an unwarranted intrusion in the scholarly conduct of a professional organisation. Such a protocol would mean that participants could be from the People's Republic of China (PRC), which was recognised by the UN, but not from the Republic of China (ROC), which was not a UN constituent member. The protocol would govern for two reasons: the Japanese National Commission for UNESCO had partially funded the Tokyo Congress, and the WCCES feared losing its coveted Non-governmental Organisation (NGO) status in UNESCO if it violated the protocol. Such a protocol would be clear evidence that academic issues were being swayed by international politics, and I wanted no part of it – even at the cost of my proposal and the hard work that had gone into it. I was repelled by the prospect of the WCCES' willingness to succumb to the political machinations of the United Nations. If Cheng's information proved true, I resolved to terminate my dealings with the WCCES.

Upon my arrival in Tokyo for the 4th World Congress, I was relieved to see Cheng's name on the preliminary programme, and assumed that Cheng was mistaken about the UN exclusionary protocol, that the protocol had been changed, or that it had been discarded by the organising committee. I was therefore prepared to move ahead with my proposal, and did so at the initial meeting of the

WCCES Executive Committee. Shortly after that meeting (which was held before other formal events of the Congress), I met Cheng, who insisted that, notwithstanding his inclusion in the preliminary programme, he was being excluded from formal participation. Cheng's assertion proved to be correct. Checking the final programme, I found that his name had indeed been omitted. I then confronted the organising committee with the matter, and that committee confirmed Cheng's exclusion.

I was then faced with a quandary. I felt that I could not allow myself under the circumstances to forge ahead with the proposal, but I had already submitted it to the Executive Committee. Moreover, this was no longer merely *my* proposal, but that of the CIES and UDEM. After considerable soul searching, I decided to withdraw the proposal anyway, feeling that at least I would act before a vote on it was cast by the Executive Committee. I therefore informed Tetsuya Kobayashi, who was chairing the Executive Committee in the absence of Masunori Hiratsuka, of that decision.

The news of my withdrawal stunned the Executive Committee. As it turned out, the Indian society (CESI), which was favoured to host the next World Congress, had decided not to submit a proposal with the result that my proposal was the only one on the table. Committee members pleaded with me to reconsider, indicating that their approval and enthusiasm for the proposal was unanimous. However, I was adamant in my refusal. That evening Joseph Katz requested a private meeting with me, and we found a quiet room in the National Women's Educational Center, the Congress venue, to discuss the matter. Katz was furious, contending that my action would jeopardise my professional career. He accused me of disloyalty not only to CIES but also to my country, and asserted that I was torpedoing the work of the World Council. I refused to yield, explaining that I could not in good conscience work on behalf of an organisation that proclaimed adherence to the highest ideals of scholarship but caved in to crass political standards. I pointed out that individuals from the PRC were fully allowed to participate, while scholars from Taiwan were not. I described this as a case of raw political favouritism, stating that the Council was committing a travesty by favouring some Chinese scholars (those from the PRC) over other Chinese scholars (those from the ROC) on the basis of a highly partisan, non-academic protocol. I was resolved to give up on all that I had worked for, and to violate the faith that both my Mexican colleagues and the CIES membership had placed in me over this issue. It was a very difficult episode in my professional life.

Although I had withdrawn my proposal, I was the official CIES representative, and therefore technically a member of the Executive Committee. I was feeling like a pariah, but was obliged as the CIES representative to attend subsequent meetings of the WCCES Executive Committee in Tokyo, including sessions devoted to discussing the crisis that I had wrought. It became clear that the Executive Committee was not yet willing to give up on my proposal, and was intent on pursuing every possible remedy. After much deliberation and searching of consciences, the Executive Committee and I reached a compromise, to the great relief of all. We agreed that I would not challenge the UNESCO protocol disallowing Taiwanese scholars from full participation in the current Congress if the Council would guarantee that in the future, the protocol would be discontinued in all matters governed by the Council, including World Congresses. This was part of an agreement that from the end of the Tokyo Congress forward, no bona fide scholar of comparative education, regardless of nationality, race, ethnicity, religion, or political creed, would ever be restricted from participation at World Council sponsored events. I demanded that this guarantee be inscribed in the Council's constitution, and the Executive Committee agreed.

I realised how big a concession this was for the Executive Committee. Several members were concerned about losing the Council's NGO status in the UNESCO over the issue, or at least diminishing their chance of moving from the lower-status category C to the higher status Category B which brought rights of consultation in UNESCO affairs. With this in mind, I thanked the members of the Executive Committee for their understanding and perseverance. The Executive Committee then voted to approve my proposal to hold the next (1983) World Congress in Monterrey, with the CIES as the host society, and nominated me before the Council's General Assembly to be President of the World Council.

The Tokyo Episode as a Defining Moment for the World Council

The episode involving my proposal and election as WCCES President was a victory that went beyond merely elevating scholarly openness above political expediency: it helped to define the nature of the World Council itself. It became clear in my altercation with Katz and in positions he took at Council meetings that he viewed the Council as becoming a sort of educational United Nations. His ideal Council was an organisation representing nation states of the world, mirroring in education the structure and function of the UN and its agencies. I reminded him that the Comparative Education Society in Europe (CESE) was a member of the World Council, overlapping with representations of the British society, Dutch-speaking society, and other European-based societies, so that the construct of Council representation could not be parallel with UN representation. It was as if not only the United Kingdom and other European countries were members of the UN, but as if the whole of Europe was a member as well. Katz's view was that this condition, though regrettable, was 'grandfathered' – that is, put into place as an unfortunate political reality about which he had no control.

I learned in later correspondence with Katz that he viewed the European societies, and in particular CESE, with disdain. He felt that they desired to dominate the field in order to further their own selfish interests. Thus, Katz opposed locating the Secretariat in Europe, and urged that it be moved to Canada where it would be out of the 'elitist' grasp of the Europeans (Katz to Epstein, 3 June 1981). According to Katz, his own successor as WCCES President, Brian Holmes, did not believe in the Council's value. In Katz's words, "Brian Holmes never did fully accept the World Council and contended for several years that the European Society could do the job and that the World Council had undermined the European Society and this despite the fact that there were internal difficulties which precluded the European Society from maintaining harmony and developing initiatives" (Katz to Epstein, 2 September 1981).

My concept of the Council, by contrast, was (and is) that of an organisation comprising representatives of national, sub-national, regional, and language-based groups of scholars and practitioners of comparative education, without regard to political affiliation. As long as a group of comparativists could show a minimum number of members on its roll; had a proper constitution that welcomed all legitimate comparative education scholars within its national, sub-national, regional or linguistic domain without regard to race, ethnicity, religion, or political creed of its members; and avowed adherence to the provisions of the World Council constitution, I felt that it should be admitted as a member of the Council. I insisted on this concept during my term as President and afterward during the years I was a co-opted member of the WCCES Executive Committee. Moreover, in my many conversations with European comparativists over the decades after the Tokyo Congress, I never encountered any of the negativism toward the World Council by the Europeans claimed by Katz. In my view, CESE and members of the other European societies worked energetically and conscientiously to further the work and ideals of the Council.

My concept of the Council and its structure was tested at various times and in several ways. Two tests were particularly memorable. First, as the Council became better known and more attractive, and as comparative education grew around the globe, several groups whose geographical domains coincided or over-lapped contended for recognition. These included most notably the Chinese groups (PRC and ROC), but also rival groups in Italy, Brazil and Great Britain. In addition, for a time a representative from a Colombian society was recognised by the Council but not by the society that he allegedly represented, and Walter Berger from Vienna even proposed that an Austrian group be admitted to the Council as a subsection of the German society (Berger to Epstein, 20 December 1980).

Of these contending groups, the rivalry between the two Chinese organi-sations proved to be by far the most vexatious and the greatest test of the Council's concept of itself. The PRC society argued insistently in favour of Katz's idea of a Council structured after the UN, and that, just as it was in the UN, the PRC organisation should be the sole representative of all Chinese scholars. By contrast, the ROC society embraced my idea of a Council consisting of com-parative education affinity groups. Despite both groups having been admitted to the Council during the early 1980s, the issue was debated over a period of two decades, mostly because the Chinese-language name of the Taiwan society was the 'Republic of China Comparative Education Society', which was not accep-table to the PRC under its 'One China Principle' (see Chapter 5). Unlike the rivalry between the Chinese societies, none of the other contending groups proved to be a serious problem for the Council. The Italians and Brazilians eventually settled on one group in each country to represent them, and the British Society and London Association of Comparative Educationists (LACE) tacitly agreed that both would be represented, though LACE disbanded some years later.

The other major test came from the Indian society. Sureshchandra Shukla, the Indian representative of CESI, throughout the 1980s argued for a kind of bicameral Council, with one part representing comparative education societies and the other composed of individuals from countries without a society to represent them. Shukla contended that the current structure disenfranchised comparativists living where there was no formally recognised comparative education society, especially in Third World and socialist countries. I argued that Shukla's proposed structure would undermine one of the Council's principal objectives: to spread comparative education by supporting the formation of national, sub-national, regional and language-based comparative education organisations. In other words, allowing individuals to have direct membership in the Council would be a disincentive to form new societies. What sense would it make, I asked, for someone to be an individual member of the World Council and concurrently a member of a national or regional organisation? Would such individuals be willing to pay dues to both organisations? Moreover, I added, no comparativist need ever be disenfranchised, since most comparative education societies, including the CIES, had open membership without restrictions on place of residence or of work. Hence, I asserted, no individual need be deprived of membership in a comparative education society simply by virtue of geographical origin.

Although Shukla's proposal was long ago put to rest, the issue has been raised in other forms. In particular, there has been the occasional suggestion at Congress planning sessions to name the Congress the 'World Congress of Comparative Education' – as if individuals as participants are the constituent members of the World Council – rather than keeping the title 'World Congress of Comparative Education Societies' and maintaining a structure of comparative education societies as constituent members. This issue arose in March 2004, when Joseph Zajda proposed a motion during a meeting of the WCCES Executive Committee to change the Congress name to 'World Congress of Comparative Education'. Being present at that meeting, I spoke against the motion, and it was soundly defeated by a vote of six to two, thereby reaffirming the World Congress as a meeting of individuals brought together by virtue of their membership in constituent societies, not by virtue of having direct membership in the Council (Minutes, Salt Lake City, Utah, 8 & 10 March 2004).

The episode relating to my withdrawn proposal for a World Congress – an episode that began just prior to my becoming WCCES President – had far reaching consequences by establishing a fundamental principle and shaping the Council's current identity. However, it should not obscure other important events that occurred during my term of office. I refer in particular to the failure of my plan to hold the 5th World Congress in Mexico.

The President's Agenda: Facing the Challenges Ahead

With my election as WCCES President at the Tokyo Congress and approval of my proposal to hold the 5th Congress in Mexico, the World Council spotlight turned on me. The Tokyo Congress had been successful, having had what was at that time the largest number of participants – approximately 450 individuals from 35 countries – and admitting four new member societies (India, Britain, the Federal

Republic of Germany, and Argentina), bringing the total membership in the Council to 13 (Minutes, Tokyo, 7 July 1980). The Council now expected me to build on this success and bring the world organisation to a new level of prominence.

The Tokyo Congress had come as I was ending my year at UDEM and preparing to return to Missouri. Once at my home university, I entered discussions with the UDEM authorities to return for another year (1982-83) of teaching in Mexico and to prepare the 5th World Congress in Monterrey. I applied for and was granted a Fulbright professorship from the US Information Agency, and was granted another leave of absence by the University of Missouri. This paved the way for me to spend my time in Monterrey in the months leading up to the anticipated Congress.

In Tokyo, the World Council was concerned with more than the venue for the next Congress and the nomination of a President. Other immediate needs included the location of the Secretariat, printing and circulation of the Newsletter, admission of new members, and financing. The Secretariat was of particular concern, because it was only temporarily being hosted by the Japan society and needed a permanent location (Minutes, Tokyo, 7 July 1980). Prior to the temporary Japan Secretariat, the WCCES Secretariat was initially housed at the Comparative Education Centre, University of Ottawa, Canada (1970-72), and was later transferred to the UNESCO International Bureau of Education (IBE) in Geneva, Switzerland with Anne Hamori serving as Secretary General from 1972 to 1978 (see Chapter 1). However, in January 1978, the IBE which had funded Hamori's office gave notice that her salary would be terminated as of June of that year (though extended to July with World Council funds). The Japan society agreed to take over from Hamori only for a brief period. Proposals to host the Secretariat were submitted by the Canadian society (with location to be at the University of Calgary) and the London society (LACE), but both withdrew their proposals in favour of an offer by Leo Fernig to return the office to the IBE in Geneva under his direction (Minutes, Tokyo, 9 July 1980). The Council agreed that the Newsletter would continue to be published by the IBE in cooperation with the Association francophone d'éducation comparée (AFEC) and supervised by Michel Debeauvais with the support of the IBE director James Chandler (see Chapter 3).

It became evident during discussions over the admission of new comparative education societies that the criteria for admission and the matter of members' voting rights were ambiguous and needed clarification. I therefore urged that these issues be addressed for the benefit of future admissions. Consequently, the Executive Committee appointed Shukla and Fernig to examine the Council's constitution and report back by the end of the Congress (Minutes, Tokyo, 9 July 1980). The matter turned out to be much more complicated than anticipated, and Shukla agreed to recommend names for a constitution committee that he would chair over the coming months.

Financing the Council's activities was another difficult issue. Until the Tokyo Congress, the Council had been supported mainly through the volunteer work of its Presidents, Secretaries General (except for Anne Hamori, who was paid), and newsletter editors (especially Michel Debeauvais). The IBE contributed office space and some miscellaneous support. In addition, monetary contributions were made by Masunori Hiratsuka and, early on, by Gerald Read, as well as small amounts by a few societies – namely, the Australian society, the CIES, and the European society (CESE). Some revenue was also generated by the sale of Council-sponsored publications (Minutes, Tokyo, 9 July 1980). The voluntary support would continue, of course, but the Council had no established mechanism for generating funds. The Council agreed that every society should make a financial contribution "somewhere between two levels, the basic fee of US$50 and the upper level of US$1 per member per year" (Minutes, Tokyo, 9 July 1980), but made no provision for enforcing this standard.

Implementing the Proposal: Preparing for the 5th World Congress
Matters relating to the Secretariat, the Newsletter, Council membership, and funding were important, but the most critical challenge was preparing for the World Congress in Monterrey, Mexico. The Council funds were so meagre that I decided against drawing on them for my own expenses. Rather, I resolved to rely on support from UDEM, my university in Missouri, whatever assistance I could secure from CIES, and my own personal savings. However, the World Council was not high on the priority list of the University of Missouri, and its support was negligible. CIES funds were available only for my travel expenses to the national meeting, where I would also hold an interim meeting of the World Council Executive Committee. UDEM was willing to pay for limited travel to Council meetings in Europe and to Monterrey for planning purposes, but not my immediate expenses while I was operating out of my Missouri office. Communications were difficult and slow: overseas telephone calls were unaffordable, leaving me to the vicissitudes of the excruciatingly sluggish, though reliable, postal service.

My first step was to appoint a Congress organising committee composed of Americans on whom I could rely and key figures from Mexico. Among the Americans, I included Gerald Read, whose knowledge of both the World Council and CIES was unmatched; Max Eckstein, CIES Vice-President and my immediate successor; Christopher Lucas, a senior colleague from the University of Missouri whom I felt could help me negotiate assistance from our university administration; and Noel McGinn, a respected scholar associated with both Harvard University and the prominent Javier Barros Sierra Foundation in Mexico. On the Mexican side, Luis Quintero was my co-organiser in charge of local planning. We were joined by UDEM Rector, Iván Espinosa; UDEM Vice Rector, Fernando Cuellar; Carmen Tamez, an UDEM faculty member; Carolina Santos de Velarde, the UDEM extension programme coordinator for education; Guillermo Gonzalez, Director of the Educational Studies Center in Mexico City; and José Esteva, Director of the Javier Barros Sierra Foundation. I convened the committee with funding from UDEM on 18 December 1980 in Monterrey.

The organisational meeting in Monterrey was extremely productive: in one day we accomplished more than most would have done in a week. The committee was highly congenial, and worked efficiently. I briefed the committee on the World Council and previous congresses, and we broke into three subcommittees to plan the budget, lodging, transportation, languages, distribution of papers, security arrangements, book exhibit, registration, and, of course, the programme and Congress theme: 'Dependence and Interdependence in Educational Development'. I mapped out a detailed schedule for implementing the plan, from the meeting that day to the Congress in July 1983, which the committee approved. The next step was to meet with the CIES Board of Directors at the annual CIES conference in March 1981 in Tallahassee, Florida, USA, to report on plans for the Congress, and then to report to the WCCES Executive Committee at its meeting in September 1981 in Geneva, Switzerland (Minutes, Meeting of the US/Mexico 1983 Congress Organizing Committee, Monterrey, 18 December 1980).

As I was now wearing two hats – as WCCES President and as CIES President-elect – I had intended to solidify the relationship between the two organisations at the CIES meeting in Tallahassee. Thomas La Belle had offered strong encouragement about the importance of that relationship the previous year. However, that encouragement would be tested by my proposal to place the World Council on a more secure financial footing by replacing the haphazard voluntary dues with a concrete schedule of membership dues collection. I assumed that my success in gaining approval for a combined CIES/World Congress would furnish the platform I needed to induce the CIES to pay its fair share as the Council's largest constituent member. As it turned out, I was wrong.

The WCCES Executive Committee in Tokyo discussed a proposal to have member societies charge US$1 to each of its individual members in support of the Council's operations. I informed La Belle of the proposal, and urged that it be considered by the CIES Board of Directors in Tallahassee. La Belle's reaction, however, was strongly unfavourable, his tone regarding the Council having changed markedly from his remarks to me before the Tokyo Congress. Without La Belle's support for the proposal on dues for the Council, I thought it best to limit my actions in Tallahassee to the Congress. I did not raise the question about dues, and my report was well received in Tallahassee without much discussion.

Pulling the Rug from Underneath: UDEM Withdraws Support

A year after the Tokyo Congress, plans were going smoothly for the 5th Congress in 1983. We had ample financing, a solid venue, and strong institutional support – or so I thought. However, on 27 August 1981, I received a call from Luis Quintero in Monterrey informing me that the Mexican economy had collapsed and that the UDEM Board of Directors were compelled to withdraw their support for the Congress. The rug was abruptly being pulled from under our feet. In one brief moment, without any forewarning, all our plans evaporated, and I felt that the trust that the Council and CIES had placed in me would be violated. Quintero's news was confirmed two weeks later in an apologetic letter to me from the UDEM's rector, Iván Espinosa (15 September 1981).

The news could not have come at a more delicate time. Only a month before, I had reported to the Council the sad news of the passing away of two figures who had had a profound influence on the World Council and their own comparative education societies, namely Masunori Hiratsuka of Japan and Joseph Lauwerys of the United Kingdom. We were beginning to think about plans to memorialise these greatly-admired individuals. And, just a month later, we were scheduled to meet in Geneva for a critical meeting of the WCCES Executive Committee, to take place concurrently with a CESE conference. I was to report on the progress we had made on our plans for the 1983 World Congress as well as confer on other matters of importance, such as the Council's finances, Newsletter, and applications for admission of new member societies. Moreover, the Council Secretariat had ceased to function over the previous nine months, causing alarm. My repeated letters to Leo Fernig during this period were left unanswered. Fearing that Fernig had fallen ill, I appealed to European members of the Council to look into the problem, with no result. As it turns out, Fernig was preoccupied with administering an international school of 2,500 pupils and could not find time to carry on his duties as Secretary General or even inform me and others of his conflict of time. Concurrently, Shukla, who had been given the responsibility to propose modifications in the Council's constitution, simply abandoned his project without explanation.

Perhaps all was not lost in regard to a Mexican Congress after all. Perhaps we could find alternative means of support and still hold the Congress in that country, though probably not in Monterrey, with CIES support. I conferred with Luis Quintero, and we arranged to meet in Geneva before the Executive Committee meeting to discuss our options and a strategy to move forward. Quintero agreed to appeal to the Mexican Council for the Advancement of Science and Technology (CONICYT) and other Mexican agencies for support.

At Geneva, the Executive Committee agreed that every effort should be made to hold the Congress in Mexico and to find alternative support, with Quintero and me to report the result of our efforts no later than the next scheduled interim meeting of the Executive Committee in March 1982, when it would convene in conjunction with the CIES annual meeting in New York City. At the same time, Executive Committee members were to explore alternatives to Mexico and have plans in hand in case a Mexican Congress proved untenable. The Committee identified France, India, and Egypt as the favoured venues, with preference given to a developing country. Because of the time lost in the crisis, the Committee moved the date of the Congress to 1984.

Notwithstanding the crisis over the Congress, we made substantial progress in Geneva on other fronts. David Turner and Martin McLean, students of Brian Holmes at the University of London Institute of Education, were appointed Assistant Secretaries General to work with Fernig. This proved to be a godsend, as Turner and McLean were both efficient and dedicated. Their work was mostly in the area of communications and arranging official meetings. With Turner and McLean to assist, Fernig again became conscientious and carried out his responsibilities effectively. I outlined a plan to elicit funds from philanthropic foundations to restore the Council's financial health, and indicated a need to produce attractive official stationery and a descriptive bilingual brochure. The Council's treasury consisted of a mere US$3,000 and SF3,000 in bank accounts that had been largely forgotten. While in Geneva, I arranged with Fernig's help to meet Anne Hamori, and together we located the accounts.

The Aftermath

The months leading up to and immediately following the Geneva meeting were some of the most intense of my professional career. Concurrently presiding over both the largest comparative education society and the world body of comparative education societies, while attending to normal duties at my university, was an extraordinary burden. In retrospect, I can only imagine how much easier it would have been had we had the internet, high-speed copiers, and word processors at that time. My files are filled with mail from all over the world. The number of matters to which I attended could only be barely grasped in this account.

Quintero and I, despite our best efforts, did not get the support we needed to secure a World Congress in Mexico. Meeting in New York City in March 1982, the WCCES Executive Committee decided to accept an offer from Michel Debeauvais and AFEC to host the next World Congress in 1984. The meeting in New York City saw other important changes as well. After Joseph Katz made some harsh criticisms about a design prepared by Leo Fernig of much-needed brochures and letterhead for the Council, Fernig abruptly resigned as Secretary General. Raymond Ryba, representing the British society, volunteered his services for the interim. The Executive Committee appointed him to replace Fernig as Secretary General in 1983. Ryba served for many years afterward with great distinction as Secretary General.

I continued to serve on the WCCES Executive Committee for almost two decades after my term ended in April 1983, first as the CIES representative and later as a co-opted member. During much of that time, I presided over the constitutional committee and was responsible for many modifications in the Statutes and By-Laws. In particular, my initiatives produced binding changes in the nature of Council officers' responsibilities, method of dues collection, obligations of member societies, enforcement of Council rules, sharing of revenues generated by World Congresses, and responsibilities of World Congress host societies. The changes also clarified the overall mission of the World Council and connections among its components.

I have dedicated my professional life to comparative education since 1962, when I became a graduate student in the Comparative Education Center at the University of Chicago and a member of CIES. My years as President of the WCCES and of the CIES, as well as my decade as editor of the CIES' *Comparative Education Review* (1988-98), were the most rewarding of my career. During the period over which I served these organisations in a formal capacity, I saw comparative education grow in scale and stature. I trust that this chapter will help to show that the field's growth and achievements have not come easily, and are the product of the good will and unselfish efforts of many individuals.

3

From Würzburg to Rio: 1983-1987

Michel DEBEAUVAIS

I am not in a position to write a fully-documented history about the five years I had the honour to chair the World Council for Comparative Education Societies (WCCES). This is mainly because the archives of the Association francophone d'éducation comparée (AFEC), including the ones I had kept on the Paris 5th World Congress in 1984, were lost during the renovation of the Sèvres Royal Porcelain Factory which housed the Centre international d'études pédagogiques (CIEP) and AFEC. This is therefore a recollection of my memories.

Election as WCCES President and Early Challenges

I was elected President of the WCCES during a Council meeting that took place in Würzburg, Germany, in July 1983 during the biennial conference of the Comparative Education Society in Europe (CESE). I had been nominated by Gerald Read, one of the founders of the WCCES. There was a need to take urgent action to announce the 5th World Congress, after the project which had been approved at the 1980 meeting of World Council during the 4th World Congress in Tokyo failed. At this Congress the WCCES Executive Committee had accepted the proposal of its President, Erwin H. Epstein, to hold the 5th World Congress in Monterrey, Mexico, in 1983. At a small Council meeting convened by Epstein in New York in March 1982 during a conference of the Comparative and International Education Society (CIES), we realised that the 5th World Congress could not be held in Mexico. I therefore reconsidered an earlier AFEC proposal to organise the 5th World Congress in Paris, around July 1984. Some years previously, I had set up both an organising committee and an international programme committee with the goal of bidding for the Congress. I went to Würzburg with a secure proposal from AFEC to organise the Congress in Paris. These measures were approved in Würzburg during the CESE Conference, which the majority of the World Council Executive Committee members attended.

My objectives were thus set within the framework of a dynamic, united and international team. I could not have committed myself to organise the 5th World Congress without being assured of the support of the CIEP and the French Ministry of Education. The CIEP Director was Jean Auba, and the Secretary General was Pierre Alexandre, concurrent Secretary General of AFEC.

Furthermore, Raymond Ryba, who had just been appointed by Erwin H. Epstein as Secretary General of the WCCES following the resignation in 1982 of Leo Fernig, was also member of the AFEC Bureau. I knew Ryba well, as he had participated in the work of AFEC since its creation in 1973, and we had a friendship that grew stronger as we worked together in the WCCES. We undertook several missions together to prepare the Congresses that ensued, mainly in Brazil for the preparation of the 6th World Congress. He was involved in all the decisions that were made during the term of my mandate, and we consulted each other several times each month on fundamental and organisational issues. It was with a view to strengthening the role of Ryba that I encouraged the Executive Committee to decide that the Secretary General would from then on be elected and not appointed by the Chairman. Ryba's advice, action and initiatives played an essential role in the life of the WCCES and its continuity. His memory should be honoured in the history of the WCCES, for he was its pillar for 20 years, from 1979 until his untimely death in 1999.

Vision for the World Council

I now come to the projects that I undertook to put in place during the time I was the Chair, with the support of Ryba and AFEC. Our development project for the World Council had several objectives, namely:

- collective international preparation of the World Congress programme;
- encouraging the creation of new comparative education societies, mainly in developing countries;
- enhancing cooperation with UNESCO; and
- encouraging comparative research that would bring together several World Council societies.

To improve the quality of the Congress debates, we set up Thematic Committees (at that time called Commissions), the moderators of which could solicit contributions from renowned comparative researchers, select papers proposed by the participants, organise discussions, make reports, and eventually widen them into publications and thus continuously further the preparation for the next congress. There was therefore long-term cooperation within the WCCES Research Committee.

Secondly, we aimed to encourage the creation of national comparative education societies, mainly in Latin America, Africa and Asia, and to draw particular attention to matters concerning the Southern regions in the Congress programmes. Focus on the developing countries was led by the increased attention by international agencies such as the Organisation for Economic Co-operation and Development (OECD) and the United Nations Educational, Scientific and Cultural Organization (UNESCO) and the World Bank. This was a new and promising field for comparative researchers, and I had underlined this theme in my speech at the 3rd World Congress in London in 1977, later published in a volume of Congress papers edited by Brian Holmes (Debeauvais 1980). Leo Fernig, who had presented the final report at the closing session, supported this orientation for the World Council.

With this leitmotif, we saw the huge potential for the field in the countries which as yet had no comparative education societies. The WCCES had only three member societies in Asia (Japan, Korea and India). I had established relations with Gu Mingyuan on a visit to China in 1980, and he had told me that he would envisage the possibility that the Chinese Comparative Education Society (CCES) formed the previous year would join the World Council. During a visit to Brazil in 1986, I worked with the Brazilian Comparative Education Society (SBEC), which had been formed in 1983. We had already envisaged the possibility of organising the 6th World Congress in Rio de Janeiro, and I had the support of Fernando Henrique Cardoso, a sociologist at the São Paulo University, Brazil. I had met him at the Sorbonne, Paris where he had been lecturing when he went into exile after the military coup. We also tried to assist both an Argentinean and a Colombian comparative education society. A society was being formed in Nigeria, but forming societies in developing countries was going at a slow rate and was filled with uncertainty, except in China and Brazil.

Our third aim was to improve relations with UNESCO. This had become especially necessary since the resignation of Leo Fernig as WCCES Secretary General at a 1982 meeting convened in New York by Erwin H. Epstein. Leo Fernig had until then provided the assistance of UNESCO's International Bureau of Education (IBE) since 1971, a year after the WCCES had been created. He had provided the IBE's institutional support to the World Council, specifically by taking charge of the publication and dissemination of a WCCES Newsletter. When he retired from the IBE in 1977, his successor, James Chandler, did not have the same interest in comparative education and in the WCCES. Having had no follow-up on the steps I had undertaken, I tried to draw the attention of my UNESCO colleagues, starting with the Director-General, Amadou-Mahtar M'Bow and the different divisions in the Education Sector. I involved them as much as I could in the programme of the Paris Congress, and reserved key roles for them in the programme.

The fourth aim was to foster relationships between comparative education societies, not only in the preparation of the Congress programme but also in joint research. I proposed to the UNESCO Director for the Division for Curricular Development, Henri Dieuzeide, to entrust to the World Council a comparative study of National Educational Research Policies, a theme that was already on the UNESCO agenda. This was the opportunity to involve the WCCES in a joint undertaking with UNESCO. Together with Ryba, we formed an international team, the first meeting of which took place in Paris during the 5th World Congress. It comprised Philip Altbach and Harold Noah (USA), José Luis García Garrido (Spain), Cândido Gomes (Brazil), R.P. Singh (India), Vittorio Telmon (Italy), Kenneth King (UK), Asuntoye Yoloye (Nigeria), and Jürgen Schriewer (Germany). We agreed to use the same problematic for each country's monograph. Later meetings took place in coordination with the sessions of the Executive Committee, for example in Garda, Italy, in 1986, and in Rio de Janeiro, Brazil, in

1987. The report of the initial undertakings was published by UNESCO in 1990 under the title *National Educational Research Policies: A World Survey* (Debeauvais 1990). Unfortunately, this programme was neither furthered by UNESCO nor taken up by any WCCES societies.

I hoped that the preparatory committees set up for the Paris Congress would ensure some sort of continuity from one Congress to another while remaining open to changes, and that they could envisage publications. Only the Commission for Theories and Methods published a book as an offshoot of the Congress (Schriewer & Holmes 1990). Other committees were created by the WCCES to ensure continuity from one Congress to another, and to look into issues such as the admission of new members, the venue for the next Congress, and the conditions for organising Congresses. Most of the preparatory groups for the committees scheduled to take place in Würzburg in 1983 had prepared papers for the Paris Congress, but also remained open to all participants.

From Paris to Rio

The theme for the 1984 Paris World Congress, 'Dependence and Interdependence in Education: The Role of Comparative Education', was complemented by six sub-themes that were to be discussed concurrently in six commissions in half of the sessions. Colleagues were contacted to form six working groups for the debates. The colleagues who had agreed to prepare papers for the six committees had a key role in encouraging comparative researchers to attend the Congress. These sub-themes were:

- dependence and interdependence in the pre-colonial, colonial and post-colonial era;
- exchanges, co-operation and dependence in education in international relations;
- dependence and interdependence in national educational policies: sexes, regions, minorities, social, ethnic and cultural groups;
- dependence and interdependence in teaching: the comparative perspective;
- new educational technologies and their impact on the relations of dependence and interdependence between countries; and
- theories and methods in comparative education.

The AFEC team took charge of the congress organisation, with the logistical assistance of the CIEP. All sessions were held at the Sorbonne University Faculty of Law, Paris, which was constructed in the 18th century at the same time as the Pantheon in the heart of the Latin Quarter of Paris. The French National Institute of Educational Research prepared an exhibition of documents on 'The Role of Comparative Education in Educational Reforms', featuring original historical works written by founders of the field such as Marc-Antoine Jullien.

The Congress was announced in the WCCES Newsletter which AFEC published in January 1984 (in French and in English), despite a number of difficulties. As mentioned, the WCCES Newsletter was created by Leo Fernig within the framework of the IBE, but its publication ceased when he was no longer its Director. AFEC took over the task of publication, and in June 1980 announced the Tokyo 4th World Congress. A second issue was published in March 1981, followed by a third bulletin in January 1984 announcing the programme and organisational modalities of the Paris Congress. Despite the short time for preparation, the Congress attracted 569 participants from 80 countries. A brochure containing summaries of 60 speeches was distributed to the participants during their registration. The commissions stimulated lively debates, and presented reports at the closing session.

I had hoped that the venue for the 6th World Congress could be agreed upon during the Paris Congress. AFEC had worked hand in hand with the incipient Sociedade Brasileira de Educação Comparada (SBEC) since 1983 with a view to drafting a well-elaborated project to be presented to the Executive Committee in Paris during the 5th World Congress in July 1984. The participation of 39 Brazilians at the Paris Congress showed the vitality of the SBEC. The choice of Rio de Janeiro was approved after long discussions, but I had to agree to remain WCCES President until the Rio Congress in 1987 because the SBEC was just newly formed. I therefore worked together with Raymond Ryba and our Brazilian colleagues for three years, in both Rio and Brasilia, and in Paris.

The Rio Congress marked a new and important step in the history of the World Council. It had a significant echo in Latin America, and entirely justified the trust that the Executive Committee had laid in the SBEC. In Rio de Janeiro, Vandra Masemann was elected WCCES President, while Raymond Ryba was appointed for a new mandate as Secretary General. The venue for the 7th World Congress was set for Montreal, Canada, and the draft project presented by Jacques Lamontagne and Douglas Ray on behalf of the Comparative and International Education Society of Canada (CIESC) was approved by the Executive Committee.

Conclusion

Despite these achievements in the institutional development of the World Council and of the field of comparative education, by the end of my term we were still far from the objectives that I had set out at the beginning of my presidency. New ways had to be found to create conditions for collaboration among the WCCES member societies, and also to ensure funding for the Council which had at its disposal only symbolic contributions from its members. Raymond Ryba worked toward this with remarkable perseverance. He secured an agreement with the SBEC about the money received from the 6th World Congress, but this was still insufficient.

After the Rio Congress, I continued to fulfil the different missions that had been assigned to me. They gave me the opportunity to participate in the work of the Executive Committee until 1996, and to maintain a close relationship between the WCCES and UNESCO.

References

Debeauvais, Michel (1980): 'The Role of International Organisations in the Evolution of Applied Comparative Education', in Holmes, Brian (ed.), *Diversity and Unity in Education: A Comparative Analysis*. London: George Allen & Unwin, pp.18-30.

Debeauvais, Michel (1990): *National Educational Research Policies: A World Survey*. Paris: UNESCO.

Schriewer, Jürgen & Holmes, Brian (eds.) (1990): *Theories and Methods in Comparative Education*. 2nd edition, Frankfurt am Main: Peter Lang.

4

The Long Road to Montreal and Beyond: 1987-1991

Vandra MASEMANN

When I look at the photograph in Chapter 30 taken at the plenary session at the 6th World Congress in Rio de Janeiro, after I was declared the incoming President of the World Council of Comparative Education Societies (WCCES), I remember thinking that a new chapter of my professional life was about to begin. Unlike most of my predecessors, I had not had a long personal association with the World Council before my election at that Congress. My presence on that stage was the result of efforts by the Executive Council of the Comparative and International Education Society of Canada (CIESC) over a period of several years to host a World Congress nearly 20 years after the first one held in Ottawa in 1970. It is only through reading the files from the WCCES archives and my personal files from the CIESC that I am in a better position now to understand why I was on that stage listening to the tumultuous applause from a room filled with Brazilian educators and colleagues from many other countries. In this chapter, I will fill in some of the background to the Canadian bid to host the 7th World Congress and the complex interplay among the various member societies, the events of my Presidency, and my efforts to reach goals similar to the ones outlined by Michel Debeauvais in the previous chapter. The experiences of the CIESC in hosting the 7th World Congress were inextricably connected with the efforts of the Chinese Comparative Education Society (CCES) to host the 8th World Congress in Beijing, China, although we did not fully realise it at the time.

Background to the Canadian Bid to Host the 7th World Congress: 1982-86

In the October 1982 CIESC Newsletter, members were urged to attend the World Congress in Paris, France. I had just been elected CIESC Vice-President, and Jacques Lamontagne of the Université de Montréal had just been elected President. In the April 1984 CIESC Newsletter, Joseph Katz and Phil Moir of the University of British Columbia were advertising the travel plans they had made to facilitate members' trips to the 5th World Congress in Paris.

Even before 1984, the members of the CIESC were contemplating hosting a

World Congress. This desire came from the wish to repeat the 1970 experience and from the concern over the failure of the plans for the Mexico Congress and the subsequent rather hurried planning of the Paris Congress. In 1983, meetings of the World Council were attended by Jacques Lamontagne, Daniel Dorotich (CIESC Past President), Joseph Katz, Michel Laferrière (Member-at-Large) and Werner Stephan (Secretary-Treasurer), so the Executive was aware of these events first-hand (CIESC President's Report, May 1984).

In March 1984, the Board of Directors of the Comparative and International Education Society (CIES) met in Houston, Texas, and discussed an invitation from the WCCES to host the 1987 World Congress. As I was on the CIES Board at that time, I knew that this idea was not warmly welcomed because they foresaw problems with the timing (their meetings were always in March) and with funding (they did not have access to government funds for such events, and would not commit any CIES funds to a co-hosted World Congress). I then suggested that the CIES and the CIESC should look into co-hosting it, and I was promptly named Chair of a committee to report back to the CIES the following year. Gail Kelly, Vice-President of CIES, wrote a memo to the then CIES President, John Hawkins, Barbara Yates (CIES Past President), and R. Murray Thomas (CIES President-Elect), with copies to me and the other Canadians later that month stating that "I support the idea of co-hosting the World Congress provided that it does not entail any financial expenditures on the part of the CIES". She wanted the committee to assess "the probability that the meeting will pay for itself" (Kelly to Hawkins et al., 17 March 1984).

I relayed this information to Jacques Lamontagne, and told him that a group of CIESC members (John Mallea, Douglas Ray, Joseph Farrell, David Wilson, and Kazim Bacchus) had met in Houston to consider the idea of co-hosting, and that there was "a generally lukewarm/favourable but not negative reaction" (26 March 1984). I replied to Gail Kelly, indicating that David Wilson, Joseph Farrell and I had been studying the feasibility of co-hosting a World Congress at the Ontario Institute for Studies in Education (OISE) in Toronto. I informed her that after discussing the preliminary proposal at the CIESC meeting in Guelph, Ontario in June 1984 with the CIESC Executive and with Bernard Shapiro, the President of the Canadian Society for the Study of Education (CSSE), our umbrella organisation, we reluctantly concluded that co-hosting the World Congress with the CIES would not be possible for the CIESC. A very major concern was that of funding. It was considered impossible to commit the CIESC to co-host the Congress on the condition that the CIES engage in no financial outlay. In addition, it was considered unlikely that the Canadian government would commit funds to a co-hosted event. The CIESC members then turned their minds to the idea of hosting the World Congress alone. I wrote to Jacques Lamontagne on 21 September 1984 that "I understand that Brazil was offering to host the next World Congress, but have not heard of any further developments on the Canadian proposal". In the same letter, I declined to be named CIESC President at the expiry of my term as CIESC Vice-President because of my lack of an institutional base [in a full-time university position] in the event that the CIESC were awarded the

Congress. I opined that "a more firmly situated President could lead the Society during the mid-80s, whether or not we are involved in the World Congress".

The October 1984 CIESC Newsletter (p.16) contained an enthusiastic report from Joseph Katz on the 5th World Congress in Paris. He noted the admission of four new societies to the World Council: Egypt, Colombia, China, and Brazil. He stated:

> The Council tentatively accepted the offer of the Brazilian Society to host the 6th World Congress of Comparative Education Societies in 1987. Negotiations for the venue of this Congress are in progress.

In his President's Report of May 1985, Jacques Lamontagne noted that I was to be President-Elect as of June 1985, for a two-year term. I had obviously been convinced to stay on. The Minutes for the June 1985 CIESC meeting in Montreal present a picture of a small society struggling with membership and income, and even discussing how to save money on postage for its journal.

An interesting outcome of the CIES/CIESC co-operation was the invitation from the CIES for me to be a member of the Planning Committee for the 30th anniversary conference of the CIES, organised by Gail Kelly, to be held in Toronto in March 1986. However, the invitation was not to me in my role as CIESC President, but rather as a Toronto-based CIES Board member. David Wilson and Joseph Farrell were also heavily involved in the planning. A World Council meeting was also scheduled at that meeting in Toronto. Gail Kelly was quite impatient with the formality and requests of the WCCES Executive members, and asked me why I "wasted my time with the World Council". That meeting did, however, signal a growing relationship between the World Council and the North American societies. Up to then, the three people most often attending World Congresses and WCCES meetings were Erwin Epstein, Susanne Shafer and Joseph Di Bona. The US participation in the affairs of the World Council has grown steadily since 1986.

By the time of the 1986 CIES conference, interest in the Brazil Congress was growing, and brochures and posters were distributed. The theme was 'Education, Crisis and Change' and the venue was the Convention Centre of the Hotel Gloria in Rio de Janeiro. As the Sociedade Brasileira de Educação Comparada (SBEC) was very young, Michel Debeauvais remained the President of the World Council and Raymond Ryba its Secretary General. They visited Brazil to help the local organisers with conference planning. Eurides Brito da Silva was named Vice-President of the WCCES. In his chapter, Michel Debeauvais states that the Association francophone d'éducation comparée (AFEC) had been working with the Brazilians since 1984 to plan their Congress. One might have wondered why the CIES had also been invited to submit a bid to host the 1987 Congress, although we were assured subsequently that the practice was to invite several proposals, sometimes with acrimonious results (see Anne Hickling-Hudson's account, Chapter 7). At that time, most of us in the CIESC were oblivious to the innermost workings of the World Council.

I attended the WCCES meeting held in conjunction with the CIES meeting in Toronto, and found it to be more formal and circumlocutory than the North American ones. It was chaired by Michel Debeauvais in both French and English, and Raymond Ryba assisted in both languages. Michel Debeauvais had invited the CIESC to submit a proposal at that meeting to host the 1990 World Congress.

In May 1986, I informed the CIESC that we had been invited to submit a bid to host the 7th World Congress in 1990, and that our proposal was to be presented to the World Council in Rio de Janeiro in 1987 (President's Message, *CIESC Newsletter*, May 1986). This was the first document to state that the CIESC was going to submit a bid as a lone society. By telephone, Douglas Ray had invited me to join him and Jacques Lamontagne in a serious effort to have the next World Congress in Canada. Jacques would chair the Congress Organising Committee, Douglas the Congress Programme Committee, and, as the then CIESC President, I would be the candidate for the WCCES Presidency. I noted that the reaction from the CIESC members who had attended the CIES meeting in Toronto in March 1986 had been very favourable to the invitation.

At the annual meeting of CIESC in Winnipeg in May 1986, Jacques Lamontagne presented the proposal to hold the Congress at the Palais des Congrès in Montreal, with the theme 'Language and Education on the World Scene/Langue et éducation sur la scène mondiale', in July 1990. It was enthusiastically endorsed by the membership. In October 1986, there was a special conference on the 25th anniversary of the Comparative Education Society in Europe (CESE) in Garda (Verona), Italy, and Douglas Ray attended that meeting to represent the CIESC and to serve formal notice that we would submit a proposal at the Rio meeting of the WCCES. It is unlikely that we were aware how much we did not know about the process of decision-making about Congress proposals, as we enthusiastically went ahead with our plans.

In March 1987, the CIESC took the proposal to the WCCES meeting in Washington held during the CIES conference. As only eight members of the WCCES attended that meeting, it was not possible to hold a vote. I wrote: "Thus I cannot report 100% success, but in the absence of any other written proposals, our [CIESC] proposal holds a very good likelihood of being accepted" (President's Message, *CIESC Newsletter*, April 1987). At that CIES meeting, I was also elected as incoming Vice-President of CIES. I hoped that by running for that office, I would be able to get the CIES to support the World Council to a greater extent than in the past. This goal was only partially achieved. For example, I was unable to get the CIES Board to agree to have their 1989 annual meeting in conjunction with the World Congress in Montreal, for reasons of timing and budget. Instead, I had to organise the CIES meeting that year at Harvard. However, many CIES members attended the Congress and have since played active roles. Jacques Lamontagne and Douglas Ray played the major role in preparing our proposal to host the 7th World Congress in Montreal. Applications for funding were submitted to the Department of the Secretary of State of the Government of Canada and to the Social Sciences and Humanities Research Council (SSHRC). The funds from the Secretary of State would support translation and interpretation, and those from the SSHRC would support the office in Canada of a major international academic society and the Congress. It was Lamontagne's plan that the World Council would have a Secretariat in Canada for the three years before the Congress and that he would be Assistant Secretary General, as Raymond Ryba had been re-appointed Secretary General at the WCCES meeting in Paris. The funding came through from the SSHRC for the first year. Although we had originally wanted to hold the 7th World Congress in the new Congress Centre in Montreal, their staff indicated that our numbers for previous Congresses were inadequate to warrant such a large venue. So it was decided to hold it at the Université de Montréal.

A few days before the meeting in Rio de Janeiro in July 1987, we were informed that the Chinese Comparative Education Society (CCES) would also be presenting a proposal in Rio. We left for Brazil feeling completely surprised. In Rio, Douglas Ray from the CIESC was working very hard with the Brazilians – Mabel Tarré Carvalho de Oliveira, Sonia Nogueira, Robert Verhine, and Roberto Ballalai – to help finalise the programme just before the Congress opened. The Congress sessions were based on the work of six Research Commissions, along the lines of the 1984 Paris Congress, and the Research Commissions were holding their organisational meetings. We were summoned by Michel Debeauvais to a late evening meeting in the Hotel Gloria attended by Raymond Ryba and the representatives from the CCES. To our amazement, the suggestion was made that we withdraw our proposal and resubmit it for the 1993 Congress. After an intense period of negotiation into the early hours of the morning, we all agreed that the CIESC could host the Congress, but in 1989, and the Chinese in 1991, so as to defer their Congress for just one year. This plan was presented to the WCCES Executive, which approved it, with a slight change of theme title: 'Development, Communication and Language/Développement, communication et langue'. Since Canada was developing strong links with China through the overseas aid pro-grammes of the Canadian International Development Agency (CIDA), and some CIESC members were doing research in China and were fluent in Chinese – among them Jacques Lamontagne and Ruth Hayhoe – the CIESC immediately planned to foster links between the organisers of the Canadian and Chinese Congresses (*CIESC Newsletter*, October 1987).

At the Rio meeting, I was elected and declared WCCES President. There-fore, I was no longer just a player in the national society. The feeling that I had on the platform did become a reality. Since that day, I have had a wider view of the world of comparative education, and I had to learn very quickly about the major issues that are described in the other chapters of this book.

Events from 1987 to 1991

The first WCCES Executive meeting that I chaired was in July 1987 in Niterói, Brazil, held at a high school venue that had been arranged for us by Roberto Ballalai. A bus had been arranged to take us to Niterói, and on that long and hot ride, Raymond Ryba sat beside me. He went through the entire meeting agenda and explained how to deal with the various issues. He and Michel Debeauvais had also ensured that I had drawn up a list of goals I intended to attain during my Presidency. That hour on the bus set the tone for all the subsequent encounters I was to have with Raymond. He was well-informed, kind, generous, articulate, constructive, well-spoken, and keen to convey to me the intricacies of World Council politics. He murmured pointers throughout the meeting so that I was able to cover all the items on the agenda.

Raymond Ryba and Michel Debeauvais must have been somewhat non-plussed to see someone who had not previously taken part in World Council business be elected to the Presidency. That system of having the Congress host society's President as President of the WCCES has become unworkable since that time because of a series of historical events beyond the WCCES' control. The present system of having a search for the Presidential candidates and a process of securing institutional support for them and the World Council avoids some of the stresses that the CIESC encountered in having its officers being responsible both as host organisers and as officers of the World Council. By that meeting at the end of the World Congress, much discussion was already underway about Lamontagne's plan to move the Secretariat to Montreal. It was only a matter of hours into my Presidency when I came to see what would grow into an intractable disagreement between Ryba and Lamontagne on the matter of the Secretariat. In the next four years, I also found myself in the middle of an insoluble situation: how to be loyal to my CIESC colleague with whom I had invested so much time and energy in getting the bid ready for the World Congress, how to make decisions that I perceived to be in the best interests of the World Council, or how to know when a matter was beyond my power to solve. This problem was never resolved, to my great regret.

At the Niterói meeting, I presented my statement of policy to the World Council:

1. Total support of the Executive Committee, the CIESC and the CCES in their preparations to host the 7th and 8th World Congresses.
2. Continued co-operation of the World Council with UNESCO Head-quarters, the International Bureau of Education (IBE), and other inter-national organisations.
3. Continued effort to promote the study of comparative education throughout the world through the holding of World Congresses, the encouragement of new member societies of the World Council, and support of existing societies.
4. Promotion of research in comparative education in various ways.
5. Improvement of communications between the World Council and its member societies through its Newsletter.
6. Improvement of communication among and between delegates at the 7th World Congress of Comparative Education Societies through the inves-tigation of translation methods and strategies at conferences.

The main features of this policy were agreed to by the members of the Exe-cutive Committee. Most of the rest of the meeting was given over to administrative matters concerning setting up Commissions (now called Standing Committees), appointing Gu Mingyuan as the Vice-President of the WCCES in addition to

Eurides Brito da Silva, appointing Jacques Lamontagne as Assistant Secretary General, appointing Michel Debeauvais as a Co-opted Member, examining the Council's finances and relations with UNESCO, and admitting the Italian Section of CESE (SICESE) (Minutes of the 6th WCCES Meeting, Niterói, 1987).

I shall now summarise the events of my Presidency in relation to the goals outlined above. While I could not personally do very much to foster the study of comparative education (items 3 and 4), my efforts in helping to encourage the formation and admittance of new societies and the promotion of World Congresses helped in the long run to achieve these goals. As Anne Hickling-Hudson discusses in Chapter 7, I put considerable effort into setting up the Commissions to run efficiently and to include members from more diverse regions of the world; and I hope that the smooth running of the Council's affairs also helped in furthering the interests of comparative education as a field.

Support for the 7th and 8th Congresses
After the 6th World Congress, preparations proceeded rapidly for the 7th World Congress in Montreal. Jacques Lamontagne produced some very fine pre-Congress and Congress letterhead and signs. They displayed the new WCCES logo, which he had had made in Montreal, showing two globes in blue and white with the words 'comparative education' and 'éducation comparée'. This logo has continued in use until the present time, and is on the cover of this book. Lamontagne maintained the WCCES Newsletter started by Anne Hamori at the IBE and carried on by AFEC in the 1980s. He introduced a computer database for publicity purposes.

A major point of discussion among Council members was the Research Commission as an organising feature of the Congresses. This model, used in previous Congresses, was not universally popular with North Americans, who favoured a more 'free market' model of submission of individual papers and panels. Since Douglas Ray as Programme Chair had much experience from the Congress in Brazil, he helped negotiate a system in which all types of submissions were acceptable, and Jacques Lamontagne allocated space for each type on the programme. The tension between the two models has nevertheless continued until today.

Member societies were quite active in helping to publicise the 7th World Congress. CESE held its biennial conference in Budapest, Hungary, in 1988, and the Congress was well publicised at that event. Since the majority of member societies were based in the North, however, publicity among countries in the South was not as effective, and the WCCES lacked travel funds to assist scholars from the South.

Preparations for the Congress had nearly reached fruition when the events in and around Beijing's Tiananmen Square took place on 4 June 1989. Gu Mingyuan, President of the CCES, was to succeed me at the Congress as WCCES President in the last week of June. My own immediate reaction on seeing the news on television was to think about the succession of the World Council Presidency and the implications for the 8th World Congress. Telephone calls were made in every direction. The first intimation I had that this situation would not be easy to resolve was when I managed to find in Norman, Oklahoma, the CCES representative, Zhou Nanzhao, who had been doing his doctoral studies at the State University of New York in Buffalo. Our conversation seemed to me surreal at the time, in that he indicated there was no problem and the Chinese were fully prepared to go ahead with their plans. I thought it extremely unlikely that the members of the Executive Committee would agree to this position.

And so it was that we went to the Montreal Congress, not being able to relish the fruits of our years of work to bid for and host the 7th Congress, but worried beyond measure about the future of the next World Congress. As an academic event, the Montreal Congress exceeded our expectations, with over 600 scholars from over 50 countries. In the words of Raymond Ryba, it was "by far the most successful of all the World Congresses in Comparative Education held so far and its organisation reached an admirable level of meticulous efficiency" (WCCES Secretary General's Report, July 1989-June 1992). The attendance was large and the papers exciting. The new format seemed to suit both kinds of presenters. The logos in blue and white were everywhere. The Government of Canada gave a generous reception with ample refreshments. The simultaneous translation was more than adequate. The Congress had the effect of energising the colleagues in North America and else-where, and we continued the links we had forged with our Brazilian colleagues.

However, the WCCES Executive Committee meetings were tense, with protests about human rights and freedom of expression. Members expressed their grave concern about the possibility of certain academics not being allowed into China for the next Congress, and of thus violating the protocol established in 1980 against disallowing bona fide scholars of any country to participate at World Congresses (see Chapter 2). The irony was that Gu Mingyuan's own students had been in Tiananmen Square. The WCCES members also expressed support for fellow academics in China. Chinese students from the United States and Canada made good use of the then-novel fax machine to importune me and the World Council to show their solidarity with the Chinese students who had been killed, by holding a moment of silence in the plenary and by voting not to hold the next World Congress in China. In the General Assembly of the World Council, a minute of silence was held in the memory of those killed in or around Tiananmen Square, and a collection was taken which yielded Cdn.$600 to pay the registration fees for six Chinese students who attended the conference and participated in academic discussions.

It was not so evident what to do about the Chinese succession. First, the WCCES debated and agreed to a statement on academic freedom, to ensure that in future all Congress host societies should guarantee unrestricted participation of all researchers, scholars, and graduate students wishing to attend, thereby con-forming with the protocol set in 1980, and a set of five principles in total that guaranteed "compliance with internationally agreed principles, such as those of UNESCO and of the United Nations in every aspect of the Congress to which these might apply" (Criteria for Confirmation of a Congress Invitation signed by Raymond Ryba and Vandra Masemann on behalf of the World Council, Montreal, 28 June 1989). On the following day, after intense hours of meetings, the World Council delivered the following very carefully-worded statement in Chinese, English and French:

- The Executive Committee of the World Council of Comparative Education Societies discussed plans for the 8th World Congress.
- On the basis of the opinions of World Council Members, decisions on the Congress will be deferred to the Madrid [Spain] meeting of July 1990. During the interim year, Member Societies can hold open and extensive consultations and formulate proposals. All proposals will be considered on the basis of the Executive Committee's established criteria.
- The term of the present officers will be extended to 7 July 1990.

Those were, without a doubt, the most difficult meetings I have ever chaired in my life. At the beginning, many members expressed anger and sorrow, and it was not evident what a solution could be. But as the hours dragged on, members tried to imagine how to "safeguard the interests of the World Council" in Raymond Ryba's words. The process of decision-making was consensual. I chalked every word of the resolution on the blackboard, and then it was translated into French and Chinese and then back into English to see that it did not lose any of its meaning in the translation in either direction. We did not stop until each member agreed to every word in all languages. By the end of the Congress, the World Council was still intact and its officers still in place until 1990.

I had been looking forward to finishing my term as WCCES President. The resolution meant that I was still faced with the question again in Madrid. I asked Michel Debeauvais to investigate the possibilities of having a Congress in Europe, and he set about contacting various academics that winter. Gu Mingyuan was still making plans to present his proposal at the Madrid meeting, and was willing to wait until 1992 (Gu to Masemann, 26 December 1989). Gerald Read, a founding and then Co-opted Member of the WCCES, wrote to Raymond Ryba and asked that his rationale for holding the World Congress in Beijing in 1991 or 1992 be read to the WCCES meeting in Madrid. His main concern was to keep the channels of communication open between the Chinese and Western educators (Read to Ryba, 15 March 1990). But he had also written to me suggesting that it might be very difficult to get people to travel to China, and that that consideration alone was a reason for finding another location (Read to Masemann, 14 March 1990). By June 1990, the CCES officials knew that the vote to hold the Beijing Congress might be defeated, but they were still hopeful that members could be prevailed upon to vote in favour of it.

In Madrid, the decision was to accept the proposal from the Czech and Slovak Pedagogical Societies' Comparative Education Section to host the 8th World Congress in Prague in 1992. The Chinese proposal was to be reconsidered for the 9th Congress. In the same meeting, the World Council admitted the Chinese Comparative Education Society-Taipei, an event that was greeted with universal jubilation among the members present. This decision was to have further ramifications which have not been settled until this day. The support for the 8th Congress was to become very much the task of my successor, Wolfgang Mitter, who was elected as Co-President with me for one year so that he could carry out these duties while I continued to represent the WCCES in the meetings leading up to the World Conference on Education for All in Jomtien, Thailand.

Continued Co-operation with UNESCO and Other International Organisations
One aspect of the work for the World Council in which I found particular enjoyment was the liaison with other international groups. As I had been elected to a three-year term in 1987 to the CIES, becoming President in 1989-90, I attended all of their Board Meetings from 1987 to 1990. I made an ongoing effort to increase CIES awareness of the desirability of co-operation with the World Council instead of considering the CIES as an international body which somehow obviated the need for a truly international federation of comparative education societies. Several WCCES Executive meetings were held in the USA during that period. Since that time, CIES members have attended World Congresses in record numbers.

Another very important part of the task was the relationship with UNESCO. As Michel Debeauvais lived in Paris, he was the World Council's primary UNESCO liaison person. We prepared a sizeable amount of paperwork, and eventually with Michel's continuing effort, the World Council was admitted to Category B Non-governmental Organisation (NGO) status with UNESCO. This designation meant that we were kept apprised of developments in UNESCO, sent an enormous amount of literature, invited to give our views on various policy matters, and given the opportunity to submit our views in writing on the drafts of various documents. As we lacked the status of the larger world organisations, our travel costs were not paid to consultations or conferences to which we were invited. The first of these that I attended was in Hamburg, Germany in 1988. It was a consultation on the next UNESCO six-year plan, and I found it extremely interesting.

One of the highlights of my term was that of being a member of the Steering Committee of the World Conference on Education for All (WCEFA) in Jomtien, Thailand, in 1990. I was asked by Nat Colletta of CIES if I was interested in participating, and I think that at the beginning, it was because of my visible role in the CIES rather than the World Council. However, I registered myself in all the documents as representing the World Council. I attended the preliminary meeting in Ottawa hosted by the Canadian Commission for UNESCO (which led to an ongoing association with that body), the meeting hosted by UNESCO in Paris, the North American regional consultation in New York City, and finally the conference itself in Jomtien. I had an unparalleled opportunity to meet representatives from many other NGOs around the world, and to participate in the drafting of the World Declaration on Education for All.

Improved Communication: Newsletter and Translations
I considered communication to be one of the most important parts of my work for the World Council. We still corresponded by regular mail, and I know that Raymond Ryba wrote a steady stream of letters during his tenure as Secretary General. The more recent use of e-mail and the WCCES website has brought vast improvement in the ability of the WCCES to communicate with its societies, and its societies and scholars with one another (Masemann 1997, p.130).

In my term as President, the continued production of the WCCES Newsletter, then called the Bulletin, was entirely in the hands of Jacques Lamontagne, as he linked it to the publicity function of the Congress. It was printed in both English and French versions in 1988 and 1989, and member societies were invited to submit news for inclusion. He identified the need to revise the WCCES mailing list, and created a computer database which he planned to hand over to the organisers of the Beijing Congress, thus deriving more value for the Council from the SSHRC grant from Canada. He also planned to invite a representative from the Chinese Congress organising committee to join him in Montreal so that the organising 'knowledge' could be passed on, as it had been by Douglas Ray and Mabel Tarré Carvalho de Oliveira from the Brazil Congress. This representative, Zhan Ruiling, did indeed spend about a month at the Université de Montréal in the early summer of 1989.

The theme of translation had been under discussion in the CIESC for several years as it attempted to become a more bilingual society. I carried this interest to the World Council in offering to chair the Language Commission. Complaints had been voiced at the Brazil Congress about the lack of translation into Portuguese, with the emphasis on the English/French languages of the WCCES. In the Canadian context, the Secretary of State gave funds for simultaneous translation of French and English only. In subsequent Congresses, some funds have been given through the French government for translation. Other modes of interpretation have also been tried, such as a personal translator who volunteers to whisper the translation in someone's ear, or a volunteer who speaks to the group intermittently throughout the delivery of a paper. However, the trend to 'Englishisation' has occurred along with the process of globalisation, and the WCCES is no exception to this trend. A recent example of this trend was the establishment of the WCCES website in 1999 and the production of publicity brochures with English being the only language used, even though they were produced in Hong Kong, China.

Conclusion

I have many other memories of the World Council, but my space has run out. Those years were full of promise, much of it realised. In his reports, Raymond Ryba voiced his anxiety that the World Council was fragile, its finances were on a precarious footing, the members were late with their dues, it did not have a regular Bulletin, its mailing list was always in need of updating, it lacked a firm support from universities in an era when budgets were being cut for higher education, and its members often had to give a great amount of volunteer time (Secretary General's Report, July 1989-1992). But the foundation that he and his colleagues laid down led to the growth and stability with which the World Council was to face the challenges of the 1990s and beyond.

Reference

Masemann, Vandra (1997): 'Recent Directions in Comparative Education', in Kodron, Christoph; von Kopp, Botho; Lauterbach, Uwe; Schäfer, Ulrich & Schmidt, Gerlind (eds.), *Comparative Education: Challenges – Intermediation – Practice. Essays in Honour of Wolfgang Mitter on the Occasion of his 70th Birthday*. Köln: Böhlau, pp.127-134.

5

Turmoil and Progress: 1991-1996

Wolfgang MITTER

My election as Co-President (with Vandra Masemann) of the World Council of Comparative Education Societies (WCCES), linked with the Executive Committee's decision to let my full Presidency begin one year later, was one of the outcomes of the emergency situation in which the Executive Committee found itself at that period. The previous decisions for Beijing, China as the venue of the 8th World Congress had been deferred, and Prague, Czechoslovakia had been presented as an alternative. In my election as Co-President, my linguistic experience and my expertise on education in Eastern and Central Europe played an essential role. Consequently, my main responsibility was identified by particular reference "to liaison with the organisers of the 1992 World Congress" (Secretary General's memorandum, 2 May 1991). I did not foresee that my whole period of office, having begun as rather an interim solution, should end up as a five-year Presidency: from 13 March 1991 (Pittsburgh) to 5 July 1996 (Sydney). During this period, re-elections had taken place in Prague (July 1992) and Boston (March 1995).

Not only did I have the urgent task of supporting our Czech colleagues in organising the 8th World Congress within an exceptionally short time and under enormous pressures, I was also aware of the complex challenges waiting for me: chairing an organisation with 'federal' Statutes and consisting of member societies which were diverse in size, inner cohesion, status within their national or regional scientific communities, and scholarly expertise. Fortunately, I was not entirely unprepared for these challenges, since I had a long experience as Head of Department and Director of the German Institute for International Educational Research, one of the internationally-acknowledged research centres for comparative education. Furthermore, I had been Chairman of the Kommission für Vergleichende Erziehungswissenschaft in der Deutschen Gesellschaft für Erziehungswissenschaft (KVEDGE) for two terms of office (1970-72 and 1987-89) and President (1981-85) of the Comparative Education Society in Europe (CESE) with preceding Vice-Presidency (1977-81). Finally, I had been active in the WCCES Executive Committee since the 4th World Congress in Tokyo, Japan and had organised several panels and workshops at the following World Congresses.

However, my strongest asset during my term of office was the support on which I could always rely from good friends and colleagues, in particular in the Bureau, the Executive Committee, the Standing Committees, and the national and local organisers of the World Congresses in Prague and Sydney. I express special gratitude to the members of the Bureau: Vandra Masemann, who gave much valuable advice in her functions as Co-President, Past President and member of the Executive Committee; Gu Mingyuan as Co-President (1992-96), with whom I entered friendly relations which have outlasted the critical negotiations around the venue of the 9th World Congress; Eurides Brito da Silva (1987-96), Jiří Kotásek (1991-96) and Christine Fox (1995-96) in their functions as Vice-Presidents; Joseph di Bona as Treasurer (1987-96); and Mark Bray as Assistant Secretary General (1994-96).

Raymond Ryba, the Secretary General throughout the years of my presidency occupied the first place among all these distinguished colleagues. He had held this focal responsibility initially on an informal basis during the presidency of Erwin Epstein, after the resignation of Secretary General Leo Fernig in 1982. In 1983, he was officially elected as Secretary General during the presidency of Michel Debeauvais and continued to serve in this post when Vandra Masemann became President. He was a highly qualified educationist and a splendid manager and organiser, always informed to the utmost degree and ready to exercise all his capacities, in particular his diplomatic skills, for the sake of the World Council. He was also distinguished by integrity, sincerity, tolerance and leadership. His very long period of office ended with my own in July 1996 in Sydney. However, the Executive Committee gladly accepted his offer to go on serving the World Council as Treasurer until his death in May 1999 after long and patient suffering from serious illness (see Mitter 1999; Brock 2001). I am proud to have been his close friend, and remember many fruitful talks during and beyond our 'official' encounters as well as our joint missions to different places including Paris, Prague and Beijing.

Meetings of the Executive Committee and General Assemblies

The Executive Committee held 10 meetings during my Presidency. In five of them, two or three sessions were convened at one venue, whereas the two meetings in Prague (1992) were enumerated separately as they took place during and after a World Congress. The agendas were always comprehensive, multi-faceted and mostly delicate, in particular with the deliberations on the lo-cations of Congresses. Consequently, the debates sometimes included contro-versy. However, the meetings were distinguished by remarkable solidarity, fair-ness and insight into the essential concerns of our world organisation.

Both the efficiency and the atmosphere of the meetings were promoted by the fact that the majority took place at the venues of the annual conferences of the Comparative and International Education Society (CIES). These arrangements permitted well-attended meetings of the Executive Committee, since they could be connected with research presentations of its members. Moreover, we had the pleasure of enjoying the hospitality of our hosts. In particular, I remember the joint dinner parties arranged for the members of both Executive Committees. In

July 1994, CESE afforded the Executive Committee the facilities to hold its extraordinary meeting in Copenhagen, Denmark.

I was mindful of recurrent matters that the World Council shares with comparable organisations. They consisted of membership development, financial and budgetary issues, the reports and proposals of the Standing Committees, and the research and publication projects stimulated by the World Council and/or conducted under its auspices. In spite of the importance of all these items, the debates on venue and preparation of the World Congresses can be considered as the focal component of most sessions, and they always demanded interminable deliberations. Less time, but equal attention, was required by the project to amend the Council's Statutes and By-Laws. The item of membership issues grew in length and complexity with the continuous debates concerning the status of the Taiwanese representation. Therefore these items will be analysed with special emphasis in this chapter.

As usual in the history of the World Council, the two Congresses that were held during my period of office gave the opportunity to convene General Assemblies attended by many participants. Though essentially advisory in its functions, the General Assembly offered direct information on developments, problems and proposals for forthcoming policies. The particular importance of the General Assembly of 1996 arose from its decision on the amendment of the Statutes following the recommendations of the Executive Committee.

The World Congresses

The World Congresses can be considered as highlights in the history of our global organisation. They are the most spectacular manifestation of its progress, which is indicated by the number of participants, their diversified geographic and academic composition, and the content of the programmes. In the light of these parameters, both Congresses held during my presidency – the 8th in Prague and the 9th in Sydney – were certainly outstanding events, the more so as both achieved success despite the short time available to the organisers.

The decision for Prague had been taken at the meeting of the Executive Committee in Madrid, Spain, in July 1990. The Czech and Slovak colleagues, who had established their national Comparative Education Society just before, were members of a nation that had entered its start into a democratic republic as the result of its peaceful transformation, known as the Velvet Revolution, at the end of 1989. It was a period of great transition, and Czechoslovakia split into two separate republics some months after the Congress. The colleagues accepted the invitation from the Executive Committee with great enthusiasm, determined to help end the intellectual isolation of their scientific community and to take an active part in the celebration for the 400th anniversary of the birth of the great pedagogue Jan Amos Comenius.

It was a severe loss for the Czech and Slovak colleagues as well as the Executive Committee that František Singule, the Chairman of the Organising Committee, passed away in August 1991, soon after the beginning of the preparatory process. He was one of the European pioneers of comparative education, had organised the 4th CESE Conference in Prague (1969), and had afterwards been persecuted and humiliated by the Communist regime. Fortunately, Jiří Kotásek (Vice-President of the World Council) and Vlastimil Pařizek (Chairman of the national Organising Committee) took up the burden. It was exceptionally heavy because the Executive Committee's decision had been taken in an atmosphere of euphoria which seriously underestimated the economic, financial and technical problems. As noted in the Secretary General's Report of June 1992 (p.3):

> From the point of view of the Secretariat of the World Council, the unusual circumstances in which these preparations took place inevitably resulted in much greater involvement than has normally been the case in the past. This was particularly so following the decision of the Executive Committee, in Pittsburgh in March 1991, to ask the President and Secretary General to act directly on its behalf in consultations and negotiations with our Czecho-slovak colleagues. This necessitated not only in a massive increase in correspondence and communication by phone and fax, but also in numerous face-to-face meetings with the Congress organisers in Prague and elsewhere. In addition, further journeys were necessary to Paris and Strasbourg to discuss support for the Congress from Unesco [sic] and the Council of Europe. We are glad to record that our Czechoslovak colleagues have been very appreciative of our efforts on behalf of the Council and that we were also successful in obtaining financial and other support for the Congress. However, despite a generous facultative grant from Unesco, these addi-tional tasks were not without their financial costs to the Council as well as their costs in time and effort.

The success of the 8th World Congress in the historic city of Prague was a reward to all who had done their best in the preparatory efforts at home and abroad. It was attended by some 650 participants from about 60 countries. The main theme had been chosen as an immediate response to the political and educational situation of the liberated host country, namely 'Education, Democracy and Development'. The exceptional importance of the event was underlined by President Václav Havel's message and the prominent speakers in the Opening Ceremony, among them the Czech Minister of Education; the Vice Rector of the Charles University; Colin Power, Assistant Director-General of UNESCO on behalf of his world organisation; and Michael Vorbeck on behalf of the Council of Europe. The plenary papers had been written by Ernest Boyer (President of the Carnegie Foundation for the Advancement of Teaching, delivered by Philip Altbach), Upendra Baxi (Vice-Chancellor of the University of Delhi, delivered by Sureshchandra Shukla), Stephen Heyneman (World Bank), Torsten Husén (University of Stockholm), Gábor Halász (Hungarian National Institute of Public Education), and Cândido Gomes (Brazilian Comparative Education Society). My Presidential Address was devoted to 'Education, Democracy and Development in a Period of Revolutionary Change', the final part of which consisted of homage to Prague and its culture, the kindness of its people, and some salient events in its history (Mitter 1993).

The 9th World Congress was very different, though with some similarities. Exceptional conditions were again created not only by the great difficulties created by distance, which necessarily limited the direct communication between the President and the Secretary General on the one hand and the national Organising Committee in Australia on the other. Moreover, the Congress had to be prepared within a very short time, in this respect like its Czech predecessor. When deciding not to hold the 9th World Congress in Beijing (see below), the Executive Committee, having convened for its extraordinary meeting in Copenhagen, Denmark, was confronted with the need for an alternative. Two options were discussed. One was Cape Town, South Africa, offered by the Southern African Comparative and History of Education Society (SACHES) for the first time at the WCCES meeting in Kingston, Jamaica (March 1993). The other was Sydney, Australia, offered by the Australian and New Zealand Comparative and International Education Society (ANZCIES), whose readiness had been open for many years but which had been deferred for reasons of distance. In Copenhagen, both proposals were considered as serious candidatures with a preference for Cape Town because of the political context. The Southern African representative gladly accepted, but soon afterwards SACHES expressed its regret at not being able to organise the Congress in 1996 for understandable economic and logistic reasons.

Avoiding further delay and making use of the Executive Committee's authorisation (in Copenhagen), I contacted Anthony Welch who signalled spontaneous acceptance on behalf of ANZCIES. This positive reply is worth recalling not only for the fact of the long overdue invitation, but also of the aforementioned time factor. In any event, our Australian colleagues organised the 9th World Congress in a splendid manner, and the pleasure in the Congress was certainly reinforced by the exceptional charm and ambience of Sydney.

The programme concentrated on the theme 'Tradition, Modernity and Post-Modernity in Education'. Considering the distance for the majority of the participants, the attendance of about 400 educationists, the presentation of 200 papers, and the organisation of 36 panels were noteworthy. The plenary sessions featured Edmund King, Anthony Welch, Victor Ordoñez, Wendy Brady, and Jill Blackmore. King's paper on 'Post-compulsory Education: A Challenge for World Education' should be particularly remembered, because it summarised his long research in this field. It was his last public appearance, which is a reason to pay explicit acknowledgment to Anthony Welch for his noble initiative to give one of the founding fathers of the World Council the opportunity to address the body with which he had been associated for many years. For me, the days in Sydney included the farewell from my long period of office. This is why I focused my Presidential Address on an autobiographical approach (Mitter 1997).

Revisions to Statutes and By-Laws

"In view of the Council's complexity, it is a periodic need to revise the organisation's rules to reflect current conditions and realities, and to ensure that constitutional members agree on expectations, objectives, and the rules by which they are to be governed." This sentence, quoted from Erwin Epstein's "Brief explanation for proposed revisions to the WCCES Statutes and By-Laws" of 29 May 1996, exactly summarised the objectives of the Constitution Standing Committee which had proposed a set of revisions to the Executive Committee at its 21st meeting in Boston (March 1995). This proposal was the successful outcome of a working process having begun in Pittsburgh (March 1991), when the President responded to Erwin Epstein's proposition and convened a Working Group, the precursor of the later Standing Committee. Its progressive negotiations had been repeatedly commented on by the Executive Committee until the By-Laws were unanimously approved. The revision of the Statutes was recommended for endorsement by the General Assembly which was effected in Sydney (July 1996) together with confirmation of the revision of the By-Laws.

The revisions of both constitutional documents were focused on corrections of inconsistencies in procedures of decision-making, definition of membership, and handling of financial matters. Furthermore, the functions and terms of office of the members of the Bureau, in particular concerning the President and the Vice-Presidents, were more specifically described in order to obviate any controversial interpretations, as had happened before under certain circumstances. By and large, as I wrote in a circular to the Executive Committee in December 1995, both amendments took into account "the World Council's development from a 'club' of a handful of members to the global umbrella organisation as it is today". The special thanks I expressed to Erwin Epstein in Boston were indeed well founded.

Membership

The membership of the World Council grew from 27 to 31 between 1992 and 1996 with the admission of the Bulgarian and Polish Comparative Education Societies, the Hungarian Pedagogical Society (Comparative Education Section), and the Southern African Comparative and History of Education Society. This trend had begun at the beginning of the 1990s with the admission of the Russian Council of Comparative Education and the Czech and Slovak Pedagogical Society (Comparative Education Section). It mirrored the opening of the World Council to Central and Eastern Europe as well as to southern Africa, as a corollary to the revolutionary events that had taken place in both regions. At the same time it signalled the progress of the World Council in living up to its name and claim which was to continue in my successors' periods of office.

The growth of the World Council must not, however, obscure the problems arising from the differences among the member societies in the aforementioned terms of size, internal cohesion, activity and the standard of comparative education in research and teaching. There has always been a gap between the large societies, such as the CIES and CESE, with their institutional embodiment in universities and solid budgets (despite the ubiquitous trend to curtailments!), and the less favoured groupings with, in the extreme cases, a few members. In this respect, the World Council acts as a global promoting agency, convening researchers, teachers and students, and launching exchange programmes. In particular, the World Congresses make an important contribution to promoting comparative education in the country and region of the organising member society. However, the Executive Committee was repeatedly confronted with problems when member societies did not respond to questions or reminders, or were in arrears with dues for more than three consecutive years and, therefore, according to the By-Laws, liable to suspension. In fact, in the given period, the Executive Committee did not execute this sanction. Instead, to this day, the World Council has accepted in-kind contributions (explicitly permitted in By-Law 2.6), as, for example, were repeatedly paid by the Bulgarian Comparative Education Society with their exemplary translation services.

As an approach to overcome the under-representation of certain regions in the World Council, in particular in Asia and Africa, the Executive Committee welcomed the efforts of David Wilson (Canada), Sureshchandra Shukla (India) and Yaacov Iram (Israel) to create a new body to be called International Associates of the WCCES. This project was repeatedly discussed, but not followed up beyond March 1994 (San Diego meeting) because the objections prevailed that such a member society might compete with the existing societies and thus complicate the World Council's structure. From the perspective of today, it seems to me that that the approach *per se* was reasonably conceived, but it was ultimately superseded by the continuing process of founding of national and regional member societies which, in their turn, had never been exclusive with regard to the national or cultural origin of their applicants.

Amidst the generally undisturbed process of adding member societies to the World Council, one case could have harmed the cohesion of the World Council. It concerned the status of the Taiwanese representation in the World Council, and was aggravated by the Executive Committee's extensive negotiations with the Chinese Comparative Education Society (CCES) about the organisation of the 9th Congress. While the decision was originally jeopardised by the other member societies' perception of the events in and around Beijing's Tiananmen Square in June 1989, it became linked during the course of the negotiations with the status of the Taiwanese society. In my view, the abandonment of Beijing as a Congress venue was highly regrettable, not only for the decision as such, but also for the fact that the organisational preparations undertaken by the CCES Organising Committee, and its intensive negotiations with the Executive Committee, had considerably and successfully proceeded. Moreover, the President's and Secretary General's visit to Beijing in the autumn of 1993 (following a visit in 1991) reinforced all these efforts: both times we were very well received by the Chinese hosts.

When the Executive Committee took its decisions in Madrid (1990), it was in the hope of pointing a solid way into the future. On the one hand, the planning of Beijing as a Congress venue had been deferred, but not cancelled, while on the other hand the application of the Taiwanese comparative educationists for the admission of their society for membership in the World Council was unanimously approved – with the CCES representatives' formal consent to the new English-language name: Chinese Comparative Education Society-Taipei (CCES-T). The Executive Committee formally recognised the 'One China Principle', and the Taiwanese colleagues provided assurance that they were not linked with the Taiwan authorities. Taking this decision, the Executive Committee believed it had done its best in observing the official standpoint of UNESCO, which was considered important for other dimensions of WCCES operation.

In fact, however, the problem had not been solved at all, chiefly because the name of the Taiwan society was very different in Chinese from that in English, and referred to the Republic of China. The authorities in Beijing declared this inconsistent with the 'One China Principle' of the People's Republic of China, and also questioned the status of the CCES-Taipei as an independent member society of the World Council as opposed to a branch society of the CCES. Initially, this standpoint was transmitted to me as President by Gu Mingyuan, the President of the CCES, in his letter of 15 February 1992. It was not accepted by the Executive Committee, who took the view that the World Council defined itself as a global umbrella organisation composed not only of national societies but also of sections within Pedagogical Societies and of regional, linguistically-based and even local associations. In Prague, this matter was not expressly discussed in an atmosphere which was determined by cooperation and compromise, and culminated in the Executive Committee's decision for the 9th World Congress to be held in Beijing in 1995, and the appointment of Gu Mingyuan as WCCES Co-President with special responsibility for matters concerned with the Beijing Congress. In Kingston, Jamaica (1993) this line was followed up, but unfortunately an exchange of letters between Co-President and President signalled the return of the controversy which became manifest again in San Diego, USA (March 1994), and did not result in any compromise on the incompatible standpoints. In this awkward situation, the Executive Committee, which I had convened in an extraordinary meeting in Copenhagen (July 1994), felt obliged to abandon Beijing as venue of the 9th World Congress.

In this context, it is necessary to emphasise that this failure was regretted by both sides, and certainly presented the World Council with a critical challenge. Fortunately, it did not shut the doors entirely. My viewpoint can be supported by the following indications:

- In its decision in Copenhagen, the Executive Committee confirmed its principles concerning the criteria of its membership but authorised the President to express its willingness for further negotiations and the hope that one of the following World Congresses might be organised in Beijing.
- Before the Copenhagen decision, the Co-President had expressed the same hope, stating that the Chinese side "believed there will be chances to work out a solution of the name problem" (Letter from Gu Mingyuan to Wolfgang Mitter, 24 June 1994).

- Throughout the years, the style of the correspondence was characterised by politeness, tact and expression of interpersonal respect. In this context I quote from Gu Mingyuan's letter of 1 June 1994:

  > What I am hoping for is that you as WCCES President, an internationally renowned scholar, and an old friend of China, will be not only understanding CCES' position but also take action in your capacity to help solve the problem.

  In my answer of 7 June 1994 I expressed my appreciations of the Co-President's words, adding that:

  > I am certainly willing to offer my help to solve the problem caused by your wish to have the name of CCES-Taipei changed. I understand that CCES takes this problem seriously as part of its allegiance to the 'One China Principle' which the WCCES supports as well.

- The Executive Committee was always aware of, and acted with respect for, both the importance and delicacy of the problem. It discussed the matter in an open atmosphere, the conduct of which may be exemplified by the following passage from the minutes of the 21st meeting in Boston, USA (March 1995):

  > Vandra Masemann suggested that ... it could be seen that the CCES colleagues operated in a political and cultural climate which was somewhat different from that which the majority of Western members were used to, and that subsequent events led the World Council to realize that what had been taken as a settling of disagreement was not in fact complete. The President agreed with this point, and felt that the World Council should be prepared to learn lessons about the different cultures within which Member Societies and their representatives operated.... Erwin Epstein stressed the need to retain sight of the fact that the WCCES had behaved entirely properly on a matter of principle.... Erwin Epstein's point was echoed by Margaret Sutherland, [who] emphasised that the Council had acted both reasonably and legitimately, and should not be over-sensitive.

In my view today, this connection between the strict observance of the World Council's Statutes and the respect for diverging standpoints, determining the policy of the Executive Committee, has paved the way to development beyond my own presidency. It has not led to settling the 'old' conflict as such, but has enabled pragmatic forms of contact and cooperation to exist between the World Council and the CCES, as well as the continuing and strengthened bonds among the comparativists on 'both sides'.

Finances, Research, Publications

Financial matters were discussed in detail at all meetings of the Executive Committee. Special emphasis was repeatedly laid on the contracts between the Executive Committee and the national Organising Committees in the countries of the scheduled World Congresses (Czech and Slovak Pedagogical Society, CCES, ANZCIES). Thanks to the observation of strict austerity, the WCCES budgets could be continuously balanced. The President and Secretary General contributed considerably to this policy by using opportunities to combine their missions on behalf of the World Council with personal obligations, such as lectures and attendance at academic conferences of which the expenses were reimbursed by the authorities concerned or by sponsoring research agencies. In any event, this policy required ingenuity during a period of declining support for universities and research institutes throughout the world. In addition to the general financial constraints, the collection of dues from the member societies continuously gave reason for correspondence and debate. The possibility of organising the World Congresses as fund-raising events materialised only after the end of my presidency at the 10th World Congress in Cape Town (1998).

Before and during my period of office, the World Council was not able to offer many financial resources to promote research under its auspices. However, it endeavoured to support projects by offering some prestige through its official sponsorship and endorsement. In the first half of the 1990s, the following five research projects, with varying objectives and deadlines, were on the books:

- National Research Policies in Education (coordinated by Michel Debeauvais),
- Women in Education (Margaret Sutherland),
- Theory and Theory Shifts in Comparative Education (Jürgen Schriewer),
- Education and Human Rights (Douglas Ray), and
- Educating All for Peace (Mark Ginsburg).

As regards publications, Raymond Ryba's agreement with the editors of *International Review of Education* (*IRE*) to publish a special issue with a set of selected papers presented to the 8th World Congress needs to be noted, the more so since this volume was reprinted as a book after successful negotiations with Kluwer Academic Publishers (Ryba 1997). This two-stage co-operation set the beginning of a fruitful strategy that was continued for the proceedings of later Congresses.

Cooperation with UNESCO

One of the legacies I inherited when taking over my presidency consisted in the cooperation between the World Council and UNESCO, to be traced back to the World Council's foundation and consistently extended by Michel Debeauvais and Vandra Masemann. It had reached its formal culmination in the Council's admission to formal NGO status, Category B. This legacy was a base for the excellent cooperation throughout my period of office. Not only was the World

Council provided with the aforementioned grant for support of attendance from Third World countries (complemented by a similar grant by the Council of Europe for participants from Central and Eastern Europe), but also the Congress itself was distinguished by the Welcome Address presented by Colin Power, Assistant Director-General of UNESCO. Representatives of UNESCO also joined many meetings of the Executive Committee.

This practice led to continuing improvement, in particular when Juan Carlos Tedesco, the Director of UNESCO's International Bureau of Education (IBE), was appointed by the UNESCO Headquarters to be responsible for its relations with the World Council (1994). Through his initiative, the World Council's column became a regular feature of *Innovation*, the IBE's newsletter. Thanks to the voluntary commitment of Seth Spaulding and Mark Ginsburg as editors, and continued by Mark Ginsburg and his editorial team at Pittsburgh, the column became a valuable medium for the World Council to address its members and several thousand readers all over the world. In this way, the long-existing plan to edit a Council Bulletin, which had to be continually delayed because of financial reasons, could be materialised.

While these activities bear witness to UNESCO's wish for cooperation, the Executive Committee, in turn formalised its efforts by establishing the UNESCO Liaison Standing Committee (formerly Commission) in Prague under Margaret Sutherland's chairmanship (until March 1995). Additionally the Association francophone d'éducation comparée (AFEC), in agreement with the World Council, appointed Michel Debeauvais to act as its Liaison Officer to the UNESCO Headquarters. He regularly provided the Executive Committee with his reports, in particular on his attendance at various UNESCO conferences on the World Council's behalf.

Some Concluding Personal Comments

In his message on the occasion of my 70th birthday on 14 September 1997, David N. Wilson characterised my term of office as President of the World Council as a "period of growth in the organisation, which was also a period of some turmoil that resulted from factors beyond the control of the World Council" (see Welch 1997, p.29). It is true that turmoil might be applicable to all presidencies in general. Nevertheless, I regard Wilson's special reference to be explicitly appropriate. Turmoil was the reason why I was unexpectedly elected as Co-President (a function that had not existed before) by the Executive Committee during its meeting in Madrid in July 1990; and the turmoil ended only in the spring of 1995, when the Executive Committee confirmed my invitation to ANZCIES to organise the 9th World Congress in Sydney in 1996. Once this important decision was taken, the World Council at long last navigated into calm waters which made me remark in my last President's Report (Sydney, 30 June 1996): "It seems as if a 'kind fairy' has decided to do good for me after the preceding years of turbulence". Looking back to this peaceful end of my presidency does not, however, mean at all that I should like to cancel the years of turmoil from my *curriculum vitae* or from my memory.

In my 1996 Sydney report, I also indicated that lights had collided with shadows, indicating gaps and deficits: "Let alone the disproportions continuing to exist in the distribution of regional membership in the World Council as a *global* organisation, it seems to me that the agenda of the Executive Committee has been too much absorbed by policy and organisation matters *at the cost of academic debates and innovatory projects*". In this respect I left "a special challenge to my successor". Yet, I added, "he will not find a *tabula rasa,* due to the initiatives of the Research Committee and, above all, to the capital, which has been accumulated by the World Council's societies and their members...". On the whole, my retrospective chapter finishes with an outlook which I consider to have been encouraging. It is true that the World Council had to cope with critical decisions, but the field of comparative education certainly made some progress.

References

Brock, Colin (2001): 'Raymond Ryba: A Tribute'. *Compare: A Journal of Comparative Education*, Vol.31, No.1, pp.7-9.

Mitter, Wolfgang (1993): 'Education, Democracy and Development in a Period of Revolutionary Change'. *International Review of Education*, Vol.39, No.6, pp.463-471.

Mitter, Wolfgang (1997): 'Challenges to Comparative Education: Between Retrospect and Expectation'. *International Review of Education*, Vol.43, Nos.5-6, pp.401-412.

Mitter, Wolfgang (1999): 'In Memoriam Raymond Ryba'. *Comparative Education*, Vol.35, No.3, pp.351-353.

Ryba, Raymond (ed.) (1997): *Education, Democracy and Development: An International Perspective*. Dordrecht: Kluwer Academic Publishers.

Welch, Anthony (1997): 'Address', in *Akademische Feier für Wolfgang Mitter zum 70 Geburtstag am 16 September 1997 im Frankurter Römer*. Frankfurt am Main: Deutsches Institut für Internationale Pädagogische Forschung, pp.25-29.

6

From Sydney to Cape Town to Chungbuk: 1996-2001

David N. WILSON

This chapter describes developments during my two-term tenure as President of the World Council of Comparative Education Societies (WCCES). In addition to facilitating improvements in the financial health of the WCCES, I negotiated upgraded status of the WCCES to become a Non-governmental Organisation (NGO) in Operational Relations with UNESCO. Several administrative measures were adopted which strengthened the WCCES: in particular, standardising World Congress contracts, streamlining dues collection, and improving communications. The organisation of World Congresses of Comparative Education Societies in Cape Town, South Africa and Chungbuk, South Korea were highlights of my tenure. My two Presidential Addresses explored the history and development of the field of comparative and international education and the WCCES (Wilson 1998, 2003).

A Defining Moment

One defining moment which had considerable impact upon my WCCES Presidency took place long before I even became President. This was the realisation on 4 June 1989 that the events in Beijing's Tiananmen Square would significantly affect the WCCES and, eventually, its President. At that time I was President of the Comparative and International Education Society of Canada (CIESC), and preparing to host the 7th World Congress in Montreal, Canada. I had also been serving as Chair of the WCCES Finance Commission since the 1986 meeting of the WCCES Executive Committee in Madrid, Spain.

The 9th World Congress was held in Sydney, Australia in 1996, hosted by the Australian and New Zealand Comparative and International Education Society (ANZCIES). I was elected WCCES President at this Congress for the customary term of either three years or until the next Congress. The 10th World Congress was held in Cape Town, South Africa, hosted by the Southern African Comparative and History of Education Society (SACHES) in 1998. I was elected to a second term as WCCES President in Cape Town. The 11th World Congress was held in Chungbuk, hosted by the Korean Comparative Education Society (KCES) in 2001, during which I completed my term.

As described in Mitter's chapter in this book, major problems arose from the co-existence in the WCCES of the Chinese Comparative Education Society (CCES) and the Chinese Comparative Education Society-Taipei (CCES-T). After initial acceptance of the name CCES-T, the CCES requested that the WCCES should force the CCES-T to change its name or revoke the CCES-T membership in the WCCES. The CCES withdrew from participation in WCCES activities, declining every personal invitation that I tendered. For example, in January 2000 a letter from CCES President Gu Mingyuan to me as WCCES President stated:

> Unfortunately, I am sorry to inform you that as the issue of the name of the Taiwan Comparative Education Society in the WCCES has not been properly solved, in accordance with our "One China" government policy, it is now impossible for me to attend the activity of the WCCES.

As WCCES President, and in consultation with the WCCES Executive, I continually replied that the CCES had agreed at the 1990 meeting of the WCCES Executive Committee in Madrid to accept the CCES-T by that name, which had been arrived at in consultation with the CCES and changed at that time to accommodate the CCES; and that while the WCCES Statutes and By-Laws contained provisions for admission of new member societies, the only provisions for the revocation of WCCES membership were because of protracted non-payment of dues.

However, I did agree, again in consultation with the WCCES Executive, to ask the CCES-T to clarify the CCES assertions that both the CCES-T constitution and web page contained different text in Chinese and English. The impasse remained unresolved not only during my Presidency but also during those of my immediate successors, though I was aware of continued efforts to address it.

During my tenure as WCCES President, I endeavoured to maintain and improve relations with CCES on a personal level, even though official channels were difficult. My correspondence with Gu Mingyuan, CCES President, and our cordial meetings at other conferences in Asia, kept dialogue open between the CCES and the WCCES. One result of this dialogue was the payment in 2000 of CCES arrears of dues. To avoid invoking suspension and revocation of CCES membership, I offered to exchange dues payments for the in-kind translation of the WCCES web page into Chinese. On several occasions, I invited CCES members to attend WCCES Executive Committee meetings when Gu Mingyuan was unable to attend. My successor continued with these invitations, which kept the lines of communication open during this difficult period.

UNESCO Relationship

Since 1972, the WCCES had been affiliated with UNESCO. It was first in Category C, and in the late 1980s in Category B. The different categories conferred increasing levels of consultative status, access to information, and invitations to meetings.

Having served twice with UNESCO while on leave from my university in Canada, I chose to strengthen the WCCES activities with UNESCO and to build links with its sister UN Specialised Agency, the International Labour Organisation (ILO) for which I had also served as field staff. Accordingly, in 1999 I represented the WCCES as an official NGO delegate at the UNESCO/ILO Second International Congress on Technical and Vocational Education and Training (TVET) in Seoul, Korea. This occasion gave me the opportunity to visit the Korea National University of Education (KNUE), which was to be the site of the 11th World Congress in 2001. Also in 2001, I represented the WCCES at a UNESCO conference on Information and Communications Technologies (ICT) in Paris while on sabbatical at the new UNESCO International Centre for Technical and Vocational Education and Training (UNEVOC) in Bonn, Germany.

As WCCES President, I regularised reporting to UNESCO, and when its relationships with NGOs were revised in 1999, I negotiated a change in category while attending the TVET Congress in Seoul. These negotiations were successful in upgrading the WCCES from Category B to the new, more prestigious, category entitled NGO in Operational Relations with UNESCO. This status was approved in November 1999, and gave the WCCES increased opportunities to participate in UNESCO activities and to be regularly consulted by UNESCO.

In this regard, I took guidance from Vandra Masemann's participation in the capacity of WCCES President as a member of the Steering Committee of the 1990 World Conference on Education for All, which was co-hosted by UNESCO, in Jomtien, Thailand. Vandra and I also prepared a WCCES position paper for the UNESCO 'Jomtien Plus 10' conference in Dakar, Senegal. The request for WCCES consultation is one benefit of the status of NGO in Operational Relations with UNESCO. The official WCCES response to the draft Dakar Framework for Action was submitted to UNESCO in April 2000. We are uncertain whether our critical perspective influenced the final Dakar declaration, although we were not alone among NGOs in our concern about the effects of external debt, military spending and the pandemic of HIV/AIDS on educational spending during the 1990s.

At every opportunity, I endeavoured to represent WCCES at UNESCO meetings, largely in conjunction with other events and at little or no cost to the WCCES. I also arranged for WCCES Vice-President Harold Herman to attend a UNESCO Ministers of Education Conference in Durban, South Africa in 2001. This type of representation gave the WCCES an enhanced role and visibility on the international scene.

In 2000, I also prepared the first Sexennial Report for NGOs to UNESCO, which is one requirement for NGOs in Operational Relations with UNESCO. This difficult task involved compilation of WCCES activities during the preceding six years. Another requirement of UNESCO affiliation has been payment of dues to UNESCO for NGO representation. This was also regularised during my tenure as President as a result of a more systematic effort on the part of UNESCO to invoice for dues after the reorganisation of the NGOs' relationship to it.

WCCES Membership

One of the less pleasant duties that I had to perform during my two-term Presidency was to operationalise the By-Laws relating to the payment of annual dues by member societies and to the negotiation of contracts for financial arrangements in the holding of Congresses. An unfortunate attribute of the WCCES had long been its weakness, both financially and organisationally. WCCES dues are structured on a sliding scale, ranging from US$400 for societies with over 600 members, US$300 for societies with 301-600 members, US$200 for societies with 101-300 members, and US$100 for societies with 100 or fewer members (WCCES 2004, By-Law 2.5). Payment of dues by member societies had never been successfully implemented. With no mechanisms in place to penalise member societies for non-payment of dues, there was no incentive for them to keep dues payments current or clear any arrears.

After prolonged and difficult debate, By-Law revisions to deal with non-payment of dues and membership were adopted. Societies in arrears for three years received an official warning that their participation in the WCCES was in jeopardy. First, voting rights were to be suspended. Second, after a three-year grace period, their membership in the WCCES was to be revoked. By-Law 2.6 stated that:

> Any constituent Society with dues in arrears for three consecutive years will have its World Council membership suspended until arrears have been paid…. Societies suspended for three years shall have their membership revoked.

During my Presidency, the virtually non-existent member societies in Nigeria, Egypt, Colombia and Argentina were suspended in 1999. Repeated attempts for at least five years to contact these societies at their last known addresses had proven fruitless. Final action on their status was placed on the agenda for the 2000 meeting of the WCCES Executive Committee in Bologna, Italy. At the same time it was also moved that letters be sent by the Secretary General to the societies in Portugal, China, India and Russia, advising them that their dues in arrears jeopardised their WCCES membership. Subsequently, after determining that the society in Portugal was either dormant or defunct, it was suspended from WCCES membership in 2002. In the interim, however, previously suspended societies were re-constituted in Argentina and Egypt.

Another provision in the By-Laws, Section 2.5, recognised the inability of small societies with limited financial resources and/or difficulties in accessing foreign exchange. The Bulgarian Comparative Education Society (BCES) was given the opportunity to exchange translation services for the in-kind payment of their WCCES dues. The BCES translated the WCCES brochure into French under this arrangement. I felt prouder of this provision than of the previous provision because it is proactive rather than reactive. Although it was never acted upon during my Presidency, I invited the CCES to translate the WCCES web page into Chinese in order to satisfy their dues in arrears during the period of estrangement.

While Chair of the WCCES Finance Commission, together with Sureshchandra Shukla of the Comparative Education Society of India (CESI), I developed a proposal and wrote a constitution for a society of individual WCCES members to accommodate comparative educators from countries unable to constitute a national society. Although this proposal was not accepted by the WCCES Executive Committee, I chose not to revive the proposal during my Presidency. One major reason was the development of two regional comparative education societies and their successful applications to join the WCCES. The Southern African Comparative and History of Education Society (SACHES) was admitted to the WCCES in 1992, and was joined five years later by the Comparative Education Society of Asia (CESA). Their establishment and admission have given many comparative educators in smaller countries in Asia and Africa the opportunity to participate in the WCCES.

Financial Initiatives

While serving as WCCES President, I encouraged my successor as Chair of the Standing Committee on Finance, David Turner (who subsequently became Treasurer), to develop proposals to strengthen the financial status of the WCCES. These proposals included the development of a regular recurrent budget, a reserves policy, and procedures for expenditures. These proposals were adopted by the WCCES Executive Committee, and the surpluses accruing from several World Congresses were used to improve the WCCES' financial status. Another innovative and noble development was the negotiated use of a portion of the Cape Town World Congress surplus to establish the SACHES Research and Publications Scheme (SRAPS) to support development of educational research capacity in the Southern African Region.

An additional matter carried over from my tenure as Chair of the WCCES Finance Commission was the improvement and standardisation of the contracts to host the World Congresses. I was placed in a difficult position while President of the CIESC, since I had to report to myself, in my role as WCCES Finance Commission Chair, on the finances of the 6th World Congress, held in Montreal in 1989. Because communications and relationships between the CIESC Executive and the Congress organiser at the University of Montreal had deteriorated, the budget and required audited financial statements were not available. When I became WCCES President, I resolved that such lacunae should never again plague either a member society or the WCCES. Accordingly, I took measures to improve the process to negotiate contracts, as well as to improve the contracts themselves. Of course, the protracted and equally difficult negotiations with the CCES also contributed to my resolve.

A related initiative arose after the 10th World Congress in Cape Town when Vandra Masemann and I arranged for the conference organiser, Penny Morrell, to write a World Congress Planning Manual. The idea for this manual was based upon the CIES Conference Planning Handbook that I had prepared while President of the CIES. The WCCES version was a much lengthier tome.

Governance
One major difficulty for the WCCES since its inception has been the nature of its governance. As an 'umbrella' body composed of member societies, the WCCES chose to reach most decisions through consensus. This procedure is rather difficult to follow, particularly when contentious issues arise. However, in most instances the WCCES has been able to make difficult choices and take decisions that have improved the Council.

While WCCES Presidents are relatively transitory, the organisational continuity provided by the Secretaries General has been essential to the WCCES. I had the pleasure of working closely with Raymond Ryba, the longest-serving Secretary General, Vandra Masemann, who followed Raymond before and after his death, and Mark Bray, who served as Assistant Secretary General with Masemann until becoming Secretary General in 2000. The interactions between Secretaries General and other WCCES officers are integral to the development, maintenance and survival of the organisation. These relationships have been examples of true collegiality.

Communications
Concomitant with my two-term tenure as WCCES President was the revolution in information and communications technology. The WCCES was significantly changed by the global extension of the internet, the development of the world-wide web, and in particular, the development of search engines (Wilson 2003). At first, communications were improved with contact by e-mail between WCCES officers, members, and societies. Then, the use of web pages to announce conferences and World Congresses added to the global presence of the WCCES. Moreover, the development of search engines put the field of comparative and international education on the global map, and the WCCES and member societies' web sites contributed to this global presence.

While the Comparative, International and Development Education Centre (CIDEC) at the Ontario Institute for Studies in Education (OISE), University of Toronto, may have established the first list server, it was originally intended to serve only our CIDEC programme. Michael Agelasto at the Comparative Education Research Centre (CERC) of The University of Hong Kong developed its ComparEd list server in 1996.While WCCES President, I encouraged the developers of ComparEd to organise the WCCES web page at CERC in 2000. One by one, WCCES member societies established e-mail addresses and web pages. Linking member society web pages to the WCCES web page created a global network for the field of comparative education. The increase in communications has been exponential, and there is no end in sight.

Conclusion
I attended the 1st World Congress of Comparative Education Societies as a young

academic in 1970, and saw the WCCES grow from an idea put forward by Joseph Katz and Leo Fernig into a viable international NGO. I was honoured to have served the WCCES for two terms as its President and several years as Chair of its Finance Commission. I am proud of the initiatives that I put forward and others that I facilitated, because I believe that these initiatives have contributed to the growth and development of the WCCES.

References

Wilson, David N. (1998): 'On Being International: Confessions of an Academic-Practitioner'. Presidential Address at the 10th World Congress of Comparative Education Societies, Cape Town, South Africa, 17 July.

Wilson, David N. (2003): 'The Future of Comparative and International Education in a Globalised World'. *International Review of Education*, Vol.49, Nos.1-2, pp.14-33.

World Council of Comparative Education Societies (2004): *By-Laws to the Statutes and Rules of Procedures* (Amendments made to the 2001 By-Laws).

7

Improving Transnational Networking for Social Justice: 2001-2004

Anne HICKLING-HUDSON

Reflecting on my three-year term as President of the World Council of Comparative Education Societies (WCCES) from July 2001 to October 2004, I consider in this chapter the adequacy of the Council's organisational arrangements and the effectiveness of its strategies for promoting comparative education research in varying regions. My overarching interest is to consider how the capacity of the WCCES could be strengthened to enhance purposeful educational cooperation and development between and among member societies and countries in the interests of social justice.

Race/Power Hierarchies and Impressions of the WCCES

My first encounter with the WCCES was the 1992 World Congress in Prague, Czechoslovakia. I had the opportunity to attend because, as an academic at an Australian university, I had some sabbatical leave which I spent at Stanford University in the USA, where I encountered the world of comparative education scholars. This was relevant to my subsequent involvement with the WCCES because my move from Jamaica to Australia enabled me to access this world. As a black, female, postcolonial academic, I stood out in the Prague gathering. I do not know what made me gather the courage to stand up and speak in the august hall of white academics. It may have been a mixture of intimidation and anger about the imbalanced scene that I perceived. I asked the panel, which had just one woman, what the policy of the World Council was on female representation. I observed that it was strange in the 1990s to see women and ethnically diverse groups so poorly represented on the platform, which consisted entirely of whites. I was painfully aware that I was one of only a handful of non-white scholars in a meeting of a 'World' Council of Comparative Education Societies. Comparative education was clearly a vitally important field for policy makers and educators, so where, I asked, was 'the rest' of the world? I learnt much later that the composition of the platform represented an important statement of collegiality in that it included both Czechs and Slovaks, at a time when the country was about to split apart. Further, the holding of the congress in Eastern Europe for the first time was a window of change introducing different academic traditions to this region.

However, the marginal place of Africans and Asians in the proceedings of this conference was evident. My Jamaican background and my experience of the decolonisation process from the 1970s causes me to see through a postcolonial lens and a Caribbean prism. This prism makes me sensitive to the colonial sources of wealth and power in Europe, North America, Australia and New Zealand, and the devastating and entrenched consequences of imperial rule across the globe. It also makes me determined to point out prevailing silences and amnesias about the colonial process. The dysfunctional state of education in many former colonies stems from the inadequacy of models left by European colonial regimes. Educational underdevelopment is perpetuated because of the oppression inherent in international economic systems controlled mainly by Euro-American business interests. Teaching in an Australian university in the State of Queensland, in which multiculturalism was poorly developed, made me aware that talking critically about race, colonialism or the imperial sources of underdevelopment was often highly unwelcome to people of European descent. Sarah White, in her article 'Thinking race, thinking development' (2002, p.407), pointed out that "talking about race in development is like breaking a taboo". Her opening paragraph is strikingly realistic in its confrontation with the issue of race:

> Concerned with economic growth and the 'war on poverty', development is determinedly colour-blind. While privately many will admit that race has 'got something to do with it', publicly there is almost total silence. The contrast with gender is striking. There is virtually no analysis of development institutions by race, showing how many people of what racial origin occupy which places in the hierarchy. There are very few programs of anti-racism or racism awareness training. There is no analysis of differential outcomes of development policies by race…. Even the powerful critiques of 'Eurocentrism' or 'neo-colonialism' in development rarely address issues of race directly.

I believe that educators in comparative and international education should carefully consider the application of White's arguments to the field. The silence about race masks the extent to which it influences comparative education (and indeed, education in general). The contradictions that constantly travelled with White in her development studies work appear almost identical to the contradictions that we meet in much comparative education research and writing.

Consider, for example, how comparative education stands with regard to these two issues on which White reflects. First, there was the issue of the *power of her whiteness over the 'Other'* (my italics).While researching women and development in Bangladesh, she was acutely aware that as a white scholar her research was privileged in a way that would never be the case for, say, a Bangladeshi scholar studying Englishwomen. In spite of her awareness of the politics of representation of 'the other', she says "my own work was nonetheless underwritten by that same privilege, and the authority of my class, nation, colour, and education which made it 'natural' that I should be the analyst of other people's lives" (White 2002, p.409). The second issue that constantly struck her was the *power imbalances of North-South relationships in studying education and development*. As she pointed out, the majority of development studies courses (and this is also true of comparative education courses) are still taught in the universities of wealthy 'first world' countries.

These observations remind us that the European and generally Western ideas of race and practices of racism which developed during 450 years of colonialism and 50 years of decolonisation in the 20th century are still strongly with us. We need to consider the extent to which they structure practices of comparative educators in the WCCES, and the extent to which we are successfully challenging those racial legacies that are bound to be part of an organisation with origins in the Euro-American elite.

Something that is very noticeable to a black person joining the WCCES meetings is the very small number, sometimes the absence, of black representatives. This absence of course has to do with the subordinated and dependent position of peoples of African, Indian and other kinds of Indigenous descent during the centuries of colonial suffering. The structuring of race and poverty on the world stage through the grossly unjust international economy which has grown out of colonial history ensures that impoverished developing countries have per capita incomes a fraction of those of the wealthy countries of Europe, North America and Australasia. This lack of financial resources affects the kinds of university courses that the poorer countries can afford. Comparative and international education is considered a luxury, and universities in these countries instead concentrate on what is seen as the basic work of teaching curriculum, pedagogy and psychology. Therefore, not many of the poorer countries have comparative education societies. Where there are such societies, their representatives can rarely afford to travel to WCCES meetings. In contrast, more universities in wealthier countries, including parts of Asia with healthy economies such as Japan, Hong Kong, Taiwan and South Korea, teach comparative education or related international education subjects, and regularly send representatives to World Council meetings (Bray 2002).

Another kind of imbalance that I had noticed in the WCCES over the years of my association since 1992 was how few members from the USA were apparently active on the Council. This was puzzling, since the US-based Comparative and International Education Society (CIES), a member of the WCCES, is by far the largest comparative education society in the world. There were Canadians in WCCES official positions, but very few Americans. An exception was Erwin Epstein, who had been a WCCES President in the 1980s and who was a Co-opted Member of the Council. I was myself a member of the CIES and became so involved in it that I was elected as a CIES Board member for a three-year term. I cannot remember WCCES issues ever being an important agenda item of CIES Board meetings or conferences. In my term of office, I wanted to see Americans – CIES members – from ethnically diverse communities active in the Executive and other committees of the WCCES.

An aspect of WCCES practice that I thought needed to be improved was the functioning of the standing committees. I was happy to have been invited to join one of these committees by David Wilson during his presidency, but I was frustrated by the low level of activities of the committee that I was in, and knew that many colleagues on other committees shared my frustration. While some committees were carrying out their roles, as could be seen by the success of the triennial Congresses, others seemed to have no clear function. Yet we were eager to have clear roles and duties, and to commit ourselves to hard work. Additionally, the racial composition of the committees was mainly white, a situation which did not reflect the international membership and goals of the World Council.

I was encouraged by colleagues in the CIES and in the Australian and New Zealand Comparative and International Education Society (ANZCIES), of which I had been President for two years, to run for the WCCES Presidency when David Wilson approached the end of his term. How far did the WCCES in the three years of my presidency address the issues of representation, access and organisational improvement? I believe that during this period, three factors started to bring about a more representative and a more racially/globally balanced body. They were the holding of the 12th World Congress in Cuba (a decision which caused some contention), our restructuring of the standing committees, and the entry of several new societies from developing countries.

Election of the Cuban Society to Host the 12th World Congress

The vote by the WCCES Executive Committee to hold the 12th Congress in Cuba sparked some disruptions which related partly to organisational flaws and partly, perhaps, to the race-and-development issues discussed above. The Executive Committee convened for its 30th meeting in London in 2002 and, after carefully considering two bids for hosting the 2004 Congress, voted for the Asociación de Pedagogos de Cuba – Sección de Educación Comparada (APC-SEC) as host. The alternative location had been Denmark, hosted by the Nordic Comparative and International Education Society (NOCIES).

The vote was very close, and the choice of Cuba left some member societies feeling upset. Subsequently the Comparative Education Society in Europe (CESE) decided at its General Assembly, held shortly after the WCCES meeting, to suspend its membership of the WCCES. The CESE President sent to the WCCES Executive Committee what she described as a Letter of Disaffection "with specific reference to the way in which the decisional process for the choice of the place of the XII World Congress *was led*" (my italics). The letter stated that the CESE Committee had assembled a proposal, through the NOCIES President, for a joint CESE- WCCES conference to be held in Denmark, and that this proposal had not been handled appropriately.

The members of the WCCES Executive Committee were surprised by this letter, having taken considerable care not only to follow due procedure but also to engage in wide consultation. At the meeting of the Executive Committee in London, the two proposals to host the 12th Congress were carefully scrutinised and discussed by all members present, and the vote was by secret ballot, counted by a member of the Congress Standing Committee and checked by others. When the majority vote for Cuba was announced, I personally was astounded, as were others at the meeting, when the representatives of three European societies strode out of the room, one slamming down papers on the table as he did so.

An hour or so after the election of Cuba to host the Congress, as WCCES President I asked the CESE President for permission to announce the result of the vote in the CESE General Assembly meeting which was about to be held. The CESE President refused permission, and made it clear that my presence would not be welcome. David Turner, the WCCES Treasurer, witnessed this exchange; otherwise I may have thought that I dreamt it. There I was, the first black WCCES President, sitting in the foyer of the University of London Institute of Education, kept out of the General Assembly meeting of the European society, waiting to be 'allowed in' only when it was time for the keynote lecture. It certainly felt as though I was experiencing 'the power of whiteness over the Other'. I found it very difficult to imagine a white male President of the WCCES being excluded from the meeting. In their meeting, the CESE leaders presented their own account of the events of the voting process which had just taken place, an interpretation which led the General Assembly to support the withdrawal of CESE from the WCCES announced in the Letter of Disaffection sent later to the WCCES leaders.

The matter of the CESE withdrawal is discussed in detail in the WCCES minutes of the 31st and the 33rd Executive meetings in New Orleans, USA, and Havana, Cuba. The Secretary General attended the CESE biennial conference in Copenhagen in July 2004, and there listened to the CESE President reporting the minutes of the 2002 CESE meeting in London. These minutes clarified the reasons for the CESE anger over the vote for Cuba. As the CESE Executive saw it and reported in their minutes:

i.   The WCCES had appealed to CESE during the 11th World Congress in Korea to host the 12th Congress.

ii. CESE had responded by asking a former CESE President, who was also a leading member of NOCIES, to prepare the bid, with NOCIES hosting the Congress in Copenhagen.

iii. The plan was to hold a double Congress, in which the 21st CESE conference would be held in Copenhagen just before the 12th World Congress. Much work had gone into arranging institutional hospitality and financial subsidies, and preparing a detailed academic proposal.

iv. Against this background, CESE and NOCIES were faced with the decision of the WCCES Executive at the London meeting to accept the Cuban bid instead.

v.   This WCCES decision produced a major problem for CESE and the plans for its 21st conference. Financial subsidies would be withdrawn, promises would have to be broken, and major reconstruction of CESE plans would be needed.

vi. The CESE Executive was deeply disturbed by this. They proposed to the

General Assembly at the London meeting to express this dissatisfaction in a formal Letter of Disaffection, and to suspend CESE's financial subscription to the World Council. The CESE General Assembly discussed these motions and voted to adopt them.

On comparing this sequence of events as reported by CESE with the minutes of the 31st WCCES meeting (New Orleans, 2003) and the report of Secretary General, Mark Bray, to the 33rd meeting of the WCCES Executive Committee (Havana, October 2004), it becomes clearer where the misunderstandings arose. At the 11th Congress in South Korea, the possibility of the 12th Congress being hosted by CESE had been raised *as one of several possibilities*. The suggestion at that time had focused on Barcelona rather than Copenhagen. On 14 July 2001, Mark Bray had e-mailed the CESE President to follow up on that suggestion. He had taken care to include in the last paragraph of his e-mail explicit reference to the possibility of proposals from "CIES, the Nordic Society [NOCIES] and possibly Cuba or Israel", and had added that the Executive Committee felt "a rather urgent need to incubate all possibilities wherever they are, and to work with the potential hosts to share the load". The paragraph had been written, he said, to ensure that all discussions were transparent (Minutes, New Orleans, 2003).

However, in spite of this correspondence, it seems that the CESE leadership had assumed that since they had been asked to prepare a proposal, their proposal (through NOCIES) would definitely be accepted. Although Mark Bray received a reply on 19 July 2001 from the CESE President, he did not receive any further communications from her to intimate that CESE would be part of a bid. The written proposal for the 12th Congress which was eventually placed on the table in London was explicitly from NOCIES and only NOCIES. The Secretary General stressed that had it been clear that CESE was a joint proposer, then the WCCES would of course have brought CESE fully into the discussions. This procedure would have been essential, not only for reasons of courtesy but also because of financial implications that would have had to be worked out and specified in the contract for the Congress (Minutes, New Orleans, 2003).

It had been made clear to all concerned that the Cuban group (assisted in their planning by some members of CIES) would put forward a bid to host the 12th Congress. Since it was well known that Cuba was going to bid, my question, still unanswered, is why the representatives of CESE and NOCIES were so angry when the majority of the WCCES Executive Committee voted for the Cuban bid. Was it that they felt betrayed? Could it be that they simply never imagined that Cuba would be voted for? Since NOCIES put forward the bid to host the Congress and not CESE, why then did the 'letter of disaffection' complaining about leadership and procedures come from CESE? As was noted by a member of the Executive Committee at the 32nd meeting in New Orleans, great care had been taken over the procedures at the London meeting, and there had been no dispute over those procedures until the results of the vote were announced. That member found it distasteful that objections were made only after the voters had selected the Congress venue which had not been the one favoured by the objectors (Minutes,

New Orleans, 2003).

CESE's actions were unfortunate and upsetting. I swallowed personal hurt at being made a scapegoat for the WCCES vote for the Cuban bid. In the WCCES constitution, the President, Secretary General and Treasurer do not have a vote, so 'the leadership' did not even vote on this matter. It was a vote of the Executive Committee, which comprises the Presidents or representatives of comparative education societies from across the globe. Yet I had to face some ugly personal remarks, as well as overt comments from a few people on their perceptions of the unfitness of Cuba to host a WCCES congress. Cuba, it was said by a member at the London meeting, was a dictatorship, and "the WCCES has always fought against the notion of Congresses being held in countries with dictatorial regimes" (Minutes, London, 2002). The reply from the Cuban representative was a restatement that, whatever the perspectives on the nature of the Cuban government, academic freedom would be respected, and the programme would not be controlled by the Cuban government machinery (Minutes, London, 2002). It was also said that the WCCES vote had been given to Cuba just because of people's desire to visit this tropical island, rather than for its ability to host a global congress. Evidently, there were some who felt the power to be as discourteous and as disparaging as they liked about the 'Other'.

At the 2003 New Orleans meeting, the Executive Committee agreed that the procedures for selecting the location of Congresses needed urgent discussion and resolution so that the complications of this situation would not recur. It was unusual for there to be more than one bid to host the Congress, and this experience showed that competition was not necessarily desirable. However, it remained difficult to see how either the Cubans or the Europeans/Nordics could have been asked to refrain from putting forward a bid to host the Congress.

Another problem was that at the London meeting in 2002 not all WCCES member societies were represented, and so some did not have the opportunity to cast their votes. I later wrote to the CESE President regretting the society's decision to suspend its membership and payment of dues to the WCCES, and asking for suggestions to improve the procedures. Though we looked forward to hearing the views of CESE on this matter, none was forthcoming: in fact, none of our letters was answered. The WCCES Executive Committee discussed the pros and cons of developing a system of soliciting e-mailed votes on important matters from societies whose representatives could not attend meetings. This procedure was put in place, and in 2005 the expanded voting procedure operated effectively for the election of the WCCES Secretary General (Christine Fox of ANZCIES).

Following the extensive discussion at the 2003 New Orleans meeting of the vote for Cuba and its aftermath, the members of the Executive Committee voted by overwhelming majority to support the following three motions:

i.   That the WCCES Executive Committee regrets the CESE decision to cease to pay its fees, which the Committee feels was based on incomplete information available to the CESE body at that time, and that the WCCES Executive Committee would welcome CESE reconsideration of that action.

ii.   That the Executive Committee fully supports the leadership of the WCCES, and has every confidence in it.

iii. That the Executive Committee seeks to mend fences and build bridges with CESE for the good of the field of comparative education.

Fortunately, the refusal of the CESE leadership to reconsider their decision to withdraw from the Council during my term of office had no impact on the 12th World Congress hosted by Cuba, which is discussed later in this chapter. At the July 2004 CESE conference in Copenhagen, which was attended by the WCCES Secretary General as a fence-mending initiative, the CESE General Assembly decided to resume regular payment of dues and constructive relationships with the WCCES as of 2005. It was well known that by this time my Presidency would have come to an end, since my period of office would have expired.

Restructuring Standing Committees and Expanding Membership

After this difficult start to my Presidency, most other situations were enjoyable despite their complex demands. I had the full support, confidence and friendship of the other Presidents of the comparative education societies, and had particularly warm and dynamic interactions with the WCCES Secretary General, Mark Bray, and Treasurer, David Turner. Together they were a tower of strength and a fund of knowledge about the World Council and its traditions, and we made an excellent team. David Turner did extremely thorough work in maintaining the WCCES accounts. Mark Bray, as Professor of Comparative Education at the University of Hong Kong, was able to contribute some of the organisational resources of his university's Comparative Education Research Centre (CERC). These resources included publicity for the WCCES in the centre's newsletter, *CERCular,* and work on the WCCES website. Some of the papers presented at the 11th Congress in Korea were published in a special issue of the *International Review of Education* and then republished as a book (Bray 2003) which CERC helped to distribute. Bob Adamson as Assistant Secretary General, first at the University of Hong Kong and then at the Queensland University of Technology, redesigned and maintained the WCCES website with the assistance of CERC's Emily Mang. He also took over from Mark Ginsburg of the CIES the writing of a regular column on WCCES activities which appeared in *Innovation*, the newsletter of UNESCO's International Bureau of Education.

Restructuring Standing Committees

During my presidency, a major task was to expand and systematise the Council's standing committees. Not only did the ethnic composition of these committees fail to reflect the international membership of the WCCES, but also the role and function of the committees needed to be rethought. This process was important since the committees were intended to carry out much WCCES work during and between meetings, and were the main instruments by which the WCCES liaised with its constituent societies. The committees were reorganised, some renamed, and some new ones established. We made strong efforts to involve committee members from a much wider range of countries than before. To coordinate and follow up these invitations was the President's responsibility, and it took considerable time and effort. The new chairpersons were prominent comparativists from Japan, the UK, the USA, Singapore, and Australia. I invited the previous leaders to become co-chairpersons, assisting the new chairpersons with advice based on their years of experience. We decided that membership of the standing committees could be renewed every three years, so that the incoming WCCES President would be able to change the membership and leadership of these committees.

New members from many constituent societies accepted our invitation to join the standing committees. The leaders and members of the Congress Standing Committee and the Research Standing Committee played particularly dynamic roles in preparing for the 12th Congress in Havana. The other four standing committees, Finance and Fund-Raising, Publications, Admissions, and Special Projects also greatly contributed to the success of the Congress. Acting on the recommendation of our 2003 Executive Committee meeting in New Orleans, we systematised the constitution of our standing committees in a By-Law.

Expanding Membership

The large gaps in the membership of the World Council were not only from Africa. They were also from South Asia, South East Asia, the Arab countries, Latin America, and the Caribbean. When I became President, the Brazilian society was the only one in Latin America, and there was none in the Caribbean. Also, the Francophone countries of Africa were represented only through the Association francophone d'éducation comparée (AFEC), which was headquartered in Europe. The WCCES was delighted to welcome four new constituent societies during the 2001-04 period: from Cuba, Mexico, the Philippines, and the Mediterranean. They helped to fill the gaps in global representation. We also prepared applications for membership from the societies of Argentina and Egypt.

I found that it was very difficult to encourage scholars in some countries to establish new societies or revitalise dormant ones. My attempts to mobilise contacts in Nigeria and Ghana were unsuccessful – there was simply no answer to e-mail messages and letters. Clearly, it would take more than just written communication to encourage the establishment of new societies. One idea was that societies already established, particularly those in the wealthier countries, should try to encourage scholars in other less wealthy countries to develop the field and establish societies. The wealthy societies could act as mentors and give some financial assistance.

However, if a country has no comparative education subjects in its university system, it is unlikely that a new society can be established and maintained. It would take the work of one or more committed and influential comparative education scholars in the particular country to provide the leadership that would contribute to a successful society. I saw that scholars involved in WCCES committees would not necessarily make the effort to launch a society in their own country. It is a voluntary task and a big demand on people's time, often not supported or rewarded by universities, so in some settings there is little motivation for academics to devote much time to it. This lack was illustrated by the fact that no systematic regional involvement in comparative education developed in the English-speaking Caribbean, despite the fact that a Caribbean-based scholar accepted my invitation to join one of the WCCES standing committees. This scholar was in an adjacent field and not really in comparative education, and did not attract other Caribbean scholars to the field of comparative education. No Caribbean society was set up, and to my disappointment not many people from Anglophone or Francophone Caribbean countries attended the 12th Congress even though it was in their own region.

The case of Cuba demonstrates a successful formal launching of comparative education, spearheaded by the hosting of the 12th Congress. This undoubtedly is the result of Cuba's highly developed educational achievements and infrastructure. The comparative education section was established as the APC-SEC, part of the already-existing 14,000 strong Cuban Pedagogical Association. The APC-SEC used the traditions and systems of that association to carry out effective work not only in organising the Congress with WCCES collaboration, but also in introducing comparative education to university educators and postgraduate students all over the country. This process took place through one-day mini-conferences on comparative education in each of Cuba's 14 provinces during February and March 2004, eight months before the Congress. I was invited, together with Rosemary Preston, Chairperson of the Congress Standing Committee, to one of these pre-Congress conferences in the province of Pinar del Rio. We were impressed by the enthusiasm of some 100 academics and post-graduate students in the presentation and discussion of draft papers. At each provincial conference, colleagues presented between 60 and 120 papers. In total, some 2,000 tertiary educators were introduced to the study of comparative education, with 1,400 preparing papers based on small research projects. The best papers from the pre-Congress conferences were selected for development and presentation by their authors at the World Congress. Cubans not selected to attend the World Congress were invited to a series of seminars and workshops about the Congress programme.

This model of national involvement was unprecedented in the history of comparative education, but was part of an APC tradition in preparing for the 'Pedagogía', a large conference of Cuban and Latin American educators that it had organised several times during the previous 15 years. The pre-conference was an approach that could benefit many other countries, but of course it demanded strong commitment and discipline. The continued work of Cuba's APC-SEC after the 12th Congress meant that by 2006 approaches to comparative education were being taught in several Cuban universities, and one was planning to offer it as a field of study. Two PhDs had used a comparative education approach, an edited book on comparative education theory and method was being prepared, some Cuban professors accepted overseas invitations to teach short education courses with a comparative education focus, and a group of eight scholars based at the

Pedagogical University of Havana was working on a comparative study of UNESCO's educational ideas in the education systems of the Americas.

It is rare to see such a flourishing of the field in countries as low-income as Cuba. The example of India illustrates a much more problematic experience. The WCCES leadership devoted considerable effort to encourage Indian scholars to revive their society, the Comparative Education Society of India (CESI). This society was still on the WCCES books as a member, but had not convened for many years and only one or two individual members had been attending WCCES meetings. Yet India's cultural diversity and its educational sophistication, co-existing with problems, were such that it could be an important centre for the comparative study of issues critical to educational development. Our hope was to see a thriving society supporting the teaching of comparative education in many Indian universities. We offered to provide funds to the Indian society to help it hold a national conference that would revitalise its functions and membership. A suggestion came from a group of Indian scholars that the existing society be by-passed and another one established. This change did not come to fruition, nor was the impasse surmounted to allow the existing society to be reconvened and revitalised. Communications with Nina Dey Gupta of CESI in 2007 have led us to hope that the Indian society may indeed be experiencing a revival. However, the question remains: if there is little or no tradition of comparative education in a country or region, how can the WCCES best help local scholars to establish the field, and support it to the point where these scholars are ready to launch a society and sustain it in a way that helps them to support their own work in the field?

The 12th World Congress in Cuba

The triennial World Congress is the principal event hosted by the WCCES, playing a vital role in bringing together its constituent societies for the exchange of scholarly work. With nearly a thousand participants from 68 countries, the 12th Congress was the largest in the history of the WCCES. Scholars organised in 14 thematic groups presented several hundred papers on the theme chosen by the host society, 'Education and Social Justice'. Publications included a special issue of the *International Review of Education* edited by Joseph Zajda, Suzanne Majhanovich, Val Rust and Elvira Martín Sabina (2006).

Recognizing the importance of the Congress, we invested a great deal of effort in assisting the host society to prepare. The Chairperson of our Congress Standing Committee, Rosemary Preston, contributed much time and her excellent organisational talent during four visits to Cuba to assist the Cuban Committee with planning. I joined her on her third visit to help with on-site planning, travelling to Havana as the invited guest of the Cuban Minister of Education and the APC. The fourth preparatory visit, in which we were both involved, took place in Havana the week before the Congress. These visits were especially important since the Cuban organisers were unable to obtain visas to the USA to attend the meetings of the WCCES Executive Committee held in conjunction with the annual CIES conferences.

We were impressed throughout by the excellent work of the Cuban colleagues. Cuba's average annual per capita income was within the range of many Caribbean countries, about US$2,500, compared to wealthy Western countries which were nearer to US$28,000. Yet, the convention facilities which were provided demonstrated significant organisational capacity, including arrangements for simultaneous translations into Spanish, English and French. With a fraction of the economic resources of wealthy countries, having been targeted by an economic blockade imposed by the USA over the previous 40 years, and with the additional difficulties of being battered by hurricanes during the summer of 2004, the Cubans pulled off a historic event that was immensely enjoyed by most participants.

The WCCES Finance and Fund-raising Committee raised US$9,600 through the contributions of societies, individuals and agencies to help 10 scholars from low-income countries, or without regular jobs, travel to Havana for the 12th Congress. This was an important transnational initiative, much appreciated by the recipients. Hundreds of papers and discussions honouring the theme 'Education and Social Justice' made a great contribution to advancing ideas on the challenges of achieving global educational equity. Additionally, three important transnational group meetings were held as part of the Congress. The 11th Seminar on Education in Cuba and the USA met, and Cuban and US educators exchanged papers and deliberations. The AFEC organised a Francophone Symposium, in which scholars from Belgium, Benin, Burkina Faso, Canada, China, France, Greece and Spain presented papers on comparative education issues in French-speaking countries. The launching of the Ibero-American Association of Societies of Comparative Education (Asociación Iberoamericana de Sociedades de Educación Comparada – AISEC), also took place, under the leadership of Ferran Ferrer (Spain). The AISEC, which included representatives from Cuba, Argentina, Mexico, Venezuela, Brazil, Spain and Portugal, made plans for future collaborative work. As Elvira Martín Sabina of the APC-SEC, one of the two WCCES Vice-Presidents, put it: "The exchange of knowledge and demonstrated scholarly rigour among participants were expressions of their degree of commitment to improve education and equity, as a necessary condition for social justice" (Martín Sabina 2006, p.2).

My presidency came to an end on 29 October 2004, when I closed the week-long 12th Congress. I will forever remember the challenging, complex and often innovative work which went into the event, the grace and comradeship with which it was carried out, and the warm friendship and hospitality which the Cubans as hosts extended to their visitors. I was surprised and honoured to be presented with the award of Member of Honour by the APC, in recognition of my services to education and to the Congress. This gives me lifetime membership in a dynamic association with some 14,000 members who are educators at all levels of the Cuban education system. It is an opportunity to work internationally for the cause of education and social justice. The Congress ended with a congratulatory letter from President Fidel Castro celebrating the event and the work of educators, bearing the somewhat rueful signature after an accident the previous week which had fractured his knee and elbow: "From Fidel, signed with my right hand at present in a cast".

Goals and Challenges

I prepared for my first meeting as WCCES President, in London in 2002, by identifying a set of goals. Endorsed and supported by the Council, they were to:

- encourage and help needy scholars financially, especially from developing countries, to attend the meetings of the larger comparative education societies, and especially the 2004 World Congress;
- encourage the teaching of comparative and international education, especially in universities in developing countries;
- promote the field of comparative and international education through publications, news items, audio-visual means, etc.;
- encourage scholars to establish societies for the promotion of comparative and international education in various countries, whether or not they have established a teaching base in the field; and
- draw on clusters of expertise in the WCCES to help with particular projects in education that need extra help, such as adult literacy and refugee education.

My overview of the 2001-04 period has demonstrated that the Council can be proud of its achievements in meeting most of these goals. Although some aspects were too ambitious and complex to be achieved in the three-year period, they remain significant, and I am confident that they can be achieved as the WCCES develops. Ongoing challenges include the need for much closer relationships and cooperation between member societies in wealthy and poorer countries, and the need to continue efforts to become more multiculturally representative. The field of comparative education is still dominated by Europeans and North Americans. The inadequacy of African participation both in the field and in the WCCES reflects Africa's weakness in the world economy. We need to redouble our efforts to help African countries develop the field of comparative education. Networking to utilise expertise takes place informally, but I would like to see the WCCES expand this and make it systematic. Supporting needy scholars to attend the Congress, as was done in Havana, is an initiative that the Council needs to expand for the future. But even raising nearly US$10,000 was not an easy task.

The "power imbalances of North-South relationships in studying education and development" (White 2002, p.409) are still problematic. Few university departments in developing countries offer comparative education as a subject at either undergraduate or postgraduate levels. It is unfortunate that they are missing out on the valuable role of comparative education in providing the evaluative and global perspectives and knowledge that is needed by all types of educators. This kind of knowledge helps us to understand our increasingly interconnected world and contribute to greater understanding, tolerance and respect both for diversity and for our common humanity.

What is important is the amount and significance of what we achieved. We systematised and revitalised the standing committees, and expanded membership of these committees across a range of countries so that they became far more reflective of multicultural and global membership than previously. We added four new societies to our membership, and had further applications in the pipeline. We promoted the field of comparative education through the scholarly activities of members in publishing and national meetings, and particularly through the way in which we co-organised, with our Cuban hosts, the 12th Congress. I congratulate all the members of the WCCES who participated in these significant achievements, and I thank them for their warm support of my role as the first black President and only the second female President of the Council in its three decades of history.

References

Bray, Mark (2002): 'Comparative Education in East Asia: Growth, Development and Contributions to the Global Field'. *Current Issues in Comparative Education*, Vol.4, No.2, pp.70-80.

Bray, Mark (ed.) (2003): *Comparative Education: Continuing Traditions, New Challenges and New Paradigms*. Special double issue of *International Review of Education*, Vol.49, Nos.1-2. Republished 2003 as book with same title, Dordrecht: Kluwer.

Martín Sabina, Elvira (2006): 'Twelfth Congress of the World Council of Comparative Education Societies (WCCES), Havana, Cuba'. *International Review of Education*, Vol.52, Nos.1-2, pp.1-7.

White, Sarah (2002): 'Thinking Race, Thinking Development'. *Third World Quarterly*, Vol.23, No.3, pp.407-419.

Zajda, Joseph; Majhanovich, Suzanne & Rust, Val with Martín Sabina, Elvira (eds.) (2006): *Education and Social Justice*. Special double issue of *International Review of Education*, Vol.52, Nos.1-2. Republished 2006 as book with same title, Dordrecht: Springer.

8

Expanding the Coverage and Hearing More Voices: 2004-2007

Mark BRAY

This chapter is primarily concerned with the period following my election to the WCCES Presidency at the 12th World Congress held in Havana, Cuba, in October 2004. My involvement with the operation of the WCCES had already been extensive, since I had been appointed Assistant Secretary General in 1994 to work with Secretary General Raymond Ryba, and continued in that role in 1997 when Vandra Masemann became Secretary General. Even more pertinently, I had taken over from Masemann as Secretary General in 2000. The appointment was for a term of five years, during which I worked with David Wilson during his last year as President and with Anne Hickling-Hudson throughout her Presidency.

The fact that I was Secretary General at the time of my election to the Presidency, with a term that had not yet expired, meant that initially I had to perform both roles simultaneously. It was obvious in Cuba that the WCCES would need a Secretary General to replace me; but it was equally obvious that an appropriate process for identifying a new Secretary General should be followed, and that it would take time. In the event, Christine Fox of the University of Wollongong in Australia was elected Secretary General in May 2005, so the period in which I held both roles lasted seven months. This chapter presents some information on that election process and its implications. It also remarks on wider achievements and challenges for the WCCES, particularly in the goal of expanding the coverage and hearing more voices.

Increasing Numbers of Constituent Societies

The 2004 meeting of the Executive Committee in Havana, with representatives of 23 of the Council's 33 societies, had the largest number in WCCES history. It was also among the largest in proportional terms.

The WCCES further expanded participation by admitting new societies. As noted by Anne Hickling-Hudson in the previous chapter, for some years the only active society in Latin America had been the Sociedade Brasileira de Educaçao Comparada (SBEC). In 2001 the Executive Committee welcomed the Asociación de Pedagogos de Cuba – Sección de Educación Comparada (APC-SEC); and then in 2004 in Cuba the Executive Committee welcomed the Sociedad Mexicana de Educación Comparada (SOMEC). These were followed by the admission of:

- the Sociedad Argentina de Estudios Comparados en Educación (SAECE) during the 34th meeting of the Executive Committee (2005),
- the Council on Comparative Education of Kazakhstan (CCEK) during the 35th meeting (2006),
- the Egyptian Comparative Education and Educational Administration Society (ECEEAS) during the same meeting, and
- the Turkish Comparative Education Society (TCES) during the 36th meeting (2006).

The admission of the Argentinean society gave pleasure not only because it expanded representation in Latin America, but also because it reflected the rebirth of organisational arrangements for comparative education in that country. In 1980, the WCCES had welcomed the Asociación Argentina de Educación Comparada (AAEC); but over the years that body had become defunct, and it was removed from the WCCES membership list in 2000. The replacement society reflected the work of a revitalised group of scholars working particularly under the leadership of Norberto Fernández Lamarra in Buenos Aires.

The welcoming of the CCEK was also significant, because it was the WCCES' first society from Central Asia. The CCEK President, Askarbek Kussainov, had trained as an engineer in Eastern Germany and spoke fluent German and Russian. The CCEK had strong delegations not only in the meeting in Hawaii, USA, in which the society was admitted but also in subsequent meetings in Granada, Spain (2006) and Hong Kong, China (2007).

The history of the Egyptian society was in some respects similar to the Argentinean one. In 1984 the WCCES had admitted the Egyptian Group of Comparative Education (EGCE), but by the late 1990s the body appeared to have become either dormant or defunct and, like the original Argentinean society, was removed from the WCCES membership list in 2000. The admission of the revitalised group was especially significant because it restored membership of a society based in an Arabic-speaking country. The Mediterranean Society of Comparative Education (MESCE) had significant numbers of Arabic speakers, and its founding President, Giovanni Pampanini, had made it a particular mission to expand membership and participation in the Arabic-speaking countries that bordered on the Mediterranean. Nevertheless, the participation of the Egyptian society gave more prominence to Arabic-speaking scholars than could be achieved through MESCE alone.

The admission of the Turkish society was significant for related reasons. Again, some Turkish scholars were members of MESCE, and indeed Fatma Gök who led the Turkish society was a founding member of MESCE. But the existence of the Turkish society, which on the one hand organised its affairs in its own language and on the other hand reached out to scholars around the world through other languages, strengthened the voice of comparative education in a country which bridged Europe and Asia.

In 2007 I learned of a further body in Asia, namely the Thailand Comparative and International Education Society (TCIES). This body had been formed two years previously, with leadership in Chulalongkorn and Naresuan Universities. I provided information on the WCCES, and encouraged its officers to apply for membership.

Alongside these bodies, moreover, were scholars in other countries who were considering forming societies. Norberto Fernández Lamarra was a great advocate of comparative education around the Latin American region, and he encouraged individuals and groups in Uruguay, Panama, Chile and elsewhere. The World Council was also aware of a group in Venezuela which had formed a society. It appeared, however, that this society was weak and, at least in the first instance, approaches to suggest that it apply for World Council membership did not bear fruit. Nevertheless, individual scholars from many countries were members of the regional societies, such as the Comparative Education Society in Europe (CESE) and the Comparative Education Society in Asia (CESA), the language-based societies such as the Association francophone d'éducation comparée (AFEC), and the large societies with international membership such as the US-based Comparative and International Education Society (CIES).

In addition to these bodies, which defined their constituencies primarily by geography or language were at least two societies which had a global remit to focus on particular specialisations. These were:

- the International Society of Comparative Adult Education (ISCAE), and
- the International Society for Comparative Physical Education and Sport (ISCPES).

The ISCAE had had various links with the WCCES. For example, several colleagues joined the World Congresses in Prague (1992) and Sydney (1996), and on the latter occasion an ISCAE officer had participated as an observer in the meeting of the WCCES Executive Committee. The ISCAE itself was formed in 1992, with Jost Reischmann of Bamberg University in Germany as the President. Various activities were organised under the ISCAE umbrella, many of which placed strong emphasis on methodology (see e.g. Reischmann et al. 1999).

In 2003 I contacted Reischmann, who was still the ISCAE President, to see whether formal links could usefully be established. The reply at that time was cordial, but he indicated that the society did not have a formal constitution or membership fees, and as such would not be able to fulfil all the requirements for admission. Nevertheless, the ISCAE remained an active even if not formally-constituted body. In 2006 I accepted an invitation to make a keynote address to an ISCAE conference in Bamberg, recognising that it would be a good opportunity to promote links between the WCCES and this group of scholars. I stressed that the participants would be welcome to join the 13th World Congress in Sarajevo, even if not as members of a WCCES constituent society.

Similar thoughts underlay approaches to the ISCPES. This body had been formed in 1978, held biennial conferences, and produced a journal and other strong publications (e.g. Fu et al. 1989). I contacted the President in 2004, but did not receive a reply. In 2006 I received an invitation to the ISCPES conference to be held in Cuba in 2007, and contacted the new President. This time I did receive a reply, thanking me for the approach and indicating that he would consult colleagues. Whether or not formal links will be established remained to be seen; but I felt that the outreach was worthwhile in the goal of expanding WCCES relationships.

Languages of Communication

During the period of my Presidency, I remained mindful of issues relating to the languages used for World Council activities. I raised this matter in a number of publications (Bray 2005, p.8; Bray & Manzon 2005, p.203; Bray 2006, p.7), noting that most formal WCCES work was conducted through English. A substantial literature has analysed and critiqued the dominance of English in international discourse (see e.g. Pennycook 1998; Johnson 2001; Crystal 2003), noting its usefulness as a common vehicle, but also the effect it has of privileging some groups over others. I considered it important for the World Council at least to be sensitive to issues, and where possible to ameliorate the dominance of one particular language.

The Statutes and By-Laws are silent on the matter of languages, and, perhaps appropriately, do not give any language official status. In the early years, the practice was to use both English and French at meetings of the Executive. With the switch predominantly to English since then, it is not insignificant that a substantial proportion of WCCES Presidents and Secretaries General have been native speakers of that language. On the one hand these individuals have felt comfortable maintaining the production of minutes and other official records in English, and on the other hand the language has perhaps been a hidden or overt discouragement to application for the posts of President and Secretary General by non-native speakers of that language.

My understanding on this matter was informed by dimensions of WCCES history, some of which are presented elsewhere in this book. When the Council was set up, considerable attention was given to the use of English and French interchangeably. This fitted well with the location of the founding meeting, since Canada is an officially-bilingual country and the hosting society, the CIESC, was an officially-bilingual society. The emphasis on both languages was maintained while the Secretariat was in the UNESCO International Bureau of Education (IBE) in Geneva, Switzerland, since that part of Switzerland is French-speaking, but the IBE conducted much of its international work in English. Raymond Ryba also paid great attention to French as Secretary General (1983-96) and an active member of AFEC, being fluent in that language; Michel Debeauvais, a native speaker, emphasised it during his period as President (1983-87). Moreover, the WCCES logo of the two 'globes', one of which has 'comparative education' written in English and the other of which has 'éducation comparée' written in French, dates from the time of the 7th World Congress in Montreal, Canada, in 1989, when Jacques Lamontagne had it commissioned.

However, by the time I became Secretary General and then President, the place of French had diminished. For reasons of tradition, and to respect a request by AFEC and the CIESC, the glossy WCCES flyer retained on the front the French version of the WCCES name (Conseil mondial des associations d'éducation comparée), even though the rest of the text was in English. Various colleagues felt, with some justification, that French did not necessarily deserve particular prominence alongside the many other languages spoken by members of WCCES constituent societies, and a later version of the flyer brought in multiple languages albeit in the background. Others still see the World Council as an officially-bilingual organisation, although that claim cannot be documented.

At the same time, efforts were made to promote the work of the WCCES through diverse languages whenever opportunities arose. As noted in the previous chapter, the 12th World Congress in Havana was primarily conducted in Spanish and English, but AFEC arranged for the resources for a French-medium strand within it. The *International Review of Education* (*IRE*), which has provided an outlet for papers from each World Congress from 1992 onwards, is willing to publish papers in English, French or German, and in addition contains abstracts in those languages plus Spanish and Russian. The special double issue of the *IRE* that was published following the Havana congress (Zajda et al. 2006) contained 10 papers, of which two had been translated with the journal's assistance from Spanish to English while one remained in its original French.

While inclusion of more than one language within the covers of a single volume is one way to reach different linguistic audiences, a more effective way can be translation of whole volumes. In this regard, particular success was achieved with the volume from the 11th World Congress in Chungbuk, South Korea. Like the others, this first appeared as a special issue of the *IRE* (Bray 2003), and was then republished as a spin-off book. All the original papers were in English, though with the usual *IRE* practice of abstracts in English, German, French, Spanish and Russian. Subsequently, translations of the whole book, each with its own context, were published as follows:

- *Japanese.* Toru Umakoshi and Yutaka Otsuka of the Japan Comparative Education Society (JCES) supervised this work, and the book was published by Toshindo in Tokyo in 2005.
- *Farsi.* This version was translated by Abbas Arani and published by Jungle Publishing House in Tehran, Iran, in 2005. It was an independent initiative by the translator, who desired to make the materials available to readers of Farsi. The WCCES did not have a constituent society in Iran, and this work was independent of the WCCES machinery *per se.*
- *Bulgarian.* This volume was prepared under the supervision of Nikolay Popov, of the Bulgarian Comparative Education Society (BCES), and published by the BCES in 2005. The WCCES accepted the translation work in lieu of hard-currency annual dues. The WCCES also made a financial contribution to printing, using revenues from sale of the English-

language book.

- *Hungarian*. This volume emerged from a similar arrangement with the Comparative Education Section of the Hungarian Pedagogical Society (HPS), and was published in 2006. The work was accomplished under the direction of Péter Tóth, Trencsényi László and Tamás Kozma.
- *Italian*. Giovanni Pampanini, who had been President of MESCE and at that time was Vice-President of the WCCES, took responsibility for this version. It was published in 2006 by the Cooperativa Universitaria Editrice Catanese di Magisterio, in Catania, Italy.
- *Chinese*. This version was translated by Peng Zhengmei of East China Normal University, Shanghai. It was published in 2007 by East China Normal University Press.
- *Spanish*. Mario Lorenzo Martínez Saldivar of the Sociedad Mexicana de Educación Comparada (SOMEC) arranged for this version to be published by Porrua in Mexico City.
- *Bosnian*. Adila Kreso, organiser of the 13th World Congress in Sarajevo, indicated her intent to prepare a Bosnian-language version in time for that Congress in September 2007.
- *Russian*. The introduction and first chapter were translated under the supervision of Elena Fedotova and published in 2004 in the journal *Education in Siberia*. Askarbek Kussainov of the Council on Comparative Education of Kazakhstan (CCEK) arranged for translation of the other chapters in order to publish the whole book in Russian.

This list is remarkable not only for its length but also for its inclusion of languages that are not among the common ones for translations of books of this type. Further, in many cases the work was achieved by graduate students as part of training exercises through which they became more thoroughly acquainted with the field. The work did indeed help the WCCES to see itself more strongly as a world body which was able to reach and serve communities of scholars in different parts of the globe.

Locations of Meetings

During my Presidency I was also conscious of the influence of the locations of meetings on the nature of participation. Over the history of the WCCES, meetings of the Executive Committee had of course been held in the places in which the World Congresses had been organised, and this practice in itself achieved diversity both in geography and in the languages of the host countries. Up to the period of my Presidency, between Congresses every meeting of the Executive Committee held since 1984 (that being the year in which the constitution created an Executive Committee distinct from the Council itself) was organised in conjunction with either the biennial conference of the Comparative Education Society in Europe (CESE) or the annual conference of the Comparative and International Education Society (CIES) (Manzon & Bray 2006). This practice, moreover, had deeper roots since it had been the normal mode of operation for the Council even before the formation of the Executive Committee.

The coordination with CESE and CIES conferences had the dual merit of promoting attendance and limiting costs, because many participants already planned to join those conferences. It did, however, introduce language biases. The CESE meetings were mostly in non-English-speaking countries, the only exception being one meeting out of nine in the United Kingdom; but the CIES meetings were mostly in English-speaking countries, the only exception being one meeting out of 15 in Mexico. Furthermore, the meetings introduced geographic biases through the fact that they were all held in either Europe or North America.

With that history in mind, I asked the Executive Committee to consider meeting sometimes in conjunction with other societies in addition to CESE and CIES. This proposal was accepted on two occasions. In 2005 the 34th meeting of the Executive Committee was held in Bangi, Malaysia in conjunction with the biennial meeting of the Comparative Education Society of Asia (CESA); and in 2007 the 37th meeting was held in Hong Kong, China, in conjunction with the biennial meeting of CESA and the annual meeting of the Comparative Education Society of Hong Kong (CESHK). Both Malaysia and Hong Kong are former British colonies in which English is widely spoken, though not as the dominant language in daily life, and in that respect they did not perhaps diversify the linguistic framework as much as other choices might have. Also, both were in Asia, which therefore left other parts of the world underserved. However, the choice of location did help to balance the work of the World Council. In addition to bringing different voices to the Executive Committee, the decision to hold the meetings in conjunction with these conferences supported the conferences and therefore the constituent societies themselves.

Also pertinent was the choice of Sarajevo as the location for the 13th World Congress. A precondition for selection of any location, of course, is availability of colleagues who, preferably with institutional backing, are willing to organise such an event. The demands of a World Congress are considerable, and the number of bids for such work is rarely large. In the case of the 13th World Congress, the WCCES was fortunate to have a proposal sponsored by MESCE and a very distinguished and capable woman at the helm in the person of Adila Kreso, who was able to mobilise the necessary support. Further, the location fitted admirably the desire of the World Council to move in sequence to different regions of the world. The event had not been held in Europe since the 8th World Congress in Prague in 1992, and in that sense it was Europe's 'turn'. Further, as explained in the bidding document, Sarajevo was especially significant as a meeting place of Islamic and Christian cultures.

However, the location was not uncontroversial. Some colleagues queried whether Bosnia and Herzegovina had sufficient political stability and infrastructure, and at least one person described Sarajevo as "the symbol of war". In making that statement, the speaker had in mind first that Sarajevo was the city in which Archduke Ferdinand of the Austro-Hungarian Empire had been assassinated in 1914, an event which had led to World War I, and second that Sarajevo had been the centre of bitter fighting in the civil war that had consumed the country from 1992 to 1995.

In order to show that these concerns were taken seriously, and thus to have confidence that the decision could be firmly grounded, the WCCES Executive Committee asked two colleagues to visit Sarajevo for fact-finding and assessment. The colleagues were Rosemary Preston, Chairperson of the Congress Standing Committee (2003-06), and Alain Carry, President of AFEC (2003-06). They were joined in Sarajevo by Giovanni Pampanini, who at that time was President of MESCE and had travelled from Italy, and worked closely with colleagues from Bosnia and Herzegovina, and in particular Adila Kreso from the University of Sarajevo. The report from that event was both thorough and positive, and the Executive Committee felt very confident in approving Sarajevo as the location.

In a related move, the 36th meeting of the Executive Committee in Granada, Spain, decided to increase collaboration among scholarly societies by working with the International Association for Intercultural Education (IAIE). This body, which dated its history to 1984, had been considering holding a conference in the same region at approximately the same season and on a related theme. It seemed appropriate for the WCCES to collaborate with the IAIE rather than to compete, and the arrangements made to do this permitted a further extension of the WCCES network both to expand the coverage and to hear more voices.

The possibility of a further exciting move to reach different communities came with the 37th meeting of the Executive Committee in Hong Kong, China. In response to a call for proposals for the 14th World Congress in 2010, colleagues in AFEC proposed Dakar, Senegal. The Executive Committee welcomed this idea, endorsing the proposal in principle pending consideration of a document with full details. The Executive Committee noted that it would be only the second time for a Congress to be held in Africa, and the first time for it to be held in Francophone Africa. Moreover, 2010 would be an especially significant year as the 50th anniversary of independence in Senegal, and the 10th anniversary of the World Education Forum which had brought leaders from all over the world to reaffirm the importance of Education for All and to make specific plans to achieve that goal. The year 2010 will also mark the 40th anniversary of the WCCES.

Uses of Technology

Advances in technology, and most notably the internet, helped to open further space for participation. As e-mail became more widespread, I found myself in regular correspondence with colleagues from all over the world at minimal cost. This was a major evolution from previous years, in which subjects for discussion by the Executive Committee had included whether the World Council could afford to send documents by air mail rather than by sea, or whether e-mail would ever prove sufficiently popular to be used as a medium of communication for the WCCES Executive Committee. The website, coupled with e-mail, permitted the WCCES to maintain and expand its network not only among scholars who had the necessary finances to join international meetings but also among ones who had much more restricted resources.

At the same time, the internet also has language biases, and in some respects it has been a vehicle for further promoting the hegemony of English (Bunt-Kokhuis 2006, p.38). Certainly my own correspondence was almost entirely in English, even though I was resident for the first part of my Presidency in Hong Kong and for the second part in Paris. In that respect, most of my direct correspondence was limited to people who could work in English, whatever their native languages.

However, the Executive Committee was again mindful of both dangers and opportunities in this domain. In Hong Kong I was ably assisted by colleagues who were fluent in Chinese and Spanish, and as necessary I could call for help with Russian, Japanese and other languages. In Paris, where I became an employee of UNESCO, the range of colleagues with different linguistic competencies was wider still. Thus, at least some of the necessary human talent was available to be harnessed with the technology when needed.

Technologies also greatly assisted with the process for electing the Secretary General in 2005. As indicated, the Executive Committee was mindful that the location of its meetings greatly influenced both the numbers and the geographic balance of the people who were able to attend meetings, which influence in turn meant that the outcomes of decision-making processes could be highly dependent on the locations in which the meetings were held. In 2005 for the first time the Executive Committee accepted electronic voting for the candidates for the post of Secretary General. The Executive Committee recognised that physical presence was highly desirable, since it facilitated debate and therefore a more informed voting process. However, the Executive Committee permitted electronic voting by societies which were not able to send representatives to the meeting. The outcome of this process was agreed to be much more participatory and fair.

Conclusions

Compared with some of the uncertain periods recounted by previous Presidents in this book, the period of my presidency was relatively stable. I worked with an excellent team, and felt that the WCCES was able to advance further in its goals of becoming a truly global body. Of course much remained to be done; but the number of societies increased, internet technology was harnessed, and attention was paid to the use of multiple languages for the World Council's work.

Throughout this process, I was mindful that almost all WCCES work was conducted as a voluntary activity. As has been the case practically throughout its history, the WCCES had no salaried personnel and operated on a minimal budget. These features, which were mirrored in almost all the constituent societies, made the achievements all the more remarkable. This chapter has mentioned the names of some key individuals in the WCCES network who helped to promote the field through organisation of conferences, translation of books, operation of websites, etc.; but within the space available the chapter could never include all the relevant names. The chief motivation for the colleagues who devoted their efforts was a sense of satisfaction in working with diverse counterparts from many cultures for the sake of "common interests and uncommon goals". The individuals within the constituent societies did feel that the global body gave another layer of meaning to their work; and the leaders in the world body were glad to provide service to the global field in this way.

Finally, I express particular appreciation of the work of Maria Manzon at the University of Hong Kong. This work began with her assisting me in some research and translation for the article which was in due course published in the *Revista Española de Educación Comparada* (Bray & Manzon 2005), and then developed into much more extensive collaboration including the co-editorship of this book. Maria Manzon assisted in the organisation of the panel on histories during the 12th World Congress in Havana, Cuba, and was of particular support during the seven-month period in which I was both Secretary General and President. Many of her contributions were provided on an informal basis, but they were formalised in her appointment as Assistant Secretary General during 2005. It has been a pleasure to see the way in which she has been inspired to embark on doctoral studies which relate closely to the themes covered in this book, and to observe the ways in which she has strengthened the WCCES through her networking in multiple languages.

References

Bray, Mark (ed.) (2003): *Comparative Education: Continuing Traditions, New Challenges, and New Paradigms*. Special double issue of *International Review of Education*, Vol.49, Nos.1-2. Republished 2003 as book with same title, Dordrecht: Kluwer Academic Publishers.

Bray, Mark (2005): 'The Evolving Field of Comparative Education: Scholarly Societies and Global Collaboration'. Keynote address at the Second Worldwide Forum on Comparative Education, Beijing Normal University, Beijing, 22-24 August.

Bray, Mark (2006): 'L'évolution du domaine de l'éducation comparée: sociétés scientifiques et collaboration mondiale'. Paper presented at the Association francophone d'éducation comparée (AFEC) colloque international d'éducation comparée, Villeneuve d'Ascq, France, 22-24 June.

Bray, Mark & Manzon, Maria (2005): 'El WCCES: Equilibrios, Misiones y Prospectivos'. *Revista Española de Educación Comparada*, No.11, pp.189-213.

Bunt-Kokhuis, van de, Sylvia (2006): 'Introduction to Filtering', in Bunt-Kokhuis, van de, Sylvia (ed.), *World Wide Work: Filtering of Online Content in a Globalized World*. Amsterdam: VU University Press, pp.15-45.

Crystal, David (2003): *English as a Global Language*. Second edition, Cambridge: Cambridge University Press.

Fu, Frank H.; Ng, M.L. & Speak, Michael (eds.) (1989): *Comparative Physical Education and Sport Volume 6*. Hong Kong: Physical Education Unit, The Chinese University of Hong Kong.

Johnson, R. Keith (2001): 'Political Transitions and the Internationalisation of English: Implications for Language Planning, Policy-making and Pedagogy', in Bray, Mark & Lee, Wing-On (eds.), *Education and Political Transition: Themes and Experi-*

ences in East Asia. Second edition, Hong Kong: Comparative Education Research Centre, The University of Hong Kong, pp.59-74.

Manzon, Maria & Bray, Mark (2006): 'The CIES and the WCCES: Leadership, Ambiguities and Synergies'. *Current Issues in Comparative Education*, Vol.8, No.2, pp.69-83.

Pennycook, Alastair (1998): *English and the Discourses of Colonialism*. London: Longman.

Reischmann, Jost; Bron, Michal & Jelenc, Zoran (eds.) (1999): *Comparative Adult Education 1998: The Contribution of ISCAE to an Emerging Field of Study*. Ljubljana: Slovenian Institute for Adult Education, and Bamberg: International Society for Comparative Adult Education.

Zajda, Joseph; Majhanovich, Suzanne & Rust, Val with Martín Sabina, Elvira (eds.) (2006): *Education and Social Justice*. Special double issue of *International Review of Education*, Vol.52, Nos.1-2. Republished 2006 as book with same title, Dordrecht: Springer.

9

The Comparative and International Education Society (CIES)

Elizabeth Sherman SWING

The Comparative and International Education Society (CIES), formerly the Comparative Education Society (CES), celebrated its 50th anniversary in 2006. From its inception it has viewed itself as international.

This chapter, which is based on material in the CIES Collection in the Kent State University Archives, begins with a prehistory: the conferences at New York University that led to the formation in 1956 of the CES. It then reviews institutional directions in the early years of the society – study tours, the first Constitution, and the launching of the *Comparative Education Review* (*CER*). Next, it examines organisation building from 1960 to 1975 – leadership and finances, constitutional reform, the name change, and the issue of meeting separately as a society. It then focuses on growth and consolidation in the years 1975 to 1990 – years when the CIES sought relationships with other societies on its own terms, established archives, created the Honorary Fellows designation, set up the Eggertsen Lectures, years also of explicit skirmishes over ways of knowing. The chapter closes with the period 1990 to 2006 – a contested election, systemic change in a new Constitution, expansion of the committee structure, and political and ideological concerns.

Prehistory, 1954-56

The New York University Conferences

The CIES evolved from annual conferences on comparative education organised by William W. Brickman at New York University in 1954. Brickman's conferences reflected the spirit of the times. The post-World War II period was an era of proliferating international educational institutions, including UNESCO, the Centre for Comparative Education at the University of Ottawa (Canada), and the Research Institute of Comparative Education and Culture, University of Kyushu (Japan). It was also an era when a distinguished group of European senior scholars, including Joseph A. Lauwerys, Nicholas Hans, Isaac Kandel and Friedrich Schneider, set a standard for what might be achieved in comparative education scholarship.

Brickman's concern was the low status of comparative education in the United States, "the apparently widespread feeling that the comparative study of foreign systems of education is decorative rather than functional and hence of little value to the teacher" (Brickman 1954, p.8). Although only 35 people participated in the initial New York University conference, Brickman labelled his edition of their papers: "Proceedings of the *First* Annual Conference on Comparative Education" (1954, emphasis added). In so doing, he signalled that this group would henceforth occupy comparative education turf in the United States.

The first objective was to rescue the term 'comparative education' from association with "junketlike tours abroad and the resultant courses" run by amateurs (Brickman 1977, p.398) – to gain for the field "recognition in the academic and professional world as a group of scholarly-minded, serious specialists with high standards of teaching, research, and publication" (Brickman 1966, p.8). Brickman's remedy was a rigorous programme of post-doctoral study, research, foreign language training, and school visits. The eminent scholar, Robert Ulich of Harvard University, who was keynote speaker at the first conference, also stressed foreign languages and travel (Ulich 1954, p.14). Like Brickman, Ulich located the field within a humanist tradition in which the frame of reference was Eurocentric, and the dominant tools were history and languages.

Humanist frame of reference notwithstanding, the focus of the New York University conferences was also prescriptive, pragmatic, and pedagogic. The theme of the first conference, 'The Role of Comparative Education in the Education of Teachers' (1954), was followed by 'The Teaching of Comparative Education' (Brickman 1955), 'Comparative Education in Theory and Practice' (Brickman 1956a), and 'Comparative Education and Foreign Educational Service' (Brickman 1957a). The Comparative Education Society which evolved from these conferences began its existence as a branch of the National Society of College Teachers of Education.

Formation of the Comparative Education Society

In 1954, shortly after the first New York University conference, William W. Brickman, Gerald H. Read of Kent State University, and Bess Goodykoontz of the United States Office of Education met in Washington DC "to explore the possibility of designing a program that would provide a significant and first-hand experience in Europe for professional educators who had a responsibility for teaching courses ... that dealt with education in other lands" (Brickman 1966, p.7). Although discussion of a formal organisation had antedated this meeting, the impetus for action was the discovery that group rates for study tours required a pre-existing group. To meet this requirement, at the close of the Third New York University Conference on 27 April 1956, Brickman and Read proposed that participants form a society (Brickman 1956b). Read's report in the minutes of the event is succinct:

> Those present voted in favour of the formation of a Comparative Education Society. The Society came into being the next day.

The CES would hold annual meetings in Chicago in conjunction with the American Association of Colleges of Teacher Education, the National Society of College Teachers of Education, and the Association of Student Teaching. In addition, it would organise a Comparative Education Section of the National Society of College Teachers of Education. Summer meetings would take place during annual study tours.

Membership in the CES was to be "open to professors and students of comparative education and other Foundations of Education, to those persons who have responsibilities in the area of comparative education in organisations other than colleges and universities, to those persons in professional education and other disciplines who are interested in comparative education" (Read, Minutes, 27 April 1956). Its goals were ambitious: to promote and improve the teaching of comparative education in colleges and universities; to encourage scholarly research in the field; to interest professors of all disciplines in the comparative and international dimensions of their specialties; to promote inter-visitation of educators and on-the-spot studies of school systems throughout the world; to cooperate with specialists in other disciplines in interpreting educational developments in a wider cultural context; to facilitate the publication of studies and up-to-date information on comparative education; to encourage cooperation among specialists in comparative education in studies, exchange of documents and first-hand description of education; to cooperate wherever possible with such organisations as UNESCO, the International Institute of Education, and the Organisation of American States". CES would "publish newsletters, monographs, yearbooks and other publications, either independently or in cooperation with other organisations". It would also sponsor programs of visitation to other lands and would even call upon its members to serve as hosts to foreign educators in the United States (Read, Minutes, 27 April 1956).

William W. Brickman was elected President; Robert Sutton, Ohio State University, Vice-President; and Gerald H. Read, Kent State University, Secretary-Treasurer. A Board of Directors was established, "with members selected from each of the various regions of the United States" (Read, Minutes, 27 April 1956). The first Board consisted of Claude Eggertsen, University of Michigan; George Z.F. Bereday, Teachers College, Columbia University; David Scanlon, Newark State Teachers College; Bess Goodykoontz, US Office of Education; Flaud Wooton, University of California; Harold R.W. Benjamin, Peabody College for Teachers; William Johnson, University of Pittsburgh; and Robert Ulich, Harvard University. Thereafter, an invitation was sent to 500 educators to become charter members of the society for a fee of US$2.00 per year. The society had 155 members after this solicitation (Read, Minutes, 27 April 1956).

Brickman later pointed out that the group who formed the Comparative Education Society consisted of junior scholars. "One might have expected an initiative from such internationally recognized scholars as Professor Joseph A. Lauwerys of England, Professor Walther Merck, Dr. Franz Hilker, and Professor Reich Hylla of West Germany; and Professors Robert King Hall, Thomas Woody, and Flaud C. Wooton of the USA, but none was forthcoming" (Brickman 1977, p.398). In Brickman's view, therefore, the founding of the society "could be regarded as an act of rashness perpetrated by a relatively younger generation rather than as the outcome of deliberation by the outstanding experts of the field". Nevertheless, Brickman persuaded senior scholars such as Flaud Wooton and Robert Ulich to join the first Board of Directors.

About the founding of the Comparative Education Society, George Z.F. Bereday, the first editor of the *Comparative Education Review*, had a similar but somewhat different perspective. In a letter to Walter F. Cronin, Office of Intelligence Research, Department of State, about his plans for the *Review*, Bereday noted that:

> Originally the Society germinated in a small group of people. Few of these have established a claim to competence in some aspects of comparative education; for most, their interest in the field was far greater than their competence. After some deliberation at the college [Teachers College, Columbia University], I have decided to join and support the Society rather than creating factions and splinter groups in the field.... At present the demand for comparative education has far outrun the supply and many teach the subject who from the point of view of training they received have no business teaching it.

Bereday went on to provide an overview of the academic interests of several founding fathers:

> At present two of the men at the helm of the Society major in research in the Soviet area. William Johnson, the vice-president, represents George Count's political-educational school. I myself represent the sociological, Harvard Russian Research Center orientation.... William Brickman, the president, has also some interest in the area. I think this is an over-emphasis.... Fortunately my first major is not Soviet but Western Europe, England in particular; David Scanlon, one of our directors is working on Africa and Fundamental Education. This points in the direction of the kind of general coverage in which I am interested for the *Review* and for the Society (Letter, Bereday to Cronin, 29 July 1957).

Defining Institutional Directions, 1956-60

Study Tours
The newly-minted CES faced an immediate challenge: to implement the programme of seminars and study tours planned by Brickman, Read and Goodykoontz. During the summer of 1956, a group of educators and academics led by Brickman and Read visited schools and universities in Denmark, Germany, Switzerland, France, the Netherlands and England. In the course of this tour, the society held its first international meeting in Geneva, Switzerland, where on 1 September 1956 tour participants heard papers on the study of education in Switzerland and in the USA

and on schools in Germany. George Z.F. Bereday (Letter to Walter F. Cronin, 29 July 1957) was concerned about "unsettledness" in the society because of foreign tours, an issue over which Isaac Kandel later resigned from the Board of Directors. Nevertheless, the society sponsored an imaginative series of excursions to Venezuela, Brazil, Argentina, Chile, Peru, Ecuador, Japan, Korea, Ethiopia, Kenya, Tanganyika, South Africa, the Republic of Congo, Nigeria, Ghana, and Liberia. During the society's first six years, Brickman and Read led groups to five continents and 24 countries. Of particular significance was the five-week trip to the Soviet Union in 1958 at a time when the US State Department had not yet obtained an exchange agreement with the Soviet Union (Bereday et al. 1960).

The First Constitution

The CES held its first annual meeting in Chicago on 14 February 1957, with 39 members present (Read, Minutes). At that time, a series of practical decisions was made. The fiscal year was to start on 1 January 1958, and those who were members at that date would become charter members. A committee chaired by Kathryn G. Heath, US Office of Education, was appointed to frame a Constitution. At the second annual meeting in Chicago, 20 February 1958, with 111 members present, drafts of a Constitution were discussed. At the third annual meeting in Chicago, 12 February 1959, the decision was made to poll the membership by mail for ratification of the Constitution. This process was officially completed on 1 June 1959.

   The first Constitution (1959) defined the shape and scope of the society. It called for annual elections and an annual professional and business meeting; a President and a Vice-President, each elected for a one-year term but eligible for a second term; a nine-member Board of Directors elected three at a time, each for a three-year term; and two Executive Committee Officers appointed by the Board, the Secretary-Treasurer and the Editor of the *Comparative Education Review*. The Constitution was amended in 1975 to provide for one-year successive terms by the Vice-President, President-Elect, and President respectively, and thus a two-year preparation for the Presidency. The society, however, has remained recognisably the organisation created in the Constitution of 1959.

   Provision in the first Constitution for election by the membership of the President, Vice-President, and the Board of Directors, rather than their appointment by a group in power, reflected the political traditions in which the Founders of the society were acculturated. The fact, moreover, of term limits for officers, board members, and appointed officers ensured that no clique would dominate the society for long. This outcome appears to be intentional. In March 1964 George Z.F. Bereday wrote a letter to Robert E. Belding of the University of Iowa in which he noted: "The founders and directors of the CES are most anxious not to dominate its affairs, hence their desire to stay in the background as much as possible". This posture, however, plus the rapid turnover of officers prescribed by the Constitution, has led to an unanticipated outcome in the years that followed: a loss on the Board of members with historical memory.

   The Constitution called for Regional Meetings (Article IV, Section 2) to be arranged by the Executive Council. What has developed instead is an active network of geographical groups whose meetings are encouraged but not coordinated by the parent organisation. The New York University conferences continued until 1959. Thereafter, Northeast Regional Meetings of the CES took place respectively at Columbia University Teachers College, Jersey City State College, the US Office of Education, Syracuse University, the Pan American Union, and the University of Bridgeport. By 1965, there were regional conferences in Pittsburgh, Pennsylvania; Madison, Wisconsin; Berkeley, California; and Montreal, Quebec (Canada).

Comparative Education Review

Article V, Section 1, of the first Constitution directed the society to publish a professional journal "which shall be distributed to members without further cost other than membership dues". On 25 April 1957, a few months after the first annual meeting, William W. Brickman, David Scanlon, George Z.F. Bereday, and William Johnson "met to discuss the probability of publishing a *Comparative Education Review*" (Read, Minutes). The journal first appeared in June 1957 with George Z.F. Bereday as Editor and Gerald H. Read as Business Editor. It has been published continuously ever since. Columbia University Teachers College financed the first issue; New York University, Harold Benjamin of Peabody Teachers College, and William W. Brickman, the next two issues. Thereafter, the journal relied on members' subscriptions and dues (Read, Minutes, 1957-1965; Bereday 1958). The first issue contained a brief introductory statement by Brickman, in which he prophesied that the *Review* would "become an organ of importance in the United States and abroad" (1957b, p.1).

Reception of the new journal was mixed. Bereday received letters of congratulation from Benjamin, Ulich, Cronin, and Eggertsen, although the latter expressed some concern that the *Comparative Education Review* might overlap with his *History of Education Journal*. A negative assessment was penned by Joseph A. Lauwerys of the University of London Institute of Education who wrote to Bereday on 13 June 1957: "I am by no means clear in my mind whether it is a good thing to have such a Review. There is already in existence the *Hamburg Journal*, our own *Year Book*, the *Journal of Education Studies*...." Bereday replied that Brickman would have put out something if he [Bereday] hadn't (Letter to Lauwerys, 19 June 1957), showing that even Founding Fathers had professional rivalries.

After seeing the first issue of the *CER*, Lauwerys expressed even greater concern. "I cannot see what good a publication of this kind can do – indeed, it is likely to do harm.... Forgive my bluntness. There are involved here academic and professional standards" (Letter to Bereday, n.d., June or July 1957). After learning more about the journal, Lauwerys recanted. "Don't get worried. All is well. I suppose as you think and say, I wrote in the heat of the moment" (Letter to Bereday, 15 July 1957). He went on to say that he would have responded differently had he known of Bereday's plans to review, in a subsequent issue of the *CER,* the *Year Book of Education,* of which he and Bereday were joint editors. He had been concerned that the British contribution to comparative education might be slighted.

Foreign Relations

Given Lauwerys' response to the launching of the new journal, the diplomatic skills displayed by Bereday in rounding up senior scholars, particularly international scholars, to give legitimacy to the fledgling *Comparative Education Review* were all the more remarkable. Both Joseph Lauwerys and Nicholas Hans eventually joined the *Review's* Editorial Board, but only after a careful balancing act. In response to Bereday, Hans had written to Bereday (15 March 1959): "I am quite willing and ready to take part in your publication on the condition that Lauwerys is also on the Board. As I am working now in his department, I would not like to represent the Institute of [Education in] London without him". Meanwhile, Bereday approached Isaac Kandel, to whom he wrote (3 March 1959):

> Your point about the younger generation not measuring up to the older in Comparative Education is well taken, humiliating as this fact is to me personally. But, in any case, we in our culture don't make nearly enough use of elder statesmen, and if our discipline is to thrive in the future, we need to have your support and blessing.... So please, please agree to being on our Board and I shall profit as I have always tried to do so in the past, from your experience and guidance.

By then, Bereday had persuaded James Bryant Conant, former President of Harvard, Franz Hilker, and Robert Ulich to join his Board; and in the next few years he enrolled Friedrich Schneider of Germany, Pedro Rosselló of Switzerland, and Torsten Husén of Sweden.

The Board of Directors of the *Review's* parent organisation, the Comparative Education Society, also reached out to established scholars from beyond the United States. During the 1960s, its Board included Edmund J. King, Vernon Mallinson, and Joseph Lauwerys, United Kingdom; Pedro Rosselló, Switzerland; Joseph Katz and Reginald Edwards, Canada; Irma Salas, Chile; and Philip J. Idenburg, the Netherlands. In addition, during this era two Canadians served as President – Joseph Katz in 1961 and Reginald Edwards in 1969. By 1962, 47 of the Comparative Education Society's 564 members, were "foreign" (Read, Minutes). In 1965 Gerald H. Read (Minutes) reported an "all-time high of 1,082 active members spread all over the world". In 1966 there were members from 44 countries (*CES Newsletter*, No.5, June 1966).

Organisation Building, 1960-75

Leadership, Finances, and Constitutional Revision

In the years following the founding of the CES, a core group assumed positions of leadership. William W. Brickman served as President from 1957 to 1959, and Gerald H. Read as Secretary-Treasurer from 1957 to 1965. Table 9.1 gives details on the organisational leadership during this period.

Table 9.1: Presidents and Secretaries-Treasurer of the CES/CIES

Term of Office	President	Term of Office	Secretary-Treasurer
1957-59	William W. Brickman	1957-65	Gerald H. Read
1959-60	William H.E. Johnson	1965-67	Franklin Parker
1960-61	Joseph Katz	1967-72	Barbara Yates
1961-62	C. Arnold Anderson	1972-75	Val Rust
1962-63	Claude Eggertsen		
1963-64	R. Freeman Butts		
1964-65	Donald K. Adams		
1965-66	David G. Scanlon		
1966-67	William W. Brickman		
1967-68	Stewart E. Fraser		
1968-69	Reginald Edwards		
1969-70	Philip Foster		
1970-71	Andreas M. Kazamias		
1971-72	Cole S. Brembeck		
1972-73	Harold J. Noah		
1973-74	Robert F. Lawson		
1974-75	Rolland G. Paulston		

George Z.F. Bereday was founding editor of the *CER*. Except for 1961-62, when he was replaced temporarily during a sabbatical leave by Hu Chang-tu of Columbia University, Bereday served as *Comparative Education Review* editor from 1957 to 1962. Harold Noah of Columbia University served as editor from 1967 to 1971. He was followed by Andreas M. Kazamias, University of Wisconsin-Madison, who served from 1971 to 1978.

This was an era of incremental financial growth. In 1957 Gerald H. Read reported a balance of US$554.11 in the society's accounts; in 1963, a balance of US$8,409.68. In 1968 there were total assets of US$21,624.02 (*CIES Newsletter*, No.10, March 1968). By then, the society was preparing for annual professional audits. There were nevertheless recurring concerns over solvency and over the need to increase membership, over the fact that officers frequently 'bootlegged' secretarial assistance from their home institutions, a theme that would echo in the years that followed. In the 1960s, however, non-financial issues dominated: constitutional revision, the question of a name change, and the decision to hold separate instead of joint meetings with groups with which the society was affiliated.

Constitutional revision was a consensus undertaking. As Gerald H. Read pointed out at the Board of Directors Meeting on 15 February 1967, the draft revision of the Constitution, which appeared in the December 1966 *Newsletter*, "formalised procedures which have been in operation for the last few years". The revised Constitution gave student members of the society the same rights and privileges as active members. It designated as officers of the society: the President, Vice-President, immediate Past President, the nine Directors, the Secretary, the Treasurer, the Editor, and the Business Manager. It also specified that the Vice-President succeed to the office of President after one year. Changes were discussed at the Annual Meeting in Chicago, 17 February 1967, and submitted thereafter to the membership by mail ballot for ratification. The *CIES Newsletter* for January 1968 reported that the revised Constitution was now official.

The Name-Change Issue

Of greater concern than the Constitution was the issue of a name change. According to the January 1966 *Newsletter*, the instigator of the change was Joseph Katz, University of British Columbia (Canada), who suggested that Comparative *and International* Education Society might better indicate the global character of the organisation. At the next annual Business Meeting on 16 February 1967, R. Freeman Butts put the issue before the membership. Twenty-four were in favour of a change, 14 against, and two abstaining. The following year the Committee on a Change of Name, chaired by Reginald Edwards, submitted, after exhaustive exploration, a very thorough report (*CIES Newsletter*, No.10, March 1968). Among names discussed in the Edwards Report were Society for Comparative and International Education, International and Comparative Education Society, International Education Society, and, of course, Comparative and International Education Society. It cannot be a total coincidence that Joseph Katz, who initiated the name change, became the first president of the Comparative *and International* Education Society of Canada, which held its first meeting in 1967.

The Edwards Report reflected a heated debate. Opinions ranged from support of no change to strong support for a change that would emphasise the idea of international education. Reasons for and against were both theoretical and practical. It was argued that responsibilities such as cultural exchanges, student exchanges, Peace Corps, UNESCO, United States Agency for International Development, the International Education Act, world colleges, and university-to-university programmes had transformed the academic discipline of comparative education as it was practised during the era of Michael Sadler and I.L. Kandel. Professionals in administration, guidance and curriculum, it was asserted, were more likely to want affiliation with an international organisation than with an exclusively academic organisation. A change in name would bring together people different from the academics attracted by comparative education, would better describe the membership of the society, and would provide a basis for special interests. There was also the practical concern that government and non-governmental agencies dispensing funding might overlook the Comparative Education Society if it did not have the word *international* in its title.

Members of the society were far from unanimous on this issue. Included in the 1968 Edwards Report is the following fervent statement (quoted in the CES Minutes, 14 February 1968):

> There are two major reasons why I would not wish to see a change of name at this juncture. The first concerns the different natures of the two topics – Comparative Education and International Education – and the second, a negative one, concerns the 'opportunist' thinking which seems to attach to some aspects of international education. It has taken rather more than ten

years to get this far in Comparative Education, and only now are we beginning to lay serious claim to being able to make any worthwhile comparisons, and to adopt methods which are presumed to underlie our studies. We have lacked good data, good methods, good training, and above all, as in so many aspects of education, we have lacked good theories. Now that these deficiencies are less obvious in Comparative Education, it might be preferable to capitalise on the skills we have acquired. In this respect International Education remains a more diffuse, more amorphous concept, and I cannot see many testable theories emerging in this area.

In an undated essay in the CIES Collection and in a 1968 letter to the Editor of *Comparative Education Review* (Vol.12, No.3, pp.376-378), Erwin H. Epstein, who was later to become editor of the journal, questioned the motives for the change. From his perspective, broadening the base of support for the field might realign factions "and even alter the nature of the field itself". For Epstein the word *international* connoted a "less analytic type of activity ... concerned more with practice and *implementing* [in contrast to the study of] policy" than was comparative education, which was more academic. These arguments still reverberate.

These concerns notwithstanding, on 14 February 1968, the Board of Directors unanimously approved a name change. The issue was put before the Business Meeting two days later, following which mail ballots were sent to the membership. The September 1968 *CES Newsletter*, reported 200 ballots returned: 149 in favour of a change and 51 opposed. "Thus, Article I, Section I, of the Constitution is now amended to read: The name of this organisation shall be the Comparative and International Education Society". The December 1968 *CIES Newsletter*, now using the new name, reported: "By vote of the membership the name of the Society has been changed to Comparative and International Education Society. From this issue onward, the title [of the Newsletter] will be *Comparative and International Education Society Newsletter*".

The Separate Meeting Issue

Until 1970 the Comparative Education Society met annually in Chicago during February, coordinating its meetings with those of the American Association of Colleges of Teacher Education, the National Society of College Teachers of Education, and the Association of Student Teaching – organisations with which it affiliated at the time of its inception. In an era, however, when George Z.F. Bereday, Brian Holmes, Harold Noah and Max A. Eckstein were exploring new methodologies in comparative education, identification with teacher education was beginning to weaken. In 1964 the Board talked of coordinating their meetings with the American Educational Research Association (AERA) while retaining identification with teacher education. By 1965, there was talk of autonomous meetings or of meetings in which the intellectual focus was oriented more toward philosophy and the social sciences than toward teacher education.

In 1966, the year William W. Brickman gave an address on "Ten Years of the Comparative Education Society", the annual February meeting was still taking place in Chicago in conjunction with the National Society of College Teachers of Education (NSCTE). There were, however, difficulties identifying a sufficient selection of useable papers; also difficulties when the American Association of Colleges of Teacher Education (AACTE) announced its own central theme (Minutes, Executive Committee, 11-12 October 1966). In February 1968, the fact that the society needed to seek permission from the NSCTE in order to plan three of its own sessions came under Board scrutiny. In October of that year, the Executive Committee examined ongoing problems of coordination, and it also discussed the "larger question of where and with whom the Society should meet annually". By March 1969, the Society was ready to experiment with a meeting independent of the AACTE/NSCTE in Chicago but to continue cooperation with the other societies on a reduced scale.

The September 1969 *CIES Newsletter* announced plans for a separate annual meeting in Atlanta in 1970:

> For the year 1969-70 our Society decided to separate the holding of a meeting in Chicago from the holding of the annual meeting. Thus, still in conjunction with NSCTE, and along with the History of Education Society, the John Dewey Society, the Philosophy of Education Society, and the American Education Studies Association, we shall also arrange a meeting at Chicago, in February 1970, in addition to the Annual Meeting to be held in Atlanta in March 1970.

It is not difficult to figure out which of the meetings was more important. The Chicago meeting would feature only graduate students, whereas senior scholars would meet in Atlanta. Meanwhile, the Executive Committee decided that the Vice-President would decide each year on the location of the Annual Meeting (Executive Committee Minutes, 10-11 October 1969).

The CIES continued to interact with education societies from its past, but in a muted way. In 1970 R. Freeman Butts chaired meetings of the Foundational Coordinating Committee, which consisted of: the American Educational Studies Association (AESA), the CIES, the History of Education Society (HES), the John Dewey Society (JDS), the Philosophy of Education Society (PES), and the Society of Professors of Education (SPE, formerly NSCTE). Three of these societies were willing to have AACTE do administration and secretarial tasks through a joint secretariat in Washington. The other three, including the CIES, were not (*CIES Newsletter*, No.17, March 1970). In March 1970 the Board discussed plans for the CIES sessions at the AACTE Chicago meeting but decided instead to hold its own Annual Meeting in San Diego in 1971. At this point, Philip Foster proposed that the site of the Annual Meeting move around the country and be located in a different region each year.

Three CIES conferences took place in 1973: San Antonio, site of the annual meeting; Chicago, where a group from the CIES met with education associations from the past; and the University of Iowa, which held a Regional Conference (*CIES Newsletter*, No.27, 1973). However, not every CIES member was happy with these geographical experiments. Philip G. Altbach called on the society "to reconsider our decision of a few years ago to hold our conventions separately from the AACTE meetings in Chicago" (*CIES Newsletter*, No.27, 1973). Altbach's concern was that recent recipients of the PhD degree needed access "to a wide range of employment opportunities", for which the AACTE format would be superior. "The situation of comparative education and that of the academic profession generally has changed greatly in the past few years and ... it would be at least a good idea to think about returning to the 'fold' of the broader community of teacher educators". Altbach also noted the central location of Chicago as an airline travel hub for faculty members in an era when travel funds appeared to be drying up.

Altbach's was not the only voice on this issue. Ursula Springer also spoke of the need to continue contact with 'foundations' societies, especially the American Educational Studies Association (AESA). In her report for the Committee on Professional Concerns (*CIES Newsletter*, No.28, May 1973), Springer noted the low visibility of the CIES in the education profession and the danger of losing support in the colleges. She also pointed out "that it would be in our professional interest to develop a set of 'competencies' that we can accept and publicise in our *Newsletter*, so that the CIES members may utilise them if their situation and interest calls for it". At the Business Meeting in 1973, a sub-committee was formed to draft this set of 'competencies', an effort that re-flected a preoccupation in the world of teacher education at that time. Concern about competencies was short-lived, but it was symptomatic of the degree to which the CIES had strayed from an earlier professional focus.

No CIES-sponsored sessions were held at the AACTE Conference in Chicago in February 1974. The Board, however, expressed "support for participation at the Conference in order to provide Mid-Western members with participatory oppor-tunities" (Minutes, March 1974). In a letter to the Board (21 May 1974), Robert Lawson, the incoming CIES President, announced San Francisco as the site of the CIES conference in 1975. There would be an extra day for sessions; but "our thought that we might arrange the meeting in cooperation with one or more other Societies could not be worked into the conference pattern". A Chicago session, coordinated with AACTE was to be run by Malcolm Campbell. In a letter to W.D. Halls, Oxford University, United Kingdom (23 May 1975), Lawson clarified the situation: "The CIES meetings held annually in Chicago are continued as a contribution to the annual meeting of the American Association of Colleges of Teacher Education. The annual CIES conference is held separately, this past year in San Francisco, March 26-29, 1975". Lawson noted that a group unrepresentative of the CIES was to be found in Chicago, thus making it clear that the San Francisco meeting represented the real CIES, an organisation with its own identity.

Growth and Consolidation, 1975-90

Relationship with Other Societies
After 1975, the CIES, although now meeting independently from other organisa-
tions, continued to seek collaborative relationships with other professional groups.
In 1980 it appointed Leo Leonard (University of Portland) and Edward Berman
(University of Louisville) to represent the CIES at the annual meeting of the Council
of Learned Societies in Education.

Throughout the 1980s, the CIES maintained relationships with organisations such as AERA, UNESCO, and the United States Office of Education
(Executive Committee Minutes, Atlanta, 16 March 1988), all professional
organisations with an international scholarly thrust (*CIES Newsletter*, No.94, May
1990). In 1990 the society had affiliations with the Council of Learned Societies
in Education; with NCATE (National Council for Accreditation of Teacher
Education), to which it contributed an annual fee of US$200; as well as with the
Alliance for Education in Global and International Studies, to which it contributed
US$150 dues.

Besides the Council of Learned Societies in Education, which consisted of
member societies in various areas of the social foundations of education, an
'umbrella' organisation of which the CIES has been a member (in fact a founding
member) is the World Council of Comparative Education Societies (WCCES). In
1974, there was concern that ratifying the WCCES Constitution would mean
endorsing a "supersociety" (*CIES Newsletter*, No.34, December 1974). However,
Robert Lawson and others successfully argued for ratification.

Moreover, the CIES has committed itself explicitly to support the WCCES. A
statement issued by the Board at the society's 1985 annual meeting, and again
endorsed by the Board at the 1986 meeting, spelled out this commitment: the CIES
encouraged members to attend WCCES congresses, to appoint CIES representation
to WCCES committees when requested to do so, to publish news of the WCCES in
the *CIES Newsletter*, to contribute dues assessed by the WCCES, and to expect that
CIES members would assume the cost of participation in committees or congresses
of the World Council. Within this framework, many CIES members regularly
attended WCCES congresses and served on WCCES committees. In 1997 the CIES
Board decided that the official CIES representative to the WCCES should be a Past
President, who would serve for two years, thus skipping a Past President every other
year (Minutes of the Board of Directors, 23 March 1997).

Establishing Historical Memory: Creation of the Archives
A measure of the growing maturity of the CIES was the establishment in 1980 of the
society's own archives. Formal discussion of the need to preserve the past dated
from a proposal by Beatrice Szekely in 1978 that was distributed to the Board the
following year by Philip G. Altbach. At that time, the Board endorsed a motion by
Gail P. Kelly that archives be established as a long-term project. To get started, the

Board voted a grant of US$600 to Beatrice Szekely for the current year and another US$600 for the following year.

Although Beatrice Szekely was subsequently unable to undertake supervision of this project, the idea slowly gained momentum. One possibility explored by President George Male would have used the "Papers in Comparative and International Education" collection at Teachers College, Columbia University, for the CIES papers. Such an arrangement, however, would have excluded Brickman, Anderson, Eggertsen, and others not connected with Columbia. It also required an initial financial outlay. Male then appointed an Archive Committee, consisting of Franklin Parker, Claude Eggertsen and William W. Brickman. Thereafter, at the urging of Philip G. Altbach (Letter to Kim Sebaly, 19 May 1980), Kim Sebaly submitted a proposal for a CIES Collection in the Special Collections of the Kent State University Archives. This proposal was promptly accepted.

The CIES Collection in the Kent State University Archives has become an important resource in the field of comparative education. It now occupies close to 81.5 cubic feet, of which 39 cubic feet are processed and included in its online inventory. The Collection holds records from before the founding of the CIES, *CER* records, issues of the *CER* and the *CIES Newsletter*, correspondence by CIES officers, minutes of Board meetings, and video interviews of past CIES Presidents. The Kent State University has, since 1996, also been hosting the WCCES archives. Kent State University Archivists, Nancy Birk, and her successor, Cara Gilgenbach, have guided the day-to-day supervision of the Collection. Of particular importance is the work of Kim Sebaly, a Kent State University faculty member and long-time CIES member who has generously donated his time and expertise to the Collection.

Societal Identity Markers: Honorary Fellows and the Eggertsen Lectures

A first attempt to honour "Elder Statesmen" was introduced at the CIES Annual Business Meeting in 1970, at which time the Board recommended an honorary membership category limited to 10 members. This proposal, which was defeated by a vote of 13 in favour, 20 opposed, was premature (Minutes, Annual Business Meeting, 23 March 1970). The idea re-emerged in 1981 in a memo to the Board from Erwin H. Epstein suggesting that CIES find a way to honour "some of our *illuminati* who have retired or are about to retire" (Epstein, Memo to Board, 7 July 1981).

In 1983, the Awards Committee proposed that the CIES appoint selected senior members as "Fellows of the CIES" (*CIES Newsletter*, Nos.67-68, April/June 1983). Thereafter, criteria for the Honorary Fellow designation were prepared by Philip J. Foster, Chair of the Awards Committee, Thomas J. La Belle and Vandra Masemann, later aided by Noel McGinn. Of particular concern was the question of posthumous awards. (George Z.F. Bereday had just died.) The membership, however, voted to reject "Posthumous Honorary Fellow" status (Business Meeting Minutes, 20 April 1985). Nevertheless, in 1990 an article in the *CIES Newsletter* (No.95, September 1990) refers to George Z.F. Bereday as an Honorary Fellow, thus confounding historical memory. The criteria agreed upon in 1985 limited the number of Honorary Fellows to five *"living* members" per year until 15 are identified (later limited to one a year, with provision for holding over nominations if more than one name is submitted). The age of 60 was set as the minimum age for an Honorary Fellow but changed in 1990 to evidence of a "long and distinguished career". All nominations, plus recommendations from at least five active members of the society, were to be forwarded by the Awards Committee to the Board of Directors, which would make the final decision.

The first two Honorary Fellows, Claude Eggertsen and C. Arnold Anderson, were appointed in 1987; the second two, Harold Noah and Philip Foster, in 1990. These were followed by Mary Jean Bowman, Andreas Kazamias, Gerald H. Read, and R. Murray Thomas – all appointed in 1991. Thereafter came Max A. Eckstein (1994), Noel McGinn (1997), Don Adams (1998), Rolland Paulston (1999), Elizabeth Sherman Swing (2000), Norma Tarrow (2001), Mathew Zachariah (2002) and Robert Arnove (2003). Joseph Farrell and William Rideout received the honour in 2007, and Vandra Masemann was announced to receive it in 2008.

Another societal marker is a lecture series inaugurated by Associates of the Social Foundations Program at the University of Michigan to honour Claude A. Eggertsen, a Founder of the CIES, its president in 1963, and one of its first two Honorary Fellows. The first Eggertsen Lecture, 'Comparative Education and Social Concern', was delivered in 1980 at the annual CIES conference in Vancouver, Canada, by Brian Holmes, University of London Institute of Education. Other Eggertsen Lecturers included: Wolfgang Mitter (1981); William W. Brickman (1982); Hans Weiler (1983); Harry Judge (1987), Ruth Hayhoe (1988); Zoya Malkova (1989); Torsten Husén (1990); and Edmund King (1991).

Epistemological Differences

The CIES has overseen its share of internecine debates over epistemology, frequently between academicians and pragmatists. During the 1980s, however, the possibility for intellectual dissonance was particularly pronounced. Two collections of articles from the *CER* illustrate the complexity of what was taking place. A book edited by Philip G. Altbach, Robert Arnove and Gail P. Kelly (1982), featured studies that illustrated "diverse methodological issues". A companion volume edited by Altbach and Kelly (1986), demonstrated a "range of orientations". In each volume the emphasis was on diversity: a diversity of scholars – World Bank pragmatists, economists, sociologists, anthropologists; and a diversity of research paradigms – structural functionalism, critical realism, conflict theory, neo-Marxism, ethnography, gender studies, human capital theory, typological theory. As the decade progressed, swords were crossed, usually in a friendly way, over paradigms. Even the annual presidential address could become an occasion for laying down the gauntlet (see e.g. Epstein 1983; Kelly 1987; Hackett 1988; Masemann 1990; Rust 1991).

In 1990 two long-time, highly respected CIES members, Vandra Masemann, an anthropologist, and George Psacharopoulos, an economist, squared off in the pages of the *CER*. Psacharopoulos (1990) attacked scholarly articles that were, in his words, "overly descriptive, in the sense that they provide long, non-quantitative accounts" (p.369). He looked instead for a theory that led to testable propositions, such as the human capital theory. In her Presidential Address, "Ways of Knowing" (1990) Masemann focused on the preference of indigenous people for experiential knowledge and their resistance to empirical positivism. She questioned the utility of quantitative methodology because, in her view, it had led to the replacement of a moral basis for schools with statistical data and to a shift away from holistic knowledge. The juxtaposition of these competing paradigms is a vivid illustration of the challenge the CIES faced then and continues to face in accommodating its disparate membership under one umbrella.

Contentious Issues and Systemic Change, 1990-2006

A Contested Election

In the 1990s, the CIES could take pride in its not inconsiderable achievements. Its journal, the *CER*, had achieved international recognition under Philip Altbach (1979-88) and Erwin H. Epstein (1989-98), who was succeeded by John N. Hawkins of UCLA in 1999, and by co-editors Mark Ginsburg and David Post, of the University of Pittsburgh and Pennsylvania State University, in 2004. Most routines were in place, including annual meetings in a new locale each year. The society was developing a responsible network of committees. Its membership was growing. It was about to receive an endowment. Nevertheless, in 1990 and in the years that followed, the CIES faced a series of contentious issues.

The most immediate issue was a contested election, an event that threw the society into uncharted territory. As Val Rust, then CIES President, pointed out to the aggrieved candidate (letter to David Wilson, 5 June 1990):

> Concern has been raised for several years that we must become more formal.... In the past we have operated almost as a large family acting with a sense that CIES members would respond responsibly and ethically with regard to the election process.... The process has been 'sloppy' in many respects.

At a meeting for incoming members of the Board of Directors on the last day of the 1990 conference, the day following public announcement of election results, a Board member, Norma Tarrow, after discussion of election anomalies, moved that the election be invalidated. This motion challenged the legitimacy of the "newly elected" members of the Board of Directors present at this meeting. Board members whose terms had expired were, of course, not in attendance. President Val Rust, therefore, ruled that a quorum was not present. In the weeks that followed, with the aggrieved candidate for Vice-President ready to pursue legal remedies, Rust contacted all members of the outgoing Board by mail for a vote on whether or not to nullify election results. The Board voted to let the election results stand, on the argument that no fraud or malice had taken place. In July in Madrid, CIES Board members who attended the Comparative Education Society in Europe (CESE) conference (too few to constitute a quorum) held an inconclusive emergency session. There was at this point no constitutional procedure for resolving the impasse.

A legal crisis was averted. The President, Val Rust, and Past President, Vandra Masemann, wrote a letter of apology to the aggrieved candidate. The following year, the aggrieved candidate allowed his name to be put into nomination for the office of Vice-President, and won. Meanwhile, reforms recommended by an Ad Hoc Elections Committee chaired by Steve Klees were put in place and in 1998 written into the By-Laws of the Constitution. Ballots would be sent only to *individuals* on the membership list, *not* to institutions. A special address sticker would be provided for the signed, sealed envelopes in which ballots were to be returned. Envelopes without the prescribed signature and address sticker, or not received by the deadline, were to be disallowed. With these reforms, elections have taken place without incident since 1990. In 2004, moreover, the CIES inaugurated an electronic voting process that appeared to be tamper-proof.

Systemic Change: The Constitution of 1998

The Constitution and By-Laws of 1998 brought systemic change to the CIES. In the past, amending the Constitution had been a cumbersome process that involved soliciting approval of two thirds of CIES members by mail over a three-month time period. In a Memo to the Board of Directors on 3 March 1991, Val Rust argued for a less complicated system:

> As you know, we have never had a set of By-Laws. Rather, as issues have arisen we have been content to change the CIES Constitution. This has resulted in a fairly complicated document that has procedural detail in it not appropriate for a constitution.

The Constitution of 1998, of which Rust was a major author, was divided into two parts: a semi-permanent, but lean Constitution, followed by the society's first set of By-Laws. Amending the Constitution still requires two-thirds approval by mail ballot. Passing or rescinding a By-Law, however, requires no more than a two-thirds affirmative vote by a quorum of the Board, a procedure that can take place during a regular board meeting (Article XII, Sections 1 and 2). It can also take place electronically (By-Laws, Article V, Section c). In 2000, using stream-lined procedures in the new Constitution, the Board amended the By-Laws to convert three newer committees from Ad Hoc to Standing Committee status: the Investment Committee, the Gender and Education Committee, and the Under-Represented Ethnic and Ability Groups (UREAG).

In addition to By-Laws, the Constitution of 1998 created a new office – Historian, an office with a three-year renewable term and Executive Committee status. The CIES Historian is charged with supervising archive maintenance, with ensuring the deposit of necessary documents therein, with advising the society on "matters of historical fact", with facilitating research projects, with coordinating communications with other collections related to the society, with serving as Parliamentarian, and with reporting annually to the Board of Directors. In 1999, the

Board of Directors appointed as its first Historian, Elizabeth Sherman Swing, whose PhD dissertation advisor was William W. Brickman, the first President of the society.

Systemic Change: Expansion of the Committee Structure

A significant development was a trend toward a decentralisation of CIES activities through expansion of the committee structure and through Special Interest Groups. At the time the Constitution of 1998 was ratified, the CIES had three Standing (permanent) Committees: the Nominations Committee, the Awards Committee, and the New Scholars Committee. The Nominations Committee (Constitution, Article VI, Section 2), which was composed of members "who are not holding office in the Society", was responsible for selecting a slate of candidates for the annual election: two each for the office of Vice-President and for three members of the Board of Directors. The Awards Committee, which came into being in 1981 in order to select the winner of an award for the best article each year in the *CER* (since 1990 called the Bereday Award), selects the Gail P. Kelly Dissertation Award winner, the Joyce Cain Award winner; and is responsible for submitting Honorary Fellow nominations to the Board for final vetting. The New Scholars Committee, which traces its origin to a student caucus at the annual meeting in 1988 (*CIES Newsletter*, No.86, January 1988), converted from Ad Hoc to Standing Committee status in 1991. At that time it changed its name from Young Scholars Committee to New Scholars Committee, "to reflect age diversity among students and scholars who are entering the field of comparative and international education". This well-established group has its own website, runs highly successful dissertation workshops, and has assumed responsibility for videotaping interviews of former CIES Presidents. Other committees had different origins. The Investment Committee, for example, was a response to a 2000 endowment of US$100,000 from George F. Kneller, a UCLA professor of the philosophy of education. Terms of the endowment included a directive that the bequest be made "in securities that will appreciate along with the factor of inflation", that it be controlled and managed "as an autonomous entity" rather than mingled with other funds, and that income from the bequest be used for an annual lecture "to be presented before the general assembly or members (and others) by a distinguished scholar or personage", and to be called The George F. Kneller Lecture (Secretariat Report, 7 March 2000).

The Gender and Education Committee represented a response to other concerns. That gender had become a dominant issue in the CIES in part reflected the women's movement in the larger society. It also reflected the pioneering work of Gail P. Kelly, a prolific scholar who was Associate Editor of the *CER* (1979-88) and President of the CIES (1986). Gender equality was not a pressing concern in the early years of the CIES. Minutes of a 1961 discussion by the Board of the characteristics looked for in a Vice-President describe the ideal candidate as "a young *man* who shows potentiality in the field of comparative education" (italics added). It was not until 1976 that the society elected its first female President, Susanne Shafer. Since then, Barbara Yates, Gail P. Kelly, Beverly

Lindsay, Vandra Masemann, Nelly Stromquist, Ruth Hayhoe, Heidi Ross, Karen Biraimah, and Kassie Freeman have served in this office. Even so, of the 46 CIES Presidents, only 10 have been women.

The structural response of the CIES to gender issues dates from 1989 when President Vandra Masemann created a Gender and Education Committee with Nelly Stromquist as Chair. Subsequent chairs were Karen Biraimah, Heidi Ross, Margaret Sutton, Mary Ann Maslak and Shirley Miske. In 1990 this Committee set out to explore what was still unfamiliar territory: participation of women on boards of professional organisations and as contributors to journals; gender issues in doctoral dissertations in comparative education; and the position of women as university professors and in international agencies. Its request, for example, that the editors of the *CER* provide them with a breakdown by gender of the number of articles submitted, accepted or rejected was the first such inquiry in the history of the *CER* (Minutes, Board of Directors, 24 March 1990). In addition to its role in setting up the Gail P. Kelly Award in 1994 for the best dissertation with social justice and equity issues in an international or comparative context, the Gender and Education Committee hosted well-attended pre-conference workshops. Tangible evidence of the increasing importance of the committee structure, and of this committee in particular, is the fact that three of the Gender Committee chairs – Nelly Stromquist, Karen Biraimah, and Heidi Ross – became CIES Presidents.

The Under-Represented Ethnic and Ability Group (UREAG) also came into being because of perceived grievances. UREAG traces its genesis to 1990 when Kassie Freeman, Paul Emongu and Victor Kobayashi petitioned to convene a committee to investigate how to ensure "greater ethnic equity in all dimensions of our professional activities". The Board unanimously approved this proposal (Minutes, 24 March 1990). Subsequently, concern over access to CIES meetings for those with physical disabilities came under the purview of this committee. UREAG leaders have not hesitated to ask that their voices be heard (Gezi 1995) or that slots be available in the conference schedule for presentations and "Global Village Dialogue". Kassie Freeman has written eloquently of the "reluctance, almost resistance, to acknowledge that there are different cultures within the USA that warrant greater understanding and inclusion" (Freeman 1995).

UREAG maintains its own website and has supported members with travel grants to attend CIES meetings. In 2000 it established an Award for Distinguished Research on African Descendants, the Joyce Lynn Cain, in honour of a faculty member at Michigan State University, "a colleague and a devoted scholar of comparative education" (*CIES Newsletter*, No.124, May 2000). Kassie Freeman, the first chair of UREAG, became a CIES President. She also ran a highly successful conference in New Orleans (2003) organised by Dillard University, a historically black institution.

Political and Ideological Concerns
During the 1990s and beyond, the CIES grappled with an increasing number of political and ideological issues. Particularly troubling was the issue of apartheid in South Africa. Should CIES welcome at its annual meeting representatives of a

regime that denied justice to a majority of its people? (*CIES Newsletter*, No.93, January 1990). A Norwegian scholar, Yngve Nordkvelle, wanted to keep all South Africans, including those opposed to apartheid, out of conferences as a way of putting pressure on a corrupt political system (Letter from Nordkvelle, 6 February 1989). Joseph Di Bona of the CIES saw a different challenge: "Nothing can be so unsettling, and therefore so morally enlightening, as face-to-face interaction with real champions of policies we detest. We need to teach our students the link between racism at home and fascist policies of South Africa" (Letter to Masemann, 5 June 1989). The society eventually decided not to adopt a boycott. What it did do was to approve a statement that subsequently appeared on much of its correspondence until apartheid ended: "The Comparative and International Education Society is opposed to apartheid in South Africa and condemns that country's laws and policies which deny basic human rights".

There were other contentious issues. After the 1989 Beijing Tiananmen Square incident, the CIES opposed selection of Beijing as the site of the next WCCES Congress. In 1997, it recorded opposition to gender discrimination in education in Afghanistan. In 2003 it wrote to US President George Bush concerning difficulties encountered by foreign students and scholars in getting visas for entry to the United States.

A different set of issues erupted over the so-called World Bank Bibliography. This database across academic disciplines called for an annotated bibliography on education reform and management resources to be prepared by members of the CIES with World Bank funding (*CIES Newsletter*, No.124, May 2000). After the first instalment was published, some CIES members questioned whether this project represented a partnership between the CIES and the World Bank – an uncomfortable prospect for a vocal group in the organisation. Once the project ended, the issue receded; but it remains an example of a fundamental difference in worldview between liberal academics and pragmatic researchers which was reminiscent of the comparative education/international education cleavage of the 1960s.

In 1992 a CIES member wrote to President Stephen Heyneman:

> I believe the welfare of the CIES mandates that individuals refrain from imposing their personal philosophical or political commitments on the society. What distinguishes the CIES from other groups involved in comparative work, in addition to its interdisciplinary reach, is both its academic base and the true sense of camaraderie among its members (Letter from Norma Tarrow, 15 February 1992).

In 1997 Gary Theissen asked whether the society should go beyond being a convener and information disseminator. Could, or should, it do a better job in representing intellectual, moral, and technical values and principles? (*CIES Newsletter*, No.114, January 1997). CIES is still grappling with an answer to that question.

Afterword

For those to whom it speaks, the CIES has become more than just a professional association. Loyalty runs deep and long. The members' list for June 1966 includes a roster of familiar names of those who remained active nearly four decades later: Donald K. Adams, Philip G. Altbach, Malcolm B. Campbell, Max Eckstein, Erwin H. Epstein, Philip Foster, Kalil I. Gezi, Edgar B. Gumbert, Andreas Kazamias, Robert Lawson, Harold Noah, Seth Spaulding, David N. Wilson, Mathew Zachariah, Gerald H. Read and Rolland Paulston. Even among the younger generation, the CIES conferences have a special ambience. Asked what the CIES has meant to her, a graduate student member of the Board of Directors offered this heartfelt testimony (Maria Fatima Rodrigues, *CIES Newsletter*, No.121, May 1999):

> The annual CIES conference creates a social space where human beings from many different parts of the world connect on topics of mutual interest and learn from one another (even from those [with whom] they may strongly disagree). The greatest value of being a member of this society has come from my interactions with people who have different frames of reference and different realities.

It is possible to argue that the CIES is still a work in progress, but it is one whose "different frames of reference and different realities" give it strength.

References

Altbach, Philip G.; Arnove, Robert F. & Kelly, Gail P. (eds.) (1982): *Comparative Education*. New York: Macmillan.

Altbach, Philip G. & Kelly, Gail P. (eds.) (1986): *New Approaches to Comparative Education*. Chicago: University of Chicago.

Bereday, George Z.F. (1958): Editorial. *Comparative Education Review*, Vol.1, No.3, pp.1-4.

Bereday, George Z.F.; Brickman, William W. & Read, Gerald H. (1960): *The Changing Soviet School*. Cambridge: Riverside Press.

Brickman, William W. (1954): 'Report on New York University's First Annual Conference on Comparative Education', in Brickman, William W. (ed.), *The Role of Comparative Education in the Education of Teachers*. Proceedings of the First Annual Conference on Comparative Education. New York: School of Education, New York University (April 30), pp.8-9.

Brickman, William W. (ed.) (1955): *The Teaching of Comparative Education*. Proceedings of the Second Annual Conference on Comparative Education. New York: School of Education, New York University (April 29).

Brickman, William W. (ed.) (1956a): *Comparative Education. A Symposium*. Proceedings of the Third Annual Conference on Comparative Education on 'Comparative Education in Theory and Practice'. Reprinted from *Journal of Educational Sociology*, Vol.30, No.3, pp.113-160.

Brickman, William W. (1956b): 'Report on New York University's Third Annual Conference on Comparative Education', in Brickman, William W. (ed.), *Comparative Education: A Symposium*. Reprint from *Journal of Educational Sociology*, Vol.30, No.3, p.113.

Brickman, William W. (ed.) (1957a): *Comparative Education and Foreign Educational Service*. Proceedings of the Fourth Annual Conference on Comparative Education. New York: School of Education, New York University (April 26).

Brickman, William W. (1957b): 'A New Journal in Comparative Education'. *Comparative Education Review*, Vol.1, No.1, p.1.

Brickman, William W. (1966): 'Ten Years of the Comparative Education Society'. *Comparative Education Review*, Vol.10, No.1, pp.4-15.

Brickman, William W. (1977): 'Comparative and International Education Society: An Historical Analysis'. *Comparative Education Review*, Vol.21, Nos.2/3, pp.396-404.

Constitution of the Comparative Education Society (1959): *Comparative Education Review*, Vol.3, No.2, pp.37-40.

Constitution of the Comparative and International Education Society of 1998 and its By-Laws.

Epstein, Erwin H. (n.d.): 'A Rose under Any Other Name'. (Undated typescript.)

Epstein, Erwin H. (1983): 'Currents Left and Right: Ideology in Comparative Education' (Presidential Address). *Comparative Education Review*, Vol.27, No.1, pp.3-29.

Freeman, Kassie (1995): 'Marginalisation on the Eve of Globalisation'. *CIES Newsletter*, No.108 (January).

Gezi, Kal (1995): 'Increasing Underrepresented Groups in Education'. *CIES Newsletter*, No.108 (January).

Hackett, Peter (1988): 'Aesthetics as a Dimension for Comparative Study' (Presidential Address). *Comparative Education Review*, Vol.32, No.4, pp.389-399.

Kelly, Gail P. (1987): 'Comparative Education and the Problem of Change: An Agenda for the 1980s' (Presidential Address). *Comparative Education Review*, Vol.31, No.4, pp.477-489.

Masemann, Vandra (1990): 'Ways of Knowing: Implications for Comparative Education' (Presidential Address). *Comparative Education Review*, Vol.34, No.4, pp.465-473.

Psacharopoulos, George (1990): 'Comparative Education: From Theory to Practice, or Are You A:\neo.* or B:*.ist?'. *Comparative Education Review*, Vol.34, No.3, pp.369-380.

Rust, Val D. (1991): 'Postmodernism and its Comparative Education Implications'. *Comparative Education Review*, Vol.35, No.4, pp.610-626.

Ulich, Robert (1954): 'Some Observations Concerning the Study of Comparative Education'. WCCES, Second World Congress, Geneva, Switzerland, June 28 – July 2, 1974. (Typed report)

10

The Comparative Education Society in Europe (CESE)

Wolfgang MITTER

The decision to form the Comparative Education Society in Europe (CESE) was initiated by 60 participants in a 1961 conference organised by the University of London Institute of Education (Cowen 1980, p.98). Draft Statutes were prepared by Joseph Katz on the model of the Comparative Education Society (CES) in the United States, and were subsequently revised at a meeting of 'provisional officers of the society'. The Statutes were formally adopted at the first CESE conference in Amsterdam, Netherlands, in June 1963 in accordance with Belgian law. The founding members included distinguished scholars such as Joseph Lauwerys who had convened the London conference, Nicholas Hans, James H. Higginson and Edmund King (England), Philip Idenburg (Netherlands), Friedrich Schneider (Germany), Franz Hilker (Germany), Edemée Hatinguais (France), Lamberto Borghi (Italy), Robert Plancke (Belgium), and Bogdan Suchodolski (Poland). The participation of Pedro Rosselló and Leo Fernig from the International Bureau of Education (IBE) in Geneva, Switzerland, and Saul Robinsohn from the UNESCO Institute for Education (UIE) in Hamburg, Germany, assured additional institutional support (García Garrido 1986; Mitter 1986; Kallen 2006).

This chapter focuses on CESE itself, and is not an analysis of the history of comparative education in Europe. However, the foundation of the society may be taken as an indicator that CESE began its activity as the representation of the scientific community of comparative educationists in Europe. This quality has been retained over the decades, notwithstanding problems which have had to be solved. Moreover, CESE's openness to comparative educationists in the rest of the world has turned out to be a lasting legacy from the founding group, which included scholars from the USA, Canada and Japan.

The Statutes consist of 10 articles. They determine the international and non-profit-making character of the society, its ordinary and honorary membership, the composition of its Executive Committee (consisting of the President, the Immediate Past President, two Vice-Presidents and two other members), the appointment and function of the Secretary-Treasurer, the membership dues, and the formation of ad hoc committees for matters of scientific or professional interest. The Statutes also define the purposes of the society (Article 3), namely:

a) promoting and improving the teaching of comparative education in institutions of higher learning;
b) stimulating research;
c) facilitating the publication and distribution of comparative studies in education;
d) interesting professors and teachers of other disciplines in the comparative and international dimension of their work;
e) encouraging visits by educators to study educational institutions and systems throughout the world;
f) cooperating with those who in other disciplines attempt to interpret educational developments in a cultural context;
g) organising conferences and meetings; and
h) collaborating with other comparative education societies in order to further international action in the field.

CESE and its European Competitors

CESE was constituted as a society of individual membership, open to comparative educationists from all parts of Europe and beyond. This principle reflected the views of the founding members, who had considered the diversity of comparative education in European universities and independent research institutes. Further, the arrangement permitted the incorporation of constituted national or other groups with equivalent purposes. Consequently, in the late 1960s, organisations of British and German comparative educationists were formed as sections of CESE, and the Italians followed during the 1980s. In 1973, French-speaking comparative educationists founded an association of their own, the Association francophone d'éducation comparée, examined elsewhere in this book, whose constitutive criterion was the use of the French language rather than a geographical dimension. The German (later German-*speaking*) section constituted a parallel membership as a Kommission in the national Deutsche Gesellschaft für Erziehungswissenschaft (German Society of Educational Sciences), and under this status joined the World Council of Comparative Education Societies (WCCES). In contrast, the British section performed a total constitutional change in 1979 by defining itself as the independent British Comparative Education Society (BCES). The development of smaller groups continued in the 1980s and 1990s throughout Western, Central and Eastern Europe. As a result, CESE and many national, regional and language-based societies existed beside each other as members of the WCCES.

For CESE, this parallelism has had both advantages and disadvantages. It has enriched European diversity in regard to scientific organisation and content. This is demonstrated by the considerable number of comparative education conferences, each attracting participants not only from their catchment areas but also from neighbouring countries and beyond. Such diversity promotes the exchange of ideas, methods and experiences. However, problems arise from parallelism and duplication of conferences and other activities. Such parallelism causes budgetary problems, since few comparative educationists in Europe are ready to engage in double membership, and most seem to make their choices in favour of their 'nearest' society in regard to distance and language. In periods of austerity, financial troubles are aggravated by significant decreases in sponsorship, whether by universities, governments, municipalities or foundations which are hesitant to include transnational societies in their sponsoring programmes. The European Union, the Council of Europe and other European institutions do not feel able to fill the gap, unlike in the 1960s and 1970s. The traditional restraint exercised by potential private sponsors in most European countries towards supporting educational initiatives hardly opens the door to compensatory action.

In spite of these factors, the common commitment of comparative educationists in Europe to their field of research and teaching has always been a stimulus for cooperation between CESE and its 'competitors' in the region. This commitment has had visible demonstration in the joint organisation of several CESE conferences. In this context, it is worth quoting the words of Brian Holmes in a letter to José Luis García Garrido (see García Garrido 1986, pp.45-46):

> When we set up the Society we hoped it would survive, but few of us could have visualised how in the hands of scholars from all over Western Europe the Society would have gone on, as it has, from strength to strength, and in the process, without animosity, stimulated the establishment of so many national societies. I am proud, as I am sure you are, to have been associated with such a society.

Geographical Distribution of Membership and Expertise

CESE's position as a 'roof above a house with no well-established rooms' partly explains its relatively small membership which has never exceeded 300. Beside the aforementioned organisational parallelism, the geographic distribution of its membership should be noted (Table 10.1). The data lead to the following remarks:

a) 'Top' positions have consistently been held by the United Kingdom (UK) and Germany, followed by France. This relative stability can be traced back to the national origin of the founding members and the state of the field of comparative education in these three countries.

b) Spain and Italy joined the top in the 1970s and 1980s. This move can partly be interpreted as the outcome of successful CESE conferences in Valencia, Spain (1979) and Garda, Italy (1985).

c) Membership from Central and Eastern Europe has been low. Before the revolutionary events of 1989, the Communist regimes did not allow their comparative educationists to join the 'Western-dominated' CESE, though Poland played an exceptional role with the membership of Bogdan Suchodolski, Mieczysław Pęcherski and others (see Mitter & Swift 1983, pp.713-719). The Czechoslovak case is worth mentioning because the engagement began with great enthusiasm in 1968, reached its culmination with the 1969 fourth CESE conference, and ceased immediately afterwards with the return of the oppressive regime. It was anticipated that the collapse of the Iron Curtain after the 1988 13th CESE conference, would cause an increase in numbers. However, the membership increased only slightly, a result which may be partly explained by the constitution of national societies in many countries in that region.

Table 10.1: Geographic Distribution of CESE Membership

	1971		1996	2004
Denmark	*		*	10
France	9		24	22
Germany	23	**	41	30
Greece	*		13	19
Italy	2		31	16
Netherlands	9		13	*
Norway	*		7	10
Spain	6		44	29
United Kingdom	28		26	31
Other Western Europe***	22		28	22
Central & Eastern Europe	12		8	17
Total Europe	*111*		*235*	*206*
United States of America	16		11	9
Canada	6		7	11
Latin America	1		3	11
Middle East	2		5	5
Asia	2		3	10
Africa	2		9	6
Australia	4		7	4
Total Non-Europe	*33*		*45*	*56*

*   Not specified, but included in Other Western Europe
**   Applies only to West Germany
*** Countries from which membership did not reach 10 in any of the reference years.

Source: Luzón (2005) and personal communication.

On the whole, the membership data indicate the extension of CESE throughout Europe, supplemented by a more or less stable presence of non-European scholars. The decreasing proportion of the USA may deserve attention, but it has never affected the cooperation between European and North American comparative educationists.

A correlation between the geographic distribution of membership and the list of CESE Presidents is reinforced by the status and rank of comparative education in the respective countries. Table 10.2 shows that Presidents have come from the UK (Joseph Lauwerys, Brian Holmes, Robert Cowen), Germany (Saul Robinsohn, Wolfgang Mitter, Jürgen Schriewer), Netherlands (Philip Idenburg), France (Denis Kallen, previously in the Netherlands), Spain (José Luis García Garrido), Denmark (Thyge Winther-Jensen), and Italy (Donatella Palomba).

Taken as a whole, the list illustrates CESE's regional focus on Western Europe. The composition of the Executive Committees modifies this general picture only slightly with members from the Central and Southeast European regions: Czechoslovakia before 1992 (František Singule, 1969-73), Hungary (Magda Illés, 1988-92), and Croatia (Zlata Godler, 1994-2002).

Table 10.2: Presidents and Secretaries-Treasurer of CESE

Term of Office	President	Institution	Secretary-Treasurer	Institution
1961-67	Joseph Lauwerys	University of London	Brian Holmes	University of London
1967-71	Philip Idenburg	University of Amsterdam	Brian Holmes	University of London
1971-72	Saul Robinsohn	Max Planck Institute, Berlin	Brian Holmes	University of London
1972-73 Interim Presidents	Sixten Marklund; Robert Plancke	University of Stockholm; University of Ghent	Brian Holmes	University of London
1973-77	Brian Holmes	University of London	Denis Kallen	University of Amsterdam
1977-81	Denis Kallen	University of Paris VIII	Henk Van daele	University of Ghent
1981-85	Wolfgang Mitter	German Institute for International Education Research, Frankfurt	Henk Van daele	University of Ghent
1985-88	José Luis García Garrido	University of Distance Education, Madrid	Henk Van daele	University of Ghent
1988-92	Henk Van daele	University of Ghent	Marc Vansteenkiste	University of Antwerp
1992-96	Jürgen Schriewer	Humboldt University, Berlin	Miguel Pereyra	University of Granada
1996-00	Thyge Winther-Jensen	University of Copenhagen	Miguel Pereyra	University of Granada
2000-04	Donatella Palomba	University of Rome Tor-Vegata	Miguel Pereyra	University of Granada
2004-	Robert Cowen	University of London	Hans-Georg Kotthoff	Freiburg College of Education

In most cases, the election of the Presidents and Executive Committee members has followed the proposals submitted by the Nomination Committee, convened by the President at the beginning of the biennial General Meeting. The Nomination Committee has consisted of Past Presidents and/or other senior CESE members, and has often included officers of the IBE and other international organisations. The Nomination Committee forms its recommendations on the basis of written inputs from CESE members. The main function of the Nomination Committee is to channel the votes by giving comments on the candidates' personal and academic qualities and, at the same time, by paying particular attention to balanced regional representation. This procedure has proved to be legitimate and opportune, taking into consideration the pluri-national and pluri-cultural structure of the society with its potential for conflict. The value of the procedure became manifest in an exemplary way when in 1973, after Saul Robinsohn's early and unexpected death, the interim succession with Robert Plancke and Sixten Marklund as Acting Presidents (1972-73) was smoothly resolved. Moreover, the acceptance of patterns by the General Meetings has been demonstrated by the fact that the two-year terms of office for the President were regularly confirmed by second two-year terms, as permitted by the Statutes.

The Statutes deal with the language issue only in an indirect way insofar as they mention, beside the English name, the French and German versions (Association d'éducation comparée en Europe; Gesellschaft für Vergleichende Erziehungswissenschaft in Europa), while the acronym CESE is used in all languages (Article 1). During CESE conferences and General Meetings, the medium of communication is more complicated. English as the dominant medium is often complemented by French and the local/national language of the venue and sometimes by German, according to the demand by participants, and availability of language competencies and ad hoc translators. Simultaneous translation (usually limited to plenary sessions) commonly plays a significant part. Since CESE is unable to make adequate budget available for translation, the solution depends on support from governmental or non-governmental institutions, mostly in favour of the local/national languages. It seems that the potential danger that Cowen (1980, p.102) observed with regard to language conflicts has decreased during the past decades. This trend may have been caused by the increasing diversity of members' linguistic descent and commitment. One can argue that CESE has settled this rather delicate issue to a remarkable degree by pursuing a strategy which modifies the monopoly of English which is found in many scientific associations.

Conferences

Since the beginning, the CESE conferences have proved to be manifestations of vitality. In spite of recurring financial and organisational emergencies, the biennial rhythm has never been interrupted with the positive exception of the special conference held in Garda (Italy) in 1986 to celebrate the society's 25th anniversary (Table 10.3). Distinctive characteristics come forth in the local and regional ambience of the venues, in the presence of eminent scholars, and in the

Table 10.3: CESE Conferences, 1963-2006

No.	Year	Place	Theme
1	1963	Amsterdam, Netherlands	Comparative education research and the determinants of educational policy
2	1965	Berlin, Germany	General education in a changing world
3	1967	Ghent, Belgium	The university within the education system
4	1969	Prague, Czechoslovakia	Curriculum development at the second level
5	1971	Stockholm, Sweden	Teacher education
6	1973	Frascati, Italy	Recurrent education: Concepts and policies for lifelong learning
7	1975	Sèvres, France	School and community
8	1977	London, UK	Diversity and unity in education
9	1979	Valencia, Spain	The influence of international educational research on national educational policies
10	1981	Geneva, Switzerland	The future of educational sciences: Theoretical and institutional issues
11	1983	Würzburg, Germany	Education and the diversity of cultures: The contribution of comparative education
12	1985	Antwerp, Belgium	The impact of technology on society and education: a comparative perspective
	1986	Garda, Italy	Comparative education today (special conference for 25th anniversary)
13	1988	Budapest, Hungary	Aims of education and development of education
14	1990	Madrid, Spain	Educational reforms and innovations facing the 21st century: a comparative approach
15	1992	Dijon, France	Evaluation of education and training: Comparative approaches
16	1994	Copenhagen, Denmark	Challenges to European education: Cultural values, national identities, and global responsibilities
17	1996	Athens, Greece	Education and the structuring of the European space: North-South, centre-periphery, identity-otherness
18	1998	Groningen, Netherlands	Education contested: Changing relations between state, market, and civil society in modern European education
19	2000	Bologna, Italy	The emergence of the 'knowledge society': From clerici vagantes to internet
20	2002	London, UK	Towards the end of educational systems? Europe in a world perspective
21	2004	Copenhagen, Denmark	Multiple identities, education and citizenship: The world in Europe, Europe in the world
22	2006	Granada, Spain	Changing knowledge and education: Communities, information societies and mobilities

participation – fortunately growing – of young educationists. They demonstrate, moreover, how progress and change in comparative education as an academic field is mirrored in plenary and workshop presentations and discussions. Many conferences have helped to consolidate comparative education in the host countries (see García Garrido 1987). In this respect, the conferences in Valencia (Spain) and Athens (Greece) were especially memorable.

Berlin, the venue of the second conference in 1965, was distinguished by the presence of many venerable representatives of the pioneer generation, including Joseph Lauwerys, Nicholas Hans, Friedrich Schneider, Franz Hilker, Philip Idenburg, Edemée Hatinguais, Pedro Rosselló and Leo Fernig. In this presentation, CESE's start "as a gathering of senior persons within the field" (Cowen 1980, p.99) was demonstrated for the last time in that completeness which needs to be mentioned with special reference to their outstanding academic or political reputations and also their interdisciplinary competencies. This comment should be underlined by reference to the key lecture given by Ernst Simon (Jerusalem), one of Martin Buber's most prominent disciples.

The fourth conference was held in Prague in the 'interim year' of 1969, between the suppression of the 'Prague Spring' which had given the decisive impulse for the choice of this venue and the return of the communist hardliners into power. The conference itself was not overtly affected by the impending political and scientific climate, but from talks during the pauses between the sessions, the foreign guests could detect predictions of what was coming. Immediately after the conference, František Singule, the organiser of the event who had been elected into the Executive Committee, was prevented by the Czechoslovak authorities from exercising his committee function and thus disappeared from the international scene for many years.

The 13th conference was held in Budapest in 1988, i.e. in Central Europe for the second time, shortly before the collapse of the Communist regime in the whole region. The somewhat expectant atmosphere was made manifest by the presence of speakers and participants from Central and Eastern Europe and the Soviet Union, in particular the prominent Russian educationist Zoya Malkova.

Two years later, at the 14th conference in Madrid (1990), this atmosphere was enhanced into a state of euphoria. This atmosphere was mirrored in some of the political speeches, although some papers were dampened by warnings of intolerant nationalism which turned out to be substantial in face of the violent events in Southeast Europe and, though in non-violent forms, in other parts of the region. Aside from such controversial dimensions, the Madrid conference signalled CESE's immediate response to the transformations in Central and Eastern Europe with their impacts on comparative educational research.

The 16th conference in Copenhagen (1994) opened CESE's explicit interest in the 'European dimension' of its scientific and political commitment which was continued in the conferences in Athens (1996), Groningen (1998), Bologna (2000), London (2002), and Copenhagen (2004). This commitment can be considered as an approach to identifying CESE as a *Europe*-centred association and, at the same time, as a concomitant of the moves on the political and academic scene at the threshold of the 21st century.

While the focus of these remarks is primarily on the political component of the venues, their whole history bears witness to the theoretical and thematic component of CESE. It indicates the readiness of comparative educationists to respond to the challenges of essential trends in the social sciences as well as in the humanities including their inherent shifts of paradigm. This comment can be exemplified by the following thematic approaches:

- recurrent education in the framework of lifelong learning (Frascati 1973);
- the discovery and revival of the intercultural component of comparative education as a response to cross-national relevance of the forthcoming migrant issue (see Mitter & Swift 1983), at a moment when that topic as a research field in Europe was growing significantly (Würzburg 1983);
- an explicit start into the empirical research domain in comparative education without abandoning its traditional domain of historical and hermeneutic studies (Dijon 1992);
- a response to the shift of paradigms in social theory, in particular systems theory and world systems theory (from Copenhagen 1994 onwards) and their impacts on comparative education (see Winther-Jensen 1996 and Kazamias & Spillane 1998).

CESE conferences also embrace workshops (until 1990 called commissions) which are related to focal themes on comparative educational trends including their contextual references. This principle is reinforced by explicit interest in middle-range research issues and their discussions in the transnational dimension. It indicates a significant difference from the way conferences of the US-based Comparative and International Education Society (CIES) are structured. This difference was especially relevant in the early history of both societies. However, CESE events have been increasingly opened to what the organisers of the 2006 Granada conference called 'free working groups, panels, symposia, poster displays, [and] workshops'.

Additional information on the conferences with their thematic and organisational components has been offered by the CESE Newsletters which were launched in 1978 and which went far beyond anticipatory and retrospective news on the conferences. The newsletters also contained reports on other events in Europe and beyond, publications, book reviews, and obituaries (see Luzón 2005).

The conference programmes are usually enriched by two special forms of presentations:

- the Joseph Lauwerys Lectures initiated in memory of one of CESE's prominent founding members and intended for outstanding European and non-European speakers in comparative education and its neighbouring fields;
- the Young Researchers' Group, which owes its existence to an initiative started by José Luis García Garrido in the early 1990s.

Mention should also be made of the CESE Women's Network founded on

Margaret Sutherland's initiative in the late 1980s. Self-organised and formally acknowledged by the Executive Committee, it helped to consolidate the position of female members in the society, and made special contributions to the agendas of the General Meetings.

Conclusions

CESE has found ways to deal with the tensions between continuity and change, and it seems legitimate to call its first four decades of history a success. In the first period the society had to occupy and assure its place among its elder neighbouring associations in the domains of pedagogics, social sciences and humanities. The second challenge was caused by the foundation of national, regional and linguistic comparative education societies, competing with CESE in attracting members and organising their own meetings. This trend posed a question about CESE's survival, after the model of sections under CESE's umbrella failed. This challenge was reinforced by the third challenge – that all these 'competing' societies joined the WCCES, thus placing CESE *beside* them as constituent members of the world body.

The success which determines the current state of the field can be essentially explained by how CESE has managed to cope with the following three problem areas that are interconnected. First, Denis Kallen's description (1981, p.3) of CESE as "a large club, but still a small society" is worth recalling. Kallen continued:

> It is no more 'a gathering of senior persons in the field', but a mixed group of 'senior persons' represented by the few professors and lecturers in comparative education in European universities, many junior staff members from universities, staff members of research institutes, of international organisations and of educational administrations.

Twenty five years later that comment had not lost its applicability. It is true that the CESE conferences attract young researchers; but compared to CIES, the 'senior persons' have held influential positions to an exceptional degree. This has been manifest in the themes of the main workshops at the conferences and also in the election of the CESE officers, exemplified by the list of Presidents. In this sense the 'club' character has not disappeared, although it has been restricted by the fact that the attendance of young researchers at the conferences goes considerably beyond their membership in CESE because they prefer to join their national associations as the organisations within their working areas.

Second, policy-oriented and practice-oriented themes have increasingly entered the conference programmes, though they have remained the domain of the 'free' working groups leaving continuing dominance of theory-based themes in the main workshops that have thus retained the feature of CESE conferences. Concerning the theoretical orientation, Cowen's analytical comment (1980, p.108) is relevant:

> The intellectual definition of European comparative education is sharply different from that of American comparative education. The major founding

fathers of European comparative education from the mid-twenties were working on themes which are comprehensible in terms of Durkheim, Weber, and Marx. The search for new methodological approaches in the United States and the confidence that American comparative educationists have had in positivist techniques drawn from other social sciences has meant that a field of study with a common name has diverged sharply.

Here again, the response should be ambivalent. On the one hand, in the 21st century the 'sharp' difference is no longer evident: empirical methodology has long gained access to comparative education theory and research in European universities and research institutes, while social theories have exerted their impact on comparative education in the USA. On the other hand, the aforementioned strong position of theory-based themes at the CESE conferences, including their representatives' dedication to European authorities of philosophical dignity, may allow the argument that the 'sharpness' of the differences mentioned by Cowen has been abandoned, while differences *per se* continue to be identified. However, some of the 'authorities' have changed in the ranking lists. Karl Marx, for example, has been replaced by Niklas Luhmann and Jürgen Habermas.

Third, the CESE conferences have increasingly demonstrated a 'European dimension' with regard to education and educational policies (see e.g. Winther-Jensen 1996). Unlike Europe-oriented debates several decades previously, the interest seemed to undergo a shift of paradigm from the more idealistic and historical considerations to the comparative re-analysis of political documents and empirical inquiries. The outcomes and effects of the Programme of International Student Assessment (PISA) sponsored by the Organisation for Economic Co-operation and Development (OECD), as well as trends in the field of intercultural education, can be adduced as significant cases. This pattern of Europeanisation may be interpreted as a corollary of the actions and debates within the bodies of the European Union. In the process, it could give CESE a unique feature in relation to both non-European and European partner associations. Moreover, it may assure CESE's distinctive place within the WCCES.

References

Cowen, Robert (1980): 'Comparative Education in Europe: A Note'. *Comparative Education Review*, Vol.24, No.1, pp.98-108.

García Garrido, José Luis (1986): 'CESE in the Past 25 Years of Comparative Education in Europe', in *CESE Publications: Comparative Education Today*. http://cese-europe.org/publications.htm, pp.41-48.

García Garrido, José Luis (1987): 'Wolfgang Mitter's Commitment to the Comparative Education Society in Europe'. *Zeitschrift für internationallerziehungs-und sozialwissenschaftliche Forschung*, pp.5-17.

Kallen, Denis (1981): 'CESE: Society or Club?'. *CESE Newsletter*, No.8, p.3.

Kallen, Denis (2006): 'A Few Remarks about the History of the CESE: The Early Years'. Unpublished manuscript.

Kazamias, Andreas with Spillane, Martin G. (eds.) (1998): *Education and the Structuring of the European Space.* Athens: Seirios Editions.

Luzón, Antonio (2005): 'La Sociedad Europea de Educación Comparada (CESE) en una Época de Cambios'. *Revista Española de Educación Comparada*, No.11, pp.215-240.

Mitter, Wolfgang (1986): 'Twenty-five Years of CESE: Experiences and Challenges', in *CESE Publications: Comparative Education Today*. http://cese-europe.org/publications.htm, pp.91-99.

Mitter, Wolfgang & Swift, James (eds.) (1983): *Education and the Diversity of Cultures / L'Éducation et la diversité des cultures / Erziehung und die Vielfalt der Kulturen. Bericht der 11. Konferenz der Comparative Education Society in Europe (Würzburg).* Köln, Wien: Böhlau. I. und II. Teilband: XXI, 719 S. = *Bildung und Erziehung*, Beiheft 2/I und 2/II.

Winther-Jensen, Thyge (ed.) (1996): *Challenges to European Education: Cultural Values, National Identities and Global Responsibilities.* Frankfurt am Main: Peter Lang.

11

The Japan Comparative Education Society (JCES)

Akira NINOMIYA

The Japan Comparative Education Society (JCES), which was established in 1965, is one of the world's oldest societies of comparative education. In Japan, it is also one of the largest academic societies in the field of education.

This chapter describes the development of comparative education in Japan, observes the way in which the JCES fits into this history, analyses the research orientations of JCES members, and comments on the challenges ahead. Most of the chapter is based on the book *Forty Years of the JCES* (Saito 2004), which was published to celebrate the society's 40th anniversary.

Aims and Organisation of the JCES

The JCES Statutes (Article 2) declare that the JCES exists "to contribute to the development and diffusion of comparative education, and to promote communication and cooperation necessary for administering research within and outside Japan". In order to achieve these aims, the JCES has organised annual conferences, published a journal, awarded a prize for outstanding publication, operated a website, and developed a research data-base. The JCES has also collaborated with counterpart societies in other countries, and with the World Council of Comparative Education Societies (WCCES).

The JCES is administered by a president, board members who are elected from each region based on the membership size in each of six regions, and associate executive members. The Secretary is nominated by the President from among the board members. The President organises an Executive Council to perform duties laid down in the Statutes. Although the members of each region elect their board members, the President is elected by the board members rather than directly by the whole membership. In 2006, the JCES had over 800 full and student members. Some of the members were resident outside Japan.

History of Comparative Studies in Education

The Pre-modern Period

As far back as the 9th Century, Japan absorbed knowledge and technology from advanced countries such as Korea and China. Several Buddhist scholars and administrators were sent to China, and one of the most famous of them, Kukai, went to the Chinese capital and brought back the sacred books of Esoteric Buddhism. In 828 he reported on the school and education systems in Chan'an in his article 'The Regulations of School of Arts and Sciences'. His article stated that China had very good universities, that each large region had regional schools, and that many villages had schools. By contrast, the article lamented, Japan had no equivalent regional school in its capital, Kyoto, although it did have a university. Kukai recommended adoption of the Chinese education system in Japan.

In medieval Japan, some Christian lords in Kyushu sent missions to Europe in 1582. Four young Japanese were sent to Rome, where they were welcomed by the Pope and others. They returned in 1590, and the knowledge and technologies that they brought back, especially in printing, contributed to the development of Japanese culture.

During the 17th century, Japan closed its doors to other countries, thereby restricting the international flow of knowledge. However, some information was disseminated by foreigners who did travel to Japan, and by 'floating' Japanese who went abroad and then returned. One of the most famous of these Japanese was 'American' Hikozo, who stayed in the United States of America (USA) and studied in a Catholic school. His 1863 book, *Floating on the Pacific Ocean*, described his school experiences (Hikozo 1955).

The Modern Period

Even before the dawn of modern Japan, the Edo Shogunate government sent missions to Europe to learn advanced knowledge. Amane Nishi, who was one of the leaders of local government of Tsuwano-han for the reform of the systems at the end of Edo period in Japan, introduced the new school system plan in his advisory report of 'Basic Guidelines of Arts and Samurai Spirit Schools' in 1870. He came back from the Netherlands in 1869 after seven years of study. In this report, he advocated the educational reforms, based on the comparative studies on education, stating as follows:

> Having compared the school systems in the four seas and in the past and present, we found that there were different histories of school reforms in the different provinces, and in the different times. But there was one common feature of school systems: there must be Universities, High Schools and Elementary Schools.

During the same period, the Meiji government sent a large mission led by Tomomi Iwakura, the Ambassador Extraordinary and Plenipotentiary, to North America and Europe from 1871 to 1873. One of the members sent from the

Ministry of Education, Fujimaro Tanaka, wrote reports on education in other countries (Tanaka 1873-75). The ideas and knowledge about education in the USA and Europe, particularly France, Germany and the Netherlands, were utilised in the establishment of modern education systems in the Meiji era.

The initial decades of the 20th century brought several important books. In 1916, Hanjiro Nakajima wrote a book entitled *Comparative Study of National Education in Germany, France, Britain and the USA* (Nakajima 1916), and discussed the merits and demerits of their education systems. The first book specifically entitled *Comparative Education* was authored by Choichi Higuchi and published in 1928, and was followed by *Comparative Education Systems* in 1936 (Higuchi 1928, 1936). Between 1931 and 1942, the Ministry of Education issued a series of reports entitled 'Studies of Education Systems in Other Countries and in Japan'.

Also of great impact during the pre-war period was the Study Group of Educational Thought at Tokyo Imperial University. Three volumes in a series entitled 'Recent Educational Thoughts of European Countries' were issued between 1921 and 1923, and 46 volumes of 'Studies of Educational Thoughts' were issued between 1927 and 1948. Academic knowledge on education in other countries was brought into the Japanese educational academy. This was almost equivalent to the Education Yearbooks (1924-44) published by Columbia University in the USA.

The Post-war Period

In the period following World War II, comparative education, together with other educational disciplines, enjoyed institutionalised development in the national universities. Not only was research in comparative education considered important and useful, but also the teaching of comparative education was valued as a way to prepare the younger generation of educational researchers and practitioners. In 1952, the first Comparative Education Institute was established in Kyushu University. Then, in 1953, the Comparative Education Systems Institute was established in Hiroshima University. Some of the professors at these universities had studied comparative education in the USA or England. They were researchers of educational philosophy, educational history, educational administration, etc., but made great efforts to teach comparative education and were eager to develop it as an important academic field together with educational philosophy, history, sociology, administration, teaching methods and curriculum studies.

It took until 1965 and 1967 for comparative education institutes to be established in Kyoto and Tokyo Universities; and it was in 1995 that the Institute was established at Nagoya University. In addition to comparative education studies in universities, the National Institute for Educational Research (NIER), which was established in 1949, focused on study of Asian and European countries.

The JCES and its Work

Informal Meetings and the Establishment of the JCES

Many educational researchers around the world who were interested in the teaching of comparative education met in New York in 1954. Two years later, a core from this meeting established the Comparative Education Society (CES) in the USA. In 1959, the Japan Society for the Study of Education, which had been created in 1941, hosted in Tokyo the first International Conference on Educational Research. A major part of the conference was devoted to 'Problems and Methodologies in Comparative Education'.

After this conference, seven professors and researchers met in Hakone, Kanagawa, to talk about the establishment of a comparative education society in Japan. They were Masunori Hiratsuka (Kyushu University), Shigeo Masui (Kyushu University), Mamoru Oshiba (Himeji University of Technology), Katsumi Yuasa (National Institute for Educational Research), Taro Yamanouchi (Tokyo University), Tetsuya Kobayashi (International Christian University), and Iwao Matsuzaki (Tokyo University).

The first conference of the Japan Comparative Education Society was held on 30 and 31 March 1965 in Miyajima Island, Hiroshima. It had over 60 participants including graduate school students. Three keynote speeches and five paper presentations were scheduled. The main theme of the public symposium raised the question: 'How can we introduce Comparative Education into the university undergraduate education programs?'.

The official establishment of the JCES was on 31 March 1965, and Masunori Hiratsuka was elected its first President. The annual membership fee was 500 yen, or 250 yen for students. Ninety four people joined the society, including 12 graduate students. Five years later, the membership increased to 202 people.

Masunori Hiratsuka held the presidency for 15 years and set up his Secretariat at the NIER rather than in his university. Although the main theme among comparative educationists who convened at the first Conference in 1965 was 'Teaching of Comparative Education', the members of the Secretariat did not show strong interest in the teaching of comparative education, perhaps chiefly because the NIER did not itself operate degree programmes. The major concern of the NIER was to carry out joint research on issues which might contribute to the policies of the national government.

The 4th World Congress

In 1980, the JCES hosted in Tokyo the 4th World Congress of Comparative Education Societies. The JCES had been one of the five founding societies of the WCCES in 1970. Prior to the Tokyo World Congress from 7 to 10 July, the Korean Comparative Education Society hosted a pre-Congress event from 3 to 5 July. The Congress attracted 402 participants from 31 countries, including 61 from the USA, 40 from Canada, 28 from Korea, 23 from the United Kingdom (UK), six from France, five from Thailand, four from Australia, and three from New Zealand.

The theme of the Congress was Tradition and Innovation in Education. The topics of the five sub-sections were Education and National Development; Innovations in Education; Issues and Problems of Teachers; Education for International Understanding and Cooperation; and Concepts and Practice of Moral Education. Several of these themes reflected the ideas of Masunori Hiratsuka, who advocated the comparative study of moral education. He was one of the outstanding leaders of UNESCO activities, especially education for international understanding and cooperation, on behalf of the Japanese National Commission for UNESCO. Education for National Development was a concern of the WCCES executive, although Japanese comparative educationists were less interested in this topic.

Developments in the 1980s and 1990s

The 1980s brought some major developments in JCES activities. For example, there were changes of the title of the JCES periodical. Originally it had been *The Bulletin of the Japan Comparative Education Society* (Vols. 1-13), but it then became *Comparative Education* (Vols. 14-16), and then *Comparative Education Studies* (from Vol. 17 onwards). In addition, from 1988 the JCES began to issue newsletters.

Perhaps even more significant was the creation in 1990 of the Hiratsuka Award for Outstanding Publication. This award, created to honour the contributions of Masunori Hiratsuka, was designed to promote comparative education studies among young researchers. The system was established through which each year a selection committee of 10 members would be asked to choose the most meritorious book or article from among those nominated.

Another important effort was the creation in 1993 of the reference database entitled Research Information for International and Comparative Education (RICE). In 2000, the database was placed on the JCES website; and by 2006 it contained over 40,000 entries.

Further Societies Related to Comparative Education

While the JCES has gradually expanded, the society has faced the birth of societies in related domains. Some JCES members have been eager to support these societies in order to extend the scope of educational studies, and/or to address urgent problems in the age of internationalisation. Particularly noteworthy among the new societies have been:

- the Japan Curriculum Research and Development Association, founded in 1975;
- the Intercultural Education Society of Japan, founded in 1980;
- the Japan International Education Society, founded in 1990;
- the Japan Association of International Education (Education for International Understanding), founded in 1991;
- the Japan Society for Educational Systems and Organisations, founded in 1993;

- the Japanese Association of Higher Education Research, founded in 1997; and
- the Development Education Association, founded in 1992.

Table 11.1: Themes of Public Symposia in Annual JCES Conferences

No.	Year	Theme
1.	1965	How can we introduce comparative education in the university undergraduate education programs?
2.	1966	University entrance examinations in other countries
3.	1967	Higher education structural reforms in other countries
4.	1968	University autonomy: its history and present state
5.	1969	University administration and management
6.	1970	Trends of secondary education reforms
7.	1971	The structure of teaching subjects of secondary schools
8.	1972	Lifelong education
9.	1973	Lifelong education
10.	1974	Problems of comparative education
11.	1975	Problems of foreign students in Japan
12.	1976	Problems of teacher education
13.	1977	Comparative study on teacher education policies and trends
14.	1978	Tradition and innovation in education
15.	1979	Tasks and prospects of university admission systems
16.	1980	The 4th Congress of WCCES (Tradition and Innovation in Education)
17.	1981	Foreign perspectives on Japanese education
18.	1982	Foreign perspectives on Japanese education
19.	1983	Proposals from comparative perspectives on approaches to lifelong education
20.	1984	Higher education in the mid 1980s: who should be educated and how?
21.	1985	Achievement issues in other countries
22.	1986	Foreign perspectives on Japanese educational reforms
23.	1987	What is internationalisation of education?
24.	1988	Educational reforms in other countries
25.	1989	Expectations on Japanese education from the perspectives of Asia and the Pacific
26.	1990	Roles of school education in the learning society
27.	1991	Problems of minority education in the world
28.	1992	The place of child culture in the world
29.	1993	The education of foreign children
30.	1994	Thinking about the future education in the world: human rights, development and environment issues
31.	1995	Gender, development and education: the new tasks of comparative education
32.	1996	Populations and education in the world
33.	1997	Identities and education in the age of living together
34.	1998	Children at risk and values education
35.	1999	Restructuring of 'knowledge' in higher education
36.	2000	Peace culture and children's books
37.	2001	Impact of the information and communications technology revolution on education
38.	2002	*Achievement issues: international comparisons*
39.	2003	Changing university management in Asia
40.	2004	The future of comparative education: the opening of new horizons

Alongside these bodies have been further societies for the study of education in such countries as the UK, the USA, France, and Germany. For example, the Societé franco-japonaise des sciences de l'éducation was founded in 1994.

The existence of these related societies has influenced the membership of the JCES. For example many of the specialists in curriculum and instruction left the JCES to join other societies. However, some of the people who joined these other societies retained their membership of the JCES.

In the past, most JCES members came from the parent-disciplines societies such as philosophy, history and sociology of education. Many JCES members remain members of their parent-discipline societies, and in this sense have multiple identities. Some scholars are members of over 10 societies which are related to comparative education.

Epistemological Understanding of Comparative Education

The titles of the public symposia during the annual JCES conferences are one indicator of the emphases of the society (Table 11.1). On two occasions, a single theme has been carried from one year to the next. Thus, in 1972 and 1973 the society considered lifelong education; and in 1981 and 1982 it considered foreign per-spectives on Japanese education. The 1965 symposium focused on teaching, but most subsequent themes were more academic. In some cases, the focus was on Japanese patterns through comparative lenses, though other themes were outward-looking.

Table 11.2: Themes of Special Issues of the JCES Journal

Year	Theme
1988	Educational Reforms and Comparative Education
1989	Curriculum
1994	30 Years of Comparative Education
1995	Methods of Educational Exchange Studies
1996	Gender, Development and Education
1997	Five Weekdays: Schools of Other Countries
1998	Educational Reforms in Japan
1999	New Development of Comparative Education
2000	Children at Risk and Educational Measures
2001	Frontiers of Area Education Studies
2002	New Trends of Public School Reforms: International Comparisons
2003	Thinking about Achievement Issues
2004	Comparative Study of Higher Education Reforms

Further indicators of emphasis are provided by the special themes in the JCES journal (Table 11.2). In most of the journal issues that had special themes, three to five articles were clustered on those themes. Only in 1994 did it become an annual practice to select a specific theme. To some extent the themes were linked to the conferences, but the links were not rigid.

Table 11.3: Geographic Focus of Articles in the JCES Journal

	Vol. 1-10		*Vol. 11-20*		*Vol. 21-30*		*Total*
Africa					Ghana	1	
					Kenya	1	
					Tanzania	1	
sub-total		*0*		*0*		3	*3*
Arab					Syria	1	
Countries					Lebanon	1	
sub-total		*0*		*0*		2	*2*
Asia &	Japan	30	Japan	15	China	11	
Pacific	Korea	9	China	8	Australia	7	
	Thailand	4	Malaysia	5	Japan	6	
	China	3	Thailand	4	Thailand	6	
	India	1	Korea	4	Indonesia	5	
	Australia	1	Indonesia	4	India	4	
	Korea, Dem Rep	1	Australia	3	Malaysia	3	
	Philippines	1	India	2	Bangladesh	2	
	Malaysia	1	Singapore	2	Philippines	2	
			Philippines	1	Korea, Rep of	1	
			New Zealand	1	Korea, Dem Rep	1	
					Singapore	1	
					Nepal	1	
					Myanmar	1	
					Australia	1	
					New Zealand	1	
sub-total		*51*		*49*		*53*	*153*
Europe/	USA	26	USA	25	USA	15	
North	England	12	England	12	England	12	
America	Germany	7	Germany	9	Germany	11	
	USSR	5	France	8	France	6	
	France	4	USSR	6	Russia	3	
	Sweden	4	Sweden	4	Canada	1	
	Ireland	1	Canada	2	Poland	1	
	Canada	1	Italy	1			
			Ireland	1			
			Netherlands	1			
			Switzerland	1			
sub-total		*60*		*70*		*49*	*179*
Latin			Mexico	1	Chile	1	
America							
sub-total		*0*		*1*		*1*	*2*

Table 11.3 (continued)

	Vol. 1-10		Vol. 11-20		Vol. 21-30		Total
Area	South East Asia	3	Latin America	2	Asia	1	
Studies	Asia	1	Europe/USA	1	Europe	1	
	East Asia	1	S.E. Asia	1	Latin America	1	
	Scandinavia	1	Oceania	1	Oceania	1	
					South East Asia	1	
					Islamic countries	1	
sub-total		6		5		6	*17*
Inter-	UNESCO	3	EC	1	EU	2	
national	OECD	2			World Bank	1	
Organi-	EC	1					
sations	ASEAN	1					
	World Bank	1					
sub-total		8		*1*		3	*12*
Others		33		32		21	86
Total		**158**		**158**		**138**	**454**

UNESCO = United Nations Educational, Scientific and Cultural Organization; OECD = Organisation for Economic Co-operation and Development; EC = European Community; ASEAN = Association of Southeast Asian Nations.

Source: Kitamura (2005), p.246.

The foci of other articles in the JCES journal provide further indicators of emphases in the society. Kitamura's (2005) analysis of the three decades since the launch of the journal showed a decrease in the number of articles focusing on Japanese education, and a sharp increase in the proportion of articles focusing on Asia and the Pacific (Table 11.3). He also observed a diversification of the countries studied, and particularly an increased interest in Southeast Asia, South Asia, China and Africa.

According to Otsuka (2005), about 10 per cent of the articles in the journal (Vol. 1 to Vol. 29) were based on field-studies and/or surveys, and field studies became especially prominent after Vol. 16 of the journal in the 1990s. In the 1980s, many scholars were more concerned with area studies of particular countries than with comparisons *per se*.

Challenges for Comparative Education in Japan

Part of the increased interest in the less developed countries of Asia, Latin America and Africa arises from the work of the Japan International Cooperation Agency (JICA). Many professors of science education, mathematics education and or other fields have become involved in JICA's development projects. At the same time, the Ministry of Education has established research and development centres in Hiroshima, Tokyo, Nagoya, Tsukuba and Naruto for the study of international cooperation in education. The JCES has welcomed members who have expertise in international cooperation in education. This pattern has parallels in the development of comparative and international education in the USA and UK, as recounted by other authors in this book.

During the mid-1990s, the JCES Executive Board made a proposal to change the name from the Japan Comparative Education Society to the Japan Comparative <u>and International</u> Education Society, and appointed a sub-committee to consider the matter. However, the committee responded negatively. As mentioned above, Japan had a separate International Education Society. Members felt that a change of the name of the JCES would cause confusion and would dilute the identity of the society. However, it is arguable that this decision missed an opportunity to expand the field of study and welcome a wide range of practitioners. Increasing numbers of young people are becoming interested in international cooperation in less developed countries. Many of these people go to England, the USA or Australia to study the phenomenon, and it is arguable that the JCES should reach out more actively to this group.

A second challenge is the fact that interests among comparative education students are becoming more diverse. Earlier generations tended to study the educational systems and policies in other countries with particular focus on such themes as social stratification in rural areas, gender inequalities, teachers' issues, higher education (especially quality assurance), curriculum and instruction, etc.. More international students are now majoring in comparative education in Japanese universities. The JCES has provided opportunities for them to make presentations in English if they wish, and they are bringing a new agenda by focusing on comparative studies on educational issues of their own countries.

Another major change came with a 2003 legal shift in the governance of universities when all national universities in Japan were privatised. The university Presidents and their executive board members were required to identify their goals and devise action plans for research and education over the next six years. The Ministry of Education retained the right to approve or disapprove these plans, and the institutions were obliged to compete for funding. This change sharply changed the environment within which departments and programmes operated. Scholars of comparative education had to answer whether their field was really necessary for training of teachers, or was really one of the most important fields in their Faculties. The shift made scholars much more pragmatic about the types of projects on which they embarked, paying close attention to availability of funds. Nevertheless, the JCES remained vigorous, with well-attended annual conferences and a membership which, at 850 in 2006, was much larger than that in many other countries.

References

Higuchi, Choichi (1928): *Comparative Education*. Tokyo: Monasu. [in Japanese]

Higuchi, Choichi (1936): *Comparative Education Systems*. Tokyo: Seibido. [in Japanese]

Hikozo (1955): *Hyoryu Ki: Floating on the Pacific Ocean*. Early California Travels Series, translated from the 1863 edition by Tosh Motofuji. Los Angeles: Glen Dawson.

Kitamura, Yuto (2005): 'Comparative Education and its Relation with Development Studies'. *Comparative Education*, Vol.31, pp.241-252. [in Japanese]

Nakajima, Hanjiro (1916): *Comparative Study of National Education in Germany, France, Britain and the USA*. Tokyo: Kyouiku-shincho Kenkyukai. [in Japanese]

Otsuka, Yutaka (2005): 'Fields as Methods'. *Comparative Education*, Vol.31, pp.253-263. [in Japanese]

Saito, Yasushi (ed.) (2004): *Forty Years of the Japan Comparative Education Society*. Tokyo: Japan Comparative Education Society. [in Japanese]

Tanaka, Fujimaro (1873-75): *Riji Kotei*. Tokyo: Ministry of Education. [in Japanese]

12

The Section for International and Intercultural Comparative Education in the German Society for Education (SIIVEDGE)

Dietmar WATERKAMP

This chapter examines the development of comparative education in Germany during the 20th and 21st centuries, identifying four overlapping periods. During the second period, the Commission for Comparative Education was formed in the German Society for Education. It was admitted to the World Council of Comparative Education Societies (WCCES) under the name Kommission für Vergleichende Erziehungswissenschaft in der Deutschen Gesellschaft für Erziehungswissenschaft (KVEDGE). Subsequent evolution led to merger with other groups in the German Society for Education, and renaming of the body as Section for International and Intercultural Comparative Education. This body then replaced KVEDGE in the WCCES under the name Sektion International und Interkulturell Vergleichende Erziehungswissenschaft in der Deutschen Gesellschaft für Erziehungswissenschaft (SIIVEDGE).

The chapter places discussion of these bodies within the broader framework of comparative studies of education. It remarks on the different patterns in West and East Germany as well as in the country as a whole. One feature of comparative education in Germany has been its incorporation into the broader academic field of education. Comparative education at universities is taught and researched in schools or institutes of education. It is often closely affiliated with the theoretical foundations and normative theories of education which are called general education (Allgemeine Pädagogik or Allgemeine Erziehungswissenschaft). General education intersects with the history of educational ideas and the history of philosophy, and sometimes also with theology and sociology. The academic field of general education kept the legacy of the early university chairs for philosophy and education, and combined it with the legacy of the teacher training institutes.

From time to time, controversies arise in the schools of education about whether general education should provide basic theories and concepts for the other branches of education, or whether it is preferable for each branch to organise its knowledge independently from theories on the general level. This question is also applicable to comparative education. The understanding of its task and scope differs according to which side is chosen. In search of a general level, comparative education might avoid general education and prefer to borrow from sociological, political or philosophical theories (Röhrs 1975).

The First Period of Development

The history of comparative education in Germany might be traced back to the 'travelling educators' in the 18th and 19th centuries such as August Hermann Niemeyer and Friedrich Thiersch (Schneider 1961). Its more recent history started when education began to be conceived as a field of university teaching.

General education at German universities often included Christian thought, because until the 1960s most elementary schools and many secondary schools were denominational. Also, some comparativists were believers. This is relevant because the Roman Catholic church and many Protestant churches had worldwide religious commitments. Friedrich Schneider, who was among the founders of the field of comparative education in Germany (see e.g. Schneider 1957), was a Catholic, and some of his writings were written from this viewpoint. Leonhard Froese, who was an influential comparativist after World War II (see e.g. Froese 1962), was affiliated with Protestant theology. A commitment to peace education which can be found among German comparativists also originates from humanistic roots, and Hermann Röhrs elaborated on this topic (e.g. Röhrs 1983, 1995). These observations point to the close interrelation between the fields of general education and comparative education.

The forces that led to an independent branch of comparative education within the academic field of education included political events which demanded many people to emigrate to countries in which several nationalities lived together. Among the migrants who came to Germany, most of whom had German origin but grew up in Eastern Europe, some contributed to the field of comparative education in their academic careers. Personal experiences encouraged reflection on cultural differences and on the educational ideas of different nations. Examples of such scholars included Sergius Hessen and Isabella Rüttenauer, who came from Russia to Germany in the 1920s, and Leonhard Froese who emigrated from Ukraine in the early 1930s (Froese 1952; Busch 1984; Willmann 1995). In a different way, a bicultural experience was the background for Oskar Anweiler who grew up in the Polish-German area which then belonged to Germany (see e.g. Anweiler 1964), and for Wolfgang Mitter who belonged to the German minority in Czechoslovakia (see e.g. Mitter 1976). Saul B. Robinsohn was a Jewish exile who, after World War II, returned from Jerusalem to his native Berlin after a stay in Hamburg. Robinsohn had a major impact on comparative education in Germany, even though he died in his early fifties (Robinsohn 1992).

Another factor in the establishment of the field was more specific to Germany, namely the division of the country into two states as a result of the Cold War. Comparative education in West Germany emphasised research on the 'East', which above all meant the USSR and the countries under Soviet influence, especially Poland, Czechoslovakia and Hungary, and to a lesser extent Romania and Yugoslavia. The German Institute for International Education in Frankfurt under the headship of Mitter was especially active in research on these countries, as was the Research Unit for Comparative Education at the University of Bochum under the guidance of Anweiler. However, the focus of comparative education in West Germany was not oriented only towards the East. For instance, the research group around Froese at the University of Marburg kept a balance between research on Eastern European and Western European countries, and also focused on the USA. Quite detailed research was conducted in West Germany on education in East Germany (Waterkamp 2004). The German Democratic Republic (GDR) was a closed state to which West Germans could not easily travel and in which contacts with university faculty or other experts were even more difficult to establish. The West German centres nevertheless collected all written materials that they could find.

This was the political background which shaped what might be called the first period of comparative education in Germany, in which a certain paradigm of research was characteristic. The most important trait was the focus on a few countries. These were on the one hand the prospering European countries such as the United Kingdom, France, Switzerland and sometimes also the Nordic states, the Netherlands and the USA. On the other hand, the communist states became objects of research because the political interest in these countries was high. Moreover, specialists were needed in West Germany to decode the news from the East because the self-descriptions of these countries were assumed to be unreliable.

The typical research design was a case study of one country, and comparisons among a limited number of countries were less common. A fairly long historical introduction was indispensable, and the study of the laws on education and other state regulations was regarded as a proper starting point. Curricula were discussed in more detail, and debates about educational topics by the public and within the scientific communities of great interest. Most investigations were based on extended reading of documents from these countries, together with discussions with experts. The publications made use of official statistics, but data collection using questionnaires and other instruments was unusual. Within this research pattern, it was taken for granted that researchers trained themselves for expertise in specific countries and should be able to treat all aspects of the education systems of those countries. Only after acquiring mastery in the knowledge of one country could a researcher add another country. Most of this research aimed to inform the politicians, to give incentives for reforms in education, and to fulfil the information needs of the public about the countries of interest. Most publications were therefore reports about recent developments in the field of education in individual countries.

The Second Period of Development

For analysis of the second period, it is even more important than in other periods to consider West and East Germany separately.

West Germany

The second period brought challenges to the historiographical pattern of presentation which was based on organising the facts and connecting them with long-term intellectual or ideological currents in the respective country. The critiques were partly fuelled by the work of leading European researchers such as Joseph A. Lauwerys and Brian Holmes, and by American scholars such as George Z.F. Bereday and Harold Noah.

When the Comparative Education Society in Europe (CESE) was founded in 1961 in London, 10 scholars from Germany participated. In 1966, a team from this group organised an association for German researchers of comparative education. It was incorporated into the recently-founded German Society for Education as a Commission for Comparative Education (Kommission für Vergleichende Erziehungswissenschaft in der Deutschen Gesellschaft für Erziehungswissenschaft). In the WCCES it was abbreviated as KVEDGE, though that acronym was not used in Germany. The Commission had its own administrative and organisational structure. Table 12.1 lists the KVEDGE Presidents over the four decades from 1966, and the Appendix presents information on conferences and other activities.

Table 12.1: Presidents of the KVEDGE

Year	Name	Location	Year	Name	Location
1966-68	Leonhard Froese	Marburg	1986-88	Jürgen Schriewer	Frankfurt
1968-70	Oskar Anweiler	Bochum	1988-90	Wolfgang Mitter	Frankfurt
1970-72	Hermann Röhrs	Heidelburg	1990-92	Hans-Peter Schäfer	Hamburg
1972-74	Wolfgang Mitter	Lüneburg	1992-94	Günther Brinkmann	Freiburg
1974-76	Siegfried Baske	Berlin	1994-96	Marianne Krüger-	Münster
1976-78	Detlef Glowka	Münster		Potratz	
1978-80	Rita Süßmuth	Düsseldorf-Neuss	1996-98	Helga Thomas	Berlin
1980-82	Friedrich W. Busch	Oldenburg	1998-00	Wolfgang Hörner	Leipzig
1982-84	Ludwig Liegle	Tübingen	2000-02	Wilfried Bos	Hamburg
1984-86	Detlef Glowka	Münster	2002-05	Dietmar Waterkamp	Dresden

The fact that this Commission was part of the overall professional organisation for educationists which embraced all fields of research on education reflected the close affiliation of comparative education with schools of education in universities. In this context, an independent association for comparativists would have harmed their strategies for keeping their positions within the schools of education. Indeed, some comparativists continued to teach in both fields. Others taught comparative education combined with another specialty within the wider field of education, such as research methods, school pedagogy, and vocational education.

The organisational networks which had been created in the 1960s enhanced the exchange of ideas among European comparativists. In Germany, it was especially Saul B. Robinsohn, then Director of the Max-Planck Institute for

Education in West Berlin, who tried to put a new research pattern into practice. He cooperated with Brian Holmes of the United Kingdom, and initiated a project to investigate school change in six countries. Each country report considered six dimensions of society in order to identify the factors that exerted the strongest impact on school change. The theoretical scope was thus no longer focussed on comparing national education systems but on comparing societal factors with respect to their strengths in moulding education systems (Glowka & Braun 1975). A similar project was conducted by the Marburg group under Froese (Blumenthal 1975). Also, the Frankfurt Institute under Mitter addressed cross-national studies in several countries (Mitter 1976, 1983, 1994). Yet neither the Marburg group nor the Frankfurt Institute approached their topics from an explicitly sociological point of view in the way that Robinsohn did. Instead, they dealt with more traditional educational aspects such as curriculum and pedagogy.

The Robinsohn project was the most ambitious of its time in comparative education in Germany. Although the final comparison was not convincing and the complicated architecture of the investigation could not be handled satisfactorily, it had an impact on the field by stressing the relevance of sociological, political and economic theories (Waterkamp 1977). Like other domains within the field of education, comparative education was challenged by the tendency to create basic theories of its own regardless of the discourses in general education. However, in some respects the Robinsohn project was premature because the available data were insufficient to answer the research questions. The obvious shortcomings of the project impeded replication of the research design, and the level of institutional strength which the Max-Planck Institute offered at that time for comparative education research was not reached again.

East Germany

In East Germany, the forces of development were partly different. Arguably the most prominent figure was Hans-Georg Hofmann, who headed the Section for Education Abroad and in West Germany which operated within the GDR's national education research body, the German Educational Central Institute. In 1990 the Academy of Educational Sciences, which was the successor to this institute was closed. This brought an end to the institutional leadership, but Hofmann endeavoured to rescue the legacy of his unit by founding a private society for comparative education.

In the GDR, the names of institutions contained clear indicators about their work. In 1958, a distinction was made between foreign countries and West Germany, because West Germany was not regarded as a foreign country. Interest in the educational developments in West Germany was high, and East German researchers wanted to demonstrate that East Germany had a better education system than West Germany. The term comparative education was not used because the research unit focused on descriptions of individual national systems. Comparing was difficult for several reasons. First, the education systems in the 'brother-nations' of Eastern Europe were not viewed as objects for evaluation or judgement by East German researchers. Rather, East German researchers mostly contented themselves with translating articles of authors from the countries themselves. Second, socialist and capitalist countries were in principle incomparable. Among the other capitalist countries as research foci, the United States and the United Kingdom were of greatest interest.

In 1963, the name comparative education was acknowledged and a Department for Comparative Education was established within the German Educational Central Institute in (East) Berlin. This lasted until 1974 when the old name, 'Education Abroad', was restored. This period was the most fruitful for comparative education in the GDR. The change was mainly due to Werner Kienitz, who worked with Hofmann and for this period headed the Department, and in 1966 founded the Section for Comparative Education within the Scientific Council of the Ministry of Education. Kienitz published the only book in the GDR which could be considered a strong example of comparative education, entitled *Uniformity and Differentiation in Education* (Kienitz 1971). This was an especially significant work considering that the opportunities for travel were limited. In this book, the East-West partition was broken and comparisons took countries from both sides of the Iron Curtain. Additionally, Kienitz stimulated a debate about the methodology of comparative education in the journal *Comparative Education* which had been edited by his section in the Scientific Council since 1965. Whereas the name of the journal was kept until the demise of the Scientific Council in 1990, the section was renamed in 1974 according to its former title because comparisons again were considered ideologically risky. Only in the Gorbachev era were new voices to be heard (Busch 1983; John 1998). Thus in 1990, at the headship of Hofmann, the Working Unit for Education Abroad was restructured and renamed the Society for Comparative Pedagogy.

In matters of vocabulary, East Germans stayed with the older term 'pedagogy' (Vergleichende Pädagogik) whereas West Germans changed to the more modern expression 'science of education' (Vergleichende Erziehungswissenschaft). This was not just an intra-German linguistic difference: it also had to do with the dominance of the term pedagogy in the USSR and other Eastern European countries. Up to the 1960s, the term 'Vergleichende Pädagogik' was also used in West Germany, as exemplified in the book by Hilker (1962); but later Walter Berger from Vienna published a textbook named *Vergleichende Erziehungswissenschaft* (Berger 1976). In line with general trends in the field of education, the change was inspired by the above-mentioned redefinition of methodology which found a clear expression in Robinsohn's writings. 'Pädagogik' indicates a collection of knowledge that is not only of interest to scholars and possibly politicians, but also to teachers and other practitioners. Like other educational disciplines which use the term 'Pädagogik', comparative pedagogy aims to remain a practical science. By contrast, the term 'Vergleichende Erziehungswissenschaft' announces an orientation to disciplinary and interdisciplinary scientific discourses.

Educational aid for developing countries was another focus in the GDR. Research in this domain started with a unit named Educational Policy in Developing Countries. It was formed in the Section for Education in Foreign

Countries and in West Germany in the Academy of Educational Sciences, and headed by Ewald Weiser. The GDR had been sending teachers and experts to selected developing countries, and Weiser's unit was designed to support this process from a scholarly viewpoint. Many written sources which originated from these activities stayed with individual experts who worked in developing countries and with the researchers, and only some of them were collected in the library of the Academy. Nevertheless, the German national agency for developmental co-operation, the Society for Technical Co-operation (Gesellschaft für Technische Zusammenarbeit), recognised the work of many development experts from the GDR.

The Third Period of Development

Although both communities of comparativists in Germany believed themselves to be operating on different intellectual grounds, their work displayed a certain parallelism due to their mutual reaction to each other. Kienitz's (1971) book *Uniformity and Differentiation in Education* stimulated and challenged the West German scholars, and contributed to the ambitious comparative projects of the 1970s. Also, the interest in developing countries had a parallelism. The West German academic community enjoyed the privilege of cooperating with the UNESCO Institute for Education founded in 1953 at Hamburg, whose directors Walther Merck and Gottfried Hausmann also held the chair for comparative education at Hamburg University. In addition, in 1963 Dietrich Goldschmidt became Director of the Max-Planck Institute in West Berlin, which later Saul B. Robinsohn also joined. Goldschmidt, like Merck and Hausmann, focused on education in developing countries. Other scholars in this domain included Hermann Röhrs and Volker Lenhart. Although the topic had existed in West German comparative education since the 1950s, it gained new momentum in the 1970s when the GDR comparativists also started to approach the theme in an organised way (Goldschmidt 1981).

In 1978, some members of the Commission for Comparative Education (KVEDGE) founded a new Commission within the German Society for Education, the Commission for Education with the Third World (Kommission Bildungsforschung mit der Dritten Welt). This was not a full break away from the community of comparativists, since many of the researchers oriented to the Third World retained their membership in the Commission for Comparative Education. However, it did indicate the wish to cultivate a different research culture. The name 'Third World' was meant programmatically in that it applied a self-conception by politicians in this group of countries, and the phrasing 'with' indicated a turn away from the illusion of objective comparative research from outside. It also became clear that the First and Second Worlds looked different when viewed from the Third World.

The discourses among the researchers oriented to the Third World were different from those among the comparativists. Comparison and the long term debate about methodology lost its appeal among the Third World group because the crucial question was about strategies for development. Neo-Marxist concepts were adopted in order to explain economic discrepancies between the First and Third Worlds, and the analysis of education was framed by political and socio-logical theories on power processes (Dias 1987; Jouhy 1988; Mergner 1998/1999). New concepts were elaborated like basic education, informal and non-formal education, human rights education, and global learning (Overwien 2000; Lenhart 2003). One of the hopes connected with the new organisational affiliation had been to access research funds from the federal ministry for international aid, since comparativists mostly aimed at the federal ministry of education. However, the relationship with the federal agency for international aid proved complex.

Although the name Education with the Third World was retained for nearly three decades, it became clear that the real topic had to be One World (Seitz 2002; Lang-Wojtasik & Lohrenscheit 2003; Scheunpflug 2003). Education in the Third World could not be investigated without analysing the relations among all three worlds, and the world as a whole had to be considered as an object of internationally-oriented research. Although this sounds more visionary than practical, it changed the outlook of the whole field including narrowly-defined comparative education.

In 2005, reflecting the fact that the two sections were in practice working together, the Commission for Comparative Education was reunited with the Commission for Education with the Third World. Wolfgang Mitter's presidency (1991-96) of the WCCES had been an influential factor, since Mitter himself and the role that he had played had conveyed a sense of global commitment to the German community of researchers in the field of comparative education.

Impetus for the merger was also provided by the work of Jürgen Schriewer from Humboldt University in Berlin. Schriewer critically examined the Stanford theory of world systems, and tried to modify it by applying an alternative approach. He moderated the assumption of growing worldwide uniformity, and emphasised the currents of regionalism and localism. Schriewer argued for a close connection between comparative education and the history of education, which he called a sociologically-enlightened type of historiography (see e.g. Schriewer 1987, 1994, 1999, 2000). The newly-formed section within the German Society for Education adopted the name Commission for International and Comparative Education, and during its short life before further merger was co-chaired by Gregor Lang-Wojtasik of Erlangen and Sabine Hornberg of Hamburg.

The Fourth Period of Development

During the fourth (overlapping) period, international and comparative education in Germany was brought into close contact with intercultural education. This field is dedicated to migration and its impact on education, and in Germany it had long been occupied with the issue of Turkish immigration. As this new field of research rapidly grew in the university schools of education, in 1992 an additional unit called Intercultural Education was formed in the German Society for Education.

Some researchers in this field have emphasised the decreasing significance for education of the nation state, and the emergence of new types of cultural amalgamation. They have challenged the tendencies of cultural homogenisation within the public school system, which they have suggested are based on a so-called monolingual habit of teachers and school officials (see e.g. Gogolin 1994). In response, researchers have addressed the curricula of several school subjects and have tried to reformulate the contents from a bicultural viewpoint. Nevertheless, the central role of the term culture has been questioned by some interculturalists because it might mislead sociological analysis into misinterpreting socio-economic discrepancies or even racist confrontations in society as cultural phenomena (see e.g. Hamburger 1994; Diehm & Radtke 1999).

Perhaps the prevalence of the term intercultural as opposed to multicultural in German educational theory points to a significant difference between research traditions in Germany compared with the USA and the UK, for example. Many German interculturalists aim at cultural and linguistic intermixes. This puts demanding expectations on the absorbing society, in which the majority might reject a challenge for change. Some theories of multiculturalism do not share this vision and instead aim at a peaceful coexistence.

In 1998, all three units within the German Society for Education which have been described here were combined into one section of the society. Its hybrid name was: Section for International and Intercultural Comparative Education (SIIVE). The society wanted to end the proliferation of commissions and groups, and pulled all of them together into 14 sections. SIIVE, having over 200 paying members, was a medium-sized section. The identities of comparativists, of researchers oriented towards the Third World, and of interculturalists were still recognised, but mutual interconnections were also noted. In 2005, the Section decided to take over membership in the WCCES from the former Commission for Comparative Education. The WCCES applied the acronym SIIVEDGE (Sektion International und Interkulturell Vergleichende Erziehungswissenschaft in der Deutschen Gesellschaft für Erziehungswissenschaft) to this restructured constituent society. Norbert Wenning from Hagen was President of the section from 1999 to 2002, and Dietmar Waterkamp from Dresden was President from 2002 to 2005.

Also to be noted is the strong foothold offered to comparativists in Germany by the International Association for the Evaluation of Educational Achievement (IEA) and the Organisation for Economic Co-operation and Development (OECD). One of the IEA founding members was T. Neville Postlethwaite, a British scholar who held a chair in comparative education at Hamburg University from 1976 to 1995 (Postlethwaite et al. 1980; Bos & Lehmann 1995). The results of IEA and OECD evaluative studies heightened public interest in international comparisons of educational systems. The OECD's Programme for International Student Assessment (PISA) aroused particular public interest, and gave a fresh impulse to comparative education (Döbert et al. 2004). In view of these developments, the SIIVE conferences in 2003 and 2005 were dedicated to this topic. Researchers in comparative education, Third World-related educational research and intercultural education could no longer afford to opt for only one of the three components. New discourses across former divisions emerged, with different styles of reasoning and also different vocabularies being brought together in new dialogues. The combination of the three components within the Section, which was not a merger but a coming together under one roof, was initially disputed but turned out to be a promising step. Both theoretical clarifications and curriculum development for university programmes which had not attracted much attention for some years were felt to be important again.

Conclusion

The field of comparative education in Germany has deep roots and a complex history. Some of the complexity, but also much of the vigour, arises from the political history of the country and especially the division and subsequent reunification of West and East Germany. This chapter has shown how the professional societies have evolved in conjunction with, and as a result of, wider developments. The time line in the Appendix helps to clarify some of the organisational changes, while also indicating the themes of KVEDGE and SIIVE conferences in specific years.

Close relationships between comparative education and other domains with the whole field of education have contributed to specialisations within comparative education which have originated from intersections of specific fields. Attention has been given in this chapter to education in developing countries and to intercultural education. Other examples include comparative vocational education, comparative adult education, and comparative special education. These branches have grown and it has mostly been specialists from those fields who have engaged in comparative work and who have invited comparativists to cooperate. These intersections are extremely important for the future of comparative education given the trend that all specialisations in education are building international networks. Conversely, some comparativists within the schools of education have begun to specialise in one of these applied disciplines in order to find partners and to demonstrate the usefulness of comparative education for educational tasks. This will be a long-term process of coming together, because it takes years to become familiar with one of these disciplines in sufficient depth as to yield fruitful comparative work.

Finally, it should be mentioned that the Society for Comparative Pedagogy (Gesellschaft für Vergleichende Pädagogik) which had been formed by Hans-Georg Hofmann and other researchers from East Germany in 1990 continued to exist as a small regional society. It collaborated with SIIVE in the 2002 conference on 'Comparative Education within the Structure of the Academic Field of Education'. Since most comparative education researchers from the former GDR had retired or left academe, this society was functioning as a network for young researchers in some universities of the former East Germany.

Appendix: Key Dates in KVEDGE and SIIVE History

March 1960:	Nine researchers met in Frankfurt and decided to form a loose working group for research on education in Eastern Europe. Among them were Leonhard Froese, Oskar Anweiler, Walter Schultze, Horst E. Wittig, Klaus Meyer, Siegfried Baske and Heinrich Abel.
May 1961:	Foundation of CESE in London. Ten German scholars participated and agreed to establish a German working group. They used the term 'comparative pedagogy' (Vergleichende Pädagogik). Among them were Franz Hilker and Friedrich Schneider, who were elected honorary members of CESE.
June 1961:	The working group for research on education in Eastern Europe met at Marburg, and Leonhard Froese recommended the participants also to join the recently-founded working group of comparativists in education. From then on, many researchers on education in Eastern Europe shared two affiliations: one with the community of researchers on Eastern Europe (in the German Society for Eastern European Studies, where they soon formed a section for education), the other with the community of comparativists in education.
German Democratic Republic 1963:	Department for Comparative Education (Vergleichende Pädagogik) established within the German Educational Central Institute in (East-) Berlin. Since 1958 there had existed only a Section for Education Abroad and in West Germany. Werner Kienitz became head of the new Department. It existed until 1974, when it became a Working Unit for Education Abroad, headed by Hans-Georg Hofmann.
February 1964:	Foundation of the Deutsche Gesellschaft für Erziehungswissenschaft (DGfE) [German Society for Education] in Frankfurt.
April 1965:	Meeting of the DGfE together with the West German Conference of Educationists at Universities (which later was merged into the DGfE) at Kassel. Franz Hilker proposed a Commission for Comparative Education in the DGfE (Kommission für Vergleichende Erziehungswissenschaft in der Deutschen Gesellschaft für Erziehungswissenschaft [KVEDGE]), which was positively received.
June 1965:	Third Conference of CESE, Berlin. German scholars decided to form KVEDGE.
April 1966:	Meeting of the DGfE together with the West German Conference of Educationists at Universities, Würzburg. The working group of comparativists in education formally became a commission within the society. The term Comparative Education (Vergleichende Erziehungswissenschaft) was used from now on instead of Comparative Pedagogy (Vergleichende Pädagogik). Leonhard Froese became the first head (President) of the Commission.
German Democratic Republic 1966:	Section for Comparative Education founded in the Scientific Council of the Ministry of Education. It was headed by Werner Kienitz and Horst Becker. It had research communities on West German Education and on Education Abroad, and working groups on developing countries, comparative education, socialist foreign countries, and capitalist countries.

January 1967:	First KVEDGE conference, Marburg, on 'Methodological Problems in Comparative Education'. 16 participating members of the Commission; 8 guests.
January 1968:	Conference on 'Methods in Comparative Education Exemplified by Ongoing Projects', Bochum.
January 1969:	Conference on 'Theory and Practice of Curriculum Development in Comparative Perspective'. Statutes formulated and agreed. KVEDGE understood itself not only as part of the DGfE, but also as a German group within CESE resembling the British group of comparativists that had been formed in CESE in 1965. Dual membership in both DGfE and CESE was seen as desirable, but membership in CESE alone gave status of an associated member with full rights in the Commission. CESE acknowledged only individual membership.
January 1970:	Conference on 'Planning and Administering Educational Reforms in Developing Countries with Explicit Consideration of Mutual Transferability between Industrialised and Developing Countries', Heidelberg.
February 1971:	Conference on 'Upper Secondary Schools and Problems of Transition into Higher Education', Frankfurt.
February 1972:	Conference on 'Methodological Questions in Comparative Education', Lüneburg.
February 1973:	Conference on 'Questions of Permanent Education', Münster.
February 1974:	Conference on 'Comparative Education in Higher Education Teaching', Berlin.
February 1975:	Conference on 'Comparative Education in Higher Education Teaching – Conclusions for the Curriculum', Oldenburg.
February 1976:	Conference on 'Methodological Problems in Comparative Education as seen in Three Recently Completed Projects', Marburg.
1976:	Members in the Commission for Comparative Education and other scholars who focused on education in developing countries formed the Working Group on German Education Research and International Education Research. In *1978* this became a new Commission of the DGfE, named Education with the Third World. First president: Karl-Heinz Flechsig, Göttingen. Some scholars were members in both Commissions. The new commission existed until 2005 when it was (re-) united with the Commission for Comparative Education.
February 1977:	Conference on 'Problems of Integrating General with Vocational Education from the Viewpoint of International Comparison', Hamburg.

[In the following years, KVEDGE sometimes abandoned the annual rhythm of conferences when it organised contributions to the biennial DGfE or CESE conferences.]

February 1979:	Conference on 'Comparative Education – An Interim Balance', Gießen.
February 1981:	Conference on 'International Tendencies in School Reforms – The Necessity of Humanising Schools', Neuss.

March 1982:	Conference on 'Education Between Cultures', Regensburg.
February 1985:	Conference on 'Comparative Aspects and International Reasoning in Academic Educational Disciplines', Münster.
March 1986:	Conference on 'New Comparative Studies Completed by Members of the Commission', Heidelberg.
March 1987:	Conference on 'Unity and Differentiation of Comparative Research in Different Fields of Research and Questions of Connecting Them', Frankfurt.
February 1989:	Conference on 'Comparative Educational Research and International Policy in Education', Frankfurt.
1990:	Hans-Georg Hofmann together with other researchers from East Germany formed the Society for Comparative Pedagogy (Gesellschaft für Vergleichende Pädagogik).
February 1991:	Conference on 'Educational Development in Germany in the European Context', Berlin.
1992:	The DGfE established a Working Group for Intercultural Education.
February 1993:	Conference on 'Regions of Europe – Challenges for Educational Policy and Research', Freiburg.
February 1995:	Conference on 'The Education System between Democratisation and Privatisation', Münster.
November 1997:	Common Conference of the Commission for Comparative Education, the Commission for Education with the Third World, the Working Group for Intercultural Education, and the Commission for Gender Research on 'The Problem of Understanding in Intercultural and International Comparative Educational Research and in Gender Research', Bonn.
March 1998:	Resolution of DGfE Assembly, Hamburg: The Commission for Comparative Education, the Commission for Education with the Third World and the Working Group for Intercultural Education together formed one of the 14 sections within the DGfE, becoming Section for International and Intercultural Comparative Education (SIIVE). It had three sub-sections: Commission for Comparative Education, Commission for Education with the Third World, and Commission for Intercultural Education.
February 1999:	SIIVE conference on 'Internationalisation in Education – New Profiles of Comparative Education and Intercultural Education', Münster.
February 2000:	SIIVE conference on 'Profiles and Quality Assurance in Teaching International and Intercultural Comparative Education', Münster.
February 2001:	SIIVE conference on 'Nation, Culture, Development: Theoretical Constructions and Operational Procedures in Educational Research', Münster.
October 2002:	Conference of the Commission for Comparative Education (together with the Society for Comparative Education which had been founded in 1990) on 'Comparative Education within the Structure of the Academic Field of Education', Dresden.
March 2003:	SIIVE conference on 'Research on International Educational Achievement as a Task for International and Intercultural Comparative Education', Soest.

November 2004:	Conference of the Commission for Comparative Education and the Commission for Education with the Third World on 'International and Comparative Education and Interdisciplinary Relations', Dresden.
March 2005:	SIIVE conference on 'Educational and Political Relevance and Acceptance of International Research on Educational Achievement', Münster.
March 2005:	Resolution in Münster of the full assembly of SIIVE to unite the Commission for Comparative Education and the Commission for Education with the Third World. Name of the new body: Commission for Comparative and International Education.
	Resolution of the full assembly of SIIVE to make SIIVE as a whole the German member society of the WCCES.

References

Anweiler, Oscar (1964): *Geschichte der Schule und Pädagogik in Rußland vom Ende des Zarenreiches bis zum Beginn der Stalin-Ära.* Heidelberg: Verlag Quelle und Meyer.

Berger, Walter (1976): *Die Vergleichende Erziehungswissenschaft: Einführung – Forschungsskizzen – Methoden.* Wien: Jugend und Volk Verlag.

Blumenthal, Viktor von (ed.) (1975): *Qualifizierung und wissenschaftlich-technischer Fortschritt am Beispiel der Sekundarschulreform in ausgewählten Industriestaaten.* Ravensburg: Maier.

Bos, Wilfried & Lehmann, Rainer H. (eds.) (1995): *Reflections on Educational Achievement: Papers in Honour of T. Neville Postlethwaite to Mark the Occasion of his Retirement from the Chair in Comparative Education at the University of Hamburg.* Münster: Waxmann.

Busch, Adelheid (1983): *Die Vergleichende Pädagogik in der DDR: Eine disziplingeschichtliche Untersuchung.* München: Johannes Berchmans Verlag.

Busch, Adelheid (ed.) (1984): *Suche nach Identität: Isabella Rüttenauer zum 75. Geburtstag.* Oldenburg: Verlag BIS.

Dias, Patrick V. (ed.) (1987): *Rediscovery of Education as 'Alternative Education' in the 'Third World'.* Frankfurt: IKO Verlag.

Diehm, Isabell & Radtke, Frank-Olaf (1999): *Erziehung und Migration: Eine Einführung.* Stuttgart: Kohlhammer Verlag.

Döbert, Hans; Klieme, Eckhard & Sroka, Wendelin (eds.) (2004): *Conditions of School Performance in Seven Countries: A Quest for Understanding the International Variation of PISA Results.* Münster: Waxmann Verlag.

Froese, Leonhard (1952): 'Sergius Hessens methodologischer Beitrag'. *Bildung und Erziehung,* Vol.5, pp.193-197.

Froese, Leonhard (1962): *Schule und Gesellschaft.* Weinheim: Beltz Verlag.

Glowka, Detlef & Braun, Frank (1975): *Schulreform und Gesellschaft: vergleichende Studien über die gesellschaftlichen Bedingungen von Schulreformen in sieben europäischen Ländern.* Berlin: Max-Planck Institut für Bildungsforschung.

Gogolin, Ingrid (1994): *Der monolinguale Habitus der multilingualen Schule.* Münster: Waxmann Verlag.

Goldschmidt, Dietrich (ed.) (1981): *Die Dritte Welt als Gegenstand erziehungswissenschaftlicher Forschung. Interdisziplinäre Studien über den Stand der Wissenschaft. Berichte, Besprechungen, Bibliographie.* Weinheim: Beltz Verlag.

Hamburger, Franz (1994): *Pädagogik der Einwanderungsgesellschaft.* Frankfurt:

Cooperative Verlag.

Hilker, Franz (1962): *Vergleichende Pädagogik. Eine Einführung in ihre Geschichte, Theorie und Praxis.* München: Max Hüber Verlag.

John, Bernd (1998): *Ideologie und Pädagogik: zur Geschichte der Vergleichenden Pädagogik in der DDR.* Köln: Böhlau Verlag.

Jouhy, Ernest (1988): *Klärungsprozesse: Gesammelte Schriften.* Frankfurt: Athenäum.

Kienitz, Werner (ed.) (1971): *Einheitlichkeit und Differenzierung im Bildungswesen: Ein Vergleich.* Berlin: Volk und Wissen.

Lang-Wojtasik, Gregor & Lohrenscheit, Claudia (eds.) (2003): *Entwicklungspädagogik – Globales Lernen – Internationale Bildungsforschung: 25 Jahre ZEP.* Frankfurt: Verlag für Interkulturelle Kommunikation.

Lenhart, Volker (2003): *Pädagogik der Menschenrechte.* Opladen: Leske und Budrich.

Mergner, Gottfried (1998/1999): *Ausgewählte Schriften.* Hamburg: Argument Verlag.

Mitter, Wolfgang (ed.) (1976): *Sekundarabschlüsse mit Hochschulreife im internationalen Vergleich: Ergebnisse einer Untersuchung über Bildungssysteme sozialistischer Staaten.* Weinheim: Beltz Verlag.

Mitter, Wolfgang (ed.) (1983): *Kann die Schule erziehen? Erfahrungen, Probleme und Tendenzen im europäischen Vergleich.* Köln: Böhlau Verlag.

Mitter, Wolfgang (ed.) (1994): *Die Zeitdimension in der Schule als Gegenstand des Bildungsvergleichs.* Köln: Böhlau Verlag.

Overwien, Bernd (ed.) (2000): *Lernen und Handeln im globalen Kontext. Beiträge zu Theorie und Praxis internationaler Erziehungswissenschaft. Zur Erinnerung an Wolfgang Karcher.* Frankfurt: Verlag für Interkulturelle Kommunikation.

Postlethwaite, T. Neville; Weiler, Hans & Roeder, Peter M. (eds.) (1980): *Schulen im Leistungsvergleich: Bedingungen für ein erfolgreiches Lernen – Ergebnisse der internationalen IEA – Untersuchungen in sechs Unterrichtsfächern.* Stuttgart: Klett-Cotta.

Robinsohn, Hilde (ed.) (1992): *Comparative Education: A Basic Approach. A Selection of Writings by Saul B. Robinsohn.* Jerusalem: The Magnes Press, Hebrew University.

Röhrs, Hermann (1975): *Forschungsstrategien der Vergleichenden Erziehungs-wissenschaft: Eine Einführung in die Probleme der Vergleichenden Erziehungs-wissenschaft.* Weinheim: Beltz Verlag.

Röhrs, Hermann (1983): *Frieden: eine pädagogische Aufgabe. Idee und Realität der Friedenspädagogik.* Braunschweig: Westermann Verlag.

Röhrs, Hermann (1995): *Der Weltbund für Erneuerung der Erziehung. Wirkungs-geschichte und Zukunftsperspektiven.* Weinheim: Deutscher Studien Verlag.

Scheunpflug, Annette (2003): 'Die Entwicklung zur globalen Weltgesellschaft als Herausforderung für das menschliche Lernen', in Lang-Wojtasik, Gregor & Lohrenscheit, Claudia (eds.), *Entwicklungspädagogik – Globales Lernen – Inter-nationale Bildungsforschung: 25 Jahre ZEP.* Frankfurt: Verlag für Interkulturelle Kommunikation, pp.129-140.

Schneider, Friedrich (1957): *Katholische Familienerziehung.* Freiburg: Herder Verlag.

Schneider, Friedrich (1961): *Vergleichende Erziehungswissenschaft: Geschichte, Forschung, Lehre.* Heidelberg: Quelle und Meyer.

Schriewer, Jürgen (1987): 'Vergleich als Methode und Externalisierung auf Welt: Vom Umgang mit Alterität in Reflexionsdisziplinen', in Baecker, Dirk et al. (eds.) *Theorie als Passion: Niklas Luhmann zum 60. Geburtstag.* Frankfurt: Suhrkamp, pp.629-668.

Schriewer, Jürgen (1994): 'Internationalisierung der Pädagogik und Vergleichende Erziehungswissenschaft', in Müller, Detlef K. (ed.), *Pädagogik – Erziehungs-*

wissenschaft – Bildung. Eine Einführung in das Studium. Köln: Böhlau, pp.407-426.

Schriewer, Jürgen (1999): 'Vergleich und Erklärung zwischen Kausalität und Komplexität', in Kaelble, Hartmut & Schriewer, Jürgen (eds.), *Diskurse und Entwicklungspfade – Gesellschaftsvergleiche in Geschichts – und Sozialwissenschaften*. Frankfurt: Campus, pp.53-102.

Schriewer, Jürgen (ed.) (2000): *Discourse Formation in Comparative Education*. Frankfurt: Peter Lang.

Seitz, Klaus (2002): *Bildung in der Weltgesellschaft: Gesellschaftstheoretische Grundlagen Globalen Lernens*. Frankfurt: Brandes & Apsel.

Waterkamp, Dietmar (1977): Differenzierung als ein internationales Problem der Schulreform. Zum Berliner Projekt. 'Schulreform im gesellschaftlichen Prozeß. Ein interkultureller Vergleich'. *Die Deutsche Schule*, Vol.69, pp.307-315.

Waterkamp, Dietmar (ed.) (2004): *Vergleichende Pädagogik und europäische Wege der Bildung: Festschrift für Klaus-Dieter Mende zum 65. Geburtstag*. Dresden: Verlag Hille.

Willmann, Bodo (ed.) (1995): *Bildungsreform und Vergleichende Erziehungswissenschaft: Aktuelle Probleme – Historische Perspektiven. Leonhard Froese zum Gedenken*. Münster: Waxmann Verlag.

13

The British Association for International and Comparative Education (BAICE)

Margaret B. SUTHERLAND, Keith WATSON &
Michael CROSSLEY

The British society for the study of comparative education has shown flexibility, and readiness to adapt to contemporary developments, by a number of name changes over the decades. Initially it was the British Section of the Comparative Education Society in Europe (CESE); then the British Comparative Education Society (BCES); the British Comparative and International Education Society (BCIES); and since 1997 the British Association for International and Comparative Education (BAICE). The British Section of CESE was represented in Ottawa, Canada, at the 1970 conference which led to the establishment of the World Council of Comparative Education Societies (WCCES), and the Council has received with equanimity its subsequent changes of designation.

This chapter documents the origins, history, rationale and activities of the British society. It explores the influence of key personnel and changing fortunes in the light of related shifts in the professional and intellectual context in recent decades. The history also shows how, in recent years, the society has contributed to a resurgence of interest in comparative and international research in education, to emergent trends in policy analysis, theory and methodology, and to creative and stimulating collaborations with related agencies including the WCCES itself.

Origins and Early Years
In the Britain of the 1960s, the prospects for the study of education, and specifically for comparative education, looked bright. The Robbins Report on the future of higher education in the UK seemed to predict the creative expansion and development of higher education, including exciting prospects for the higher education of teachers (Robbins 1963). The potential growth of courses in comparative education, not only in university departments of education, but also for Bachelor of Education (BEd) students at the college level, seemed to be the beginning of a positive new era. Unfortunately this period was relatively short-lived.

Certainly there was a feeling of optimism, even of exhilaration, among participants at a conference at the University of Reading in September 1965 on 'The Place of Comparative Education in the Training of Teachers' (Mercier 1966). In 1961 a group of specialists in comparative education had already met in London to found CESE. This European society was at that time a small and rather exclusive body, largely being the preserve of specialist researchers, but some of its members also contributed greatly to the success of the 1965 conference at the University of Reading. Some 70 participants met in Reading, with a fairly even distribution from university departments of education and from colleges of education that focussed entirely on the training of teachers. This core of people resolved to found a comparative education society, of which the constitution and formal membership would be determined at a further conference to be held in Reading in the following year. Participants who wished to do so were then to be enrolled as foundation members. At the suggestion of Brian Holmes of the University of London Institute of Education, it was agreed that this new society would be a section of CESE, though few people believed that any problems would be likely to arise if, in Holmes' phrase, this British organisation were to 'go it alone'. The British society has diverged considerably over the years from its European parent body particularly in embracing a more international and development orientation.

The British Section of CESE was thus duly established at the conference held at the University of Reading in September 1966. It was perhaps an indication of the awareness of the common interests of both the university and college constituencies that the first Chair, N.K. Growcott, came from a college of education (Bolton), while the first Vice-Chair, Margaret B. Sutherland, came from a university department of education (Queen's University, Belfast). When Margaret B. Sutherland became Chair of the society in 1968, the next Vice-Chair, H. Gillmann, also came from a college of education (Doncaster). This alternation between the two sectors of higher education lasted until 1980, when representatives from university departments of education began to dominate. The shift reflected changes in the climate of higher education.

Aims of the New Society

The aims of the new society were indicated to a considerable extent by the eight addresses presented at the 1965 conference. Joseph Lauwerys, of the University of London Institute of Education, outlined the history of the study of comparative education, downplaying the French (and positivistic) influence of Jullien (1817), and emphasising the more socio-cultural and historical orientations pioneered in England by Matthew Arnold and Michael Sadler (Higginson 1979). Other speakers provided not only statements of the benefits likely to result from the study of comparative education, but also possible methods of study and research, with examples of provisions then being made in different countries. For example, Vernon Mallinson of the University of Reading included in his discussion of the potential of comparative education, a plea for the study of small countries such as

Belgium in addition to the customary attention given to large countries such as the USA, France and the USSR. This issue has remained important. It has been picked up by other British comparative educators as concerns have increased about the growing influence of multilateral organisations, such as the World Bank, that underplay the importance of context sensitivity and differences in scale (Bacchus & Brock 1987; Bray & Packer 1993; Crossley & Holmes 1999). Brian Holmes spoke about research strategies and his own problem approach to comparative study (Holmes 1965). W.R. Fraser (Woodbroke College, Birmingham) outlined the possibilities of the area studies approach; W.D. Halls (University of Oxford) commented on the potential of field studies; and Edmund King (King's College, University of London) favoured an applied orientation to comparative studies. The other two speakers focused on how teaching could be adapted to different types of students of comparative education. Ken Smart (University of Reading) discussed the characteristics and needs of overseas students, especially from the Third World, and C.H. Dobinson (also University of Reading) considered the particular needs of students taking the new BEd courses.

More than one speaker referred to the beneficial effects expected from the study of comparative education. The main emphasis was on insights into the social forces determining education systems, echoing the views expressed by Sadler at the beginning of the 20th century (Sadler 1900). Discussing the question of the academic respectability of the field, Lauwerys recognised the potential of contributions from specialists in other forms of educational studies – history, sociology and economics. He nevertheless concluded (Mercier 1966, p.31) that students of comparative education:

> would begin to see more clearly how social forces shape educational systems and practices. In this way they would gain insight into the nature and function of their own – and perhaps be less dominated by routine and tradition because they would see that these are not always justifiable rationally.

Vernon Mallinson (cited in Mercier 1966, pp.33-34) similarly affirmed that the student of comparative education must:

> accept … the implication of the cultural background of the society in which he lives.… He (sic) must know what limits are set to his freedom and what are the limits of his creative potential in terms of the whole culture pattern. He must know about other culture patterns, how they arose, and what limiting factors they in turn impose. The student will come to recognise different solutions to common problems, and arrive at a better understanding of nationalism (the role of the schools in fostering 'national sentiments') and internationalism, as well as international co-operation. Comparative education properly taught must, by constructively challenging the myths and objectively assessing a given culture pattern, lead to more effective international understanding and to a greater measure of communication.

Unlike previous, and future, generations of comparativists, the speakers at Reading gave little attention to the possibility of improving one's own educational system as a result of comparative studies. W.D. Halls, however, having warned of the need to ensure academic independence and integrity by avoiding "being too involved with official agencies" (Mercier 1966, p.110) while carrying out research, did emphasise that independent comparative education research might indicate to policy-makers the probable results of proposed changes in their provision of education. Halls was prescient in this respect since this issue has exercised the minds of many British comparativists – especially because so much comparative and international research has been funded by governments and international agencies (Preston & Arthur 1996; McGrath 2001a, 2001b).

Various speakers at the Reading conference also exhorted researchers to ensure that comparative education would be studied not simply through documents and statistics but also by visits and study tours that generated personal knowledge of the cultures and systems in question. Such background knowledge could be increased, Mallinson suggested, by the reading of fiction or other books written in the country being studied. He developed this 'humanities inspired' approach in an article published in the journal *Comparative Education* (Mallinson 1968). For similar reasons, Halls suggested the need to be proficient in a foreign language, though the ideal that he indicated – four European languages in addition to English – was perhaps somewhat over-ambitious. This interpretive/hermeneutic concern for differences in cultural context added considerably to the existing stock of research strategies and priorities that writers such as Bereday (1964) advocated in his then influential book on *Comparative Method in Education*.

A final observation from the inaugural conference in Reading was made by W.R. Fraser. He argued that, in addition to the possible enlightenment that could result from increased awareness of other cultures and the many facets of social life that could be taken into account, one other aspect had run throughout all the discussions at Reading in 1965, namely that comparative and international studies "are, most of the time, not just bewildering, but also very enjoyable!" (cited in Mercier 1966, p.108). The Reading Conference thus marked an enthusiastic and vibrant start for the British society, and reflected the influence of strong, applied, historical and humanistic traditions that have continued to shape much of its intellectual spirit and landscape.

Changing Contexts and Changing Constituencies

Once established, the British Section of CESE thrived. The list of the themes chosen for annual conferences provides a conspectus of the key topics engaging the interest of British comparative educators. They included reforms in secondary education; the changing school curriculum; trends in teacher education; priorities in educational planning; the politics of education; higher education reform; and education in multicultural societies. Initially, the venues for the annual conferences alternated between Reading and other selected universities. Gradually, however the choice of venue came to depend more on whoever was willing and able to organise and host the conference rather than deliberately alternating the venue (Brock 1986a).

Significant changes during the 1970s and 1980s had a lasting impact on the nature and shape of comparative education in the UK. First among these was the Conservative government's 1972 White Paper, 'A Framework for Expansion' (Department of Education & Science 1972). Although this document foresaw an expansion in nursery, technical and vocational education, within two years the trends it had set in motion led to the closure and/or merger of many UK colleges of higher education. This was partly due to a predicted drop in population growth, but was compounded by the educational and financial crisis of the mid-1970s. Such was the perceived state of education that in 1976, Prime Minister James Callaghan launched what came to be known as the Great Education Debate, an examination of what kind of education system the country needed for a post-industrial future.

Unfortunately many of the positive ideas and hopes generated were dashed by a financial crisis that hit Britain in 1977. Inevitably this led to a squeeze on funds for higher education, not least for teacher education, and to the beginning of tighter regulation on the education of teachers (McDade 1982; Brock 1986b). This continued in subsequent decades, and by the time of Watson's (1982) study of the state of comparative education in 'British Teacher Education', it had become apparent that traditional teaching in the comparative field of study was being squeezed out from colleges of education and was barely surviving in some universities. Watson wrote (1982, pp.196-197) that:

> there has been a crisis of confidence in the value of comparative education as well as its place in educational institutions. While there has undoubtedly been much valuable research work undertaken during the 1970s, there was a considerable sense of gloom and despondency in the 'state of the art' issue of *Comparative Education* in June 1977, largely because of cutbacks in funding for research and travel, both essential ingredients for the further-ance of practical and realistic studies in comparative education.... For far too many teachers and administrators, comparative education is regarded as an interesting luxury, a 'frill', but an unnecessary ingredient for a common core teacher education curriculum.

By the mid-1980s, therefore, not only was comparative education in decline in the UK (as were other 'foundation studies'), but this had had a detrimental impact on membership of the national society.

Another influence on the development of the field and the society was the decision by Holmes and a group of supporters in London to establish the London Association of Comparative Educationists (LACE) in the mid-1970s. To what extent micro-political motives relating to leadership of the British Section of CESE or intellectual disagreements over research priorities and methodology inspired this organisational conflict will probably never be known. From an intellectual standpoint, the dispute over territory nevertheless reflected differing views over the nature and direction for British comparative research and ongoing tensions between positivistic trends and more interpretive traditions. LACE conducted some interesting work, mainly on methodology and theory (Turner 2004). It continued for about a decade, but its existence was partly instrumental in the decision taken at the 14th Annual Conference of the British Section of CESE, held at the University of Bath in 1979, to form a separate British Comparative Education Society (BCES).

The BCES existed for only a few years before its title was again changed. In 1983, under the Chair of Keith Watson (University of Reading) and the Vice-Chair of Colin Brock (University of Hull), the decision was taken by an overwhelming majority to change the society's name to the British Comparative and International Education Society (BCIES). This reflected the growth of the international development constituency and the increased significance of its contextual and professional focus (Watson & King 1991). Some comparativists, especially in London, opposed the move, but the vast majority of members understood the reasoning behind the decision. A similar (and also controversial) name change had been made in 1968 in the US-based society.

In short, the introduction of the word 'International' into the name of the society was an acknowledgement of changing geopolitical and intellectual realities. Since the 1950s there had been an emerging division between the work of those who saw themselves primarily as comparativists, mainly concerned with the industrialised nations, and those who worked in the newly independent developing countries. For example, when the Colonial Department (later the Department of Education in Tropical Areas and, later still, the Department of Education in Developing Countries) was established at the University of London Institute of Education in 1927, its main concern was to support good policy and practice in the colonies (Little 2004). The comparativists based in London as part of the Department of Comparative Education, on the other hand, predominantly focused on Europe, North America, the Soviet Union and Japan. Two distinct but parallel fields of study were thus emerging. The latter, comparative education, emphasised theory, methodology, and research in industrialised countries, while those involved in the study of education and development emphasised the improvement of educational planning, policy and practice in the developing world. The latter were often less concerned with theory and more focused upon the practicalities of what worked on the ground in poor countries, drawing evidence from different contexts with which they were familiar. Influential British scholars such as Edmund King (1967, 1989) made efforts to bridge the gulf between such groups, and pioneered ways in which the two sub-fields could work together. The division nevertheless continued to influence developments in the field in the UK.

Moreover, as more colonies gained their independence during the 1960s, and as the Commonwealth Secretariat together with the British Council began sending scholars to the UK to take courses in educational policy-making and planning, educational administration, science education, English language teaching, technical and vocational education, and rural development, a significant shift in both the student body and the focus of funding began to take place. Student numbers from poor countries were growing faster in the international education field than those from the rich and industrialised world. Government departments, such as the UK Ministry of Overseas Development (ODM) (later the Department for International Development, DFID), together with the British Council, decided to designate 10 universities and three colleges of education (technical) as special 'centres of excellence' for such work. Inevitably those 10 universities began recruiting staff who had had developing-country experience. Many of these staff became members of the British Section of CESE and the BCES. Eventually they outnumbered the more theoretically oriented comparativists, and began to argue that the methodology and research techniques of comparative education should be applied more internationally to the developing world. In many ways such developments were supported by work being pioneered in the USA on modernisation theory and its challenges in the form of dependency perspectives. The name BCIES was, therefore, seen to be a more appropriate title for much of the work and research interests of the UK constituency at this time.

Society News and Communications: The Birth of *Compare*

From 1969 onwards, attempts to keep members of the society informed of ongoing developments were strengthened by the circulation of a bulletin three or four times a year. Initially this was a modest, cyclostyled document that offered news of members' activities, arrangements for study tours, book reviews, and other materials. The scope of the bulletin grew to include, for example, proposals for a research project on school textbooks in different countries, and responses to a questionnaire asking members for information about books and visual aids used in their courses on comparative education. It was also in this Bulletin that members received from the then Chair, Margaret B. Sutherland (1971), a report on the 1st World Congress of Comparative Education Societies held in Ottawa, Canada, in 1970, and on the proposal made there to create "a Council and a continuing Congress". Later issues highlighted the 3rd World Congress of Comparative Education Societies, held at the University of London Institute of Education in 1977. This event was organised by the main body of CESE rather than by the British Section of CESE, and was both the 3rd World Congress and the 8th biennial CESE Congress.

From the modest publication of the Bulletin, there developed a more scholarly production, the journal *Compare*. This became the official journal of the British society in 1970. Initially *Compare* was published by a small firm in Liverpool called Dejall and Meyorre. This publisher kept changing the size of the volumes, and although the content of some papers was extremely good, university libraries found it hard to find the appropriate shelf space. In 1976, *Compare* was taken over by Carfax Publishers in Oxford, and it has since evolved into one of the leading, internationally peer-reviewed journals in the field. The Founding Editor was Leon Boucher of Chester College. A useful history of "*Compare*" was written by Higginson (2001) and is available elsewhere. The journal expanded from two to three issues per year in 1992, and from three to four issues in 2003. With the

Taylor and Francis Group's subsequent incorporation of Carfax, the quality of production and marketing contributed much strategic support for *Compare*; and this in turn assisted the growth and robustness of BAICE.

Initially, it seemed as if the new journal would include with its scholarly articles, the types of communications with members which the original bulletin had provided. Certainly the production of the separate bulletin fell into abeyance in the mid-1970s. However, in 1981 this kind of communication was revived in the form of an annual Newsletter which contained information on members' activities, conferences and projects, and book reviews. This series continued until 1989. More recently, communication with members has been through an annual Chairperson's letter which provides information about changes in the society, past and forthcoming conferences, and the like. In due course, e-mail and the website (www.baice.ac.uk) became more important.

Numerous other publication developments for BCES/BCIES took place from the 1980s. Reports of the annual conferences, including the papers delivered during them, had been published in cyclostyled format from 1966 to 1979, much like the regular conference reports from CESE. However, beginning in 1981 the annual conference papers were published in book form by Croom Helm publishers. The themes that commanded attention at this stage included: Politics and Educational Change (1981); Changing Priorities in Teacher Education (1982); Youth, Education and Employment (1983); Dependence and Interdependence in Education (1983); Education in Multicultural Societies (1984); and International Academic Interchange and Co-operation in Higher Education (1987). When Croom Helm was absorbed into a larger publishing house, this arrangement ceased and conference papers were produced by the host institution for each annual conference. After the late 1990s, Symposium Books in Oxford published some of the society's annual conference papers. Occasional papers from one-day seminars have often been reproduced in simpler format, made available in web-based forms, or published in *Compare* or related journals. Indeed, the work of members has long been represented in the wider educational literature, and in other comparative and international journals and books. The journal *Comparative Education*, for example, was founded in the UK in 1964 and it has developed a distinguished profile of its own, led by key figures from CESE, BCES, BCIES and BAICE (see Crossley et al. 2007).

Alliances, Mergers and Renewed Growth

Running parallel to the above developments was the British Association of Teachers and Researchers in Overseas Education (BATROE). This body brought together academics who were involved in teaching this sub-field, together with some of their students. BATROE also sought to hold annual conferences where both scholarly papers were presented and pastoral matters pertaining to the many Commonwealth and British Council scholars could be addressed. The British Council was always well represented, and the Chief Education Adviser at the ODM usually talked about government thinking on educational aid and development. Most of the students attending these meetings were taking diploma or master's courses in the UK.

During the 1980s and early 1990s, two government policy changes had a major impact on the position of overseas students. In the early 1980s, the Conservative government courted anger from the academic community by developing a policy towards overseas students whereby they were expected to pay 'full-cost' fees. This policy was seen to discriminate against poor international students and to tarnish Britain's enviable reputation for dealing equally with overseas students. Following a public outcry, students from Hong Kong, Malaysia, Cyprus and the European Union (EU) were exempted from the increased fees for a period of three years. The policy paper on the 'Power of Change' (Overseas Development Administration 1992), then advocated a reduction in the number of Commonwealth and British Council scholars coming to the UK for long courses. Instead it recommended that they should be trained in another developing country. This policy paper was widely criticised for its short-sightedness and its likely impact on British higher education (Watson 1994). Given these policy changes, it was inevitable that the size and influence of BATROE itself would decline. Thus both BCIES and BATROE were facing major challenges at about the same time.

In 1979, two Birmingham businessmen/project management consultants, the Ozanne brothers, decided to launch a new education journal, the *International Journal of Educational Development*, to fill a perceived niche in the market. They were concerned about the cynicism that they encountered in the developing countries with regard to the so-called 'experts' who arrived for brief visits and then felt able to write definitive reports. They were also concerned that the importance of education in the development discourse was being squeezed out by economists. They therefore aimed to publish a journal containing articles based on research into policy and practice in the developing world which might influence policy-makers. The first two volumes of the journal were published by W.I. Ozanne and Associates Ltd., and were printed by a firm in Hong Kong, but it became apparent that this system was economically not viable. Bill Ozanne, therefore, approached Pergamon Press in Oxford to see if they would like to add the journal to their social science portfolio. They agreed enthusiastically, beginning with Volume 3, Number 1. Elsevier Science Ltd. later took over the Pergamon imprimatur and continued to publish the journal, which is now recognised as one of the leaders in the field. Both this journal and *Comparative Education* are available to members of BAICE at reduced subscription rates, and in the case of *Comparative Education*, to individual members of some constituent societies of the WCCES. To celebrate the first 10 years of the *International Journal of Educational Development*, it was agreed to host a conference in Oxford. Thus the first International Oxford Conference on Education and Development was held in September 1989 and attracted over 80 participants from 26 different countries (Watson 1990).

Meanwhile, several academics and individuals concerned about the apparent decline in the number of British personnel involved in international education met to see how to increase collaboration between the different constituent groups. The key figures were Beverley Young (British Council), Peter

Williams (Commonwealth Secretariat), Kenneth King (University of Edinburgh), and Keith Watson (University of Reading). Bill Ozanne was also involved in later discussions. These discussions led to the creation of the United Kingdom Forum for International Education and Training (UKFIET), which eventually brought together professional associations such as BCIES, BATROE and BALID (British Association for Literacy in Development); non-governmental organisations such as Education for Development, Action Aid and Oxfam; and agencies such as the British Council, DFID and the Commonwealth Secretariat, to share ideas and organise a biennial international conference on education and development (Watson and King, 1991). It was agreed that, in addition to organising Oxford conferences, UKFIET would hold colloquia/ seminars on key educational issues. The underlying idea was that while organisations such as BCIES and BATROE would continue to hold their own annual conferences in one year, they would benefit from coming together every second year as part of a larger event. This would include delegates from international bodies such as the World Bank, UNESCO, DFID and the EU together with academics and researchers from around the world.

The first UKFIET-sponsored Oxford International Conference on Education and Development (though in reality it was the second such event), was held in 1991. Since then it has gained in importance and prestige with the result that the seventh conference in 2003 had over 400 delegates from over 70 countries and the eighth one in 2005 was larger still. These biennial conferences had clearly become an important landmark for both British and international scholars and practitioners involved in comparative, international and development education (see www. ukfiet.org).

The success of UKFIET and the first two Oxford conferences thus facilitated closer co-operation between different groups involved in comparative and international education in the UK. It also coincided with major changes in funding for educational research, moves towards greater collaboration between institutions and organisations, and the decline in funding for overseas students. With the obvious benefits of such alliances, negotiations took place during the mid-1990s between the officials of BATROE and BCIES to combine as a new and larger association of interested professionals. Rosemary Preston (University of Warwick), the then Chair of BCIES, together with Thelma Henderson (also of the University of Warwick), the then Chair of BATROE, Bill Ozanne, the Secretary of both UKFIET and BATROE, Peter Williams (formerly Commonwealth Secretariat), and Keith Watson, the then Chair of UKFIET, undertook to draw up a new constitution for a reformulated society. This was achieved in September 1997, and the new name was confirmed as the British Association for International and Comparative Education (BAICE). This was ratified at the inaugural BAICE conference at the University of Reading in September 1998.

Looking back, it was highly appropriate that Reading should have been the venue for the first BAICE conference since this was another new beginning and it was here that the original British Section of CESE had been formed in 1966. Moreover, the three keynote papers prepared for the inaugural conference collectively formed a launch symposium appropriately titled 'Reconceptualising Comparative and International Education'. This was convened by Michael Crossley (University of Bristol), Keith Watson (University of Reading) and Rosemary Preston (University of Warwick), and contributed much to the intellectual rationale that underpinned the formation of BAICE itself. Indeed Crossley (2000) and Crossley and Watson (2003) subsequently developed these themes, building on the efforts of earlier generations of UK comparativists, to encourage greater co-operation between 'comparative' and 'international' colleagues and constituencies. They have also articulated ways in which a fundamental 'reconceptualisation' of the field could be pursued further in theoretical, methodological, substantive and organisational terms. Selected papers from the inaugural BAICE conference were published first in Volume 29, Number 3 of *Compare* (1999), and subsequently in a book edited by the conference convenor (Watson 2001).

The renewed aims of BAICE reflected the combined traditions upon which it was founded. To cite the official society brochure (2004, p.2), the association aimed to encourage the growth and development of international and comparative studies in education by:

- promoting teaching and cross-disciplinary research;
- facilitating research publication;
- networking with other professionals and professional organisations;
- supporting students;
- organising conferences and meetings; and
- being a resource to policy makers.

A new constitution was introduced in 1997. The BAICE Executive Committee, elected by the full membership, normally meets three times a year, and an elected Chair and Vice-Chair each hold office for two-year periods. The Vice-Chair normally succeeds the Chair, to maintain continuity. A President is also elected annually, the main role being the presentation of a Presidential Address at the annual conference. While the Executive Committee deals with most ongoing society business, an Annual General Meeting held during the conference ratifies key decisions and provides further representation and guidance. An honorary BAICE Secretary provides administrative support. Over the years, therefore, many traditions and structures first developed for the British Section of CESE have been maintained, though working procedures have been formalised and systematised, reflecting increasing transparency and organisational maturity.

Further Developments

Reflecting renewed national and international interest in comparative and international research throughout the social sciences, worldwide as well as UK membership of BAICE has grown steadily, and research student engagement has been especially noticeable. Since 2005 the BAICE Executive Committee has included a research student representative, and other student members have played a key role as Membership Secretaries. Regular day conferences have increasingly been targeted at student members. These include the first joint day conference of BAICE and the British Educational Research Association (BERA) on 'Globalisation, Culture and Comparative Education', held at the University of Bristol in 2003, and a dedicated BAICE/BERA research student event at the University of Oxford in 2004. BAICE has thus continued to reach out to other research constituencies – including UKFIET, the UK Academy for Learned Societies in the Social Sciences, research councils, and several non-governmental organisations. Most teaching in the field is now focussed at the postgraduate level, and related closely to research and consultancy work; but the BAICE constituency continues to grow. Nevertheless, within the society much remains to be done. For example, a formal archive would be a considerable asset and remains a priority for future development.

Links with the WCCES have always been strong. Brian Holmes, Professor of Comparative Education at the University of London Institute of Education was a founder member of the WCCES and its second President (1974-77). Edmund King, Professor of Education at the University of London King's College, was also a founder member of the WCCES and Chairperson of the Research Committee (1987-89). These distinguished figures in the field of comparative education later served as Co-opted Members of the WCCES and remained as active and valued founder members until the end of their lives. Raymond Ryba, from the University of Manchester, was the third Secretary General for a long period (1983-96). Mark Bray, who had joined the British Section of CESE in 1978 while teaching at the University of Edinburgh, remained a member of the society in its various manifestations after his move to the University of Hong Kong (via the Universities of Papua New Guinea and London) in 1986. In 1994 he was appointed WCCES Assistant Secretary General to work with Raymond Ryba; in 2000 he became the fifth Secretary General; and in 2004 he was elected the 10th President of the WCCES. David Turner of the University of Glamorgan, who had been Assistant Secretary General from 1982 to 1985, became Chair of the WCCES Finance Standing Committee in 1997 and WCCES Treasurer in 2000; and Rosemary Preston of the University of Warwick played a major role in the 2004 12th World Congress in Cuba, in her capacity as Chair of the WCCES Congress Standing Committee. BAICE contributed funds to this very successful event which were earmarked for young scholars facing financial hardship.

Factors that have influenced the contemporary revitalisation of the field include changing geopolitical relations that have reshaped global politics and challenged dominant world views; the intensification of globalisation that has transformed priorities and perspectives worldwide; and paradigmatic developments that draw increased attention to the importance of cultural and contextual differences. More specifically, international competition has heightened interest in international rankings of academic achievement (and in critiques of them); and the growing influence of international development agendas such as the Millennium Development Goals has attracted both widespread attention and sustained critical analysis. Details of the changing intellectual landscape of BAICE can be found in Watson's (1996, 1998) reviews of the varied fortunes of comparative and international education. Indeed, the boundaries of comparative education have become increasingly diffuse as both new and experienced researchers have developed comparative dimensions to their work (see e.g. Alexander 2001). The two linked special millennial issues of the journal *Comparative Education* (Crossley & Jarvis 2000, 2001) illustrate these trends well. They also articulate the diversity of British perspectives on the field, and present an insightful international response. Links between UK comparativists and CESE have also continued to develop, reflecting ongoing European studies by researchers such as Patricia Broadfoot, David Phillips and Marilyn Osborn (see Alexander et al. 1999, 2000); and direct organisational involvement, such as Robert Cowen's (University of London) election to the CESE Presidency in 2004.

While the history of BAICE is complex and multifaceted, improved awareness of this history can do much to enhance understanding of contemporary issues and debates. From the early beginnings related closely to teacher education, the field has transformed itself in ways that have seen the research orientation emerge more strongly. Reflecting and inspiring broader intellectual trends, the dominance of the nation-state as the primary unit of analysis has been challenged by arguments favouring greater methodological diversity and more globally and more locally framed analyses (Bray & Thomas 1995; Arnove & Torres 2003; Crossley & Watson 2003). BAICE and its members have played an active part in this broader international revitalisation and reconceptualisation; and in the light of this, the future is both challenging and encouraging.

Acknowledgements

Many people have assisted with this chapter. Particular thanks are due to Colin Brock for invaluable information on the early history, to Thelma Henderson for insights into the formation of BAICE, and to members of the BAICE Executive Committee including Clive Harber and Elizabeth McNess.

References

Alexander, Robin; Broadfoot, Patricia & Phillips, David (eds.) (1999): *Learning from Comparing: New Directions in Comparative Education Research – Contexts, Classrooms and Outcomes*. Oxford: Symposium Books.

Alexander, Robin; Osborn, Marilyn & Phillips, David (eds.) (2000): *Learning from Comparing: New Directions in Comparative Educational Research – Policy, Professionals and Development*. Oxford: Symposium Books.

Alexander, Robin (2001): 'Border Crossings: Towards a Comparative Pedagogy'. *Comparative Education*, Vol.37, No.4, pp.507-523.

Arnove, Robert F. & Torres, Carlos A. (eds.) (2003): *Comparative Education: The Dialectic of the Global and the Local*. 2nd edition, Lanham, Maryland: Rowman & Littlefield.

Bacchus, Kazim & Brock, Colin (eds.) (1987): *The Challenge of Scale: Educational Development in the Small States of the Commonwealth*. London: Commonwealth Secretariat.

Bereday, George Z.F. (1964): *Comparative Method in Education*. New York: Rinehart & Winston.

Bray, Mark & Packer, Steve (1993): *Education in Small States: Concepts, Challenges and Strategies*. Oxford: Pergamon Press.

Bray, Mark & Thomas, R. Murray (1995): 'Levels of Comparison in Educational Studies: Different Insights from Different Literatures and the Value of Multilevel Analysis'. *Harvard Educational Review*, Vol.65, No.3, pp.472-490.

Brock, Colin (1986a): 'BCIES – Coming of Age: A Resume of the History of the British Comparative and International Education Society and its Antecedents', in Corner, Trevor E. (ed.), *Learning Opportunities for Adults*. Proceedings of the 21ˢᵗ Annual Conference held at the University of Glasgow, 12-14 September 1986.

Brock, Colin (1986b): 'Comparative Education: What do we Think of it so Far?', in Corner, Trevor E. (ed.) *Learning Opportunities for Adults*. Proceedings of the 21ˢᵗ Annual Conference held at the University of Glasgow, 12-14 September 1986.

Crossley, Michael (2000): 'Bridging Cultures and Traditions in the Reconceptualisation of Comparative and International Education'. *Comparative Education*, Vol.36, No.3, pp.319-332.

Crossley, Michael; Broadfoot, Patricia & Schweisfurth, Michele (eds.) (2007): *Changing Educational Contexts, Issues and Identities: 40 Years of Comparative Education*. London: Routledge.

Crossley, Michael & Holmes, Keith (1999): *Educational Development in the Small States of the Commonwealth: Retrospect and Prospect*. London: The Commonwealth Secretariat.

Crossley, Michael & Jarvis, Peter (eds.) (2000): 'Comparative Education for the Twenty-first Century'. Special Millennium Number of *Comparative Education*, Vol.36, No.2.

Crossley, Michael with Jarvis, Peter (eds.) (2001): 'Comparative Education for the Twenty- first Century: An International Response'. Special Number of *Comparative Education*, Vol.37, No.4.

Crossley, Michael & Watson, Keith (2003): *Comparative and International Research in Education: Globalisation, Context and Difference*. London: RoutledgeFalmer.

Department of Education & Science (1972): *A Framework for Expansion*. London: Her Majesty's Stationery Office.

Higginson, J.H. (1979): *Selections from Michael Sadler: Studies in World Citizenship*. Liverpool: Dejall & Meyorre.

Higginson, J.H. (2001): 'The Development of a Discipline: Some Reflections on the Development of Comparative Education as seen through the Pages of the Journal *Compare*', in Watson, Keith (ed.), *Doing Comparative Education Research: Issues and Problems*. Oxford: Symposium Books, pp.373-388.

Holmes, Brian (1965): *Problems in Education*. London: Routledge & Kegan Paul.

Jullien, Marc-Antoine (1817): *Esquisse d'un ouvrage sur éducation comparée*. Paris: de Fain. Reprinted by the Bureau international d'éducation, Genève, 1962.

King, Edmund J. (1967): *World Perspectives in Education*. London: Methuen.

King, Edmund J. (1989): 'Comparative Investigation of Education: An Evolutionary Process'. *Prospects*, Vol.19, No.3, pp.369-379.

Little, Angela (2004): 'Seventy-five Years of Education Partnerships with Developing Countries'. Paper written for the 75ᵗʰ anniversary of the Institute of Education's work with developing countries, in *Education and Developing Countries, 75 Years*. A commemorative CD-ROM, London: Institute of Education, University of London.

Mallinson, Vernon (1968): 'Literary Studies in the Service of Comparative Education'. *Comparative Education*, Vol.4, No.2, pp.177-181.

McDade, Daniel F. (1982): 'The Things that Interest Mankind: A Commentary on 30 Years of Comparative Education'. *British Journal of Educational Studies*, Vol.30, No.1, pp.72-84.

McGrath, Simon (2001a): 'Confessions of a Long Distance Runner: Reflections from an International and Comparative Education Research Project,' in Watson, Keith (ed.), *Doing Comparative Education Research: Issues and Problems*. Oxford: Symposium Books, pp.265-282.

McGrath, Simon (2001b): 'Research in a Cold Climate: Towards a Political Economy of British International and Comparative Education'. *International Journal of Educational Development*, Vol.21, No.5, pp.391-400.

Mercier, P.J. (ed.) (1966): *The Place of Comparative Education in the Training of Teachers*. Reading: University of Reading, Institute of Education.

Overseas Development Administration (1992): *The Power of Change*. London: Overseas Development Administration.

Preston, Rosemary & Arthur, Linet (1996): *Quality in Overseas Consultancy: Understanding the Issues*. London: The British Council.

Robbins, Lionel (1963): *Higher Education: Report of the Committee appointed by the Prime Minister under the Chairmanship of Lord Robbins, 1961-63*. London: Her Majesty's Stationery Office.

Sadler, Michael (1900, reprinted 1979): 'How Far can we Learn Anything of Practical Value from the Study of Foreign Systems of Education?', in Higginson, J.H. (ed.) (1979): *Selections from Michael Sadler: Studies in World Citizenship*. Liverpool: Dejall & Meyorre, pp.48-51.

Sutherland, Margaret B. (1971): 'Chairman's Report'. *Bulletin of the Comparative Education Society in Europe, British Section*, Vol.2, No.4, pp.7-10.

Turner, David (2004): 'The London Association of Comparative Educationists (LACE)', unpublished paper, University of Glamorgan.

Watson, Keith (1982): 'Comparative Education in British Teacher Education,' in Goodings, Richard; Byram, Michael & McPartland, Michael (eds.), *Changing Priorities in Teacher Education*. London: Croom Helm, pp.193-225.

Watson, Keith (1990): 'Information Dissemination: The Role of the *International Journal of Educational Development* 1979-89'. *International Journal of Educational Development*, Vol.10, Nos.2/3, pp.95-114.

Watson, Keith (ed.) (1994): '*The Power of Change: A Response*'. Reading: University of Reading on behalf of the United Kingdom Forum for International Education & Training.

Watson, Keith (1996): 'Comparative Education', in Gordon, Peter (ed.), *A Guide to Educational Research*. London: The Woburn Press, pp.360-397.

Watson, Keith (1998): 'Memories, Models and Mapping: The Impact of Geopolitical Changes on Comparative Studies in Education'. *Compare: A Journal of Comparative Education*, Vol.28, No.1, pp.5-31.

Watson, Keith (ed.) (2001): *Doing Comparative Education Research: Issues and Problems*. Oxford: Symposium Books.

Watson, Keith & King, Kenneth (1991): 'From Comparative to International Studies in Education: Towards the Co-ordination of a British Resource of Expertise'. *International Journal of Educational Development*, Vol.11, No.3, pp.245-253.

14

The Comparative and International Education Society of Canada (CIESC)

Suzanne MAJHANOVICH & ZHANG Lanlin

The Comparative and International Education Society of Canada/Société cana-
dienne d'éducation comparée et internationale (CIESC/SCECI) was established
on 5 June 1967. As an educational society in an officially-bilingual country, the
society from the outset has been a bilingual organisation with its Constitution in both
English and French. Conference papers may be in either language, and the society's
journal also publishes in both English and French. In 1970 the 1st World Congress of
Comparative Education Societies was held in Ottawa; and in 1989 the CIESC
hosted the 7th World Congress in Montreal.

This chapter presents a history of the development of the CIESC, touching
on its context and epistemological foundations. The society's characteristics are
discussed and its activities are presented. The foci include CIESC members'
international leadership, the journal, awards, and academic endeavours. The concluding section comments on challenges and future directions.

Birth and Development of the CIESC

The birth of the CIESC was itself a story of international education development.
Andrew F. Skinner, the first CIESC Vice-President and the second President,
reported in the first issue of the society's journal (1972, p.4), *Canadian and
International Education*, that the society was "conceived in Vancouver, born and
named in Chicago, confirmed in Ottawa, and fostered by a loyal and keen nucleus
of founding members and by much appreciated financial sustenance from friendly
encouraging sources".

The initiative to form the CIESC was taken by Joseph P. Katz of the
University of British Columbia. In March 1966, Katz contacted a number of
Canadian educators to express his conviction that there was a place for such an
organisation in Canada, either as a branch of what was then called the Comparative
Education Society (CES) in the United States, or as a separate though co-operating
entity. Many founding members were graduates from the United States and

members of the CES. Katz proposed seven objectives for the society (Gillett et al. 1967, p.9):

- to promote comparative analyses of educational systems within Canada;
- to contribute to better overall planning in education;
- to establish better and more frequent communication among Canadian colleagues in the field of comparative and international education;
- to plan Canadian overseas education seminars;
- to facilitate the exchange of students in the field of comparative and international education;
- to explore ways and means of cooperating with the various organisations and agencies working in international education; and
- to assist in the development of programs for accommodation of foreign students in Canadian colleges and universities.

The founding meeting at Chicago was planned by Katz as a regional gathering during the annual CES conference. The Director of the Comparative Education Center at the University of Chicago, C. Arnold Anderson, agreed to schedule a half day on 14 February 1967 for papers from the nascent Canadian group. Three papers provided overviews of education in Quebec, Ontario and Western Canada. Subsequently the three papers, plus a fourth by Colin H. Smith about adult education in Mid-Western Nigeria, appeared in the first CIESC publication entitled *Founding Papers: The New Look in Canadian Education* (Gillett et al. 1967). Katz was unanimously elected Provisional Chairman by the 20 Canadians present in Chicago. Participants discussed whether the proposed Canadian society should be an independent association or a regional chapter or affiliate of the CES. Gerald Read, the CES representative, noted that the US society welcomed all interested members, and suggested that the Canadian society might wish to begin as a local chapter of the US society and decide later whether to form a separate and independent association (Gillett et al. 1967, p.11).

As a result of this discussion, the following motion was proposed: "That a provisional committee be formed to explore the best type of organisation and purpose for a Canadian group; such exploration should cover the possibility of becoming a local chapter of the Comparative Education Society, or an independent Canadian society, or some other type of association". The motion was carried unanimously. The other elected members of the Provisional Committee were Margaret Gillett (McGill), Secretary; Robert Lawson (Calgary), Treasurer; and Andrew F. Skinner (Toronto) and Colin Smith (Simon Fraser University), Members-at-large. Two other members were subsequently co-opted to represent Francophone Canada and the Atlantic Provinces: Edouard Trudeau (Collège Jean-de-Brébeuf, Montreal) and Alexander S. Mowat (Dalhousie).

The provisional committee opted for an independent Canadian society, albeit one that would seek contact and possible affiliation with the US and European societies. At the Learned Societies Conference at Ottawa in June 1967, at the request of Joseph Katz, Anthony Paplauskas-Ramunas who was then director of the Comparative Education Centre of the University of Ottawa scheduled the Canadian-based meeting which reviewed programmes and un-animously adopted the English and French versions of the CIESC Constitution. According to Article 1, Section 2 of the Constitution (Gillett et al. 1967, p.18), the purpose of the society was to encourage and promote comparative and international studies in Canadian education by:

1. promoting and improving the teaching of comparative education in institutions of higher learning;
2. stimulating research;
3. facilitating the publication and distribution of comparative studies in education;
4. interesting professors and teachers of other disciplines in the comparative and international dimensions of their work;
5. encouraging visits by educators to study educational institutions and systems throughout the world;
6. co-operating with those in other disciplines who attempt to interpret educational developments in a broad cultural context;
7. organising conferences and meetings;
8. co-operating with comparative and international education societies and with governmental and private agencies in order to further common objectives; and
9. co-operating with other Canadian educational societies to further common objectives.

The *Founding Papers* listed as members 42 people and one institution, the Ministry of Education of the Province of Quebec (Gillett et al. 1967, pp.74-76). Greetings to the new society were sent from the comparative education societies of Japan, Europe, and the United States, from the UNESCO International Bureau of Education (IBE) in Switzerland, and from Joseph Lauwerys of Great Britain who was a Past-President of the Comparative Education Society in Europe (CESE). The Provisional Executive elected at Chicago was confirmed in office and augmented by the election of Edouard Trudeau and Alexander S. Mowat as Vice-Presidents. It was decided to publish a periodical newsletter.

The international education component of the society was acknowledged from the very outset, not only in the constitution but also in the Ottawa conference. The conference programme included an address by a member of the Governmental External Aid Office, W.D. Coombs, on activities of his office and on funding possibilities. Colin Smith spoke of his experiences as an educational adviser in developing countries, and subsequent discussion revolved around ways that the CIESC could contribute to international education development through evaluation of aid programmes (Gillett et al. 1967, p.14).

During the initial years, CIESC meetings were held in conjunction with the annual meetings of the Conference of the Learned Societies. Hence, after the founding meeting in Ottawa in 1967, the first actual conference of the CIESC took place on 31 May and 1 June 1968 at the University of Calgary. The theme was

'The International Mosaic in Canadian Education', which included talks on Canada's external aid programmes, International Action Groups, CUSO (Canadian University Service Overseas), CYC (Company of Young Canadians), Peace Corps, VSO (Voluntary Service Overseas), a report by Roger Magnusson on the status of comparative education in Canada based on a survey, and a panel entitled 'Foreign Influences in Canadian Education' with papers outlining Scottish influence (Andrew Skinner), French influence (Louis-Philippe Audet), English influence (Willard Brehaut) and American influence (Rudy L. Schnell) for which Gerald Read was discussant (Braham et al. 1968, pp.87-88).

Joseph Katz was not only the driving force behind the establishment of the CIESC, but also an important initiator of international activities related to comparative education. David Wilson (1994a) recalls a heated 1964 exchange between Anderson and Katz at the Comparative Education Center in Chicago, USA, which in part contributed to the change of name of the Comparative Education Society in the United States to the Comparative and International Education Society (CIES).

As early as 1960, Katz had advanced the idea of the International Education Year. His idea was realised a decade later. In order to mark this event, he proposed the formation of the World Council of Comparative Education Societies (WCCES). (For further details, see Chapter 1.)

Lifelong learning was an important theme of the 1970 International Education Year, with a focus on adult and higher education. The theme of the 1970 CIESC conference, held in Winnipeg during the Conference of the Learned Societies was 'Comparative Studies in Higher Education'. Papers addressed issues of community colleges, federal-provincial relationships, changing roles of universities, teacher preparation, and a comparison of higher education in Australia and Canada (Skinner 1970a, pp.115-116). The Canadian Society for the Study of Higher Education (CSSHE) was also founded in 1970, and the CIESC invited members of that society to attend its meeting (Skinner 1970b, p.8). The connection between the CIESC and the CSSHE as well as the Canadian Society for Studies in Adult Education (CSSAE) continues, with some members active in both the CIESC and either or both of the other associations. During the annual conference, later called the Congress of Humanities and Social Sciences, it became common to have co-sponsored sessions by the CIESC and the CSSHE or the CSSAE.

The year 1972 saw two events of significance for the CIESC. First, the society launched its journal *Canadian and International Education* (*CIE*) published by the Ontario Institute for Studies in Education (OISE) and "devoted to the publication of articles dealing with education and society in Canada and other nations" (inside cover, Vol.1, No.1). The word 'Comparative' did not appear in the title of the journal, but it is clear that the founders of the journal expected that articles dealing either with issues in Canadian education or in an international context would employ comparative approaches. As Skinner (1972, p.5) noted regarding the early publications of the CIESC and its journal:

> It may be observed, and observed correctly, that in these publications attention has to a great degree been focussed upon education in Canada and its provincial and interprovincial features and issues. This is not surprising, indeed it was a matter of deliberate policy. Canada itself, within its own very extensive boundaries, offers wide scope and opportunity for enlightening comparative studies in education. (…) On the other hand a substantial number of other papers offer international content and sustain international perspective, dealing as they do in comparative terms with problems and features in both developed and developing countries.

Since then the journal has normally been published twice a year in June and December, although some years have seen three issues including one special guest-edited issue.

In the first issue the Editor, Shiu Kong, offered the journal as a place where "Canadian comparative educators [could] share their thoughts, research findings, and insights with educators abroad, and ... invite interchange of ideas and experience" (p.1). Andrew Skinner provided a "transition note for the record" (Skinner 1972), celebrating that the new CIESC organisation had developed to the extent that it had moved beyond the publication of mere papers from the annual congress as a Proceedings to the point where it could launch its own journal. Seven articles included focus on the multicultural curriculum (Katz 1972), the politics of language and teaching in Quebec (Farine 1972), and education in China, Romania and developing areas. The *CIE* journal has had several homes besides the Ontario Institute for Studies in Education. These include the University of Western Ontario, the University of Saskatchewan, Ryerson University, the Chinese University of Hong Kong in conjunction with Brandon University (while the editor, Jack Lam, a Brandon professor was on an extended leave of absence from his home university and was working at the Chinese University of Hong Kong), and Queen's University.

The second momentous event of 1972 was the founding of the Canadian Society for the Study of Education (CSSE) which was organised during the Montreal Conference of the Learned Societies. The CIESC was one of five founding associations, and Avigdor Farine was a member of its first executive board (*CIESC Newsletter*, June 1972). The CSSE is an umbrella organisation for various education society affiliates. Hence membership in both the CSSE and the CIESC is a requirement for CIESC members – something that could cause difficulties for international scholars interested only in the CIESC. The June 1973 *CIESC Newsletter* reported that the CSSE had revised its structure to accommodate the CIESC members. CSSE members could elect to join any or all of the affiliated groups, but international members concerned only with the activities of the CIESC could apply directly to the CIESC for membership, and would receive a subscription to the *CIE* journal as part of the membership fee (*CIESC Newsletter*, June 1973). The affiliation of the CIESC to the umbrella CSSE has been part of a structure which has been different from that of independent comparative education societies, but which resembles the structure in some other countries.

The two other societies that retain very close ties to the CIESC, namely the Higher Education and Adult Education Societies, never became affiliates of the CSSE but remain independent organisations even though their annual conference coincides exactly with the dates of the CIESC/CSSE conference. There have been many discussions as to whether the CIESC should be an independent society or remain an affiliate of the CSSE. The CIESC executive was not unanimous in the decision to become an affiliate of the CSSE. The January 1973 edition of the newsletter reported (p.6) that:

> The discussion among the executive committee revealed that hopes are high for the CSSE, but there are some strong reservations too. Members are urged to consider this matter very carefully.

Many members still harbour reservations, but there has been no overt attempt to secede from the CSSE. The larger CSSE association recognises the connections the CIESC has to international research and development, and it is always a member of the CIESC who is named the CSSE representative to the Canadian National Commission for UNESCO. When CIDA wishes to hold a symposium during the annual Humanities and Social Sciences conference, normally the CIESC programme will list and co-sponsor the event in recognition of the ongoing work by CIESC members in CIDA projects.

The CIESC newsletter has reported on activities of members in the international education area as well as on the development of courses and programmes in comparative and international education. For example, the November 1969 issue announced McGill University's new MA in Comparative Education. It also reported that the University of Alberta was continuing with its comprehensive school training programme for experienced teachers from Thailand; and the University of Western Ontario highlighted a pilot programme for returned CUSO volunteers in which the returnees could take an intensive course to prepare them for teaching certification for Ontario schools. The newsletter has also included occasional short articles, and has been used to publish minutes and reports from the Annual General and Executive meetings, and to list members with their current research interests. A version of the newsletter was placed on line as a link to the CIESC website (www.edu.uwo.ca/ciesc).

Epistemological Grounding

Throughout its evolution and development, the CIESC has demonstrated an ongoing exploration of the epistemological base, asking what it means to engage in comparative and international education. Some members have questioned whether comparison of different regions of Canada qualifies for the field. However, as Andrew Skinner noted (1970b, p.7), in comparative education "a first essential is to know one's own system of education as thoroughly as possible, historically and contemporaneously; and second that within the provinces of Canada itself there is plenty of scope for comparative educational studies". Referring to the papers in the 1970 edition, Skinner remarked that "while there is revealed a desirable readiness now for comparative studies that range through other countries, Canada remains sensibly the essential base of reference and comparison". David Radcliffe, editor of the *CIESC Newsletter* in the early 1970s, reflected on the research interests of Canadian comparativists as developing "from an initial concern with our intraconfederal comparisons, to a steady broadening of interest to more international studies", citing the community education of CIDA and the evolving functions of the International Development Research Centre (IDRC), among many other indications (*CIESC Newsletter*, May 1973, p.2). Radcliffe also playfully commented on methodologies used in comparative education studies:

> Do we detect a return swing of the pendulum, from comparative educator as key-puncher extraordinary (as a well-known educational economist said, "Many are the transgressions of those who do regressions") to Yogi-Guru? Or perhaps it is a sign of maturity when one hears a distinguished authority remark that it is time we stopped fussing about the appropriate methodology to give our discipline respectability and got on with the job; for method-ology emerges naturally from the object of study.

A review of the CIESC presidential speeches may further illustrate how Canadian comparativists have viewed the inter-connection of international and comparative studies. David Wilson, a past President of the CIESC (1987-1991), of the US CIES and of the WCCES, was much involved in documenting the history of the institutions, key players, and the field. In his CIES presidential address, he commented on how comparative and international education in North America merged in the 1960s (Wilson 1994a). This theme intertwines the field even today.

According to Suzanne Majhanovich (2003), President of the CIESC from 2001 to 2003, a dichotomy continued to exist with the comparative side being viewed as the scientific, theoretical component focused on explaining the pheno-mena of the field. The international counterpart on the other hand has been associated with the practical-descriptive field-based activities including the all-important work championing education for all, human rights, peace, and cultural understanding. Former CIESC presidents expressed concerns in research metho-dologies that involve comparative and international education issues in the field. For example, Douglas Ray (President 1973-1975) gave a report (1997) on the ongoing project in Russia on democracy and education, *Russian-Canadian Cooperation in Curriculum Development: Russian Civic Education, 1990-1996* which provided an example of exemplary international research and development. K.P.Binda (President 1999-2001) also showed this aspect of comparative and international education research when he argued the case for aboriginal education in Canada legitimised through comparative and global perspectives (2001).

These examples reflect the way comparative and international theory and practice overlap and confirm Wilson's message in his 1994 CIES presidential address, 'Comparative and International Education: Fraternal or Siamese Twins?' (Wilson 1994a). As he pointed out, "our twins have been inseparable since their birth, and both the names of each twin and their activities have been inter-changeable at various periods in their life cycles" (p.483). Comparative and international education can also make important contributions to the illumination of educational policy.

Some Features of the CIESC

At the founding meeting in 1967, the English and French versions of the CIESC Constitution were approved. The Constitution was revised in 1975 to reflect CSSE membership and was further revised in 1993. According to the 1993 version, the following are eligible for membership:

- teachers, research workers, and graduate students in comparative edu-cation, international education, development education, native education, cross-cultural education, and related fields; and
- persons working in government and non-government agencies and organisations concerned with studies in comparative education, interna-tional education, development education, native education, cross-cultural education, and related fields.

CIESC members fall into four categories: regular members (who join the society as part of their membership of CSSE), student members (who are designated by their advisors who are members of the society), world members (teachers or researchers in comparative and international education who reside outside Canada and who join by applying to the Secretary-Treasurer), and honorary members (who have rendered long and distinguished service to comparative and/or international education and related fields).

The Executive manages the business of the society between Annual General Meetings, and consists of the President, Vice-President (who is considered as President-Elect), Immediate Past-President, Secretary-Treasurer, the Programme Chairperson, and two or three Members-at-Large (who take on specific portfolios with the society such as membership, liaison with CSSE, newsletter editorship, or other tasks deemed necessary by the Executive). The President, Vice-President and the Members-at-Large are elected for a term of two years, and the Secretary-Treasurer is elected for three years. Over the decades from 1967 to 2007, CIESC members elected 21 presidents (Table 14.1).

CIESC members hold their annual conference in late May or early June during the dates assigned to the Canadian Society for Studies in Education by the Congress for Humanities and Social Sciences which in 2000 took over responsi-bility for the Annual Congress from the Conference of the Learned Societies of Canada. Following the tradition of the Learned Societies Congresses, the Conference is hosted by a different university in Canada every year. The CIESC represents the CSSE every few years in the American Educational Research Association (AERA) at the annual conference whereby each affiliate of the Canadian umbrella organisation – the CSSE – provides a dedicated session in the AERA annual programme on a rotating basis.

Table 14.1: Presidents of the CIESC

Name	Years	Name	Years
Joseph P. Katz	1967-1969	Vandra L. Masemann	1985-1987
Andrew Skinner	1969-1970	David N. Wilson	1987-1989
Lionel Desjarlais	1970-1971	David N. Wilson	1989-1991
Roger Magnuson	1971-1972	Ralph M. Miller	1991-1993
Avigdor Farine	1972-1973	Deo H. Poonwassie	1993-1995
Douglas Ray	1973-1975	Eva Krugly-Smolska	1995-1997
John R. Mallea	1975-1977	Peter Fan	1997-1999
Margaret Gillett	1977-1979	K.P. Binda	1999-2001
Shiu Kong	1979-1981	Suzanne Majhanovich	2001-2003
Daniel Dorotich	1981-1983	Cecille DePass	2003-2005
Jacques Lamontagne	1983-1985	Allan Pitman	2005-2007

In 1988 the CIESC conferred its first Michel Laferrière Thesis Award in memory of an Associate Professor from McGill University and Associate Editor of the *CIE* journal who died at 38. The first recipient of the award was Susan Bayley of McGill University. The award was conferred to the best research conducted by either a Master's student or a PhD student. Later the society decided to confer two awards: one for the best Master's thesis, and one for the best PhD dissertation. In 1990, Andrew Skinner made a monetary award to CIESC which serves as a travel stipend of Cdn$100 to award winners to help them attend the conference. Starting from 2000, Douglas Ray also made a similar monetary contribution to fund an award to the best graduate student paper presented at the annual conference. Award winners receive a Certificate of Accomplishment and a cash award. They are also entitled to a one-year free membership of the CIESC.

International Leadership

Several distinguished leaders of the CIESC have played significant roles in the WCCES and the US-based CIES. Although the extraordinary contributions of Joseph Katz regarding the founding of both the CIESC and the World Council have been mentioned above, it is fitting to include at this point a special tribute to him because he was so central to the development of the field in Canada. Joseph Katz graduated from the University of Chicago, USA, in 1941, and started the comparative programme at the University of British Columbia, Canada, in 1956. At the founding stage of the CIESC, he was the recognised driving force.

Although the early proposal for the CIESC to have a special relationship with its US counterpart was never formalised, continuing scholarly exchanges between the two societies have benefited both organisations. The majority of CIESC members are also members of the CIES, and several Canadians have served as CIES Presidents, beginning with Joseph Katz and continuing with Reginald Edwards, Robert Lawson, Mathew Zachariah, Joseph Farrell, Vandra Masemann, David Wilson and Ruth Hayhoe. Ratna Ghosh has been a Board Member of the CIES.

Formal CIESC international linkages continue to be maintained with the WCCES with the CIESC President serving as a member of the Executive

Committee. In addition to David Wilson, former CIESC President, Vandra Masemann served as President of the Council as well as Secretary General; Douglas Ray served as Chair of two World Congress Programme Committees in Rio de Janeiro and Prague, and Jacques Lamontagne was Chair of the Organizing Committee for the 7th World Congress in Montreal, and was also Assistant Secretary General of the WCCES.

The CIESC grew from its 43 founding members through a peak of 204 members in 1989 (because of the Montreal Congress), to just over 100 members in 2006. The capacity of the society to organise activities related to the field of comparative and international education has expanded. In 2003, a cross-Canada research group, the Citizenship Education Research Network (CERN) joined the CIESC as a Special Interest Group (SIG). Their projects on citizenship education in Canada's plural and diverse society closely match the society's goals as set out in the Constitution.

Table 14.2: Special Issues of *Canadian and International Education*

Year	Issue	Theme	Editor(s)
1979	Vol.8, No.2	Education in Asia	Shiu Kong
1983	Vol.12, No.1	Education and The World Bank	Stephen P. Heyneman
1983	Vol.12, No.3	Development Education in Canada in the Eighties: Context, Constraints, Choices	Mathew Zachariah
1985	Vol.14, No.1	Race, Culture and Ideology in Canadian Education	Richard Heyman
1987	Vol.16, No.1	Chinese Educators on Chinese Education	Ruth Hayhoe & Ralph Miller
1991	Vol.20, No.1	New Challenges for Development Education in Canada in the Nineties	Cecille DePass, John L. McNeil & Mathew Zachariah
1991	Vol.20, No.3	On the State of Higher Education	Michel Saint-Germain
1996	Vol.25, No.2	Citizenship Education: Canadian and International Dimensions	Alan Sears & Murray Print
1999	Vol.28, No.2	Multiculturalism	Rosa Bruno-Jofré & Evelina Orteza y Miranda
2002	Vol.31, No.2	The OECD Indicators. International Comparisons of Education Systems	Nelly McEwen
2004	Vol.33, No.1	Educational Restructuring in the Era of Globalisation	Goli Rezai-Rashti
2005	Vol.34, No.1	Values, Human Rights and Citizenship Education in Transnational Perspectives	Yvonne Hébert, Glen Eyford & France Jutras

Continuing Challenges and the Future

Reviewing the comparative education courses offered by Canadian universities in the early 1990s, Wilson (1994b, p.17) commented that the field was fragmented:

> Most Canadian comparative educators are hired to teach courses other than Comparative Education and no stand-alone Department of Comparative Education exists in the country. While this is deplorable on the one hand, the other side of the equation is that interest in the comparative study of education is quite widespread at the Canadian post-secondary level.

A decade later, the situation had worsened in terms of the number of courses specifically designated as comparative education. Although some comparative education courses were offered by colleges rather than universities (for example Lethbridge College and Fanshawe College), and some educational courses were offered outside Faculties of Education (for example in York University, where comparative education was offered in the Department of Sociology), the number of courses appeared to have declined. However, this picture might have reflected changes in course names and expanded areas of research in comparative and international education. For example, at the University of Western Ontario, only one graduate course that specifically included 'comparative education' in the title was listed, but at least four other graduate courses treated areas of interest to comparative education, such as the issues of globalisation.

Comparative and international education in Canada has become an eclectic discipline in the most positive sense of the word. It is concerned with international matters and development around the world, and is involved in research using a variety of methodologies into such global issues as human rights, peace studies, cross-cultural studies, literacy, numeracy, multilateral initiatives such as Education for All as well as national (Canadian) education issues of second language education, immigration and the education of immigrants, citizenship, academic assessment, educational restructuring and many other issues currently under focus in education. Hence, even if there are very few courses or programs explicitly labelled comparative education, the field pervades the study of education.

The challenges facing the CIESC in its fourth decade include increasing membership, particularly student membership; encouraging Canadian practitioners of international education to participate in CIESC activities; promotion of comparative education in all Canadian faculties of education; liaison with other learned societies interested in comparative and international studies; and coming to grips with the realties of globalisation. Comparative and international educators in Canada are active in almost every area of education, and the experience they bring from other milieux can add different perspectives lacking in those who have not been privileged to experience the world from the reality of others. This is among the strong contributions that comparativists can bring to the study of any educational matter. It is the responsibility of the CIESC and its members to live up to that challenge.

Note: This chapter was expanded in 2004 from an earlier version in 1989 by Song Yijun and David N. Wilson. David N. Wilson died on 8 December 2006.

References

Binda, K.P. (2001): 'Aboriginal Education in Comparative and Global Perspectives: What has Research and Practice done for Aboriginal Education in Canada?'. *Canadian and International Education*, Vol.30, No.1, pp.1-16.

Braham, Mark; Brehaut, Willard; Skinner, Andrew F. & Zachariah, Mathew (eds.) (1968): *Papers: The International Mosaic in Canadian Education*. Comparative and International Education Society of Canada.

Comparative and International Education Society of Canada. *Constitution*: Approved 5 June 1967. In Gillett, Margaret; Katz, Joseph; Lawson, Robert & Skinner, Andrew F. (eds.) (1967): *Founding Papers. The New Look in Canadian Education*. Toronto: University of Toronto Press, pp.18-23 (later revised 6 June 1975 and 6 June 1993; archives of CIESC).

Farine, Avigdor (1972): 'La politique de la langue et de l'enseignment au Québec'. *Canadian and International Education*. Vol.1. No.1. pp.51-58.

Gillett, Margaret; Katz, Joseph; Lawson, Robert & Skinner, Andrew F. (eds.) (1967): *Founding Papers: The New Look in Canadian Education.* Comparative and International Education Society of Canada.

Katz, Joseph (1972): 'A Multicultural Curriculum for a Cosmopolitan Citizen'. *Canadian and International Education*, Vol.1, No.1, pp.7-14.

Majhanovich, Suzanne (2003): 'Making Sense of Decentralisation in Education Using a Comparative Lens'. *Canadian and International Education*, Vol.32, No.1, pp.1-18.

Ray, Douglas (1997): 'Russian-Canadian Cooperation in Curriculum Development: Russian Civic Education 1990-1996'. *Canadian and International Education*, Vol.26, No.1, pp.1-13.

Skinner, Andrew F. (ed.) (1970a): *Papers: Comparative Studies in Higher Education.* Comparative and International Education Society of Canada.

Skinner, Andrew F. (1970b): 'Foreword', in Skinner, Andrew F. (ed.), *Papers: Comparative Studies in Higher Education.* Comparative and International Education Society of Canada, pp.7-9.

Skinner, Andrew F. (1972): 'Transition: A Note for the Record.' *Canadian and International Education*, Vol.1, No.1, p.4.

Wilson, David (1994a): 'Comparative and International Education: Fraternal or Siamese Twins? A Preliminary Genealogy of Our Twin Fields'. *Comparative Education Review*, Vol.38, No.4, pp.449-486.

Wilson, David (1994b): 'On Teaching the Methodology of Comparative Education: Why are there so few Courses in Canada?'. *Canadian and International Education*, Vol.23, No.1, pp.13-24.

15

The Korean Comparative Education Society (KCES)

LEE Byung-Jin & KWON Dong-Taik

This chapter focuses on the role and contributions of the Korean Comparative Education Society (KCES) within the wider context of the field of comparative education. It remarks not only on the domestic contribution, but also on the international one. The KCES was a founder-member of the World Council of Comparative Education Societies (WCCES) in 1970. It played a supporting role with an event prior to the 4th World Congress of Comparative Education Societies in 1980, and then hosted the 11th World Congress in 2001. Officers in the KCES have also played leadership roles in the Comparative Education Society of Asia (CESA).

    The chapter will also show ways in which the KCES has made these and other domestic and international contributions to the field. In order to explain the context, the chapter begins with some historical perspectives in the Republic of Korea (hereafter in this chapter simply called Korea).

Development of the Field

Comparative education can be considered to have a long history in the sense that policy-makers and others have looked outside the country to learn lessons from other parts of the world. As a clearly-identified field, however, the history dates only from the second half of the 20th century. The paragraphs that follow conceptualise the development over the decades.

The First Period (1950s and 1960s)

After the Korean War (1950-53) left the country in ruins, the pursuit of modernisation and economic recovery was of utmost importance. Based on the conviction that education was a key force behind modernisation, improving domestic education was a priority. The process involved understanding education in developed countries and the relationship between education and national development (see Lee Byung-Jin 1995, 1998). During the period following the Korean War, many universities incorporated comparative education in their lectures. Indeed, it became an official course for students majoring in education. Articles introducing foreign education policies were published in journals and newspapers, and some scholars wrote theses on foreign education.

Historians commonly highlight the lecture on comparative education delivered by Rim Han-Young in 1953 at the Department of Education of Yonsei University. Many professors followed him in the teaching of comparative education, and in 1961 a textbook on comparative education was published (Rim 1961). This book introduced the work of Nicholas Hans as well as theories of comparative education. However, little information was provided on the features of education systems in other nations.

In 1963, comparative education began to be a part of the curriculum with the establishment of graduate schools. Each graduate school offered a major in educational administration and emphasised the study of comparative education. The most active scholars during this period, in addition to Rim, were Kim Seung-Hwa (Seoul National University), Yoo Hyung-Jin (Sookmyung Women's University), Lee Kyu-Hwan (Ewha Women's University), and Kim Jong-Cheol (Chung Ang University).

The establishment of the KCES was proposed by several of these scholars plus Hahn Ki-Un, Lee Nam-Pyo, Ahn Sang-Won and Kim Jung-Hwan. On 24 February 1968, they held a ceremony to mark the official inauguration of the KCES. During this event, Yoo Hyung-Jin was elected the first President. The inaugural symposium was held on 30 March 1968 on the theme 'Characteristics and Recent Trends of Comparative Education'.

The KCES was initially established as an independent professional society. However, in July 1970, the KCES became part of the Korean Society for the Study of Education (KSSE) as its research section of comparative education. This notwithstanding, the KCES has retained its original name to signify the continuing pursuit of its foundational spirit. In this light, the KCES has cultivated research on comparative education in a global perspective.

The Second Period (1970s)

During the 1970s, zealous comparative education scholars started to build the scholastic cornerstones. The KCES began to be in the limelight in the global arena, and significant research on comparative education in Korea was produced. For example, the 1971 thesis by Lee Kyu-Hwan was noteworthy as the first comparative study of the influence of foreign education in Korea.

Comparative studies undertaken in Korea included a number of other significant works. They included the work by Yoo Hyung-Jin (1970) on education in England, and the study by Lee Kyu-Hwan (1970) on educational reform in West Germany and Sweden. Three years later, Hahn Ki-Un wrote 'A comparative study of the educational philosophy in Korea, China, and Japan' (1973); and on the occasion of the 10th anniversary of the KCES in 1978, Hahn Ki-Un presented 'The research and prospects of comparative education in Korea'.

The Third Period (1980s)

In the 1980s, the KCES increased its interchanges with various comparative education societies across the world, and projected its research achievements by hosting academic conferences and seminars both domestically and internationally. Of particular importance was the pre-Congress for the 4th World Congress of Comparative Education Societies, which the KCES hosted in Seoul from 3 to 5 July 1980. The decade also commenced with publication of a strong book by Lee Kyu-Hwan (1980).

Holding the pre-Congress in Korea gave the KCES fresh impulse for development, and boosted its confidence to step onto the global stage. The decision to appoint the KCES as the host of the event had been confirmed by the WCCES Executive Committee during its 1979 meeting in Valencia, Spain. The event was significant not only for the KCES but also more broadly in Korea. It gave the opportunity for educators and scholars from around the globe to visit Korea and study Korean education. Participants from 36 countries joined the pre-Congress, including the prominent British scholars Brian Holmes and Edmund J. King.

The Fourth Period (1990s)

To note its 25th anniversary, in December 1993 the KCES organised a conference entitled 'Innovations in School Education in Asia'. In addition to the intrinsic interest of the event, 12 scholars from eight countries in Asia joined a forum to discuss the formation of the Comparative Education Society in Asia (CESA). They signed a memorandum, which was one of the steps leading up to the establishment of CESA at the University of Hong Kong in May 1995.

The decade of the 1990s was also important for the preparations leading to the hosting of the 11th World Congress of Comparative Education Societies. The KCES was first officially proposed to host the 11th World Congress during the 9th World Congress in Sydney, Australia, in July 1996. The WCCES Executive Committee held its first screening of proposals for the 11th Congress in Mexico City in 1997. Finally in July 1998, during the 10th World Congress in Cape Town, South Africa, the KCES was announced as the host of the 11th World Congress. Hosting this event meant for KCES substantial improvements in the quality of its international exchanges with academic societies around the world.

The Fifth Period (Since 2000)

The 11th World Congress was held from 2 to 6 July 2001 at the Korean National University of Education in Chung'buk, on the theme 'New Challenges and New Paradigms: Moving Education into the 21st Century'. It attracted approximately 400 scholars from 38 countries. Participants were honoured by a video message of welcome from the President of the Republic of Korea, and by the attendance of the Deputy Prime Minister, who was also Minister of Education and Human Resources Development, at the opening ceremony. Part of the spirit of the Congress was captured in the speech by the Deputy Prime Minister, who stressed the qualitative side of education (Han 2001, p.2):

> In this age of information, I believe educators must realize the significance of wisdom as "know-why" as well as knowledge as "know-how". Knowledge is not merely a sum of information. And wisdom is more than a sum of

knowledge. Wisdom, knowledge and information should always go together, but the most valuable among these is wisdom.

The Congress had seven plenary addresses and two symposia. A special issue of the *International Review of Education* (Vol.49, Nos.1 & 2, 2003) collected some papers and was subsequently republished as a book (Bray 2003).

Despite the great achievement of hosting the Congress, in the years that followed the KCES felt that it still faced major tasks in cultivating the field of comparative education. It noted fundamental weaknesses due to a lack of infrastructure to support the field. These became a focus in the years that followed.

KCES Activities and Leadership

The KCES members include persons who majored in education during college or graduate school, and especially those with interest in comparative education, in-service teachers (elementary, middle or high school) who are interested in comparative education research. In 2007 the KCES had 400 members, and had over the years seen the growing involvement of professors, scholars, education administrators and school teachers. The KCES has organised many academic conferences and seminars, totalling over 170 during the first four decades of its existence.

In 1992, the periodical that had been launched in 1971 under the title *World Culture and Education* was retitled *Korean Journal of Comparative Education*. Since then, it has been published at least twice a year. The journal strives to propose a theoretical framework for the academic development of comparative education and provide extensive information on education in other countries. It follows a strict screening process evaluating the importance and originality of submissions.

For this historical account it is useful also to identify each of the presidents and their periods of office. As mentioned, Yoo Hyung-Jin led the formation of the KCES and served first as its founding President (1968-70). He contributed to the establishment of the WCCES, and was an active representative of the KCES in the WCCES. During the period 1978 to 1982, Yoo Hyung-Jin became President again and led the pre-Congress event in July 1980. In June 1985, he died at age 60.

The second President of the KCES was Hahn Ki-Un, who was a philosopher of education. In 1971 the periodical *World Culture and Education* was launched as a result of his efforts.

Lee Kyu-Hwan, an educational sociologist, was the third President. He also was very active in WCCES and other international affairs. In 1976 he produced the second edition of the periodical that had been launched by Hahn Ki-Un. He later served two further terms, the bridging the 1980s and 1990s.

The fifth President was Park Jun-Hui, an educational psychologist. He especially contributed in fostering the interchange among scholars of comparative education in Asia. The close mutual relations that he developed with Japan and China sowed the seeds that were to bear fruit in the formation of CESA.

The sixth President of KCES was Shin Kuk-Bom. Using his wide international network in the field of education administration, his election to office was with the expectation that he would contribute to the globalisation of KCES. However, he was appointed as the educational secretary to the President of Korea, and stayed in office as KCES President for only six months.

Succeeding him as seventh President was Kim Sun-Ho. As a comparative educator, he strengthened the KCES from within and planned to connect it with on-site education by gathering more members and conducting research on academic exchanges.

Lee Byung-Jin was elected for four consecutive terms. After majoring in educational leadership, he used his experiences in elementary education and educational administration to lead the KCES to new heights. During the organisation of the KCES' 25th Anniversary International Congress in 1993, he contributed not only to the KCES but also to CESA. He was in due course elected the second CESA President. Lee Byung-Jin also organised 11th World Congress in 2001.

Lee Hyun-Chung took over as the next President. As Secretary General of the Korean Council for University Education, he was able to use his extensive domestic and foreign networks to contribute to the society.

Conclusions

Despite the work of the KCES, comparative education has not been able to develop institutionally in Korea's university system. It has not been well understood by academics, let alone by policy makers. Although comparative education used to be a compulsory programme of academic programmes, this is no longer the case. Ironically, this may reflect the fact that Korea has become more prosperous and more international, and no longer sees so strong a need to learn developmental lessons from other countries in order to climb out of its underdeveloped mode.

The KCES nevertheless has much to be proud of. One major highlight was the hosting in 2001 of the 11th World Congress of Comparative Education Societies, and both before and since the KCES has maintained a strong journal.

One approach considered by the leadership for strengthening the KCES has been broadening the membership base by accepting teachers who are interested in the society's activities. Scholars and the school teachers can cooperate to study, implement, and evaluate tasks together. Many elementary and secondary school teachers in Korea are fluent in different foreign languages. The number of teachers holding doctoral degrees in education is also increasing. These offer potential sources for recruitment of society members.

Of course sufficient funding is crucial for the successful implementation of any task. The KCES largely depends on the annual membership fees and some donations from the staff members of the society. One of the major challenges is that the KCES, like most other academic societies in Korea, is not a juridical foundation or a corporate body and donors are therefore not entitled to tax deductions. Nevertheless, the society is confident that the necessary funds can be gathered if it is able to demonstrate the relevance and usefulness of its work.

Education has been a key component of Korea's spectacular economic and social development. This stimulated interest in comparative studies, and has relevance not only nationally but also internationally (see Lee Byung-Jin 1996, 2003). The role of the KCES has evolved over the decades, but remains as important in the 21st century as it was in the 1960s.

References

Bray, Mark (ed.) (2003): *Comparative Education: Continuing Traditions, New Challenges, and New Paradigms*. Special double issue of *International Review of Education*, Vol.49, Nos.1-2. Republished 2003 as book with same title, Dordrecht: Kluwer Academic Publishers.

Hahn, Ki-Un (1973): 'A Comparative Study on the Educational Philosophy in Korea, China and Japan'. Paper presented at the 37th seminar of the KCES. [in Korean]

Hahn, Ki-Un (1978): 'The Research and Prospects of Comparative Education in Korea'. Paper presented at the 10th anniversary conference of the KCES. [in Korean]

Han, Wan-Sang (2001): 'Congratulatory Address', 11th World Congress of Comparative Education Societies, Chung'buk, Korea, 2 July.

Lee, Byung-Jin (1995): 'The Current and Past of the Study of Comparative Education in Korea and Japan'. *Korean Journal of Comparative Education,* Vol.5, No.1, pp.111-130. [in Korean]

Lee, Byung-Jin (1996): 'Analysis on the Situation of Comparative Education in Korea'. *Korean Journal of Comparative Education*, Vol.6, No.1, pp.1-7. [in Korean]

Lee, Byung-Jin (1998): 'Comparative Education', in Education Research Institute of Seoul National University (ed.), *The Encyclopaedia of Education*, Seoul: Howdongseol, pp.1332-1341. [in Korean]

Lee, Byung-Jin (2003): 'Comparative Education and Prosperity of Asia in the World'. Paper presented to the 4th Comparative Education Society of Asia (CESA) Biennial Conference, Bandung, Indonesia.

Lee, Kyu-Hwan (1970): 'The Comparative Study of Educational Reform in West Germany and Sweden'. Paper presented at the 19th seminar of the KCES. [in Korean]

Lee, Kyu-Hwan (1980): *The Educational System of Developed Countries*. Seoul: Baeyoungsa. [in Korean]

Rim, Han-Young (1961): *Comparative Education*. Seoul: Modern Educational Books Press. [in Korean]

Yoo, Hyung-Jin (1970): 'A Study on the Middle School Educational Reform of England'. Paper presented at the 15th seminar of the KCES. [in Korean]

16

The Francophone Association for Comparative Education (AFEC)

Margaret B. SUTHERLAND

The Association francophone d'éducation comparée (AFEC), which is commonly translated into English as either the French-speaking or the Francophone Association for Comparative Education, came into being in 1973. The Association was established in the place which has been its home during most of its existence, the Centre international d'études pédagogiques (CIEP) – the International Centre for Educational Studies – in Sèvres, France. This was a particularly suitable place for the beginning of a comparative education society, since the Centre has since its inception received people from all over the world who are interested in education. Since courses at the CIEP may frequently open with exchanges of experiences of education and discussions of the educational background of the participants, they have thus in effect been exercises in comparative education.

The CIEP has ensured in the Association a strong sense of French identity, since it is in a place of considerable historical interest. Modern occupants of this building, which was constructed in the 1750s, find reminders of French civilisation at every turn. The building was first designed as a porcelain factory, and at the end of the 19th century served as a teacher training college – the École normale de jeunes filles. Wider European relationships are recalled in the Marie Curie Room, where the eminent scientist taught for some years. Thus, even if it is not the most convenient place for committee meetings of people resident in Paris, and even if increasing bureaucracy has meant that it has been less used for AFEC meetings than at the outset, the CIEP remains an influential part of AFEC's life. It is bound into the history of AFEC since it has provided a distinctive setting for many AFEC events and international contacts.

Origins and Early Activities of AFEC

AFEC was created at the CIEP on 19 January 1973. A two-day colloquium on the education of teachers had been taking place, and on the second afternoon the organisation and Statutes of the Association were discussed and agreed upon. In due course the Statutes were lodged at the local Prefecture. Michel Debeauvais was the first President; the two Vice-Presidents were Jean Auba and Michel

Girard; the Secretary General was Aimé Janicot; and the Treasurer was Renée Lescalie. Jean Beaussier was responsible for international relations, and Jean Corpron for internal relations. Responsibility for documentation and the publication of the Bulletin lay with Michèle Tournier and Alberte Maera.

The aims of the Association as defined in the Statutes were (a) in countries which were totally or partly French-speaking, to unite people interested in the problems of comparative education; (b) to encourage these people to share their experiences and research in order to improve the practice and teaching of comparative education; (c) to provide administrators, researchers and teachers with information or ideas which might help educational renewal and innovation in their respective countries; and (d) to encourage exchanges of all kinds with national, regional and other bodies concerned with comparative education.

The Secretary, who was also Deputy Director of the CIEP, wrote about the Association in the first issue of the Bulletin. He recognised that while the status of comparative education in France was not strong – which indeed was also true of educational studies in general – there was a real need for the services that AFEC could offer. He emphasised that the association was open to people at all levels of education, and that it would fail if comparative education simply became a university subject or if AFEC were concerned only with the training of teachers. He also wrote, disarmingly, that "we will try not to take ourselves too seriously as we know that if our aims are ambitious, our means are limited".

Comparative education societies were coming into existence in a number of locations at that time, particularly serving specific countries such as Japan, Korea and Canada. By choosing to be francophone, and thus to cut across national boundaries, AFEC showed open-mindedness and willingness to develop international contacts. This strategy also increased the potential membership of the Association. The choice was welcomed by many comparativists who were happy to be members not only of their own national societies but also of this international association. Two members of the 'wide committee' of AFEC nominated in 1973, Brian Holmes and W.D. Halls, had been founder members of the British Section of the Comparative Education Society in Europe (CESE). Joseph Lauwerys, another founder member of the British Section of CESE, was elected (as was Maurice Debesse) as an Honorary Member of AFEC. Subsequent developments of AFEC's activities tried to reinforce international contacts.

Two forthcoming conferences attracted AFEC members at the time of the creation of the Association. One was the CESE congress which was to be held in Frascati, Italy, in June 1973. The second was the conference of the International Association for Educational Research (later renamed the World Association for Educational Research) due to take place in Paris in September 1973. A study day (journée d'étude) to prepare for participation in that conference was organised by Michel Debeauvais in Sèvres on 23 June 1973.

AFEC rapidly established itself by hosting the 1975 CESE congress in Sèvres; and in 1984 it hosted the 5th World Congress of Comparative Education Societies in Paris. An active presence in the affairs of the European and world bodies became habitual.

International and National Aspects

The international outlook of AFEC has also been evident in its choice of Presidents. Michel Debeauvais of France held the presidency from 1973 to 1979. He was followed by Denis Kallen from the Netherlands (1979-85); an Italian, Ettore Gelpi (1985-88); an Englishman, Raymond Ryba (1985-91); and a Scotswoman, Margaret B. Sutherland (1991-94). Then came a French President, Jean-Michel Leclercq (1994-2000), who was followed by a Belgian, Mariane Frenay (2000-03) and another French President, Alain Carry (2003-06). Régis Malet, also a French national, took over in 2006.

The position of Vice-President has also demonstrated the international approach, notably in the case of another Belgian, Henk Van daele, who was Vice-President from 1994 to 2000. Van daele substituted for the President (Jean-Michel Leclercq) at the AFEC conference and General Assembly in Lyon in 1996, the President being abroad on a mission.

The office of Secretary has served perhaps to safeguard the French aspects of the Association. Devoted service has been given in this office by Pierre Alexandre (at one time also Deputy Director of the CIEP, and initially involved in AFEC's affairs through the CIEP), Michel Soëtard, and Henri Folliet. Similarly the office of Treasurer was kept resolutely French by Jean Auffret and then Pierre-Louis Gauthier. These appointments have not only ensured that Association documents have appeared in good French, but have also provided 'insider' knowledge to deal with French legal requirements, financial conventions, and Ministry regulations.

The friendly collaboration of Directors of the CIEP who have facilitated AFEC's use of the Centre has also been important in maintaining French characteristics. Jean Auba, for many years Director of the Centre, has been one of AFEC's most important members. His successors – Jeannine Feneuille, Michèle Sellier and Gilbert Léoutre – have in their various ways also supported AFEC.

Meetings

From its inception, AFEC has given special attention to the careful preparation of its academic meetings, especially by its journées d'étude. These study days have preceded the conference proper so that, some weeks in advance of the main meeting, members have had the opportunity to become acquainted with the conference theme and to begin to develop it more thoroughly. In the early years, the traditional French enjoyment of lengthy discussions somewhat disconcerted members reared in other traditions. Such members found that listening to uninterrupted talk for three or more hours was rather beyond the usual limits of their endurance. Possibly as a result of foreign though francophone influences, the lengthier sessions of the early years gave way to the custom of the coffee break.

Initially, AFEC proceeded to engage its members in an annual conference held at Sèvres. However, it was increasingly felt that the proud title of French-speaking should be demonstrated in a more obvious way, and in 1994 the conference was held in Montreal, Canada. The University of Montreal hosted the event, which benefited greatly from the work of Marie Mc Andrew, Manuel Crespo and Claude Lessard.

Subsequent conferences continued this trend, showing flexibility in the choice of venues. The 1997 conference was in Louvain-la-Neuve, Belgium; in 2000 it was in Geneva, Switzerland; in 2001 in Brussels, Belgium; and in 2004 a conference was attended in Ouagadougou, Burkina Faso. Within France, conference sites have included Strasbourg, Caen, Lyon and Lille.

Publications

Among the activities proposed for AFEC when it first came into existence was the publication of a Bulletin and other papers on comparative education. As noted, Michèle Tournier (of the comparative education section of the Institut national de documentation et de recherche pédagogique, Paris) was appointed Editorial Secretary at the inaugural meeting. She was responsible for the publication of the first Bulletin in May 1973, in which she indicated the possible contents of future Bulletins: articles and research reports, accounts of conferences, information about AFEC activities, information about other comparative education societies, and book reviews. It was intended that the Bulletin – which was later, in a rather more substantial format, given the title *Éducation comparée* – would appear four times a year. It would be free to members, but could be bought by non-members.

This first edition of the Bulletin kept to the proposed pattern and was cyclostyled. In due course, editions became more substantial and more firmly bound; but regular annual production did not continue. *Éducation comparée* became essentially compilations of papers delivered at the annual conferences, sometimes spread over two issues and not always appearing in the same years as the conferences. The continuity of numbering was maintained even in the 1990s when the responsibility for publication was undertaken not by the AFEC Secretary but by the people or the university departments responsible for the organisation of the conferences. For example, the innovative 1994 conference in Montreal led to a two-volume publication of proceedings entitled *Pluralisme et éducation* and published by the University of Montreal and the University of Quebec at Trois Rivières, yet it was duly given its place in the AFEC series as No.48. The conference report *Éducation et handicap*, which presented papers from the 2003 conference in Lyon, similarly fell into the sequence of *Éducation comparée* as issue No.58. In this conference, as editor Denis Poizat pointed out, AFEC had usefully collaborated with another organisation concerned with a neglected aspect of education, the Collectif de recherche sur les situations de handicap, l'éducation et les sociétés (CRHES).

Nevertheless, from its inception it has been felt that AFEC should promote the publication of a French language journal of comparative education which would be not simply a publication of conference papers but a learned journal open to contributions from all scholars of comparative education. During his presidency, Raymond Ryba particularly supported this policy. However, progress toward finding a suitable publisher and financing was slow until in 1999 the solution seemed to have been found in collaboration with the Institut européen d'éducation et de politique sociale (IEEPS). A contract was established for the publication of the journal *Politiques d'éducation et de formation: analyses et comparaisons internationales* by De Boeck in Belgium. This publication, intended to be of three issues per year, duly began in 2001 with supportive financing from the Ministries of Education in France and Belgium. However, differences in policy soon became evident, and disagreements emerged concerning finance. The partnership with IEEPS ended after only two years, though the review continued in publication under the joint auspices of IEEPS and EPICE (Institut européen pour la promotion et l'innovation de la culture dans l'éducation).

A similar attempt at journal publication was also short-lived. The project, entitled Réseau européen de dissemination en éducation comparée (REDCOM) proposed collaboration among three organisations – AFEC, the IEEPS and the Spanish comparative education journal, *Revista Española de Educación Comparada*. The intention was to present European Commission research projects on a website; to have a joint seminar; and to publish an issue of a journal representing the three associations. The project was approved by the European Commission's Director General of Research; but shortly after withdrawing from the collaborative journal *Politiques d'éducation et de formation*, AFEC also withdrew from REDCOM. Again, differences of opinion on policies and financing had proved insuperable. The Spanish participants withdrew too, but IEEPS maintained the project with new collaborators – EPICE and a German journal.

But, an important and distinctive 'publication' activity emerged in the e-mail provision of AFEC-Info, by which regular bulletins provide information about comparative education activities, conferences, offers of scholarships and posts, books and journals. The service has achieved considerable popularity, in 2005 having 1,300 registered users in 92 countries. Obviously, different parts of these regular news bulletins have been of interest according to individual preferences and occupations; but for some young scholars especially, the bulletins have provided important information and have encouraged participation in comparative education conferences and research. Alain Carry was particularly influential in fostering this development.

La Francophonie: AFEC and the French Language

In its conferences, AFEC has remained resolutely true to its French-speaking nature, though in the conditions proposed for the 2005 conference it indicated willingness to receive scripts in English provided that summaries in French were also given. In the course of AFEC history there have been attempts to organise bilingual conferences, or at least conferences in England to be conducted in both languages; but unhappily, possibly because of the reluctance of some English comparativists to engage in close encounters with the French language, arrangements for these proposed conferences had to be abandoned.

By virtue of its situation and language, AFEC seems well qualified to serve the World Council of Comparative Education Societies (WCCES) in its communications with UNESCO, whose headquarters are in Paris. AFEC has been able to send to UNESCO meetings representatives able to transmit information from the international organisation to the World Council and also to make known to UNESCO, where appropriate, the views of members of the World Council. During her period as Chair of the WCCES Standing Committee on Liaison with UNESCO, Margaret B. Sutherland invited Michel Debeauvais to serve as the WCCES representative in UNESCO meetings for NGOs. Michel Debeauvais gave devoted service, as did his successor, Pierre Laderrière. Other members of AFEC have also occasionally served on UNESCO committees as NGO representatives.

At the World Council, members of AFEC have endeavoured to maintain the status of the French language. It is one of the two languages in which the Statutes were originally written; but using French at meetings has rarely been easy. While AFEC representatives can introduce themselves in French as well as in English at meetings of the Council, English has become the operational language of the WCCES Executive Committee.

Problems have also arisen in the matter of simultaneous translation at World Congresses. Given the daunting costs of this service, the need for translation in the language of the host country if that is not English has been readily recognised, but the need for provision in French has been questioned. AFEC has therefore made efforts to obtain from French official sources the necessary funding, as, for example, for the 1998 World Congress in South Africa. AFEC has also encouraged the use of French during Congress sessions, in part by seeking finance to enable francophone African comparativists to meet the expenses of conference attendance. In addition, arrangements have been made to ensure that some Congress or conference sessions are conducted in French. This was effectively done at the 2004 World Congress in Cuba, from which publication of papers was organised separately.

In 2005, AFEC learned with considerable pleasure that it was being given consultant status with the Organisation internationale de la francophonie (OIF), being one of few NGOs to have this status. In 2005, AFEC was happy also to learn of the election of its candidate, Moussa Daff of Cheikh Anta Diop University in Senegal, to the presidency of the fifth Francophone Conference of the Organisations internationales non-governmentales (OING) and of the committee following up the Conference. The Conference was organised by the Agence intergouvernementale de la francophonie (AIF).

Taking Stock

Towards the end of the 20th century, the creation of a new Association in France possibly indicated the desire of some comparativists for a greater variety of activities than AFEC's traditional annual conference supported by one or two journées d'étude. At its foundation in 1998, the Association pour le développement des échanges et de la comparaison en éducation (ADECE) expressed the wish to improve knowledge of other systems in a practical way through exchanges and other interactions with other countries. Communication was to be encouraged by conferences, seminars, a newsletter and a website. In its later form as the Association française pour le développement de l'éducation comparée et des échanges (AFDECE), this new association obviously shared objectives with AFEC and indeed had some eminent AFEC members on its Board of Directors. It was also, in 2004, admitted to membership of the WCCES. Whether, in view of the restricted opportunities for expansion of the study of comparative education, it is helpful to have two societies with similar aims and membership (and AFDECE even adopted the CIEP as its official address), was questionable. It would seem improbable that the use of the term 'French' rather than 'French-speaking' in AFDECE's title would indicate the intention to be national rather than international in nature, the more so as AFDECE's statement of aims affirmed the wish to offer all those interested in the problems of comparative education and exchanges "an international forum relevant to the field of our concerns". In times when extension of the study of comparative education was difficult, it might have seemed more sensible to have combined forces.

At the beginning of the new millennium, however, AFEC engaged in a kind of stocktaking, considering the extent to which the original aims had been achieved and what further developments seemed desirable. The committee also drafted, for approval at the 2003 Annual General Meeting in Lyon, Standing Orders for the Association – a provision which, for some reason, had not been made during the decades of its existence. Members considered that in many important respects the Association had been successful in achieving the aims stated when it was founded. Effective conferences had been organised, collaboration with other organisations had been effected, and at that time it seemed as if the publication of an international French-language journal of comparative education had been achieved. On the other hand, the creation of a closely-knit network of French-speaking comparativists had not been achieved; AFEC's participation in the WCCES and CESE conferences had not been as impressive as it might have been; and AFEC was not attracting enough members in the younger age groups.

In view of the original decision to focus on a common language rather than on common nationality as defining membership, the participation of members from other countries is obviously of considerable importance. While the Canadian conference was highly successful, it has not proved easy to develop extensive membership in Canada (Lessard et al. 1998). Canadian members have the advantage of a bilingual society at home, namely the Comparative and International Education Society of Canada; and inter-continental travel remains costly. Investigations of the situation of comparative education in other partly French-speaking countries, notably in Belgium and Switzerland (Frenay et al. 1999; Carry et al. 2005) suggested that difficulties in attracting members would continue. In these countries, while considerable developments in the teaching and study of comparative education are evident, there remain problems in the recruitment of students. The vocational advantages of the study of comparative education are not evident, and many universities are reluctant to create and maintain Chairs and Departments devoted to this study.

However, some encouraging developments in Africa may be reported. In 2001, a meeting of African comparativists in Dakar considered the formation of a Senegalese Society for Comparative Education. Pierre-Louis Gauthier explained the work of AFEC, and discussions led to creation of an African Section of AFEC called AFEC-Afrique. At the inaugural meeting, there were 25 members of this association. The decision to hold the 2004 colloquium at Ouagadougou, in collaboration with other associations, was further indicative of AFEC's interest in African studies. In 2007, AFEC went further with a proposal to the WCCES Executive Committee to host the 14th World Congress of Comparative Education Societies in Dakar in 2010. This proposal was strongly welcomed by the Executive Committee, which noted that it would take the Congress to Africa for only the second time in its history, and to French-speaking Africa for the first time in its history.

As a result of such forces, the membership profile of AFEC in 2005 had some interesting features. Among the 99 persons who had paid their subscriptions, French nationals comprised 53 per cent, while other nationals comprised 47 per cent. Just over half the members were working in universities, while 37 per cent were in non-university education and 12 per cent were in other occupations including research. By gender, membership was closely balanced, with men comprising 52 per cent and women 48 per cent.

Prospects for the Future

In a longer-term analysis of future developments, what factors seem important for the healthy progress of AFEC? What is its place in the growing network of comparative education societies? AFEC has acquired status in Europe, and has maintained good relationships with CESE. Though not officially as AFEC representatives, members of AFEC including Henk Van daele, François Orivel and Denis Kallen have served as members of the CESE Executive Committee. Yet it has been necessary to make a determined effort to ensure that the contribution of AFEC members to such international conferences is made in French. Similarly, in the WCCES the place of the French language is less than satisfactory from the point of view of those supporting it. The proposal to hold the 2010 World Congress in Senegal seemed to be a very positive way to reverse that position.

Nevertheless, it is hard to see how to overcome the neglect of official provision for comparative education in French-language universities and in particular for the absence of requirements for the study of comparative education in courses of teacher education in France and other French-speaking countries. It may be, of course, that the links being formed between European countries and the increased facilities for European students to study in other countries will inevitably lead younger generations to be curious about other systems of education because they will experience some differences first-hand. In addition, teachers of modern languages should find it necessary to be well informed about the countries whose languages they teach, and to pass on such knowledge to their pupils. However, institutional recognition of the need to provide systematically for this aspect of the education of students and of school teachers remains hard to develop. Individual contacts have certainly been made, but cannot in themselves be enough.

Difficulties in achieving the recruitment and retention of a strong membership of comparative education societies may indeed be encountered particularly because of some characteristics of the discipline of comparative education. Within scholarly circles, comparative education may be less highly regarded because it cannot claim to have its own distinctive methods of research. Thus it is sometimes described as a 'second-hand' science, depending on the results obtained by other disciplines with more specific research methods.

On the other hand, the many facets of comparative education may mean that it is widely used without adequate recognition by scholars specialising in other aspects of education such as sports education and language teaching. In these cases, isolated pieces of information about educational provision in other countries may be taken at face value without the realisation that to understand this information correctly it is necessary to have studied those systems thoroughly. Thus prospective members may be lost – and comparative education undervalued – because of the failure to realise the need for a scholarly approach to information about a particular aspect of education. A decision to create special interest groups within AFEC may be seen as recognition of this kind of motivation.

However, for better recognition of the value of comparative education, and for an increase in the numbers of those concerned with the discipline, some more subtle difficulties need to be overcome. There is the problem of the general understanding of the nature of educational studies (les sciences de l'éducation) and the need to eliminate suspicion in some parts of academe that the status of these subjects is questionable. It is perhaps unfortunate that the plural term 'sciences de l'éducation' has been generally accepted, for attention to 'sciences' tends to distract attention from the underlying reason for their existence, the study of education. All these 'sciences' are required for the full understanding of this activity.

Popularising the study of comparative education is thus made difficult by the failure to recognise that individual branches of educational studies need to be combined if the whole process of education is to be understood. Comparative education has the difficult task of recognising and synthesising the contribution of many different aspects of systems of education.

A role that has been widely claimed for comparative education is assistance with improvement of individual countries' systems of education. In turn, this role has commonly been highlighted as a justification for recruiting members to comparative education societies and for soliciting government support for their activities. It has increasingly been recognised that knowledge of what is done in other countries – including social, economic, psychological, historical factors – may be comprehensive, but that its influence on change in educational systems must ultimately depend on value judgments, on the country's essential aims. In various instances it has been evident that borrowings of individual elements of education are likely to fail if they are brought into an alien environment animated by other values. Consequently, while international surveys offer material for comparison of the effects of education in different countries, interpretations are by no means straightforward and immediate transformations cannot be expected. Comparative education cannot provide instant remedies for possible weaknesses in systems of education; yet it remains all the more important to provide by comparative methods expert interpretation of the results of international surveys, and to disentangle the underlying factors and aspirations. An original aim of the founders of AFEC was to help administrators and others in education by making available skilled interpretations of international data. This objective does seem to merit further development.

Nevertheless, even if it no longer seems fitting to claim that comparative education research can lead to large-scale amelioration of educational systems, there does remain the possibility of small-scale improvement of what is offered in education. Individual teachers are not normally in a position to make major alterations in the systems in which they work; yet the comparative study of education can help individuals to understand those systems and their aims, and so to perceive possibilities of better approaches. Such study can thus enable individuals to make some improvements within their schools – or even, through teacher associations' activities, to introduce wider changes in whole systems.

Conclusion

AFEC can and should continue to promote the study of comparative education, because this study is in itself liberating and enjoyable. For individuals, the benefits include awareness of the worldwide experiment of education – an experiment whose variables are not scientifically controlled and whose results have not been systematically recorded. This awareness of the worldwide endeavour to educate is refreshing. It seems indeed to satisfy a natural interest in educational differences in different countries, an interest which has been a human characteristic not simply since the 19th century but since classical times. AFEC members can therefore look forward to continuing developments and progress in the Association as they recall the metaphor of the great concert of planetary pedagogy proposed by Aimé Janicot (1973, p.8), AFEC's first Secretary General:

> In their classes, teachers (whether of young pupils and adolescents, or as trainers of teachers) will find benefits from comparative education. [They] will be reassured by learning about the difficulties faced by their colleagues in other countries, and encouraged by their successes. They are neither directors of operas nor conductors of orchestras, but will assume with greater confidence and finesse their functions as first violinist or fifth flautist in the grand concert of planetary pedagogy.

AFEC can also find satisfaction in the assertions of many members that they have both profited from and greatly enjoyed its activities during the decades of its existence.

References

Carry, Alain; Frenay, Mariane; Pérez, Soledad & Gorga, Adriana (2005): 'L'éducation comparée dans l'éspace francophone: tendances et perspectives'. *Revista Española de Educación Comparada*, Vol.11, pp.135-159.

Frenay, Mariane; Mc Andrew, Marie; Perez, Soledad & Lessard, Claude (1999): 'La situation de l'éducation comparée en belgique, au canada francophone et en suisse', in Leclercq, Jean-Michel (ed.), *L' éducation comparée: mondialisation et spécificités francophones*. Sèvres: Association francophone d'éducation comparée; Paris: Centre national de documentation pédagogique, pp.125-148.

Janicot, Aimé (1973): 'Réflexions du secrétaire géneral à l'issue de la création de l'association'. *Bulletin de l'association francophone d'éducation comparée*, No.1, May, pp.7-8.

Lessard, Claude; Mc Andrew, Marie; Mapto, Valèse; de Grandpré, Marcel; Joffe-Nicodème, Arlette & Lamontagne, Jacques (1998): *L'éducation comparée en langue française au canada: un bilan des activités à l'université de montréal*. Paris: Association francophone d'éducation comparée.

17

The Australian and New Zealand Comparative and International Education Society (ANZCIES)

Christine Fox

The Australian Comparative Education Society (ACES) was founded in 1973. Beginning as a national society in Australia, it soon formed links with scholars in neighbouring New Zealand. In its 10th year, the society became a regional body and was renamed the Australian and New Zealand Comparative and International Education Society (ANZCIES). It was the second regional member society of the World Council of Comparative Education Societies (WCCES), after the Comparative Education Society in Europe (CESE). At the 2006 annual conference, participating scholars from Australia, New Zealand, Fiji, Papua New Guinea, Indonesia, Korea, Japan and Vietnam called for ANZCIES to become even more regionally representative. This call may portend a new era for comparative and international education in the region, and echoed earlier proposals to hold conferences in Fiji as a means to foster regional participation. Although still of modest size, ANZCIES has exercised strong influence in comparative and international scholarship, and is helping to develop a new generation of internationally-oriented scholars throughout the Asia-Pacific region.

This history has been compiled largely through the recollections of ANZCIES members who have remained with the society since its beginnings, from a search through minutes of meetings and members' personal archives, and through the annual conference proceedings where available. ANZCIES has not maintained full records of its history, but it is hoped that the society will continue to gather historical and contemporary data as a result of this WCCES Histories Project.

Beginnings

The first conference was convened by Ron Fitzgerald at the University of Sydney in 1973. Some 100 people attended the conference, including the invited keynote speaker, Joseph Katz from the University of British Columbia, Canada. Katz was one of the founders of the Comparative Education Society (CES) of the United States, and became its President in 1961. He was also the first President of the

Comparative and International Education Society of Canada (CIESC), and a driving force behind the formation of the World Council of Comparative Education Societies. He strongly encouraged the formation of other societies, and was enthusiastic about coming to Australia to speak to the assembly.

Phillip W. Jones (2007) from the University of Sydney was at this first conference, and he has recollected that time vividly:

> Joseph Katz was keen to see that a national society was established in Australia. His opening speech was notable for the emphasis on consultancy and political engagement with governments and with the media. He stressed the impact that the world body and its constituent societies could have, highlighting the strong UNESCO link, especially in the context of developing countries. There was a lot less emphasis in his address on intellectual engagements in research and discourse between scholars. He saw comparative education very much in applied terms as having an immediate impact on policy and development systems. And I remember his punch line at the end of the speech, that this was a time for action not for words.

The convener of the 1973 conference, Ron Fitzgerald, was a senior researcher in the Australian Council for Educational Research (ACER). Fitzgerald envisaged a society that would include government officials and researchers such as himself, not only the academic community. He believed that an Australian comparative education society could motivate and coordinate Australian expertise to support the applications of comparative education overseas. This idea dominated the discussions at the inaugural annual general meeting, where a society was established formally. Phillip W. Jones (2007) recalled some of the debate:

> On the second or third day of the conference there was a major intervention by Ron Price from La Trobe University, Victoria. He lambasted the orientation of both Katz and Fitzgerald, saying that at the heart of the matter was the commitment to research, commitment to truth, commitment to building up knowledge, comparative knowledge of education systems irrespective of how that knowledge could be applied. And so Price put up an alternative model of the society, which was one grounded in academic discourse and academic engagement. He maintained there could then be a multiplicity of generic applications of that model, but the primary point was to bring scholars together. Eventually Ron Price's model was supported, but the discussion was acrimonious and Ron Fitzgerald did not come back to the newly-formed society. It was one of those crucial defining moments where the assembly in its wisdom opted for intellectual research engagement, to the extent that those who had a different vision for the society felt excluded. That's my overwhelming memory of how ANZCIES began.

The naming of the society reflects the ongoing debate about its aims and purposes. In 1975 the Australian Comparative Education Society (ACES) became the Australian and International Comparative Education Society (AICES), and in 1976 the Australian Comparative and International Education Society (ACIES).

The word International symbolised the contentious debate over the role of applied work, a debate paralleled in the United States when the Comparative Education Society (CES) in 1968 became the Comparative and International Education Society (CIES). As Phillip W. Jones recalled (2007):

> International education [was seen to be] something that you do; comparative education was a methodology as it was called back then, a basic way of studying and thinking about educational phenomena.

In 1983, the society's name changed again, to the Australian and New Zealand Comparative and International Education Society, following the first annual conference in New Zealand. At the event in Hamilton, Rosita Holenbergh was a key player, and subsequently vigorous New Zealand contributions came from such scholars as Roger Dale, Roger Peddie and John Barrington. The research interests of ANZCIES scholars have thrived in both comparative education and parallel fields such as the history of education. Several original members of ANZCIES were also prominent in the Australian and New Zealand History of Education Society (ANZHES). Other scholars were members of the Sociology Association of Australia and New Zealand (SAANZ), the Philosophy of Education Society of Australia (PESA), and other allied bodies.

Early Researchers and Centres

Key educational researchers who were present at the 1973 founding meeting included John Cleverley from the University of Sydney and Robin Burns, Ron Price and Barry Sheehan from La Trobe University in Victoria. La Trobe University was the powerhouse of comparative education in the 1970s and 1980s. With a staff of about 10 until the mid-1990s, the Centre for Comparative Education had a global reputation. The demise of the La Trobe Centre in 1994, and the gradual break up of the group of scholars at the University of New England (UNE) in New South Wales, left the University of Sydney as the principal centre for the field of comparative education. However, UNE subsequently experienced something of a renaissance in part through the leadership of Peter Ninnes (President 2003-05) and Brian Denman (President 2005-07).

Ron Price was a multilingual scholar who believed that comparative research required knowledge of the language to understand education in other cultures. He came to La Trobe from London, and was respected in European comparative circles for his work on Marx and education (e.g. Price 1977, 1987).

Robin Burns also had a significant influence in ANZCIES, and with Barry Sheehan in 1984 ran perhaps the most successful conference in the society's history on the theme of 'Women in Education'. Her 1992 book edited with Anthony Welch was among the first to problematise issues such as the state as prime unit of analysis (Burns & Welch 1992). It also addressed comparative methodology and the ethics of research; the role of international agencies; the challenge of inequality; and the nexus of comparative education and educational practice. Other noteworthy works include Burns (1975, 1990) and Burns and Aspeslagh (1996).

John Cleverley's work in both the history of education and comparative education gave ANZCIES a high profile in the 1970s and 1980s. His publications in the 1970s included focus on education in Australia and in Papua New Guinea (e.g. Cleverley & Lawry 1972; Cleverley & Wescombe 1979). Subsequently he became known for work on China (e.g. Cleverley 1985, 2000). In 1976, Cleverley wrote with Phillip E. Jones (who has sometimes been confused with Phillip W. Jones) *Australia and International Education,* an ACER publication that was an early attempt to survey the field from an Australian perspective. Phillip W. Jones wrote an ACER book with a similar title a decade later (Jones 1986). Subsequent books by Phillip W. Jones include important works on United Nations bodies and education (e.g. Jones 1988, 1992, 2005, 2006).

A third key centre in the 1970s was the University of New England where scholars included James Bowen (who, although principally a historian, also worked on Soviet education) and Phillip E. Jones, whose book *Comparative Education: Purpose and Method* (1971) was widely known. Other UNE researchers included Russell Francis (a South Pacific specialist), Zvi Halevy (from the USA and Israel), whose 1976 book *Jewish Education under Czarism and Communism* was a rare contribution to that field of comparative scholarship, and Toh Swee-Hin, a peace education and development specialist. After the tragic early death of Phillip E. Jones in 1976, Anthony Welch, newly graduated from the University of London Institute of Education, joined UNE. In the following years Welch became one of Australia's leading comparative educators, based at the University of Sydney from 1990. One of Welch's publications, *Australian Education: Reform or Crisis?* (1996) was published separately in Europe as *Class, Culture and the State in Australian Education.* Welch's Australian work echoed that of Phillip E. Jones and John Cleverley, and illustrated the close and ongoing engagement of some ANZCIES scholars with their own national system. With other authors, Welch went on to complete a second work on Australian education entitled *Education, Change and Society* (Connell et al. 2007). Among his prominent works in comparative education are Welch (2003) and Mok and Welch (2003).

Several other scholars also deserve specific note. Roselyn Gillespie and Colin Collins established a strong research base at the University of Queensland. Joseph Zajda, based in the Melbourne campus of the Australian Catholic University, became known internationally for his work on Russian history textbooks among other themes; and other early researchers who contributed regularly to ANZCIES and organised annual conferences included Kelvin Grose (UNE), Roger Hunter (Griffith University, Queensland), James Liesch (Macquarie University, New South Wales), and Bob Bessant (La Trobe University).

In New Zealand, the country's proximity to the neighbouring Pacific Islands and the need to accommodate different ethnic groups in its education system provided a different type of stimulus for comparative studies of education. In contrast to Australian patterns, much early comparative education in New Zealand was broad-based and applied in focus (Burns 1990). Among the active New Zealand members of the ANZCIES, Roger Peddie published on language policies and assessment (e.g. Peddie 1993; Peddie & Tuck 1995), and prepared the proceedings of the 1998 ANZCIES conference (Peddie 1998). Roger Dale has published on issues of globalisation and the role of international organisations (e.g. Dale 1999, 2000; Dale & Robertson 2002).

Changes and Challenges from the 1980s to the Present

Centres of comparative education scholarship and teaching in Australia and New Zealand flowered most vigorously between the late 1970s and the mid-1990s. During the first part of this period, it was not uncommon for undergraduate classes in comparative education to have over 200 students. During the mid-1980s, Australian universities diversified their intakes and opened their doors to full-fee-paying international students. ANZCIES conference themes reflected these moves. In 1986 the theme was 'Education as an International Commodity', and in 1987 it was 'Educational Exchanges and their Implications: Challenge and Response'.

In the 1990s, ANZCIES interests reflected the growing emphasis on diversity, on cultural and social constructions of education, and on qualitative approaches to comparative and international education. Debates ensued on the name of the society, with calls to move away from comparative to a focus on cultural analysis. Other attempts were made to bring in more scholars interested in internationalisation and educational development in the region. The annual conference themes again reflected the positioning of ANZCIES in the international debate. By 1999, the focus was on 'Culture, Crisis and Education', and the first conference of the 21st century was labelled 'Comparative Education in Question', followed in 2001 by 'Comparative Education on the Edge'. Table 17.1 lists the conferences and their locations between 1997 and 2006. Only one during that decade was in New Zealand, though a decision was reached to hold the 2007 conference again in Auckland, New Zealand.

Peter Ninnes was among those who challenged the society to reconsider its name. In 1995 he noted in the ANZCIES Newsletter that:

> Using the term 'comparative' fails to adequately and inclusively describe the whole range of work that goes on in the field. Recent research into the field ... has shown that much of the work that is published in major comparative education journals is not explicitly comparative, and in many cases at best only implicitly comparative. On the other hand, to limit the use of the term 'international' only to educational exchanges also omits studies that have some kind of international focus. What we need is a term that more inclusively reflects what actually happens in 'Comparative and International Education'.

At this time, ANZCIES had just agreed to host the 9th World Congress of Comparative Education Societies at the University of Sydney in July 1996. The WCCES had hoped to hold the Congress in Beijing, China, but that proved im-

Table 17.1 ANZCIES Annual Conferences, 1997-2006

No.	Year	Theme	Location
25	1997	Education, Equity and Transformation in a Postcolonial World	University of Ballarat, Victoria, Australia
26	1998	Looking at the Past, Looking to the Future: Educational Change in Comparative Perspective	University of Auckland, New Zealand
27	1999	Culture, Crisis and Education: Comparative Perspectives for the New Millennium	University of Melbourne, Victoria, Australia
28	2000	Comparative Education in Question	University of Sydney, New South Wales, Australia
29	2001	Comparative Education on the Edge: New Views, New Positions, New Discourses	Curtin University, Western Australia
30	2002	Internationalising Education in the Asia-Pacific Region: Critical Reflections, Critical Times	University of New England, New South Wales, Australia
31	2003	Education & Social and Cultural Change in the Asia-Pacific Region	University of Wollongong, New South Wales, Australia
32	2004	Global Pedagogies: Equity, Access & Democracy in Education	Australian Catholic University, Victoria
33	2005	Questioning 'Best Practice' in Education: Benefits and Disadvantages, Debates and Dilemmas	Coffs Harbour, New South Wales, Australia
34	2006	Global Governance, Educational Change, and Cultural Ecology	Canberra, Australian Capital Territory

possible because of complexities linked to the simultaneous membership in the WCCES of the Chinese Comparative Education Society (CCES) and the Chinese Comparative Education Society-Taipei (CCES-T). Anthony Welch, who was at that time part of the WCCES Membership Committee, liaised with the WCCES and ANZCIES about the possibility of stepping into the breach. Christine Fox, President of ANZCIES 1994-96, presented the successful bid at the meeting of the WCCES Executive Committee in March 1995. Fox became a WCCES Vice-President, and Welch took on the task of Congress Convenor. The Congress theme, 'Tradition, Modernity and Postmodernity in Education', reflected the ongoing intellectual debate of the 1990s, and attracted over 700 registrations from over 50 countries. A special issue of the *International Review of Education* contained some of the papers and was reprinted as a book (Masemann & Welch 1997).

The 21st century brought further discussion on the comparative-international foci, again reflected in conference themes. As Phillip W. Jones (2007) observed:

> International education has taken on an increasingly important policy weight in Australia but that's not really reflected in the constitution or membership of the society. It's reflected in the content of papers but not in the nature of the society itself.

The debate also reflected the fact that many society members, like their counterparts elsewhere in the world, taught and researched across a number of educational fields. ANZCIES members have also retained a strong interest in internationalisation of education as evidenced in the increasing numbers of overseas students in Australia. For example, the 2002 conference at UNE on internationalisation of education led to a book edited by Peter Ninnes and Meeri Hellstén (2005).

ANZCIES continues to play a major role in international circles and in the WCCES. The WCCES Executive Committee has for many years seen Anthony Welch, Joseph Zajda, Christine Fox, and Anne Hickling-Hudson take on important roles in the standing committees for publications, research, and congresses. Both Phillip W. Jones and Anthony Welch have been WCCES Vice-Presidents; and in 2001 Anne Hickling-Hudson, a prominent ANZCIES member and 1996-98 President, was elected to the WCCES Presidency. Hickling-Hudson was only the second female to be WCCES President, and the first black female. She led the WCCES from 2001 to 2004, her term concluding with the 12th World Congress in Havana, Cuba. Based at the Queensland University of Technology, she published in the areas of globalisation, post-colonialism, and comparative studies of the Caribbean (e.g. Hickling-Hudson 2003; Hickling-Hudson et al. 2004). A further ANZCIES link came in 2005 when Christine Fox was elected to the post of WCCES Secretary General for a five-year term. She moved the Secretariat from the University of Hong Kong to the University of Wollongong, where she was employed. Fox's publications focused on education in low-income countries, intercultural communication and narrative enquiry, and gender and equity in comparative perspective (e.g. Fox 1996, 2003, 2004).

The Structure and Governance of ANZCIES

Australia is a large country with its 40 universities scattered across a vast territory, and is 3,000 kilometres from New Zealand. Yet the society has remained a small, closely-knit community of scholars who meet every year at the annual conferences and with a growing regional contribution by graduate students and scholars from the Asia-Pacific region. For most years since the society was founded, there have been fewer than 100 members. Under the leadership of Peter Ninnes, ANZCIES established a website on which key information was posted; and the newsletter shifted from a paper to an electronic publication. In the 1970s, 1980s and to some extent in the 1990s, the newsletter was the main avenue for communication. It was mailed to all members, and contained news, articles, book reviews, and editorials. In 2007, ANZCIES took over the *International Education Journal* from Flinders University in South Australia, and renamed it the *International Education Journal: Comparative Perspectives*. This fulfilled a longstanding aspiration of the society to run its own journal.

The ANZCIES constitution calls for a committee that includes a representative of each Australian state as well as from New Zealand. With the advent of e-mail, the committee has been better able to confer on society matters, most of which have focused on the annual conferences. As Phillip W. Jones (2007) remarked:

> People have always said that ANZCIES is a society whose conference provided a space that was safe. Young scholars in particular ... could make presentations without too much trepidation about how others might react. When a young researcher myself, there were many meetings where I really felt I had to watch what I said, both in sessions and in the corridor. But the ANZCIES conference was always a relatively supportive space conducive to people's development as scholars.
>
> What was very good about many of the [early] meetings was that they were small enough for there to be a single program. You might have 30 people around a big table over two or three days having a conversation. There was a real cohesiveness and unity in this mutual and extended exploration of ideas, in contrast to the necessarily fragmented program of larger conferences. There have been real benefits from small size.

The ANZCIES membership still reflects its origins as an association of academic comparative and international education researchers, with a small number of members actively engaged in international development. Over the last 30 years there has been a steady decline of what used to be called the foundations of education, i.e. the history of education, sociology, philosophy and comparative education. Fewer universities have undergraduate courses in these foundations, and the University of Sydney is among the last institutions to retain them. In other universities, the decline of courses has generally caused the loss of a cohesive cohort of lecturers in the field. As a result it has become common for only one person to come to the annual conference from any one university, and many researchers no longer identify themselves as comparative educators. Phillip W. Jones (2007) noted that internationally there has been both a decline and a revival. Speculating on the form of a possible revival in Australia, he remarked:

> Whether it would involve a return to such a curriculum structure as 'comparative and international studies in education', I don't know. I would doubt it, but who knows? For me, the issue of our future is bound up with the future of teacher education in Australia, and whether we wanted to put teacher education on less of a local and more of an international footing – so that here we would provide a qualification that was globally recognised. That in itself would require more cross-cultural experience on the part of all our students, and researchers in education who were more internationally skilled and experienced. So I'm not writing off the future of the field at all, but I think it might take on a quite different configuration.

ANZCIES seems set to remain a forerunner in the field for Australian and New Zealand comparativists, internationalisation and globalisation researchers, specialists in postcolonialism and intercultural concerns, and practitioners in education and development. Publishing among members of ANZCIES has increased in the comparative education field, and the active engagement of ANZCIES members in the WCCES is striking. More educational researchers in

Australian universities and research centres are building international perspectives in their work. ANZCIES is well positioned to continue to make a significant impact on the field.

References

Burns, Robin (1975): *Higher Education and Third World Development Issues: An International Comparative Study*. Rome: Action for Development/Food and Agriculture Organization.

Burns, Robin (1990): 'Australia, New Zealand and the Pacific', in Halls, W.D. (ed.), *Comparative Education: Contemporary Issues and Trends*. Paris: UNESCO, and London: Jessica Kingsley, pp.227-256.

Burns, Robin & Aspeslagh, Robert (eds.) (1996): *Three Decades of Peace Education around the World*. New York: Garland.

Burns, Robin & Welch, Anthony (eds.) (1992): *Contemporary Perspectives in Comparative Education*. New York: Garland.

Cleverley, John (1985): *The Schooling of China: Tradition and Modernity in Chinese Education*. Sydney: Allen & Unwin.

Cleverley, John (2000): *In the Lap of Tigers: The Communist Labor University of Jiangxi Province*. Lanham: Rowman & Littlefield.

Cleverley, John & Jones, Phillip E. (1976): *Australia and International Education: Some Critical Issues*. Hawthorn: Australian Council for Educational Research.

Cleverley, John & Lawry, John (eds.) (1972): *Australian Education in the Twentieth Century: Studies in the Development of State Education*. Melbourne: Longman.

Cleverley, John & Wescombe, Christobel (1979): *Papua New Guinea: Guide to Sources in Education*. Sydney: Sydney University Press.

Connell, Raewyn; Campbell, Craig; Vickers, Margaret; Welch, Anthony; Foley, Dennis & Bagnall, Nigel (2007): *Education, Change and Society*. New York: Oxford University Press.

Dale, Roger (1999): 'Specifying Globalization Effects on National Policy: A Focus on Mechanisms'. *Journal of Education Policy*, Vol.14, No.1, pp.1-14.

Dale, Roger (2000): 'Globalization and Education: Demonstrating a 'Common World Education Culture' or Locating a 'Globally Structured Agenda for Education''. *Educational Theory*, Vol.50, No.4, pp.427-448.

Dale, Roger & Robertson, Susan L. (2002): 'The Varying Effects of Regional Organizations as Subjects of Globalization of Education'. *Comparative Education Review*, Vol.46, No.1, pp.10-36.

Fox, Christine (1996): 'Listening to the Other: Mapping Intercultural Communication in Postcolonial Educational Consultancies', in Paulston, Rolland G. (ed.), *Social Cartography: Mapping Ways of Seeing Social and Educational Change*. New York: Garland, pp.291-306.

Fox, Christine (2003): 'The Question of Identity from a Comparative Education Perspective', in Arnove, Robert F. & Torres, Carlos A. (eds.), *Comparative Education: The Dialectic of the Global and the Local*. 2nd edition, Lanham: Rowman & Littlefield, pp.133-145.

Fox, Christine (2004): 'Tensions in the Decolonisation Process: Disrupting Preconceptions of Postcolonial Education in the Lao People's Democratic Republic', in Hickling-Hudson, Anne; Matthews, Julie & Woods, Annette (eds.), *Disrupting Preconceptions: Postcolonialism and Education*. Flaxton, Queensland: Post Pressed, pp.91-105.

Halevy, Zvi (1976): *Jewish Schools under Czarism and Communism: A Struggle for*

Cultural Identity. New York: Springer.

Hickling-Hudson, Anne (2003): 'Beyond Schooling: Adult Education in Postcolonial Societies', in Arnove, Robert F. & Torres, Carlos A. (eds.), *Comparative Education: The Dialectic of the Global and the Local.* 2nd edition, Lanham: Rowman & Littlefield, pp.229-251.

Hickling-Hudson, Anne; Matthews, Julie & Woods, Annette (eds.) (2004): *Disrupting Preconceptions: Postcolonialism and Education.* Flaxton, Queensland: Post Pressed.

Jones, Phillip E. (1971): *Comparative Education: Purpose and Method.* St. Lucia: Queensland University Press.

Jones, Phillip W. (1986): *Australia's International Relations in Education.* Hawthorn: Australian Council for Educational Research.

Jones, Phillip W. (1988): *International Policies for Third World Education: UNESCO, Literacy and Development.* London: Routledge.

Jones, Phillip W. (1992): *World Bank Financing of Education: Lending, Learning and Development.* London: Routledge.

Jones, Phillip W. (2005): *The United Nations and Education: Multilateralism, Development and Globalisation.* London: Routledge.

Jones, Phillip W. (2006): *Education, Poverty and the World Bank.* Rotterdam: Sense Publishers.

Jones, Phillip W. (2007): Interview by Christine Fox.

Masemann, Vandra & Welch, Anthony (eds.) (1997): *Tradition, Modernity and Post-Modernity in Comparative Education.* Special double issue of *International Review of Education*, Vol.43, Nos.5-6. Reprinted in book form Dordrecht: Kluwer.

Mok, Ka-ho & Welch, Anthony (eds.) (2003): *Globalization and Educational Restructuring in the Asia Pacific Region.* Basingstoke: Palgrave Macmillan.

Ninnes, Peter & Hellstén, Meeri (eds.) (2005): *Internationalizing Higher Education: Critical Explorations of Pedagogy and Policy.* CERC Studies in Comparative Education 16. Hong Kong: Comparative Education Research Centre, The University of Hong Kong, and Dordrecht: Springer.

Peddie, Roger (1993): *From Policy to Practice: The Implementation of Languages Policies in Victoria, Australia, and New Zealand.* Auckland: Centre for Continuing Education, University of Auckland.

Peddie, Roger (ed.) (1998): *Looking at the Past, Looking to the Future: Educational Change in Comparative Perspective.* Proceedings of the 1998 Annual Conference of The Australian and New Zealand Comparative and International Education Society. Auckland: University of Auckland.

Peddie, Roger & Tuck, Bryan (1995): *Setting the Standards: The Assessment of Competence in National Qualifications.* Palmerston North: Dunmore Press.

Price, Ronald F. (1977): *Marx and Education in Russia and China.* London: Croom Helm.

Price, Ronald F. (1987): 'Convergence or Copying: China and the Soviet Union', in Hayhoe, Ruth & Bastid, Marianne (eds.), *China's Education and the Industrialized World: Studies in Cultural Transfer.* Armonk, New York: M.E. Sharpe, pp.158-183.

Welch, Anthony (1996): *Australian Education: Reform or Crisis?.* Sydney: Allen and Unwin. Separately published in 1997 as *Class, Culture and the State in Australian Education: Reform or Crisis?.* Frankfurt: Peter Lang.

Welch, Anthony (2003): 'Technocracy, Uncertainty, and Ethics: Comparative Education in an Era of Postmodernity and Globalization', in Arnove, Robert F. & Torres, Carlos A. (eds.), *Comparative Education: The Dialectic of the Global and the Local.* 2nd edition, Lanham: Rowman & Littlefield, pp.24-51.

18

The Dutch-speaking Society for Comparative Education (NGVO)

Sylvia van de BUNT-KOKHUIS & Henk VAN DAELE

When the Comparative Education Society in Europe (CESE) started in 1961, three scholars from the Low Countries [Netherlands and Belgium] participated as founding members: Philip Idenburg, Helena Stellwag, and Robert L. Plancke. Idenburg organised the first CESE conference in Amsterdam in 1963, and Plancke organised the third CESE conference in Ghent in 1967. It was the beginning of comparative education as an academic field in the rather small Dutch-speaking part of Western Europe.

Birth and Development of the NGVO

During the 1970s a younger generation from the Netherlands and from the Dutch-speaking part of Belgium decided to start a scientific society for comparative education using their native language. The *Nederlandstalig Genootschap voor de Vergelijkende Studie van Onderwijs en Opvoeding* (NGVO), which in English could be called the Dutch-speaking Society for Comparative Education, was founded in Leuven, Belgium, in April 1973. The first President was a Belgian, Cyriel De Keyser, and the presidency then alternated between the two countries. De Keyser was followed by Elzo Velema from the Netherlands, Willy Wielemans from Belgium, Joop Branger from the Netherlands, and Henk Van daele from Belgium.

The NGVO started as a small group of academics working in the field. Only 33 people joined the first conference, in May 1974, on the methodology of comparative education; but soon the NGVO conferences attracted the attention of teachers, school superintendents and even policy makers. The second conference, in Amsterdam in April 1977, was about 'Unity and Diversity in Education', the same theme as the joint CESE conference and 3rd World Congress of Comparative Education Societies later that year in London. In March 1978 the NGVO organised a three-day conference in Antwerp, Belgium attended by about 250 people, about the role of the teacher. The meeting in March 1979 focused on primary education.

In the early 1980s, Wim van Velsen, Director of Development and Planning of the Katholiek Pedagogisch Centrum (KPC) in 's-Hertogenbosch, was appointed NGVO Secretary. Van Velsen enhanced activities with the support of the KPC infrastructure. In September 1981 the NGVO discussed intercultural education during its conference in 's-Hertogenbosch. A working group continued to discuss this theme for several years, and attracted a large group of interested researchers and policy makers. This period also brought the first NGVO Newsletter to existence.

Other conferences followed. The October 1982 conference was organised in Ghent, Belgium by Karel De Clerck on comparison of higher education in the Netherlands and in Flanders [Dutch-speaking Belgium]. In February 1985 an NGVO symposium on education and the economy was organised at KPC with speakers including Jo Ritzen (who later became Dutch Minister of Education) and Fons van Wieringen (later Director of the Dutch Educational Council, de Vlaamse Onderwijsraad). During the 1980s, close collaboration was established with the British Comparative and International Education Society (BCIES [which later became the British Association for International and Comparative Education – BAICE]). In June 1986 a joint conference was organised at Hull University) in the United Kingdom, where topics included 'Education and Colonial Legacies', 'The Legacy for Education in the West Indies', 'Education and Contemporary Society', and 'Policy and Quality in Education'. The BCIES speakers included Colin Brock, Patricia Broadfoot and Trevor Corner. The NGVO speakers included Joop Branger, Denis Kallen, Wouter van der Bor, and Sylvia van de Bunt-Kokhuis.

The NGVO also took the responsibility to host two CESE conferences. In 1985 the Flemish members of the NGVO organised the 12th CESE Conference in Antwerp, Belgium. The theme was 'The Impact of Technology on Society and Education'. Thirteen years later, in July 1998, the Dutch members of the NGVO organised the 18th CESE Conference in Groningen, Netherlands. The theme was 'State-Market-Civil Society: Models of Social Order and the Future of European Education'. This conference was widely considered one of the most successful CESE meetings. Working Groups included focus on the European welfare state and deregulation policies in education, alternatives to state-run public educational systems, and equity and effectiveness in the perspective of empirical cross-national research.

New Directions in the 21st Century

Reorganisation of the NGVO with the advent of the new millennium permitted revitalisation and reaching out in new directions with the help of the internet. The website of the World Council of Comparative Education Societies (WCCES) provided the platform for an NGVO site, and in 2001 the NGVO Board declared the following renewed society objectives:

1. to promote the teaching, research, policy and development of international and comparative education in the Netherlands and Flanders;
2. to disseminate ideas and information, through seminars and publications in the Netherlands, Flanders, and abroad;
3. to link up with other scholarly associations of comparative education abroad;

4. to establish a vital and social network for students to find internships abroad;
5. to provide students with an opportunity to present and discuss their research progress;
6. to arouse the interest of web visitors in comparative and international studies; and
7. to raise funds by members' donations and otherwise to carry out the above objectives.

The Board aimed to establish a society panel or resonance group on the internet to share relevant knowledge and insights, and to give students and professionals the opportunity to chat on specific themes. In addition the NGVO wanted to gather some comparative and international issues for further exploration in discussion groups, workshops, etc. Topics included online learning in Northern and Southern universities, teaching styles across different cultures, and education and language learning.

It was decided that the individual membership of the society would be free of charge. Twice a year, the members/web readers received an online bulletin through subscription on an electronic distribution list. Corporate membership was envisaged for organisations with a comparative outreach, such as university departments, ministries, educational councils, international consultancy firms, etc. It was expected that these organisations would benefit from the network offered by the society, and therefore would be willing to contribute financially to the society.

Activities during the following years included:

- In 2001, the NGVO organised seminars in conjunction with the Onderwijs Research Dagen [Education Research Conferences] on topics such as 'The Relevance of International Comparative Studies' chaired by Sjoerd Karsten. Presentations included focus on educational inspection agencies within Europe by Roger Standaert (Standaert 2001), market reforms in New Zealand by Sietske Waslander, and cross-cultural indicators in education by Jules Peschar.
- Another Onderwijs Research Dagen seminar was organised in 2002 at the University of Antwerp, Belgium on school choice in a multi-ethnic society, with participants from Flanders and the Netherlands. Other issues raised during the NGVO sessions were cross-cultural indicators in education, and the school performance of ethnic minorities in schools.
- In 2004 a study visit was organised to the European Parliament in Brussels, Belgium with speakers on the history of educational policy and the impact of Europe on national educational policies, and an international symposium 'Globalisation and the Freedom of Knowledge'.
- In 2005 an international symposium on lifelong e-learning was organised at Middlesex University in the United Kingdom in collaboration with the NGVO, and supported by the European Commission.

The Secretariat and responsibility for the NGVO Newsletter moved in 2003 to the

Haagse Hogeschool/TH Rijswijk in The Hague, Netherlands. The internet allowed the NGVO to reach larger audiences of professionals interested in comparative education.

In addition to its corporate activities, some NGVO members have also contributed to the field of comparative education through their publications. These include the works of Van daele on the history of the field (1993; 1999), various comparative studies on European education (Karsten & Majoor 1995; Wielemans & Roth-van der Werf 1997; Peschar & van der Wal 2000; Sun 2003), and van de Bunt-Kokhuis' work on lifelong e-learning (2006).

Conclusion

The alternation in the organisation of activities between universities in the Netherlands and Belgium is evidence of the good fellowship that has long existed among the comparativists of the Low Countries. Comparison of patterns in the two countries has itself been a major focus of work, in addition to comparisons of education in other parts of the world.

Although the NGVO has always been a rather small group, its members have been active in larger bodies as well as in the NGVO itself. Most obvious has been the role in CESE, for which NGVO members have organised several biennial congresses. Other explicit links have been with the BCIES, and some NGVO members have also had strong links with the Comparative and International Education Society (CIES) and the Association francophone d'education comparée (AFEC). The NGVO has valued its membership of the World Council of Comparative Education Societies (WCCES), which has given the NGVO a voice on the global stage.

References

Bunt-Kokhuis, van de, Sylvia (ed.) (2006): *World Wide Work: Filtering of Online Content in a Globalized World.* Amsterdam: VU University Press.

Karsten, Sjoerd & Majoor, Dominique (1995): *Education in East Central Europe, Educational Changes after the Fall of Communism.* Berlin: Freie Universität.

Peschar, Jules L. & van der Wal, M. (eds.) (2000): *Education Contested: Changing Relations between State, Market and Civil Society in Modern European Education.* Lisse: Swets & Zeitlinger.

Standaert, Roger (2001): *Inspectorates of Education in Europe: A Critical Analysis.* Leuven: Acco Leuven.

Sun, Hechuan (2003): *National Contexts and Effective School Improvement: An Exploratory Study in Eight European Countries.* Groningen: Groningen State University.

Van daele, Henk (1993): *L'éducation comparée.* Paris: Presses universitaires de france.

Van daele, Henk (1999): 'Introduction: de Jullien aux sciences de l'éducation', in Leclercq, Jean-Michel (ed.), *L'éducation comparée: mondialisation et spécificités francophones.* Sèvres Association francophone d'éducation comparée, pp.13-15.

Wielemans, Willy & Roth-van der Werf, Trudy (1997): *Onderwijsbeleid in Europees perspectief.* Leuven-Apeldoorn: Garant.

19

The Spanish Comparative Education Society (SEEC)

Luis M. NAYA & Ferran FERRER

A discussion of the history of the Spanish Comparative Education Society (Sociedad Española de Educación Comparada – SEEC) allows one to discover unexplored dimensions which had not previously received sufficient focus, while helping to trace the trajectory of a community of persons and institutions who had contributed to the society in a decisive way. In our case, this challenge is augmented by the fact that the authors have been Secretary and President of the society. Luis Naya has been a member since 1995, and Ferran Ferrer since 1982. The work for this chapter brought reflection on events that they had experienced without then occupying positions of responsibility and, as a consequence, without all the first-hand data necessary to have a meaningful understanding of the evolution of the society. Now, with a grasp of the contextual elements and with the distance given by the passage of time, the analysis of the evolution of the SEEC becomes more complex and is thus enriched.

Various documents have been employed to accomplish this task. The first category includes minutes of the meetings of the Executive Committee and the Assemblies, financial statements, membership records, Bulletins, correspondence from the Presidents and Secretaries, and other documents in the archives. The second category embraces publications of and about the society: issues of the Spanish Journal of Comparative Education (*Revista Española de Educación Comparada* – REEC), proceedings of the national congresses, and the SEEC homepage. Also in this category are works by such authors as Marín (1985), González (1989), González et al. (1996), Valls (1998), Ferrer (2002), Martínez (2003), and García Garrido (2005). After analysing this invaluable documentation, the authors thought it appropriate to divide the history of the SEEC into different stages and to use a descriptive typology for each era. The following paragraphs show different ways of conceptualising and directing the society – and the field of comparative education – depending on the period of reference.

The history of the SEEC can be conceived as in three stages: the first starting from its establishment in 1974 until 1979; the second from 1979 to 1994; and the third from 1994 to the present. During the first two stages the society was called the Spanish Comparative Pedagogy Society (Sociedad Española de Pedagogía

Comparada – SEPC). Each stage must be understood within the political, educational and other contexts in which it developed. Furthermore, each stage is an offspring of the preceding one.

To provide a summary of leadership and a framework for what follows, Table 19.1 lists the Presidents and Secretaries over the decades. Of course many other actors were also important, but they cannot all be named here. At the time of writing, the society had approximately 150 members. This had grown steadily since just over 100 in 1996. It was considerably below the peak of 250 reached in 1988, but not all members at the peak period actually paid their subscriptions.

Table 19.1: SEPC/SEEC Presidents and Secretaries

Period	President	Secretary
1974-1977	Juan Tusquets	Emilio Redondo
1977-1981	Ricardo Marín	Justo Formentín
1981-1988	Ricardo Marín	Jose A. Benavent
1988-1989	Ricardo Marín	Francesc Raventós
1989-1994	Ricardo Marín	Mercedes Vico
1994-1998	José Luis García Garrido	Ángel González
1998-2002	Ángel González	Ferran Ferrer
2002-2006	Ferran Ferrer	Luis M. Naya
2006-	Vicente Llorent	Inmaculada Egido

First Stage: The Beginnings of the Society (1974-79)

This stage commences with an important figure in comparative education in Spain, Juan Tusquets, Director of the Instituto de Pedagogía Comparada (Institute of Comparative Pedagogy), which since 1964 has been affiliated with the Consejo Superior de Investigaciones Científicas (Spanish National Research Council) and the Universidad Central de Barcelona. This scholar gave a decisive push to the formation of the society in 1974. Tusquets had been linked to the World Council of Comparative Education Societies (WCCES), and this linkage was among the factors that led to the establishment of the SEPC. One venue through which Tusquets called for a society was the journal of the Instituto de Pedagogía Comparada, *Perspectivas Pedagógicas*. Tusquets urged (1971, p.377) not only that the society be established but also that "an authentic pluralism inspire the Statutes of the Sociedad Española de Educación Comparada whose creation cannot be delayed if we want to avoid the risk of not being represented in the World Council of Comparative Education Societies". In this article Tusquets used the term 'Educación Comparada' in the title of the proposed society, though in the initial decades 'Pedagogía Comparada' was used by the body formed in 1974.

Also important during this early stage was Victor García-Hoz. After establishing the Instituto de Pedagogía Comparada and becoming a member of the Comparative Education Society in Europe (CESE), in 1965 Tusquets handed over his role as the Spanish representative in CESE to García-Hoz (Tusquets 1979).

The Spanish society made its first international public appearance during the 2nd World Congress of Comparative Education Societies in Geneva, Switzerland, in 1974; and the second appearance was in the 7th CESE Conference in Sèvres, France, in 1975.

The location of the headquarters of the new society was of no lesser importance. Tusquets favoured establishing it as a section of the Spanish Pedagogical Society (Sociedad Española de Pedagogía) with its office in Madrid, but García-Hoz, Marín and Angeles Galino argued for its establishment in Barcelona given the pivotal role of the Institute in the field of comparative education. Finally, this latter proposal was accepted, and Tusquets became the first President of the society. When Ricardo Marín was elected SEPC President in 1977, he transferred the seat of the society to the Universidad de Valencia where he was a professor.

The idea of a Bulletin for the society was first raised officially in a letter sent by Marín to the members in December 1978. The inaugural issue was published in 1979, though it took 1978 as its year of publication. Subsequent issues followed until 1987, the year of its last issue (no.10).

This historical period of the society can thus be characterised as follows:

- The personification of Spanish comparative education in Juan Tusquets, through the Instituto de Pedagogía Comparada, and more especially through its journal *Perspectivas Pedagógicas*, strengthened the links of the field with international societies and helped in its international recognition.
- During this stage, the SEPC consisted of a small nucleus of internationally-renowned university professors who were deeply identified with the field.
- Because of its small size, during this period, the SEPC was able to operate without a clear set of normative Statutes. The Statutes were not formally approved until 1980.
- The society's Bulletin played a role similar to that of the newsletters of other societies such as CESE.

Second Stage: The Period of Consolidation (1979-94)

During this entire period, Ricardo Marín was SEPC President. This gave great continuity, though there were changes in the Board of Directors. The office of the SEPC remained in the Universidad de Valencia until the end of this period.

The era began with the first large event sponsored by the society. This was the 9th CESE conference, held in Valencia in June 1979 on 'The Influence of International Educational Research on National Education Policies'. The idea of hosting this conference in Valencia had been broached by the CESE President, Denis Kallen, in a telegram to Marín in June 1978. Ultimately, the Instituto de Ciencias de la Educación (ICE) of the Universidad Politécnica de Valencia hosted the event under the leadership of José Luis Castillejo. The conference was attended by 180 participants, the majority coming from Europe.

During this conference, the different European societies of comparative education organised several parallel sessions. The SEPC together with the Italian society chose the theme 'International Influence on the Regionalisation of Educational Policy'. Tusquets, by that time Honorary President of the SEPC, delivered the inaugural address on 'The Idea of Europe in the Mind of Spanish Comparative Educators'. Kallen stated in his opening address that the choice of Spain as the host of this conference had been determined partly by political factors, meaning newly-established democracy after many years of military dictatorship, and partly by the fact that the Spanish scholars had recently formed their comparative education society (Kallen 1979, p.5).

All these events undoubtedly led to the definitive takeoff of a society of which the members were increasing in number, despite an ongoing debate about its official name. The minutes of the meeting of the SEPC Executive Board on 19 January 1980 stated that:

> In view of the suggestion to change the name of the Sociedad Española 'de Pedagogía Comparada' to 'de Educación Comparada', it was decided to opt for the former terminology since it was considered more precise and more authentically European.

A provisional version of the Statutes had been prepared in 1978, and a copy had been sent by Marín as SEPC President to Anne Hamori, Secretary General of the WCCES. The Statutes were approved two years later after having been revised upon the request of the Ministry of Interior Affairs. The Statutes were finally registered on 28 March 1980, and the society was entered in the Registry of Associations as a 'cultural and research association'. Most of the members were university professors from different areas in the field of education (e.g. school guidance, special education, general pedagogy, history of education, educational research, didactics), and were not specifically from the area of comparative pedagogy. A resolution passed by the General Assembly in 1983 opened SEPC membership to students in the fifth year of their undergraduate degree who were studying comparative pedagogy at Spanish universities. A 50 per cent discount on membership dues was offered to student members.

The Statutes envisaged centres of comparative pedagogy outside the official headquarters of the SEPC in Valencia. More specifically, Article 4 indicated the possibility of establishing "social centres in other cities by entering into an agreement with the Board of Directors". This provision reflected a policy which was actively promoted by the society's officers, and was in line with the trend towards deconcentration of power that matched developments in Spain's political context during this period. The first centres to be approved, in 1980, were the Universidad Central de Barcelona, Universidad Autónoma de Barcelona, Universidad de La Laguna, Universidad Complutense de Madrid, Universidad de Palma de Mallorca, Universidad de Navarra, Universidad de Salamanca, Universidad de Santiago de Compostela, Universidad de Tarragona, and Universidad de Valencia. The initiative continued to widen, resulting in a total of 15 centres in 1986. The centres organised seminars, colloquia and other activities specific to comparative education, and some centres, such as the Instituto de Pedagogía Comparada at the Universidad Central de Barcelona, were very active. The membership dues were collected through these centres. Half of the amount was retained by the centre for its discretionary use, while the other half was remitted to the SEPC Treasurer as the centre's contribution to the SEPC.

The society also organised National Congresses. The first was held in Valencia in 1979 in conjunction with the CESE conference, and entitled 'The Influence of International Educational Research on National Education Policies'. Subsequent events were freestanding, as follows:

- 2nd National Congress: 'Secondary Schooling from a Comparative Perspective', Universidad de Granada, 1984.
- 3rd National Congress: 'The University Today in an International Context', Universidad de Málaga, 1987.
- 4th National Congress: 'Educational Reforms and Innovations at the Threshold of the 21st Century', Universidad Nacional de Educación a Distancia, Madrid, 1990.

The idea of publishing a journal was also being contemplated by the society, but did not materialise during this period. José Luis García Garrido formally proposed this initiative during the 1984 General Assembly in Tarragona. After debate, with some in favour but others proposing a publication in book format, it was decided to adopt the latter commencing with a book on secondary education. The editorial board comprised one member from each affiliated centre – with a view to fostering an even more territorialised image of the society – and with Marín as its Chief Editor. A Proceedings from the congress on the theme of secondary education was published, but after several attempts no further books were produced. Further, over a decade elapsed before a product in journal format finally emerged.

During this period, SEPC members participated actively in CESE affairs. During the 1979 conference in Valencia, Tusquets was elected an honorary member of CESE, and Marín was elected to the CESE Executive Committee. Then in the 10th CESE conference in Geneva in 1981, García Garrido was appointed CESE Vice-President. He later became its President from 1985 (12th CESE conference in Antwerp, Belgium) until 1988 (13th CESE conference in Budapest, Hungary). In 1985, García-Hoz was also appointed an honorary member of CESE. In 1981 the 10th CESE conference in Geneva, Switzerland, was attended by 24 SEPC members.

The links between the SEPC and the WCCES were likewise very strong. García Garrido was the SEPC representative in the WCCES Executive Committee throughout the 1980s and the early 1990s. In 1980, the 4th World Congress of Comparative Education Societies in Tokyo, Japan, welcomed 25 SEPC partici-pants, with 11 paper presentations.

This phase of the history also continued discussion on the name of the society. It was widely recognised that 'Comparative Pedagogy' better reflected the vision that SEPC members had of the field. Nevertheless, some members expressed the need to change it to 'Comparative Education'. Among the most explicit examples was the suggestion in 1984 by Julio Ruiz Berrio during the Ordinary Assembly on the occasion of the 2nd National Congress in Granada. He proposed that the new name be Sociedad Española de Educación Internacional y Comparada (Spanish Society of International and Comparative Education), like the US-based Comparative and International Education Society (CIES). Since the proposal required an amendment of the Statutes, thereby requiring a special Assembly, no decision was taken and the matter was deferred.

In summary, the salient characteristics of this period in the society's history were:

- its formal consolidation as the Sociedad Española de Pedagogía Comparada through the approval of its Statutes;
- growth in the number of members, with a clearly dispersed profile of specialisations although all belonged to the field of pedagogy;
- convergence in a view of comparative pedagogy as a proper sub-specialisation of pedagogy;
- consolidation of a democratic structure for running the society, wherein the Board of Directors was accountable to its members, and these in turn elected the candidates for the different positions with no formal requirement other than 'one voice, one vote';
- publication of the Bulletin as a means of communication among the members; and
- shaping of the society led by the formation of affiliated centres based in the Spanish universities that applied for it.

Concerning the last of these points, the members of the affiliated centres automatically became members of the SEPC. This was a strength insofar as the society was composed of university professors from very diverse disciplines, but the fact that many members did not identify academically with the field of comparative education caused difficulties in collecting fees from a substantial portion of the membership.

Third Stage: The Period of Specialisation (after 1994)

The discussion on this period examines various factors that exerted a direct influence on the development of the society, some of which were endogenous and others exogenous. Starting with the latter, two factors must be highlighted. The incorporation of Spain into the European Union brought a heightened interest in international affairs both in political circles and in society at large; and the government set out general curriculum guidelines for accreditation of degrees in pedagogy in all Spanish universities (*Boletin Oficial del Estado*, No.206, 1992). Comparative education appeared in these guidelines as a subject under the category of compulsory foundation (troncal) courses to be taken in the third or fourth year for the Bachelors Degree in Pedagogy. A minimum of six credits (60 class hours) was required, and this could be increased at the discretion of each university. This regulation obliged many universities that had not previously offered the subject to add it to their programmes, and resulted in an increase in the number of professors who were teaching comparative education.

As to the endogenous factors, the beginning of this era in the history of the society was typified by two important events. First, new Statutes in 1994 brought the significant change in the society's name to Sociedad Española de Educación Comparada (SEEC). This name change was basically motivated by two practical reasons. On the one hand, as explained in the previous paragraph, comparative education became a compulsory subject in all Spanish universities offering a degree in Education. On the other hand, the term 'comparative education' had gained wide usage in the Spanish educational literature. It was thus apposite to change the name of the society to adapt to the changing times. The second major event during this period was the launch in 1995 of the society's journal, the *Revista Española de Educación Comparada*, edited by the Department of History of Education and Comparative Education of the Spanish National University of Distance Education (Universidad Nacional de Educación a Distancia – UNED).

García Garrido, chair professor of Comparative Education in UNED, was elected SEEC President in 1994, and the headquarters of the society were transferred to the UNED in Madrid. García Garrido set in motion a series of projects, many of which were completed immediately. Among them were an informative bulletin, a scientific journal of comparative education, regular congresses, networking, and strengthening the direct participation of the members in the society. This task of profound renewal of the society – one could even speak of a second founding – took its first step with an Assembly in 1994, during which it was decided to change the name of the society and to grant it new Statutes that were more responsive to the prevailing socio-educational situation in Spain.

The bulletins became an effective means of communication during these years, comprising 18 issues published in 11 years. In 2003 the format was redesigned to permit full colour printing, making them more attractive. The possibility was raised of replacing the printed copies an electronic version, thereby reducing costs and speeding up communication among the SEEC members.

In the 1994 Assembly, it was also announced that, after a five-year hiatus, the 5th National Congress of Comparative Education would be held the following year in Valencia. The theme was 'Education, Employment and Professional Formation', and the event attracted over 150 participants from 20 universities, with 42 paper presentations. After this event, the congresses again became more regular. The next, in Seville in 1998, was entitled 'Focusing on Early Childhood and Educational Space: Comparative Dimensions'. It was probably the best attended National Congress of the SEEC, attracting over 500 participants.

During this event, Ángel González, chair professor of comparative education in the Universidad de Murcia took over from García Garrido as President. The new leadership conscientiously assumed its mandate, and in 1999 organised the 2nd Scientific Seminar on Comparative Education in Murcia for the purpose of reflecting on the teaching of comparative education in the Spanish universities, and presenting the academic panorama of the field. The 3rd Scientific Seminar took place in Seville in 2001 on the theme 'Youth, Environment and Education'. The following year, the 7th National Congress was held in Murcia with the title 'Reality and Prospects of Higher Education: A Comparative Perspective'.

The next congress took place in Salamanca in 2002 on the theme 'Compulsory Education in Spain and Latin America: Current Situation and Future Prospects'. On this occasion, a new Executive Committee was elected, chaired by Ferran Ferrer. This leadership focused on deepening the society's relationship with the WCCES and on new strategic directions including convocation of awards and publication of a new bulletin. Moreover, and as a result of a legislative change in Spain, a new set of Statutes was drafted. These were unanimously approved in the Assembly held in Seville in October 2003, and were inscribed in the National Registry of Associations of the Ministry of Interior Affairs in March 2004.

The 9th National Congress was held in March 2005 in the Universidad de Granada on the theme 'Convergences in Higher Education in the European and Latin American Sphere'. The theme aimed to address and respond to the concerns and challenges that the Bologna Process had introduced in the European university setting, as well as the evolution of this theme in the Latin American world. It was followed by the 10th National Congress in San Sebastian in 2006, on 'The Right to Education in a Globalised World'.

In another initiative, in 2004 the SEEC inaugurated the Pedro Rosselló Prize with the aim of providing an incentive to students whose doctoral theses were methodologically and/or thematically relevant to comparative education. Pedro Rosselló was a distinguished comparativist of Spanish nationality who worked for nearly 30 years (1929-1967) at UNESCO's International Bureau of Education in Geneva, Switzerland. The winners of the 1st Pedro Rosselló Prize in 2004 were María Rosa Oria Segura for her thesis on 'Legal, administrative and organisational structures for managerial practice: Comparative case studies of England, France, Italy and Spain'; and Javier Manuel Valle López for his thesis on '50 years of Educational Policy in the European Union (1951-2001): Foundations and Actions'. In 2006, the 2nd Pedro Rosselló Prize was awarded to María Teresa Terrón for her thesis on 'Education within the family setting of Moroccan immigrant children in the Province of Huelva. A comparative study with Moroccan families in their home country from the mothers' perspective'. The award of €600 was to be made available every two to three years.

Another fundamental element that guided the work of this stage of the society's history was the publication of the *Revista Española de Educación Comparada*. It operated under the editorial leadership of García Garrido, and aimed to fill the vacuum left by the discontinuation of *Perspectivas Pedagógicas*. The journal also counted on a Secretary, Javier M. Valle, and an editorial advisory board which had a representative from each university department that collaborated with the journal. Most issues of the journal had four distinct parts: the Monograph Section coordinated by an expert who was responsible for soliciting contributions from authors of the coordinator's choice; the Studies and Research section, which presented unsolicited articles received by the Editorial Advisory Board, after having been approved by two blind peer reviewers; a third section on New Publications, containing critical reviews of recent books; and a final section entitled Documents which presented legislative innovations in education reforms in different countries.

In the first 10 issues of the journal, 69 articles were published in the Monograph Section and 29 in the section on Studies and Research, with over 120 contributors. This decade of work showed a plurality of themes, types of studies and units of comparison. The articles also showed the co-existence of diverse methods of investigation, although with the marked dominance of "the qualitative over the quantitative and the strictly comparative studies" (Martínez & Valle 2005, p.87). During this decade, the journal made comparative research visible in the Spanish-speaking world. The journal achieved the objectives for which it was created in 1994, and seemed set to continue doing so in its forthcoming issues. The titles of the Monograph Section of the first 12 issues were:

1995: Education Reforms in Europe: East-West
1996: Education, Training and Employment in Developed Countries
1997: Concept, Methods and Techniques in Comparative Education: A Tribute to Jullien de Paris on the150[th] Anniversary of his Death
1998: Education in the 21st Century
1999: Higher Education in the Knowledge Society
2000: Educational Prospects in Latin America
2001: Secondary Education
2002: Society, Education and Cultural Identity
2003: Early Childhood and Human Rights
2004: New Educational Perspectives in the 'New Europe': Challenges and Trends in Education Policy in the Context of a Wider European Union
2005: Ten Years of the REEC: Comparative Education between Two Centuries (1995-2005).
2006: The Bologna Process. Dynamics and Challenges facing Higher Education in Europe at the Beginning of a New Era

Another element that was useful in making comparative education in Spain even more visible was the launch in 2000 of the society's website, with the address www.sc.ehu.es/seec. The website consisted of a pyramidal complex of more than 50 pages with over 2,000 external and internal hyperlinks. It was organised in two big blocks: one containing internal information about the society (Statutes, Board of Directors, bulletin, journal, application form, etc.); and the other, the more substantial part, offering links with other websites in the field. It was displayed in Spanish and an important part in English, and within six years of its launch had received over 40,000 visitors. An analysis of the visits revealed that it had become a frequently-used tool for teaching and research in the field (Naya 2005, p.249). The homepage also received prizes from the Association of Webmasters and Website Designers.

The SEEC played a leading role in the initiative to form the Asociación Iberoamericana de Sociedades de Educación Comparada (AISEC), which was established during the 12th World Congress of Comparative Education Societies in Havana, Cuba, in 2004. The association, coordinated by the SEEC President as its inaugural chairperson, was initially modest but expected to grow in strength and stature. It established contact with the Organización de Estados Iberoamericanos (OEI), with the aim of obtaining financial assistance.

In summary, the major features of this epoch were:

- a change in epistemological orientation, expressly manifested in a change of name, not only of the society but also of the field;
- a significant increase in membership to the extent of achieving a stable nucleus of around 140 specialists who regularly paid their dues, many of them clearly linked to the field of comparative education, and supported by the fact that all Spanish universities offering a degree in pedagogy were obliged to offer comparative education as a compulsory subject;
- in line with the previous point on having members who were specialists in comparative education in contrast to preceding periods where most members were outsiders interested in the field, discontinuation of the practice of university-linked centres, recognising that very few were active in 1990 and that the majority had become dormant years earlier;
- maintenance of a democratic structure in the management of the society, continuing the tradition initiated in the previous period;
- continued functioning of the Bulletin as an organ of internal communication among the members; and
- a more visible international profile of the society achieved through the launch of the society journal in 1995 and the website in 2000.

Conclusions

The evolution of the SEEC took place within the context of the political, academic and cultural transformations that Spain underwent during the decades from 1974. It is therefore important to understand the society's development by locating both the information and the decisions taken at each moment within their contexts. It is equally important to underscore that the SEEC has always been very conscious of the international thrust of the society and of the field. This consciousness took on different hues and directions in each period, but the effort was ongoing.

The SEEC has always shown interest in developing occasions for meeting among its members, which, while pursuing a clear professional objective, were also a means to project the national and international image of the field. These have been achieved in particular through the national congresses, seminars and symposiums.

Looking at the future, the society faces significant challenges. In the internal sphere (although it also has important external implications), it is indispensable to make the society more visible on the internet. In this respect, the translation into English of a part of the homepage has helped. The conversion of the current printed version of the Bulletin into an electronic version is another project that has been envisaged. The expected cost savings and the faster circulation of news to be achieved with this innovation are the key elements warranting this change. In this same sphere, the society is considering the possibility of publishing such research work and/or teaching materials in electronic format, as it may be less easy to get them published in the traditional manner.

At the same time, in the area of university teaching, Spain is on the verge of new reforms in the degree conferment system. Likewise, the discourse about the curriculum for tertiary education – which will reopen debates about the compulsory and optional subjects, among them comparative education – should place the SEEC in a position to participate in the discussion and contribute its expertise. In addition, teaching approaches are likely to change radically, gravitating towards student-centred learning instead of teacher-centred approaches. This change is necessary, but will certainly generate tensions among academics including professors of comparative education.

Finally, an important element to which the SEEC will have to contribute is a more profound cultivation of comparative education as a field of study. We cannot remain at the level of "talking there about what is done here, and talking here about what is done there". It is imperative for comparative education scholars to do the real work of comparison and to transcend the barriers of mere description, aiming for more analytical and explanatory approaches, and even seeking new objects of study that would result in expanding the current boundaries of comparative education.

References

Ferrer, Ferran (2002): *La Educación Comparada Actual*. Barcelona: Ariel.

García Garrido, José Luis (2005): 'Diez Años de Educación Comparada en España'. *Revista Española de Educación Comparada*, No.11, pp.15-35.

González, Angel (1989): *Lecturas de Educación Comparada*, Barcelona: Promociones y Publicaciones Universitarias.

González, Angel; Sáez, Juan & Encabo, Jesús (1996): *La Comparación en Educación y Lecturas de Pedagogía Comparada*. Murcia: Diego Marín Librero.

Kallen, Denis (1979): Opening Address, in CESE: *IX Conferencia de la CESE, 25-29 Junio 1979*. Valencia: Instituto de Ciencias de la Educación/Universidad Politécnica de Valencia.

Marín, Ricardo (1985): 'Sociedad Española de Pedagogía Comparada (SEPC)', in Ruiz Berrio, Julio, *Diccionario de Ciencias de la Educación: Educación Comparada*. Madrid: Anaya, pp.192-194.

Martínez, María Jesús (2003): *Educación Comparada: Nuevos Retos, Renovados Desafíos*. Madrid: La Muralla.

Martínez, María Jesús & Valle, Javier M. (2005): '10 Años de la REEC: Una Mirada en Perspectiva'. *Revista Española de Educación Comparada*, No.11, pp.37-93.

Naya, Luis M. (2005): 'La Educación Comparada en los Nuevos Espacios Virtuales (1995-2004)'. *Revista Española de Educación Comparada*, No.11, pp.241-272.

Tusquets, Juan (1971): 'La Personalidad, el Pensamiento y la Obra de P. Rosselló'. *Perspectivas Pedagógicas*, No.27, pp.333-381.

Tusquets, Juan (1979): 'La Aportación Española al Comparativismo Pedagógico'. *Revista de Educación*, No.260, pp.115-131.

Valls, Ramona (1998): *Pedagogos Comparatistas Catalanes del Siglo XX: Rosselló, Tusquets, Sanvisens: Una Visión Prospectiva*. Barcelona: Facultat de Pedagogia/ Universitat de Barcelona.

20

The Chinese Comparative Education Society (CCES)

Gu Mingyuan & Gui Qin

The Chinese Comparative Education Society (CCES) was founded in 1979, and admitted to the World Council of Comparative Education Societies (WCCES) in 1984. It has undergone remarkable changes over the decades, and its history has instructive messages for wider understanding of the nature and purpose of the field.

This chapter is partly based on previous studies, including those by Jin and Zhou (1985), Chen (1992), Bray and Gui (2001), and Gu (2001, 2003a, 2003b). It is also based on interviews and discussions with key actors, and on the authors' personal experiences. The discussion is contextualised within the wider political, socio-cultural, and intellectual settings.

The first part of the chapter is an account of the birth of the CCES. The focus then turns to the name and nature of the society, and to leadership and membership. The next part focuses on functions and activities, and the final parts of the chapter address challenges and directions.

Birth of the CCES

The birth of the CCES was linked to the creation in 1979 of the Chinese Society of Education (CSE), which is China's largest learned society in the field of education. The CCES evolved from a national conference on foreign education as discussed below.

Embryonic Form of the CCES

After the downfall of the radical leftists known as the Gang of Four, paramount leader Deng Xiaoping was reinstated to all his previous posts in August 1977. Under his leadership, the Ministry of Education resumed work that it had been forced to stop during the 1966-76 Cultural Revolution. As early as August 1977, a symposium on Foreign Education Study was organised in Beidaihe, Hebei Province. Participants included scholars from Beijing Normal University (BNU), East China Normal University (ECNU), Northeast Normal University (NENU), and Hebei University (HU). Participants in the symposium considered directions and approaches for research on foreign education in the new context.

Following the symposium, the Foreign Education Research Institute at BNU convened a national meeting on foreign education in July 1978 in co-operation with the other three universities plus South China Normal University (SCNU). It was a particularly significant event since it was still difficult in that era to organise national meetings. The Institute had to rent bedding for a total of 50 participants, and had to secure additional rice from the Food Department since food was strictly rationed. During the conference, participants discussed the research plan drafted during the symposium in Beidaihe, exchanged ideas about the roles of each university, and decided to hold an annual conference by taking turns among the five institutions.

The CCES Founding Conference

Following the plan made in 1978, a National Conference on Foreign Education Research was held in Shanghai from 24 October to 3 November 1979. The body which evolved into the CCES was founded during this conference.

Prior to the Shanghai meeting, further political changes had taken place. In December 1978, the Third Plenum of the 11th Party Congress Central Committee launched the Reform and Open Door Policy; and within weeks China established official diplomatic relations with the USA. The Central Committee of the Communist Party of China (CPC) decided that the major focus would shift from political class struggle to economic construction. The 1979 New Year editorial in the official newspaper *People's Daily* declared that in order to accelerate development, import of all advanced sciences and technology was encouraged regardless of their origins. Education was recognised as a key instrument, and the Ministry of Education collaborated with the National Social Science Academy to organise a conference from 23 March to 13 April 1979 during which the CSE was established. It mobilised educationalists nationwide to conduct research by setting up their own associations affiliated to the CSE.

Because foreign education research became even more important in the context of the reform and open door policy, programmes in foreign studies within the universities were enlarged, and some were promoted to become independent institutes. The Foreign Education Research Institute at BNU was one of them. In addition, in July 1979 the China National Institute of Educational Research (CNIER) was reopened, and foreign education study was established as a research division within the Institute. Because education was permitted as a degree major in 1978 by the Ministry of Education, and comparative education became a required course in teachers' colleges, more scholars and institutes became involved with the field. In 1979, training of graduate students majoring in comparative education started in both BNU and ECNU. That year, seven students were admitted to the programmes.

There was also a need for institutes and scholars to cooperate to prepare textbooks. In February 1979, the Ministry of Education, Ministry of Foreign Affairs, and Ministry of Finance released a policy entitled 'Contemporary Methods and Regulations for Strengthening Importing Textbooks from Abroad'. In March, the Ministry of Higher Education organised some universities to discuss editorial work. In order to accelerate the provision of texts in comparative education, a strategy which combined importing from abroad and editing by Chinese scholars was accepted. Kandel's (1955) book *The New Era in Education*, and Kazamias and Massialas' (1965) book *Tradition and Change in Education* were chosen for translation by teams in six universities. At the same time, preparation of a Chinese textbook was initiated.

When the second national conference was held in Shanghai in October 1979, over 90 scholars attended, i.e. nearly twice the number of the first meeting. They came not only from the five universities involved in the first conference, but also from the CNIER, the People's Education Press, and teachers' colleges across the nation. Participants discussed what they should do according to the government's draft 'Outline of National Development Planning in Educational Science'. They decided to create their own national association affiliated to the CSE which would have more authority to organise national activities.

Following this decision, the CCES was set up. Liu Fonian, as the President of ECNU and the Vice-President of CSE, was elected President. The Secretariat was placed in the CNIER because its location in Beijing and its status as a national institute made it more representative than any individual college or university. The Board of Directors decided to focus on the following three activities:

- list the institutes and researchers involved in foreign studies nationwide, in order to recruit members for the society;
- implement the academic plan for the coming year, including symposia on preparation of a textbook on comparative education and on education in the Soviet Union; and
- publish *Foreign Education* as an official journal of the Society, with the editorial office being located in the CNIER and that body providing financial resources.

Name and Nature

When established in 1979, what later became the CCES was officially named the Foreign Education Research Sub-commission of the CSE. Four years later it became the Comparative Education Sub-commission of the CSE. These names reflected the wider environment and its evolution.

CCES as Foreign Education Research Sub-commission of CSE

The name itself reflected epistemological and teleological characteristics of the society. First, the focus was more on foreign education than on comparative education *per se*. As Chen (1992, p.278) pointed out, the proportion of journal articles and books in which comparisons were made among different countries or areas was small. Among the journals he studied, this proportion was less than 20 per cent. All institutes specialising in comparative education were named Institutes or Centres of Foreign (rather than Comparative) Education Research; and key journals had such titles as *Foreign Education Conditions* (published by

BNU), *Foreign Education* (published by CCES), and *Journal of Foreign Education Studies* (published by ECNU).

Second, the name indicated that as a branch of CSE, the CCES should share the mission and regulations of the CSE. The mission of CSE was to unite and organise the numerous educators who were focused on research, and to carry out theoretical and practical studies under the guidance of Marxism-Leninism and Mao Zedong Thought. The CSE was committed to promoting educational reform, developing the educational cause, establishing the educational system with Chinese characteristics, and building up socialist modernisation. The mission of the CCES fitted within this framework (Chen 1992, pp.121-122). The core princeples included leadership by the CPC. This meant that even as a non-government academic organisation, all CCES activities had to fit with CPC policies. In this linkage to a political body, the CCES differed from most other member societies of the WCCES.

CCES as the Comparative Education Sub-commission of CSE

The name changed from Foreign to Comparative in 1983 during the society's fourth national conference in Changchun. The change reflected changes of understanding about the nature of comparative education, particularly as a result of the programme in BNU. In 1980, a document entitled 'Rules about Chinese Academic Degree System' had been promulgated. This document classified comparative education as a sub-discipline of educational science. In order to have deeper understanding, the Ministry of Education invited Hu Chang-tu, a professor from Teacher's College, Columbia University in the USA, to lecture on comparative education at BNU.

Gu Mingyuan as President of the CCES, Dean of the College of Education, and Director of the Institute of Foreign Education Research took responsibility for the matter. He invited comparative education teachers from 10 universities across China to attend the course, which lasted for three months. At the end of the course, these teachers decided to prepare a textbook of comparative education. In order to ensure the quality of the work, Gu as chief editor invited two other senior scholars to join him: Wang Chengxu of Hangzhou University and Zhu Bo of South China Normal University. The book was finally published under the title *Comparative Education* by the People's Education Press (Wang et al. 1982), and was the first such work to be published since 1949. It was reprinted many times, and by 2001 had sold 112,700 copies. The book disseminated the concept of comparative as opposed to foreign education. It defined comparative education as a discipline aiming to provide reference for educational reform in one's country or area by seeking general laws and specific regulations in the development of education through comparative analysis of different countries or areas. As part of this shift of emphasis, in 1981 the Institute of Foreign Education in ECNU was renamed the Institute of Comparative Education.

Because the name Comparative Education Sub-commission of the Chinese Society of Education was rather long, it was often abbreviated. When the society joined the WCCES, it was under the English-language name of China Comparative Education Society. However, in contemporary times in English it is more commonly called the Chinese Comparative Education Society.

Leadership and Membership

Leadership

The leading body of the CCES is its Board of Directors. It manages the affairs of the society within the framework of general procedure established by the Regulations. One of the Board's most important duties is to elect the President, Vice-Presidents, and Secretary General from its membership.

According to the CCES Regulations, consideration should be given to each municipality, province and autonomous region when the Board of Directors is being elected. Such regulations reflect efforts to respond to unbalanced geographic development. In 1990, the 40 members of the Board came from 16 provinces and municipalities; and among the 40 members, 13 were from Beijing and six from Shanghai (Chen 1992, pp.136-137). By 2004, membership had increased to 48 because of the emergence of comparative education institutes in other cities. The members came from 17 provinces and municipalities, which was almost the same as in 1990, but only 10 came from Beijing and three from Shanghai.

Other changes occurred in the age structure of the Board of Directors. In 1990, 20 of the 40 members were over the age of 60, 15 were aged 50 to 59, four were aged 40 to 49, and one was aged 30 to 39 (Chen 1992, p.138). In 2004, by contrast, only four of the 48 members were over the age of 60, and most were aged between 35 and 45 (Gui 2005). This change reflected the expansion of the field among young scholars.

The Executive Committee exercises authority when the Board is not in session. In 1990, the Committee had 11 members who had been elected from and by the Board; but in 2004 the Committee had expanded to 30 (Gui 2005). According to the regulations passed at the 12th National Conference of the CCES in 2004, consideration was to be given not only to geographic distribution but also to the academic level of institutes. It was decided that Committee members should come only from institutes which had doctoral and master's programmes in comparative education. Since all institutes with doctoral programmes also had master's programmes, those institutes were given two seats on the Executive Committee. In 1990, only three institutes were permitted to provide doctoral programmes in comparative education, but by 2005 the number had increased to seven.

A close relationship exists between administrative positions and the nomination or election of members, in part because members who hold administrative positions in their institutions can more easily obtain financial and other resources to support the CCES activities. Therefore, the administrative position rather than academic degree or professional position becomes the most important criterion to be considered in the nomination and membership of the Board of Directors and Executive Committee.

Administrative position is also very important in the election of the President. During the two and a half decades from 1979, the CCES had five Presidents: Liu Fonian (1979-81), Zhang Tianen (1981-83), Gu Mingyuan (1983-2001), Liang Zhongyi (2001-03), and Zhong Qiquan (2004-). Liu and Zhong came from

ECNU in Shanghai; Zhang came from the CNIER in Beijing; and Liang came from NENU in Changchun. Gu's tenure of nearly 19 years was much longer than others, and showed a pattern which differed from that in many other WCCES constituent societies.

Membership

The CCES membership increased from 90 in 1979 to 343 in 1985 (Jin & Zhou 1985) and then 683 in 1990 (Chen 1992, p.139). In 2004 it was slightly lower at around 500. The membership is both institutional and individual. According to the Constitution, any institute or individual who agrees with the society's Constitution and who works in the field of comparative education can apply to become a member. Institutional members should obtain approval from the Board of Directors, and individual members should be recommended by a member of the society and then gain approval from the Board. In practice, scholars who work in organisations which are institutional members consider themselves to be CCES members. As a result, there are very few individual members. The CCES in this sense is a national mass academic organisation based on institutional members. Most of the individual members are overseas students.

According to the Constitution adopted in 2004, each member of the Executive Committee should pay 400 yuan per year, and each member of the Board of Directors should pay 200 yuan per year. Other institutional and individual members are not required to pay membership fees. Such regulations aim to motivate people to join the society, while stressing the responsibility of the leading members.

Among the institutional members, BNU has always played a very strong role. In 1991 its journal, *Comparative Education Review*, became an official publication of the CCES. In 1993, a book entitled *Methodology in Comparative Education* written by Xue Liyin, the third doctoral student supervised by Gu Mingyuan, drew attention to the differences among the terms 'international education', 'development education', 'global education', and 'comparative education'. Scholars in the field increasingly felt a need to stress international education within the field of comparative education. In 1995 under Gu's suggestion, the Institute of Foreign Education Research in BNU was renamed the Institute of International and Comparative Education. One year later, the Institute of Comparative Education in ECNU was renamed, and other institutes followed.

Functions and Activities

Functions

When it was founded, the CCES was expected to:

- advise local chapters in each province, municipality, and autonomous region;
- coordinate studies and projects in order to serve policy makers and educators;

- select and disseminate information;
- encourage promising young scholars; and
- develop two-way rather than one-way international exchanges.

During the following decades, much evolution occurred. The 2004 revised regulations indicated that the CCES would:

- organise academic conferences;
- publish the CCES journal;
- conduct academic exchange among members of the society;
- carry out academic and educational exchange with Hong Kong, Macao and Taiwan;
- improve academic and educational exchange and cooperation with other countries;
- provide advice for educational policies and practice; and
- advocate transformational activities, including publication, training and operation of experimental schooling.

One major difference in these two lists was the removal in 2004 of the provision of advice to local chapters. By 1990, nine chapters had been set up around the country. When the CCES Constitution was revised in 2004, the Board of Directors felt that the society should not have local chapters since it was itself a sub-association or chapter of the CSE. However, to avoid dampening the enthusiasm of the local groups, the CCES still permitted them to conduct activities.

A second change was the stress on dissemination and use of knowledge in comparative education in more ways, including the operation of experimental schools. This could never have been imagined in 1979, but had been made possible by the market-economy policy promulgated by the CPC Central Committee in 1993.

In addition, cooperation and exchange with Hong Kong, Macao and Taiwan was expressed explicitly because of the return to China of Hong Kong and Macao in 1997 and 1999 respectively, and the strong national desire for further unification with Taiwan. The greater stress on international academic exchange and co-operation reflected the impact of globalisation and internationalisation, especially after China's 2001 entry to the World Trade Organisation.

National Conferences and Symposia

Organisation of conferences and symposia has always been one of the most important activities of the CCES. Table 20.1 lists the national conferences convened between 1978 and 2004. Although the frequency had been expected to settle down to a biennial pattern, it was sometimes disturbed by the political situation and the society's financial condition. For example, the fifth conference was held in 1986 instead of 1985, in part because the national campaign against spiritual pollution in 1983 and 1984 discouraged activities related to foreign studies. The 1986 conference was inspired by the 1985 *Decision on National Reform in Structure of Education*. Subsequently, the sixth conference was post-poned to from 1988 to 1990. Although shortage of funds was one important reason for the postponement, the campaign against bourgeois liberalisation initiated by the student movement in 1986, and the political disturbance in 1989, were more important factors. The conferences could thus in a way be seen as a kind of barometer indicating the status of comparative education in China.

Table 20.1: CCES National Conferences, 1978-2006

No.	Year	Location	Theme
1	1978	Beijing	Exchange information and ideas about foreign education research; discuss division of labour and cooperation among the five main institutes
2	1979	Shanghai	Foundation of the CCES and work plan until the next conference
3	1981	Baoding, Hebei	Relationship between education and economy; educational administration and law; educational structure reform; teacher education trends; higher education reform trends; recent developments in foreign pedagogy; issues related to preparation of the textbook on comparative education
4	1983	Changchun, Jilin	Disciplinary building of comparative education; compulsory education; combination of education and production; higher education reform in China.
5	1986	Wuhan, Hubei	Learning international lessons, discussing structural reform in education
6	1990	Tianjin	Educational reform, retrospect and prospect of comparative education
7	1993	Beijing	Comparative education towards the 21st century
8	1995	Jinan, Shandong	Education in Asia Pacific and economic development
9	1997	Huangshan, Anhui	Cultural tradition and educational modernisation
10	1999	Beipei, Chongqing	Training of talent in different countries in the century of transformation
11	2001	Guilin, Guangxi	Lifelong learning in China
12	2004	Zhuhai, Guangdong	Chinese educational reform in the context of globalisation
13	2006	Shanghai	Teacher education, curriculum reform, and international collaboration

The locations of the conferences are also worth mentioning. Some were held in Beijing and Shanghai, but the rotation to other cities had a great impact because it provided opportunities for participants from different locations. During the first two decades, the organisers had to limit the number of participants because they had to take responsibility for buying tickets, and meeting and seeing off all participants. Purchase of tickets was really difficult because at that time the trains were crowded and seats could not be booked in advance. Moreover, the conference organisers were expected to provide daily meals and welcome and departure banquets. Since the organisers could not expect to gain funds from the participants, they had to seek sponsors. The rotation of locations not only spread the burden but also gave opportunities to regional institutions to host participants from elsewhere.

Also significant was the evolution in conference themes. The first four conferences were based around issues to be discussed rather than themes *per se*. The introduction of themes from 1986 onwards reflected growing maturity. From that date, prospective presenters were required to address the conference themes, and proposals were accepted or rejected by the conference organising committees.

The seven issues discussed during the 1981 conference reflected concern with practical issues, especially educational reforms at all levels in other countries. However, the 1983 conference was more concerned with the disciplenary building of comparative education, which led to the change of the society's name. Discussion focused on the nature of comparative education, which had been listed as a key national research project under the direction of Zhu Bo. There were altogether seven key national research projects in the field for the sixth five-year educational research plan.

The fifth conference, held in Wuhan in 1986, was much larger than previous events in part because it was stimulated by the CPC Central Committee education reform document. For the first time, some Japanese comparative educationalists were invited. At the conference, preparation of a new version of the standard textbook was discussed. Participants recognised the need to include China, as well as the value of including a focus on India and other less developed countries.

The 1990 conference was the first to focus on the history of the field. Events since the 1986 conference, and in particular the political movement associated with Beijing's Tiananmen Square in 1989, encouraged members to look back at the development of the field since 1979. Participants discussed three problems in the previous decade. First, comparative education researchers had paid much attention to foreign education but little attention to what was happening in China. Second, the research lacked strong theoretical frameworks; and third, scholars had paid insufficient attention to the construction of the discipline. Although in the initial decade several textbooks on comparative education had been published, these works had not broken away from the conventions of the 1950s and 1960s in either methodology or content. The textbooks could be used only as introductory materials for newcomers to the field, and they reflected neither the development of comparative education as a sub-discipline in educational science nor a manifestation of the characteristics of comparative education in China (Gu 1991, pp.5-8). In order to stress comparative study and attempt to overcome the above problems, the name of the journal was changed from *Foreign Education Conditions* to *Comparative Education Review* after it was selected as the official publication of the CCES.

The themes of subsequent conferences were directly related to key national research projects, such as 'Cultural Tradition and Educational Modernisation', which was a project in the eighth five-year national educational research plan. The theme of the 2004 conference was 'Chinese Educational Reform in the Context of Globalisation', which had become a major issue in the field.

In addition to the national conferences, many symposia were organised either solely in the name of the CCES or were co-hosted. About 30 symposia during the 1980s focused on issues such as The College Entrance Examination in Foreign Countries (1982), Educational Reform in the Soviet Union (1984), The New Revolution in Technology and Educational Reform (1985), and Educational Reforms in Foreign Primary and Secondary Schools (1987). Most were small events, but during the 1990s they became larger. During the decade and a half from 1990, the BNU Institute of International and Comparative Education organised 26 conferences and symposia. The 1999 event on private education was the largest, and attracted 310 participants.

The conferences and symposia provided a platform for scholars to discuss their research plans, collect information and ideas on particular issues, find potential partners, and disseminate their findings. This function was extremely important when transportation was not easy and information was limited. Papers on methodology and disciplinary construction were normally published in a special section in the CCES journal after each conference. Apart from these special sections, few articles focused on this topic in any of the journals.

Publications

The CCES has produced three types of publications: the official journal, collections of conference papers, and books. The initial journal, *Foreign Education*, was launched in 1979 and ceased publication in 1991. It was published bimonthly and had a circulation of about 10,000. At the sixth national conference in 1990, according to the policy of the CPC Central Committee made after the 1989 political movement that each institute was permitted to publish only one journal in each field, the CCES decided to stop publishing *Foreign Education* edited by the CNIER because the CNIER also published a major journal entitled *Educational Research*. Instead, BNU's *Foreign Education Conditions*, which had been informally circulated as a bulletin since 1965 and had been given permission for formal publication in 1979, was selected as the CCES official journal.

The BNU journal also had a circulation of about 10,000. However, the circulation dropped to 5,000 when its name was changed to *Comparative Education Review* in 1992, even though both names had been on the journal during 1991 in order to allow readers to become familiar with the new name. The fall in circulation reflected the lower interest in the academic field of comparative education compared with the more factual domain of foreign education. Nevertheless, by 2001 the journal's circulation had risen to 5,600. Articles in the journal were typically five to seven pages in length (maximum 8,000 Chinese characters). This permitted a large number to be published, but the waiting list remained long. In order to reduce the pressure, during the 11th national conference in 2001 the committee decided to double the number of annual issues from six to 12; and two years later the number of pages in each issue was increased from 64 to 96. The journal also functioned as a window for scholars in mainland China to note developments in Hong Kong. From 1999 to 2001, a special section of the journal was devoted to Chinese translation of articles from *CERCular*, the newsletter of the Comparative Education Research Centre at the University of Hong Kong.

The CCES has also regularly published collections of papers from the national conferences. Most were produced by the host universities, but a special collection entitled *Vertical and Horizontal Study of International Education: Collection of Chinese Comparative Education* was produced by the CCES after the sixth conference, and was published in 1992 by the People's Education Press. The collection contains 62 articles published between 1979 and 1990 as a retrospect on the development of the field since the establishment of the CCES.

Subsequently, the CCES sponsored various books. In 1992 during the 90th anniversary conference of BNU, the CCES obtained support from the People's Education Press for a book series. Gu Mingyuan as the CCES President became the Chief Editor, and Zhou Nanzhao of the CNIER and Lu Da of People's Education Press became his deputies. Ten books were published in 1997 and 1998. In 2000, in order to reflect new research findings and achievements, the CCES produced two sets of volumes. One set contained works written by Chinese scholars, and the other contained translated works written by foreign scholars.

International Activities and Impact
During the first decade, the international activities of the CCES mainly consisted of Chinese scholars going out of the country rather than external scholars coming in. In order to become part of the international community and to learn about the wider field, the CCES sent delegates to all the Congresses of the WCCES during the 1980s. In 1980, Gu Mingyuan, Jin Shibo and Su Zhen attended the fourth congress held in Tokyo, and submitted the CCES' application to join the WCCES. In 1984, Ma Jixiong of ECNU from Shanghai and Liu Wenxiu of Hebei University from Baoding attended the fifth congress in Paris, when the CCES became a formal member of the WCCES. In that year the CCES also sent a delegate to Japan to attend the 20th conference of the Japan Comparative Education Society (JCES).

In 1987, the 6th World Congress in Brazil was attended by Jin Shibo, Zhou Nanzhao, Wu Fusheng, Meng Xiande and Gu Mingyuan. At this conference, the CCES delegates expressed their desire to organise a world congress in Beijing. The 7th World Congress held in Montreal, Canada, in 1989 was attended by Zhou Nanzhao, Zhan Ruiling, Wu Fusheng, Bi Shuzhi, Wang Yingjie and Gu Mingyuan. At the congress, because of the 1989 political movement associated with Beijing's Tiananmen Square, the climate for a congress in Beijing was not favourable. As a result, the 8th World Congress was held in Prague, Czechoslovakia. In 1990, Gu Mingyuan and Zhou Nanzhao went to Spain to attend the meeting of the WCCES Executive Committee which was held in conjunction with the biennial conference of the Comparative Education Society in Europe (CESE). Their particular objective was to discuss the 9th World Congress which they still proposed to host in Beijing. At that meeting, Gu Mingyuan was elected Vice-President of the WCCES.

In 1992, Zhou Nanzhao, Wu Fusheng, Zhan Ruiling and Gu Mingyuan attended the 8th World Congress in Prague. During the Congress they discussed how to organise the 9th World Congress in Beijing; but by this time the Office of Hong Kong, Macao and Taiwan Affairs in the State Education Commission (Ministry) in Beijing had called attention to the fact that the Taiwan society was a member of the WCCES under the Chinese-language name of Republic of China Comparative Education Society. The English-language name was the Chinese Comparative Education Society-Taipei (CCES-T), but the existence of this English-language version did not satisfy the authorities in Beijing. Since the Taiwan society refused to change the Chinese-language version of its name, and the WCCES Executive Committee did not feel able to force the Taiwan society to do so, the officials in Beijing indicated that the CCES could not participate in WCCES affairs.

Because of this problem, the plan to hold the 9th World Congress in Beijing again failed. During subsequent years, while CCES scholars were allowed to join WCCES events on a personal basis, the CCES did not send official delegations to WCCES events. This was a great loss to all sides. The CCES lost the official opportunity to present the Chinese voice among WCCES members, and to see and experience developments in the global field; and the WCCES lost the active involvement of one of its largest members.

To help compensate for the loss, the CCES began to organise more international conferences and symposia for which it invited foreign scholars to China. Leading members of the CCES had been founding members of the Comparative Education Society of Asia (CESA), which was established at the University of Hong Kong in 1995; and the second CESA conference was co-hosted by the CCES and held in Beijing in 1998. Over 200 participants from 13 countries in Asia, North and South America, Australia, and Europe attended this conference. In 2002 BNU hosted the First Worldwide Comparative Education Forum on the theme 'Globalisation and Educational Reform'; and in 2005 it hosted the Second Worldwide Comparative Education Forum on the theme 'Globalisation of Education: Government, Market, and Society'.

Challenges and Directions

Challenges

Some of the challenges facing the CCES arise from the wider context, and have evolved over time. When the society was established, none of the five institutions working in the field of foreign education research was pre-eminent in authority. The CCES, as a national academic organisation, thus had more legitimacy than any single institution to organise national activities. However, this situation changed during the 1990s when BNU began to play a dominant role in the CCES. Balances were challenged when BNU's Institute of International and Comparative Education became a National Research Base in the Discipline of Comparative

Education in a prestigious 'Project 211' funded by the national government. The issues could be seen even more clearly when Gu stepped down as President in 2001, because the existence and vitality of the CCES could mainly be recognised through the activities organised by BNU. Even when the activities were organised in the name of the CCES, such as the Worldwide Comparative Education Forums in 2002 and 2005, the real organiser was BNU and the CCES was just one joint sponsor among others. Gu was followed as President by Liang Zhongyi of Northeast Normal University, but he died two years later. The election of Zhong Qiquan of ECNU to the CCES presidency in 2004 created a new set of balances since ECNU already had a vigorous comparative education journal of its own, and since the CCES Secretariat also moved to Shanghai.

Other changes occurred in the identities of some of the bodies which had institutional membership of the CCES. The Institute of Comparative Education in Northeast Normal University became independent in 1986, but was merged into the School of Education in 1993; the Institute of Comparative Education in ECNU was first merged with the Institute of Curriculum and Instruction in 1998, and then in 2000 merged into the Department of Curriculum and Instruction which was a part of the School of Education; and the BNU Institute of International and Comparative Education was merged into the School of Education in 2001. The loss of independence of these institutes exacerbated problems of identity for the field of comparative education.

When China's door had just opened to the world in the 1970s and 1980s, scholars in comparative education who wished to work from anything other than translated sources had to master a foreign language. Most of the early scholars indeed came from the foreign language institutes. As knowledge of foreign languages became more widespread, this characteristic ceased to be the special advantage of comparative educationalists. Further, with increased international exchange and the rapid development of information technology, materials about foreign education could be obtained with increasing ease. Scholars in comparative education could still have maintained their distinctive contributions if they had been able to undertake extensive fieldwork, but opportunities for such work were limited. Further, the scholars in comparative education paid inadequate attention to conceptualisation and methodology. Therefore, it seemed that comparative studies could be conducted by any scholar who knew a foreign language or had foreign education materials. This dilution created a problem of identity recognition in the field. Many graduates took comparative education as a major, but they did not strongly identify with the field. Most specialised in other branches of education, such as preschool education, curriculum, management, higher education, and sociology of education, in order to improve their opportunities for employment. As a result, few involved themselves in the activities of the CCES.

Directions

Given these challenges, the future vitality and development of the CCES will depend on the role that it can play during the coming decades. New themes are emerging, and the CCES has many opportunities.

Since the mid-1990s, internationalisation of education in the context of globalisation has become a key issue of comparative education research in China. Scholars recognise that new questions about resources, information and structures should be studied in relation to internationalisation. These issues were stressed during the 12th national conference of the CCES in 2004, and the construction of the discipline with Chinese characteristics was regarded as an important and urgent task (Gu 2005, p.2). Internationalisation has been considered one of the most rapid ways for China to develop, but the field of comparative education did not seem to be in a strong position to play a leading role. It is true that since the mid-1990s some scholars had tried to strengthen the construction of the discipline (see e.g. Xue 1993; Gu & Xue 1995; Wang 2005; Gui 2005). However, much remained to be done. One way to do this was through the internationalisation of comparative education itself, with the recruitment of more international scholars and students to the research institutes, and a stronger external interflow.

It is also arguable that the CCES should further modify its regulations. In addition to geographic criteria, members of the Board of Directors could be selected to bring in a wider range of research interests; and in addition to (or instead of) administrative positions, scholars' academic reputations could be regarded as important criteria. Sub-groups could be set up to address tasks such as theory and methodology; knowledge production and dissemination; lifelong learning; global pedagogy; and international exchange. Efforts could also be made to attract scholars from different branches of education.

Conclusions

This chapter has examined three decades of the CCES history within the wider political, socio-cultural and intellectual contexts. The establishment of the CCES was a response to the need for resumption and development of international communications when China's reform and open door policy were launched in the late 1970s. The characteristics of the CCES were shaped by its mission under the leadership of the CPC, guided by Marxism-Leninism, Mao Zedong Thought and, later, Deng Xiaoping Theory. Its evolution also reflected the developmental stages of comparative education in China, from foreign education to comparative education – though in practice much work would still fit more easily under the old label than the new one.

Over the decades, several factors contributed to the strong development of the society. These factors included its authority as a national body with official approval, the system of institutional membership, and, particularly in the early years, the pressure for applied study which would generate lessons for national development. However, these factors also brought challenges. The link to the government and the CPC required the CCES to withdraw from official participation in WCCES affairs pending resolution of the Chinese-language name of the Taiwanese society; and scholars in the field did not always relate their work to the needs of education in China. Inadequate attention was given to conceptualisation in the field; and the roles of institutions sometimes overshadowed the roles of the society. The future directions for the CCES will be strongly influenced by the forces of globalisation. Leading scholars are at the same time keen for China to assert its own identity in the field, and thus to construct a discipline with Chinese characteristics. Much has been achieved within a relatively short time; and many further achievements can be predicted as China continues its trajectory of internationalisation and economic development.

References

Bray, Mark & Gui, Qin (2001): 'Comparative Education in Greater China: Contexts, Characteristics, Contrasts and Contributions'. *Comparative Education*, Vol.37, No.4, pp.451-473.

Chen, Shuching (1992): *Comparative Education Studies in the People's Republic of China*. PhD Dissertation, State University of New York at Buffalo.

Gu, Mingyuan (1991): 'Comparative Education: Retrospect and Prospect'. *Comparative Education Review* (Beijing), Vol.67, No.1, pp.5-8. [in Chinese]

Gu, Mingyuan (2001): *Education in China and Abroad: Perspectives from a Lifetime in Comparative Education*. CERC Studies in Comparative Education 9, Hong Kong: Comparative Education Research Centre, The University of Hong Kong.

Gu, Mingyuan (2003a): 'The Mission of Comparative Education in the Era of Knowledge Economy'. *Comparative Education Review* (Beijing). Vol.152, No.1, pp.1-5. [in Chinese]

Gu, Mingyuan (2003b): 'Identity of Comparative Education: Crisis and Solution'. *Comparative Education Review* (Beijing), Vol.158, No.3, pp.1-4. [in Chinese]

Gu, Mingyuan (2005): 'Comparative Education and Me'. *Comparative Education Review* (Beijing), Vol.176, No.1, pp.1-4. [in Chinese]

Gu, Mingyuan & Xue, Liyin (1995): 'The Internationalisation of Education and Issues of Comparative Education'. *Comparative Education Review* (Beijing). Special Volume, October, pp.12-18. [in Chinese]

Gui, Qin (2005): 'Dichotomy or Unity? Implications of Change Theory in Ancient China'. Paper presented at the 49th Annual Conference of the Comparative and International Education Society, March 22-26, Stanford University, USA.

Jin, Shibo and Zhou, Nanzhao (1985): 'Comparative Education in China'. *Comparative Education Review* (Beijing), Vol.29, No.2, pp.240-250. [in Chinese]

Kandel, Isaac L. (1955): *The New Era in Education: A Comparative Study*. Boston: Houghton & Mifflin.

Kazamias, Andreas M. & Massialas, Byron G. (1965): *Tradition and Change in Education: A Comparative Study*. Englewood Cliffs, New Jersey: Prentice Hall.

Wang, Changchun (2005): 'On the Harmony in Differences Again: The Orientation of the Development of Chinese Comparative Education in the Context of Globalization'. *Study of Foreign Education*, Vol.32, No.9, pp.1-6. [in Chinese]

Wang, Chengxu; Zhu, Bo & Gu, Mingyuan (eds.) (1982): *Comparative Education*. Beijing: People's Education Press. [in Chinese]

Xue, Liyin (1993): *Methodology in Comparative Education: Comparative Education as a Forum of International Communication in Education*. Beijing: Capital Normal University Press. [in Chinese]

21

The Brazilian Comparative Education Society (SBEC)

Marta Luz Sisson de Castro

In Brazil, as elsewhere, the field of comparative education is gaining relevance as an academic area in the globalised world because of the interdependence between nations and the similarity of educational challenges faced by many countries. Technological advances have facilitated access to information about education systems in different regions and countries. One limitation for Brazilians is the lack of knowledge of English and other foreign languages, but increasing numbers in the young generation are well prepared for communication in foreign languages.

The Brazilian Comparative Education Society (Sociedade Brasileira de Educação Comparada – SBEC) was founded in 1983 by a group of professors of education, and is relatively young in the Brazilian educational context. The more traditional societies, such as the National Association of Policy and Educational Administration (Associação Nacional de Política e Administração da Educação – ANPAE), are over 40 years old. The SBEC seems to be reaching adulthood if we compare it with the ages of humans; but in several respects the society is still in its adolescence, trying to find a role and identity in the social environment.

The main objective of the SBEC is the promotion of comparative studies through the teaching of comparative education and the networking of researchers. The society had 121 members in 2005, and one objective of its leadership was to increase both the membership and the visibility of the SBEC. Most members have some form of international background and/or have studied abroad. Most speak at least one foreign language, usually English, and most are related to the academic world. Meetings and seminars are the society's main activities, and some people become members during those events. The society has long published a bulletin three times a year, and has planned a digital journal.

The Early Years

Eurides Brito da Silva, who was SBEC President from 1983 to 1990, was very active, and participated strongly in the affairs of the World Council of Comparative Education Societies (WCCES). During an interview which was a source of information for this chapter, she indicated that the society had been founded to express the interests of a group of professors of school administration within the ANPAE. There were two groups of professors: one from the University of Brasilia and another from Rio de Janeiro. Jacira Câmara, Eurides Brito da Silva and Clélia Capanema formed the Brasilia group, which was later enriched by the participation of Cândido Gomes. The group from Rio de Janeiro had professors from different universities in the region: Sonia Nogueira and Mabel Tarré Carvalho de Oliveira from the Federal University of Rio de Janeiro, and Fátima Cunha from the Federal Fluminense University, Niterói. In 1981 and 1982, a seminar was held in Brasilia with the presence of international scholars including Robert Cowen from the University of London Institute of Education. This seminar stimulated interest in international education and comparative themes.

In one ANPAE meeting, this group decided to organise the society. The initial members were professors of educational administration who had attended international meetings promoted by the World Council, and they brought the experiences from the World Council to the Brazilian society. They shared common interests in comparative education, and were well acquainted with journals such as the *Comparative Education Review* published by the US-based Comparative and International Education Society (CIES). They had links with scholars in Europe, including Brian Holmes from the University of London Institute of Education. The society organised support from different scholars around Brazil, including Roberto Ballalai from the Centre for Comparative Education at the Federal Fluminense University in Niterói, Cândido Gomes in Brasilia, and Maria Luiza Chaves from the Federal University of Ceará. In addition, Robert Verhine from the Federal University of Bahia had very good contacts in the University of California at Los Angeles (UCLA) in the USA, which helped the society in its initial phase.

Eurides Brito da Silva, the first President of the SBEC, was a well-known figure in Brazil. Perhaps because of her political position, the society was considered conservative by other educational associations. She commented that some traditional societies openly opposed the formation of the SBEC as a new academic society, partly reflecting the difficult period in Brazilian history. In 1964 a military coup had brought an authoritarian political regime which had lasted until 1985 when elections were held. With these events the country moved in the direction of a democratic government, and everything had to be black or white, leftist or rightist. The fact that the SBEC was considered rightist created unnecessary resistance to the society.

The role of Roberto Ballalai as Secretary General during Brito's presidency was very important. The Centre for Comparative Education in Niterói, where Ballalai worked, provided the institutional support for the activities of the society.

The 6th World Congress

A major event in the history of the SBEC was the 6th World Congress of Comparative Education Societies hosted by the SBEC in Rio de Janeiro in 1987. The World Congress brought the theme of comparative education to the Brazilian educational arena.

The decision to organise the Congress partly arose from discussions that Eurides Brito da Silva and Sonia Nogueira had had with Michel Debeauvais, who was WCCES President between 1983 and 1987. Debeauvais had raised the idea, and the Brazilian team decided to respond proactively. Brito, looking back at the experience, described it as an act of courage and an effort to disseminate comparative education in the Brazilian context. The first big decision was about the location for the meeting. Rio de Janeiro was selected because it was a tourist attraction and because it had a group of scholars able to promote the event. The meeting was organised in a cooperative way by the two initial groups in Brasilia and Rio de Janeiro.

One challenge was to secure finance for the Congress. In 1986 the organisers approached national funding agencies without initial success, but in 1987 Brito and Nogueira went to the Ministry of Education and received sufficient funds to pay for air tickets and accommodation for the invited international speakers. That support was essential for the success of the Congress.

The theme of the Congress was 'Education, Crisis and Change'. Participants from 73 countries joined the event, and the SBEC achieved a three-fold increase in membership. Approximately 500 papers were presented, and the SBEC President was elected Vice-President of the World Council. The Brazilian participants were exposed to international scholars in education, and the event was a national landmark. The Brazilian participants came from diverse universities around the country, and the theme of comparative education was disseminated to a large number of Brazilian professors. An edited book was published as a result of the Congress (Verhine 1989).

The 1990s and Beyond

Although the expectations were very high of the effects of the Congress, during subsequent years activity declined. Nevertheless, Brazilian involvement in World Council events was sustained. For example, Sonia Nogueira took charge of a Commission in several subsequent Congresses, and the number of Brazilians participating in comparative education events was maintained.

Cândido Gomes was President of the society from 1990 to 1993. During the interview for this chapter he recalled two seminars in Brasilia, one of which was held in the Senate in 1992. It discussed the relations between research and educational policy and involved Brazilian educational leaders including Darci Ribeiro and João Calmon. The other event was held at the Catholic University of Brasilia in 1994, and focused on diminishing resources for education. The proceedings were published in the *Revista Universa* published by the Catholic University of Brasilia.

During his presidency, Gomes presented a paper about education in Latin America at the 8th World Congress of Comparative Education Societies, which was held in Prague, Czechoslovakia, in 1992. In the paper, which was subsequently published in a special issue of the *International Review of Education* and then republished in a book edited by WCCES Secretary General Raymond Ryba, Gomes highlighted the technical, managerial and financial problems challenges for education in Latin America (Gomes 1993, 1997). He finished the article with a statement about interdependence that two decades later he considered to be of continuing relevance to the understanding of comparative education (Gomes 1993, p.539):

> Fortunately or not, today's world is so small that all of us depend on each other. Comparative and international education knows and teaches this lesson well. If Europe's discovery of America was disturbing to the world of its time, the greatest finding of this century is the growing understanding of our global interdependence. Each of us is a link in a chain of being.

From 1993 to 1997 Clélia Capanema was the President of the society. She felt that her presidency was very difficult because the Secretary General left, and she was alone to do all the work. It was a difficult time not only for the SBEC but also for academic societies in Brazil in general.

In 1997 Robert Verhine became President. He served for two terms, until 2003, which were marked by activities in consultancy, research, publications and seminars. He participated in several international events, keeping the society connected with international scholars. In 1997 the SBEC organised a seminar on New Tendencies for Education in the Third Millennium. It was held at the Federal University of Bahia, and attracted a great audience. Another event was organised in Salvador, Bahia, in 2001 with a focus on International and National Tendencies in Educational Evaluation. The journal *Gestão em Ação* published some of the papers presented at the meeting. A website for the SBEC was developed, and an electronic Bulletin was produced with news about events, reports on research, and short articles.

Other SBEC events, in 1999 and 2003, were held at the Pontifical Catholic University of Rio Grande do Sul, and brought scholars from around the Latin American region. From the 1999 conference a book was published (Castro & Werle 2000), and from the 2003 conference a special issue of the *Revista Educação* was published in 2004.

Marta Luz Sisson de Castro was elected President in 2003, at the SBEC's conference in Porto Alegre, the theme of which was Construction of a Latin American Identity. Marta Luz Sisson de Castro worked with colleagues to develop a new web page at the address www.sbec.org.br. It contained information on the officers and members, the papers from the Congresses in 1999, 2000, 2001 and 2003, a number of publications, and links to the WCCES and other bodies. The Porto Alegre meeting brought the collaboration of scholars from Portugal, Spain, Argentina and Italy as well as Brazil, and stimulated a proposal to produce a book which could become a reference for comparative education in the Portuguese language.

Conclusion

Comparative education used to be part of the curriculum of majors in education in

Brazilian universities. That is no longer the case, but a study of publications in Brazilian journals provided evidence that comparative education was a growing interest (Werle & Castro 2000). Nevertheless, a subsequent study on national educational publications observed that nearly three quarters of the articles classified as comparative focused only on issues in Latin America (Werle & Castro 2004). The most common themes were educational reform, higher education, pedagogical trends and globalisation. Continued efforts were needed to broaden both geographic and subject-matter horizons.

Brazil can learn from other countries' experiences, but can also itself be a model. Among the lessons are ones on tolerance and openness. The WCCES must itself be a model of openness, giving voice to different languages, ethnic groups and countries. The SBEC is glad to contribute to that goal.

References

Castro, Marta Luz Sisson de & Werle, Flávia Obino Corrêa (eds.) (2000): *Educação Comparada na Perspectiva da Globalização e da Autonomia*. São Leopoldo: Editora Unisinos.

Gomes, Cândido A. (1993): 'Education, Democracy and Development in Latin America', *International Review of Education*, Vol.39, No.6, pp.531-540.

Gomes, Cândido A. (1997): 'Education, Democracy and Development in Latin America', in Ryba, Raymond (ed.), *Education, Democracy and Development: An International Perspective*. Dordrecht: Kluwer Academic Publishers, pp.69-78.

Verhine, Robert (ed.) (1989): *Educação: Crise e Mudança*. São Paulo: Editora Pedagógica e Universitária Ltda.

Werle, Flávia Obino Corrêa & Castro, Marta Luz Sisson de (2000): 'Administração Comparada uma análise de publicações na América Latina', in Castro, Marta Luz Sisson de & Werle, Flávia Obino Corrêa (eds.), *Educação Comparada na Perspective da Globalização e da Autonomia*. São Leopoldo: Editora Unisinos, pp.93-108.

Werle, Flávia Obino Corrêa & Castro, Marta Luz Sisson de (2004): 'Administração Comparada como área temática: Periódicos Brasileiros 1982-2000'. *Revista Educação*, Vol.27, No.2, pp.417-437.

22

The Comparative Education
Society of Hong Kong (CESHK)

WONG Suk-Ying & Gregory P. FAIRBROTHER

In March 1989, several academics from Hong Kong's two major universities, the University of Hong Kong (HKU) and the Chinese University of Hong Kong (CUHK), went separately to Boston, USA, to attend the annual conference of the Comparative and International Education Society (CIES). Without any prior arrangement, these academics bumped into each other while attending each other's presentations, and were excited about what each other had to say. The fervour for some form of intellectual exchange in a comparative context led to the birth of the Comparative Education Society of Hong Kong (CESHK) that same year.

When the founding President of the CESHK, Bernard Luk (1989-91), gave this vivid description of the founding of the society at the 2005 annual conference, one could still detect his intellectual concern for a body of which the founding members had held a visionary agenda. It was a time of much attention to the political and social development of China, especially after the outbreak of the social unrest in and near Beijing's Tiananmen Square in June 1989. Hong Kong was still a colony of the United Kingdom, but since it was scheduled to return to Chinese sovereignty in 1997, the population was very sensitive to political developments in China. The Tiananmen incident penetrated almost all dimensions of life in Hong Kong. Looking back, Luk (2005) recalled:

> At that time there was very little communication across the Harbour [i.e. between the two universities]. The few of us at the Chinese University of Hong Kong got together and decided to form a CESHK. I took a pen and paper and wrote a first draft of the constitution. The other two colleagues went to the police station to register [it in] Spring 1989. Up north bigger things were happening. All of Hong Kong's attention was focused on Beijing/Tiananmen. Nobody did any work. I was on sabbatical then so I helped draft the constitution, and sent colleagues to register it with the police. That was it.

Building Comparative Education as an Institution

In Search of a Role Identity

Recalling the origins of the CESHK, Luk (2005) added that the intellectual climate in 1989 intensified the uncertainty about the future of Hong Kong:

> It was a time that academia in Hong Kong began to articulate its role and identity. And the identity for comparative educationists was not only about the place of Hong Kong vis à vis the rest of the Chinese-speaking world. It was also about how these intellectuals looked at education. In the 1980s the most active academic group concerned with education in Hong Kong was the Hong Kong Educational Research Association (HKERA). It was ... dominated by quantitative researchers who focused on the psychological dimensions of education. There was a need for those who were interested in a qualitative approach, highly motivated to further expand the horizon of inquiry to a macro level, to be more assertive.

In this attempt to assert the role and identity of a specific group of university professors and researchers, the CESHK was founded on the basis of promoting an alternative approach for framing educational inquiries and the methodological strategies. Luk (2005) was convinced of the need and advantages for doing comparative education in Hong Kong especially when taking into consideration the colony's unique trajectory:

> If not taking into account the issue of 1989 and as a colonial society, Hong Kong's education has always been *implicitly* comparative. In Hong Kong there is more than one education tradition. People usually identified two strands of education in Hong Kong: English strand and Chinese strand. However, if you look at the history of education in Hong Kong until the 1980s, there have always been more than the Chinese and English strands. A good many of the most important educators in Hong Kong have been Italian, French and German. What did they bring into Hong Kong's education setup?

Luk felt that many dimensions of the implicit comparativeness in Hong Kong education had been neglected. He maintained that the first person who consciously did comparative education was Cheng Tung Choy, who had first-hand experience in the colonial English-speaking education system and the nationalist Mandarin-speaking education system in China. Cheng proceeded to a Master's degree at the University of London Institute of Education, where his thesis compared education in Chinese communities in Hong Kong, Singapore and the Dutch East Indies (Cheng 1949). He continued his career as a civil servant and university administrator, and he gave Luk his first job at the CUHK upon Luk's return from his MA and PhD studies overseas. Cheng was by the mid-1970s the head of the School of Education at the CUHK. When Luk was appointed, Cheng said to him: "We have to add comparative education as one of the options for Masters degrees at the CUHK."

While Luk's remark on the implicit comparativeness in the educational experience of the colony is noteworthy especially in laying the foundation for the establishment of the CESHK, some forms of comparative education research in Hong Kong can be dated back to the 1920s. As noted by Sweeting (1999), in 1926 the University of Hong Kong published an article that was at least contiguous with the field of comparative education. The earliest university course in Hong Kong with a comparative education focus was in the programme of the postgraduate diploma in education at HKU. By the 1980s, while the Faculty of Education at the CUHK had become active in research on comparative education, its counterpart at HKU had also invested substantial resources in the field through offering courses and recruiting academic staff. It was at this time that legitimate programmes in comparative education began to take shape and were institutionalised at the masters' degree level at both universities. The initiatives to launch a programme of study at the postgraduate level was partly due to the elaborate training in comparative education that those faculty members had received from major centres of comparative education (London, Columbia, etc.) at the time. They were the direct cultural carriers of comparative education in higher education institutions in Hong Kong. The demand for applying their disciplinary training in the context of education was also in place. Those who had formal training in social sciences or humanities also found comparative education a viable platform to substantiate their research and professional interests in education.

Consequently, much effort was directed toward the location of comparative education as an alternative and then supplementary field in the higher education sector. Disciplinary identity and role functioning were not clearly differentiated at that point, nor was it a major concern for academics and educational professionals. However, the initial undertaking gave room for interested scholars to position their scholarly interests, and some might even have possessed a positive outlook towards the handover and found a mission for their academic careers. Most importantly, it might have created a reservoir for preserving these intellectuals who might have left the community when Hong Kong faced political and social instability. Commitment to Hong Kong among academics could not necessarily be taken for granted, with 33 per cent of academic staff in the seven institutions funded by the University Grants Committee (UGC) employed on non-local terms, though foreign nationals constituted only 2 per cent of Hong Kong's total population (Postiglione 1996).

The institutionalisation of comparative education as a field of teaching and research was definitely enhanced by the establishment of the CESHK. By the time Bernard Luk completed his presidency of the society, his successor, Leslie Lo (1992-94), a professor in Comparative Education and Educational Administration & Policy Analysis in the CUHK, had a distinct goal of identifying the disciplinary nature of comparative education and its role in a transforming society. As advanced by Lo (2005):

> Being in its infant stage, the society was small, constituted by a number of interested scholar-teachers and some of their research postgraduate students at the CUHK and HKU. The scholar-teachers were relatively young people

who were trying to establish comparative education as a viable field of study in their respective institutions. The efforts, though not concerted by any means, came under many guises: educational development in Chinese societies, education in small states, education and national development, and more. I think we had a critical mass to sustain comparative education as a viable field of study in the Hong Kong academia; but the interests were so diverse and work agendas so different that opportunities for cross-institutional endeavours were not readily available.

In addition to its stated purpose, I did have a vision for the society: to find theoretical footing in the empirical context of Hong Kong's education, then initiate comparison with certain localities in the Chinese Mainland, and then expand comparison to include Taiwan and Macao in order to afford a more comprehensive view of educational change in the Chinese societies. With that secured, comparison with other societies could be confidently conducted. This initial vision has been gradually fulfilled with the nurturing of PhD students and the participation of scholars in the disciplines, such as economics and sociology of education. However, its fruition has taken much longer than I had anticipated.

Lo felt that the scope of comparative education should be focused on the greater China region as an initial departure, highlighting his concern and vision for the legitimacy of the field while the colony was approaching the transition. The CESHK had by then incorporated members from other tertiary institutions, and the third President, Gerard Postiglione (1994-96), was an American-born sociologist from the University of Hong Kong who had done most of his work in the context of comparative education. He highlighted the role that the CESHK could play in Hong Kong's political transition by providing the community with a better understanding of education in China (Postiglione 1995, p.4). A decade later, Postiglione recalled his concern and support for intellectual freedom when Hong Kong was experiencing a period of decolonisation during his tenure as President (Postiglione 2005).

If the initial effort had been devoted to the positioning of comparative education as a field in the academic domain within which an organised community emerged to reinforce its legitimacy of presence, the subsequent effort consolidated both the intellectual identity and role functioning of comparative educationists. The historical juncture that Hong Kong encountered was an important factor; and patterns also demonstrated the dynamics of the Hong Kong academic community. The society has lived up to the expectation of being an international mix which serves as a force for its continued existence.

Functioning of the CESHK

The Hong Kong Educational Context

A review of Hong Kong's educational context helps in the understanding of several factors related to the development of the CESHK. Both before and after 1997, Hong Kong society, politics and education underwent changes related to the resumption of Chinese sovereignty. Among the changes in education were those in the curriculum, including the incorporation of new subjects, adaptations to existing subjects, and increased emphasis on civic and moral education, especially with regard to national identity (Bray 1997; Vickers 2005). Pressure in the pre-1997 period for a shift from English to Cantonese as a medium of instruction led the government in 1998 to require such a change for schools that were deemed to be better able to serve students by teaching in Cantonese (Cheng 2002). In 1999, the new government embarked on a wide-ranging set of reforms of the primary and secondary education systems and curricula with the goal of adapting Hong Kong education for the knowledge economy (Education Commission 2000).

The period after 1989 also saw a rapid expansion of Hong Kong's higher education system, nearly doubling the number of students admitted to first-degree courses by 1994/95 (Postiglione 1998). Before 1991, Hong Kong maintained only two universities: HKU and the CUHK. The newly-founded Hong Kong University of Science and Technology (HKUST) began to enrol students in 1991. By 2004, Hong Kong had nine publicly-funded degree-granting university-level institutions. The expansion was partly driven by the government's goal of providing equal access to higher education and the strong social demand for higher education. The expansion was also viewed by many as an attempt to boost confidence in Hong Kong as the colony approached the 1997 change of sovereignty (Yung 2004).

The expansion of higher education was one demonstration of the indirect influence that mainland China had on Hong Kong's education system. However, postcolonial Hong Kong also saw a need to be more receptive to both the sovereign motherland and the international community in the process of searching for its identity. Hong Kong's reunification with China was accompanied by Beijing's encouragement of closer links between Hong Kong and mainland universities, continuing a trend of increasing academic exchanges since the late 1970s (Law 1997; Postiglione 1998). UGC allocations for Hong Kong-mainland academic exchanges nearly doubled to HK$4.4 million (US$0.56 million) between 1992 and 1996, and new visa policies made it easier for Hong Kong's universities to recruit mainland academics returning from having earned their doctorates abroad. In the area of student exchange, the number of postgraduate students from mainland China studying in Hong Kong's universities nearly doubled from 948 to 1,868 between 1998 and 2001 (Li 2004).

Exchange with mainland China represented a new arena for Hong Kong's external academic links which traditionally had focused on Australia, Canada, the UK and the USA. One manifestation of such links was the high proportion of foreign academics working in Hong Kong's universities, as well as a large number of overseas Chinese and locals who had earned their doctorates abroad (Postiglione 1998). In an international survey of the academic profession, 85 per cent of Hong Kong respondents claimed that connections with scholars in other countries were very important to their professional work (Boyer et al. 1994). In the same survey, Hong Kong academics ranked third in terms of both the amount of time served as a faculty member in another country and agreement to the necessity of reading books and journals published abroad in order to keep up with developments in their fields.

Contrary to the expectation of pessimists that Hong Kong's social and cultural institutions would be interrupted after the handover, postcolonial Hong Kong became more dynamic in presenting a transnational orientation by playing an active role in the international arena while being conscious of the optimal link with China. This was especially prominent in higher education, and was evident for example in recruitment of students and academic staff, student exchange, and financing. Postcolonial Hong Kong would not have been as exciting and challenging had the development of China not commanded much attention in the world map. The various organisational goals that had been identified by the CESHK posed more compatibility than contradiction to the aspiring effort of the Hong Kong Special Administrative Region government in terms of the positioning of Hong Kong. The postcolonial framework described as 'one country, two systems', which allowed Hong Kong to be part of China but to operate differently from the mainland, easily accommodated both a local/culturalist and international outlook into the agenda-making of comparative education.

This context raised several salient points with regard to the CESHK's development. First, the expansion of higher education and teacher education had implications for the membership and leadership of the society. Most of the founding members of the society had been drawn from the two university-level teacher education providers, the CUHK and HKU. By the second decade in the society's history, it was drawing members from these two institutions as well as from the Hong Kong Institute of Education, Hong Kong Baptist University, City University of Hong Kong, and others. Second, the international composition of academic staff in Hong Kong's universities, because of colonialism as well as the recruitment of foreign and overseas-trained mainland Chinese and Hong Kong academics, was reflected in the make-up of the CESHK's membership. Third, increased links with mainland China, among faculty and also demonstrated by increasing numbers of mainland Chinese postgraduate students, were reflected in the research interests of society members, the composition of the membership, and the direction and nature of its activities. Finally, the overall traditional internationalism of Hong Kong's tertiary education sector demonstrated the importance of and interest in cross-societal research and scholarship in education. All of these factors have meant that Hong Kong's small geographical and academic territory has been host to a society which is characterised by multiculturalism and multilingualism.

On Membership

It only took three years for the society to go beyond the local and regional context. In 1992, the CESHK became a member of the World Council of Comparative Education Societies (WCCES). This membership became a crucial milestone for the development of the CESHK, since it represented a leap forward for the society in becoming a legitimate member of the largest community of comparative education at the international level. Throughout the remaining years of the 1990s, CESHK membership grew steadily and by 2005 the society had approximately 80 members. While this might not be seen as a large number, it was impressive in proportion to the size of the total population. The geographical representation of the members was not confined to Hong Kong, but included researchers and professionals in Australia, mainland China, Japan, Macao, Philippines, the UK and the USA. The membership fee remained HK$150 (US$19) for regular members and HK$90 for student members, which was modest in terms of general costs in Hong Kong.

Despite its small size, the efforts of the society's executive committees and membership have ensured its flourishing, avoiding the fate of other small comparative education societies which have collapsed. Part of the explanation for the society's success, among other factors noted by Bray and Manzon (2005), has been a motivation to continue holding a series of activities which provide a platform for scholarly exchange both locally and internationally and among educational researchers and practitioners.

On Activities

The objectives of the CESHK set out in its Constitution are as follows:

- to promote the study of comparative education in Hong Kong;
- to disseminate ideas and information, through seminars and publications and other means, on recent developments, in Hong Kong and abroad, of comparative education scholarship; and
- to liaise with other scholarly associations of comparative education and of other areas of educational research, in Hong Kong and abroad.

The fifth President of the society, Mark Bray (1998-2000), at that time Director of the Comparative Education Research Centre (CERC) at the University of Hong Kong, revitalised attention to these objectives. Bray had a distinct mission of taking the CESHK further beyond the local context, which was partly achieved through the links with the WCCES. Bray's address at the CESHK's 10th anniversary conference highlighted the impressive output of Hong Kong scholars in the prominent English-language and Chinese-language journals of the field, namely *Comparative Education Review* (Chicago), *Comparative Education, Compare, International Journal of Educational Development, International Review of Education*, and *Comparative Education Review* (Beijing). Hong Kong scholars, Bray pointed out, were doing much to promote the visibility of Hong Kong itself, and also mainland China, Macao and Taiwan, in the international literature. He added that they had particular strengths in being able to publish in Chinese-language as well as English-language journals. However, Bray underscored the need for stronger attention to methodology, and urged CESHK scholars to reach further beyond local case study research into the broader conceptual arena (Bray 1999).

During Bray's presidency, the CESHK began its tradition of holding conferences on a regular annual basis rather than on a somewhat *ad hoc* pattern. The conferences have typically attracted 50-70 participants, and have benefited from the relatively informal atmosphere that that size has permitted. The CESHK has made efforts to rotate the location of the conferences around the tertiary institutions in Hong Kong in order to promote a broad sense of ownership of the society.

The society has also benefited from close links with the HKU's Comparative Education Research Centre (CERC), founded in 1994, which serves as the society's Secretariat and hosts its website (Bray 2004). Lee Wing On, Mark Bray, Bob Adamson, and Mark Mason have served as both Directors of CERC and Presidents of the CESHK, and other CERC members have served as officers of the society. Emily Mang, the CERC Secretary and a graduate of the HKU Master of Education programme in comparative education, has worked as the CESHK Secretary and Manager of the website and archive. CERC's publications, including the book series co-published initially with Kluwer and then with Springer, have served as a very visible outlet for the works of comparative education scholars based not only in Hong Kong but worldwide, and have been made available to CESHK members at discounted prices.

Some of the activities organised by the society have served as useful platforms for younger scholars to identify and substantiate their interest and knowledge in comparative education. The annual CESHK conference has provided an opportunity for postgraduate students to practice presentations for larger conferences and to learn from each other not only in terms of content but also in presentation styles. Opportunities to practice presentations are certainly available among colleagues and students at students' own institutions, but the cross-institutional and international participation at the conference has helped widen the range of feedback and brought in the voices of academics within participants' own specialisations as well as perspectives from those previously unfamiliar with their work. These factors help to reduce the anxiety of presenting for the first time at larger conferences. The CESHK conferences have also provided for students a forum to present their developing ideas and frameworks for their dissertations, and to test their research conclusions and get an idea of potential challenges during the period of waiting before their final dissertation defences. Selected conference papers have been published in the CESHK *Newsletter*, which was first issued in March 1993, and evolved into the *Comparative Education Bulletin* in May 1998.

Other activities deserving mention are seminars and study trips. The seminars have commonly been co-hosted by the CESHK and the tertiary institutions. In many cases, the institutions have paid the expenses of visiting scholars, and invited the CESHK to co-host in order to support the society and expand the audience for the events. Some study tours have been to international schools in Hong Kong, thus substantiating Luk's point, made above, about the potential for instructive comparisons even within Hong Kong (see also Bray & Yamato 2003). Study tours have also been undertaken as day trips to Macao and Shenzhen. These cases have again illustrated the potential for the field of comparative education to gain insights from neighbouring locations, and have demonstrated that it is not necessary to travel to distant countries in order to undertake meaningful cross-border comparative studies of education.

Further, the CESHK has collaborated with other WCCES member societies in the organisation of various events. In 2002, and again in 2005, the CESHK supported the Chinese Comparative Education Society (CCES) in its partnership with Beijing Normal University to host the first and second Worldwide Forums of Comparative Education. These events attracted several hundred participants, and were a demonstration of collaboration in the Chinese-speaking community. Regionally, in 2007 the CESHK joined hands with the Comparative Education Society of Asia (CESA) in hosting the 6th CESA biennial conference in conjuncttion with the CESHK annual conference.

Conclusion

It was during the presidencies of Mark Bray and Bob Adamson that the CESHK gained substantial prominence in the international arena. The growth of the society had continued in terms of the establishment and regularisation of activities such as the annual conference, study trips, the website and the publication of the Bulletin which replaced the older Newsletter. The society's finances had also become much healthier, chiefly because of the willingness of institutions to absorb various costs and the willingness of enthusiastic supporters to work volun-tarily. As successors to the Presidential office, Ip Kin Yuen, Mok Ka Ho and Wong Suk-Ying all worked conscientiously to continue these activities while advancing their own visionary agendas for the society. Further synergies and international visibility were achieved by Wong Suk-Ying between 2005 and 2007 with the CESA partnership, achieved through her dual role as President of the CESHK and co-President of CESA. Mark Mason at HKU, who had become the CESHK President in 2006, played a major role in hosting the CESHK/CESA conference in 2007.

The CESHK has undergone various stages of development during which emphases were modified and advanced. It has also handled well the constraints of being a small organisation. Nevertheless, it is salient that the society has relied on a small group of committed volunteers. Furthermore, the Presidents frequently became the defining and mobilising force for society activities. The increasing intensifica-tion of work in the higher education institutions exerted some threat, which was related to Lo's (2005) observation that the society somehow had missing links:

> The identifiable contribution to comparative education is mostly linked to individuals rather than the society. My involvement for a time in the editorial board of the *Comparative Education Review* and Mark Bray's involvement in the WCCES and the *International Journal of Educational Development* [as the Corresponding Editor, 1983-90; and Editor for Asia Pacific, 1990-2005] were cases in point. Some of the scholarly work that members performed for comparative education was mostly linked to the institutions. Academic papers and books published, websites for related areas, and even visits by overseas scholars in the field were identified as the fruits of labour by individuals in certain institutions. For example, visits by Philip Altbach, Torsten Husén and Wang Chengxu to the Chinese University did not always involve members of

the society. Be that as it may, the infant society existed as a useful platform for individual scholars in the field.

My last personal observation: while it seems conveniently logical to have someone 'in power' in institutions to run the society, it may not bring the kind of benefits that have been anticipated. Deans and department chairmen who serve as officers of the society may help to establish comparative education as a viable field of study in their institutions, and they may have some resources to channel to worthy activities of the society. But they are also very busy people with numerous tasks to attend to, and the society's affairs are only one of those tasks. As officers of the society, they may be constantly distracted from its developmental needs. This was my own situation, though other former Presidents may have different impressions of their roles and performance.

Among the special features of the CESHK is its bilingual identity in both English and Chinese. This has particularly promoted links with scholarly communities in mainland China, Macao and Taiwan. The conference presentations and articles in the Bulletin have given more prominence to English than Chinese; but the fact that both languages can be used has helped with cross-fertilisation and collaboration. The historical identity of the CESHK in Hong Kong's colonial era has been carried forward as an asset in the postcolonial era.

The trajectory of the CESHK has demonstrated that much effort has been devoted to attending and adapting to the conditions that would have made possible the maintenance and development of the society. Likewise, changes of organisational goals of the CESHK might have reflected the society's effort to locate its meaning of presence by playing a unique role of promoting either a local/culturalist or international identity. With the rapid changes in China and the increasing interest in education as a global phenomenon, the CESHK has reached the juncture of not only working to safeguard the continual presence of the organisation but also to expand and consolidate its role identity and function through bridging both academic and practical endeavours of education within the intellectual realm of comparative education.

References

Boyer, Ernest L.; Altbach, Philip G. & Whitelaw, Mary Jean (1994): *The Academic Profession: An International Perspective*. Princeton: The Carnegie Foundation for the Advancement of Teaching.

Bray, Mark (1997): 'Education and Colonial Transition: The Hong Kong Experience in Comparative Perspective'. *Comparative Education*, Vol.33, No.2, pp.157-169.

Bray, Mark (1999): 'Comparative Education Research in Hong Kong: A Decade of Development, and an Agenda for the Future'. *Comparative Education Bulletin* [CESHK], No.3, pp.2-7.

Bray, Mark (2004): *Comparative Education: Traditions, Applications, and the Role of HKU*. Lecture presented on the occasion of the 20th anniversary celebration of the Faculty of Education at the University of Hong Kong, and the annual conference of the CESHK, 7

February. Hong Kong: Faculty of Education, The University of Hong Kong. Available on www.hku.hk/education.

Bray, Mark & Manzon, Maria (2005): 'Comparative Education and Teacher Education in Singapore and Hong Kong: Comparisons over Time as well as Place'. *Comparative Education Bulletin* [CESHK], No.8, pp.13-28.

Bray, Mark & Yamato, Yoko (2003): 'Comparative Education in a Microcosm: Methodological Insights from the International Schools Sector in Hong Kong'. *International Review of Education*, Vol.49, Nos.1 & 2, pp.49-71.

Cheng, Tung Choy (1949): 'The Education of Overseas Chinese: A Comparative Study of Hong Kong, Singapore and the East Indies'. MA Thesis, University of London.

Cheng, Kai Ming (2002): 'Reinventing the Wheel: Educational Reform', in Lau, Siu Kai (ed.), *The First Tung Chee-hwa Administration: The First Five Years of the Hong Kong Special Administrative Region*. Hong Kong: The Chinese University Press, pp.157-174.

Education Commission (2000): *Learning for Life, Learning through Life: Reform Proposals for the Education System in Hong Kong*. Hong Kong: Education Commission.

Law, Wing Wah (1997): 'The Accommodation and Resistance to the Decolonisation, Neocolonisation and Recolonisation of Higher Education in Hong Kong'. *Comparative Education*, Vol.33, No.2, pp.187-209.

Li, Mei (2004): 'Policies of Hong Kong and Macao Higher Institutions on Recruiting Mainland Chinese Students: Divergent or Convergent', in Zheng, Xinmin; Cheng, Guohai & Li, Mei (eds.), *Research Studies in Education*. Hong Kong: Faculty of Education, The University of Hong Kong, pp.76-85.

Lo, Leslie N.K. (2005): Unstructured Question Survey conducted by Wong, Suk-Ying and Fairbrother, Gregory P.. Hong Kong: Comparative Education Society of Hong Kong.

Luk, Bernard (2005): 'Address at the History of CESHK Panel'. Annual Conference of the Comparative Education Society of Hong Kong, January 29.

Postiglione, Gerard A. (1995): 'Comparative Education Studies and the Role of a Comparative Education Society in Hong Kong'. Paper presented at the International Symposium on Education and Socio-Political Transitions in Asia, Comparative Education Research Centre, The University of Hong Kong.

Postiglione, Gerard A. (1996): 'The Future of the Hong Kong Academic Profession in a Period of Profound Change', in Altbach, Philip G. & Boyer, Ernest L. (eds.), *The International Academic Profession: Portraits of Fourteen Countries*. Princeton: The Carnegie Foundation for the Advancement of Teaching, pp.191-227.

Postiglione, Gerard A. (1998): 'Maintaining Global Engagement in the Face of National Integration in Hong Kong'. *Comparative Education Review*, Vol.42, No.1, pp.30-45.

Postiglione, Gerard A. (2005): Unstructured Question Survey conducted by Wong, Suk-Ying and Fairbrother, Gregory P.. Hong Kong: Comparative Education Society of Hong Kong.

Sweeting, Anthony (1999): 'Comparative Education at HKU: The Early History'. *CERCular* [Newsletter of the Comparative Education Research Centre, The University of Hong Kong], No.1, p.8.

Vickers, Edward (2005): *In Search of an Identity: The Politics of History as a School Subject in Hong Kong, 1960s-2005*. Hong Kong: Comparative Education Research Centre, The University of Hong Kong.

Yung, Man Sing Andrew (2004): 'Higher Education', in Bray, Mark & Koo, Ramsey (eds.), *Education and Society in Hong Kong and Macao: Comparative Perspectives on Continuity and Change*. 2nd edition. Hong Kong: Comparative Education Research Centre, The University of Hong Kong, and Dordrecht: Kluwer Academic Publishers, pp.61-72.

23

The Comparative Education Section of the Czech Pedagogical Society (CES-CPS)

Eliška WALTEROVÁ

Comparative education has become a vital component of Czech educational research, and an important starting point of educational reforms. Interest in the education of other countries has deep roots. Situated in the heart of Europe, the country and its cultural context had favourable conditions for the field's constitution. However, political circumstances and the ensuing social climate led to deficits in the organisational development of the field. The rather weak formal academic status of comparative education reflects the political situation and cultural discontinuity. The original Comparative Education Section (CES) of the Czechoslovak Pedagogical Society (Československá pedagogická společnost – CSPS), which was established in 1964, was dissolved in 1970 as a consequence of the 'normalisation' that followed the violent oppression of the 1968 Prague Spring political movement. Its re-establishment as a section of the Czech Pedagogical Society (CPS) in the 1990s was a confirmation of an intellectually mature era. Support also came from outside the country, including the World Council of Comparative Education Societies (WCCES).

This chapter examines the challenges of the development of comparative education in the Czech Republic, and the professional community's struggle for recognition. The discussion takes into account not only the formal and organisational history of the Comparative Education Section but also the development of the field as a whole. Collecting documents and reconstructing the history of the society for this chapter was a very challenging project. The society's archives disappeared during the 'normalisation' period, and the personal memories of the founders and former members were therefore of particular importance.

Historical Background

Early traces of Czech comparative education can be found in past centuries, when philosophy on the one hand and practical education experiences on the other provided a humanistic interest in a variety of educational approaches and stimulated the transfer of educational practices. John Amos Comenius (1592-1651) was a forerunner of Czech comparative education. He believed that to know differences meant to understand the essence of phenomena. The philosophical orientation in his pedagogical works together with the lessons about school reform which he learned from Poland, Hungary, Sweden, England and the Netherlands are still considered an epistemological foundation of contemporary Czech comparative education.

Other early works are also worth noting. The journal *Slavonic Educator* (1872-74), edited by Jan Mašek, a Czech teacher, was probably the first international multilingual set of comparative studies published in various Slavic languages. Comparative education as a field of educational research emerged near the end of the 19th century when systematic analyses of education abroad started to appear. The first Czech *Encyclopaedia of Education* (1891-1909) included approximately 100 entries on school systems from all continents as well as on the regional systems in the Austrian monarchy.

The classic era of Czech comparative education was between 1918 and 1938. It exhibited a progressive development based on values of national identity, democracy and freedom in the new Czechoslovak Republic. Support for study trips and scientific communication with the rest of the world enabled the application of research methods based on experiences from Europe. The epistemological base was enriched by contemporary theories. Ideas of such leading comparativists as Michael Sadler, Isaac Kandel, Friedrich Schneider, Nicholas Hans and Sergej Hessen were well known, and their works were translated and reviewed. In addition to numerous monographs on European education, particular attention was given to the USA. Otakar Kádner's four-volume series entitled *Development of Contemporary School Systems* (1929-38) was representative of Czech comparative education during this period. The series examined education in 35 European countries, the USA, and Japan.

The promising development of comparative education was interrupted by the occupation of the Czechoslovak Republic and World War II. After the war, the field stagnated. The political bipolarity of the world was reflected in 'socialist education' from the 1950s through the 1980s: a strong and uncritical orientation to the East and overestimation of Soviet education, and one-sided criticism of Western education. An epistemological unification under the ideological umbrella of Marxism-Leninism did not permit the development of objective and methodologically transparent comparative research. Political isolation behind the Iron Curtain interrupted international contacts. Nevertheless, notable studies were published in the 1960s during the warmer social atmosphere before the 1968 Prague Spring.

In this context, the CSPS was established as an association of specialists in educational research. As an academic organisation, the society was a member of the Czechoslovak Academy of Sciences. Despite its academic thrust, the society viewed education as a powerful tool for social development. The importance of the scientific background in political decision-making concerning education was stressed alongside academic freedom in educational research. This approach represented a radical methodological change and an effort to abandon ideologically dogmatic education.

The name of the society followed the continental-European tradition, in which education developed as an autonomous and largely mono-disciplinary field. A specific hermeneutic approach influenced mainly by philosophy and psychology allowed the establishment of the first autonomous Czech chair in pedagogy at Charles University, Prague in 1882. Educational theory and practice were both denoted by the term 'pedagogy'. This differed from the tradition in Great Britain, France and the USA, where educational sciences were multidisciplinary and anchored in the social sciences (Schriewer & Keiner 1992; Průcha 2002, pp.21-32).

The initiative to establish the CSPS came from the Scientific Board for Pedagogy and Psychology. The constituent assembly was held in Prague in October 1964 for the Czech part of the society, and in December 1964 for the Slovak one. The first President was Ludovít Bakoš, the first Secretary was Jiří Kotásek, and the members of the Executive Committee were also leading scholars. Membership was open only to scholars publishing in the field, with exceptions for publicly influential teachers and school administrators. The CSPS worked on a decentralised basis, and its organisation was extended to seven regional branches in the Czech regions and three in Slovakia. Internally the society was divided into 12 specialised sections, and the Comparative Education Section, led by František Singule, was of great importance.

One of the main aims of the society, as stated in Section 3 of the Statutes, was to "represent Czechoslovak education in international organisations either by the society or by individual members, and to support international cooperation in educational research". When the constituent assembly criticised the isolation from the international community and the absence of critical analysis with alternative ideas, a special commission for international relations was appointed and led by Vlastimil Pařízek. During the following period of the section's existence, international contacts grew rapidly. The main activities were lectures, discussions, seminars and conferences.

From 1965, the bulletin *Prospects of the Czech Pedagogical Society* was distributed to the members of the society, who numbered 142 in that year. Twelve issues were published from 1965 to 1970. The bulletin was a source of information on educational research, and offered members a platform for scientific discussions. A substantial part of every issue was devoted to comparative education, international relations and/or members' participation in events abroad. Regular surveys of foreign publications and references to international resources, particularly of UNESCO, supported the development of comparative education. An effort was made to balance the orientation between East and West. Contributors to the comparative section of the bulletin represented leading institutions of comparative and international education: the Comenius Institute of Education in the Czechoslovak Academy of Sciences; the Department of Comparative Education, Sociology of Education and Psychology in the Faculty of Social Sciences of the University of Seventeenth November (which mostly educated students from developing countries); the Department of Education in the Faculty of Philosophy of Charles University; and the Institute of Teacher Education of Charles University.

An international exhibition of educational literature from 12 countries in

1965 was a great success, and contributed to the acceptance of the society. The Comparative Education Section initiated the exhibition, held under the aegis of UNESCO. The exhibited books were later donated to the Comenius National Pedagogical Library.

The Comparative Education Section was also active during annual conferences and general assemblies. The first CSPS conference, held in 1965 in Trnava, analysed the development of education and pedagogy in Czechoslovakia from 1945 to 1965. Using international comparisons, critics identified the weaknesses of domestic education. The second conference in 1966 in Olomouc concentrated on theoretical and methodological questions including interdisciplinary relations. Participants from six European countries and Canada joined the conference, and Jarmila Skalková was elected President.

The Comparative Education Section subsequently organised intensive lecturing and study visits abroad. Developments were influenced by patterns in the USA and Western Europe. In the 1960s, the US Comparative Education Society organised several study trips of American scholars to Europe. Groups led by Gerald H. Read, Secretary of the US society, visited research institutions and met with Czech and Slovak comparativists and teachers.

Conferences focusing on Comenius were also integral to comparative education in Czechoslovakia. The 1967 conference in Olomouc devoted to Comenius' work *De Rerum Humanarum Emendatione Consultatio Catholica* (General Consultation on the Remedy of Human Matters) gathered 140 scholars, half of whom came from abroad. Comenius' view of education as the central starting point of global change substantially enriched the epistemological foundation of educational research. Comeniology was a rare platform during that period for international encounters of educationalists from the entire world.

Another important thrust came from the Comparative Education Society in Europe (CESE). Its 3rd conference, held in Ghent, Belgium, declared a goal of cooperation with the socialist countries. Singule was the Czechoslovak comparative education representative. He promised to organise the 4th CESE conference in Prague in 1969, and duly did so.

The 1968 Prague Spring offered a suitable climate for comparative education. An interdisciplinary group, led by Radovan Richta from the Czechoslovak Academy of Sciences, organised an international conference in 1968 in Mariánské Lázně. The humanistic concept of civilisation in the age of technology as a central theme of the conference stressed the role of education in social and personal development. The resulting publication (Richta 1969), which was based on comparative studies, projected an interdisciplinary view of education. Its identification of determining factors of social change differed fundamentally from the prevailing dogmatic views on 'social revolutions'. This orientation led to the subsequent political rejection of the book.

In December 1968, the 3rd Congress of the CSPS was held in Prague. The Congress reflected the new social atmosphere, and discussed questions of orientation of educational research in national, European and global contexts. Kotásek's keynote speech evaluating the scientific, political, cultural and social responsibility of education was warmly received. The congress marked the official end of the Czechoslovak Pedagogical Society (CSPS). The society was divided into two autonomous organisations: the Czech Pedagogical Society (CPS) and the Slovak Pedagogical Society (SPS), based on the new federal state order. Kotásek was elected President of the CPS, which gave particular emphasis to educational policy, cooperation with teachers, and international contacts. Its main task for 1969 was the strengthening of comparative education and preparation for the CESE Congress.

Also significant in 1968 was the International Conference on the Further Education of Teachers, held in Prague. It was part of a series of working meetings, and in 1969 the series culminated in an international meeting of experts at the UNESCO Institute for Education in Hamburg. A substantial study, *Current Trends and Problems in Teacher Education* (Kotásek 1970) was published in English, though by that time CPS activities and the author's domestic publications had been prohibited.

Several other publications and activities in this period also deserve mention. Singule (1966) presented a fundamental theoretical analysis of Western education theories, movements and reforms; and Pařízek (1967) compared pedagogy in the USSR, USA, Cameroon, and England and Wales. Another theme concerned lifelong learning. The UNESCO conference in Prague opened discussions on the concept, and contributed to the report *Learning to Be* (Faure 1972). However, the first Czech synthesis on lifelong education by Kotásek was not allowed to be published in Czech. A French translation was issued later in Paris (Kotásek 1972).

The 'swan song' of the CPS in this period was the 4th CESE conference in 1969 in Prague. One hundred specialists from 19 European and four other countries participated in the congress together with 50 Czech and Slovak scholars. It was the largest international comparative education meeting in Czechoslovakia since World War II, and the first congress of comparative education in the Eastern bloc. The conference focused on curriculum issues, and was hosted by the Comenius Institute of Education, Charles University, and the University of Seventeenth November. The Comparative Education Section of the CPS organised special seminars on Czech education and discussions with congress participants. Singule, who had organised the conference in his capacity as Vice-President of the CPS, was elected to the CESE committee, and the congress increased the number of CESE members from Czechoslovakia and other socialist countries. The congress invited leading European scholars, including Saul B. Robinsohn, Gaston Mialaret, Torsten Husén, Wolfgang Mitter, and Wincenty Okoń. A special congress volume in English was planned, but political intervention halted it. A detailed analytical report (Singule 1969) and a Czech translation of some papers were published in the journals *Pedagogika* (1969, No.2) and *Prospects* (1969, No.10).

The return to intellectual emancipation and a renewal of international contacts for Czech scholars were prevented in the following two decades by political forces. In this period, education studies were prone to ideology, avoided comparisons, and were mostly limited to education in the Eastern bloc. A group of leading members of the CPS had publicly criticised ideologically determined and politically monopolised education. In the article 'Pedagogy and Pedagogists' (Literature Sheets, 2 May 1968) a critical view was strongly expressed and signed by 13 persons. The critics called for a revival process, and supported international activities. After the Soviet Army invasion of Czechoslovakia, criticism against concerned persons and against the CPS was misused. Signatories were blacklisted and in the 1970s demoted from positions. The activities of the Comparative Education Section stopped in 1970 when the SPS was abolished.

From the 1970s some Czechoslovak scholars took part in the Commission on Criticism of Bourgeois Education led by Soviet experts. Paradoxically, the publications of this group, in spite of misinterpretations and class ideology, were significant sources of comparative data on education for the Czech community. The series *Education Abroad* (1974-91) and the series *Education in Socialist Countries* (1974-89) issued by the Institute for Information in Education provided 35 case studies of education systems, curricula and research in the USA, Canada, Australia, Japan and other countries. UNESCO documents also offered data and information. Possibilities to participate in UNESCO conferences or to study in UNESCO's International Bureau of Education (IBE), although rare, contributed to the survival of the field even though it lost its vitality. In the late 1980s, a more relaxed social atmosphere permitted partial improvements, but dramatic stimulation of comparative education came only after the political reversal in 1989.

Restoration of the Society and Comparative Education in the 1990s

A serious effort to overcome isolation, discontinuity and weakness started soon after the 'Velvet Revolution' in 1989. Social change, democratisation, and a new political orientation sparked educational transformation. The call for educational reforms to take into account European and global trends underlined the need for the revival of comparative education.

First, the informative role of comparative education was emphasised. Studies were conducted of problems, shifts, innovations and trends, particularly in countries with developed education systems. Numerous articles and reports were published in Czech journals. However, the prevailing approach was descriptive and oriented mostly toward the structure of education systems. Higher education received most attention (see e.g. Vašutová 1990a, 1990b).

New travel opportunities for educational researchers and practitioners fostered international contacts and mobility, offering an inside view of education abroad. Comparison inspired the grass roots movement of Czech innovative schools. The characteristic feature of this short period was a prevailing admiration for 'borrowing' from foreign experiences to support educational transformation.

The strict political shift to the West and an effort to reach a qualitatively comparable education with leading European and developed countries influenced the choice of countries for comparison. A noteworthy comparative study published in the Czech Republic at this time was *Views on Danish Schooling, Alias Travelling in Educational Paradise* (Rýdl 1993). Also, citations of Western authors increased rapidly. Ježková (1997, p.44) reported that among 2,789 citations in the Czech journal *Pedagogika* during the period 1990 to 1994, 53 per cent were of foreign authors. Among the foreign-language citations, 65 per cent were in English, 19 per cent in German, and 6 per cent in French.

The Department of Comparative Education in the new Institute for Educational and Psychological Research (IEPR) of the Faculty of Education of Charles University was established in 1990. It was initiated by the Dean of the Faculty, Jiří Kotásek, and the Director of the Institute, Jan Průcha; and it was headed by Eliška Walterová. In the same year, the CPS restored its Comparative Education Section, and in 1993 the comparative section of the Czech Association of Educational Research held its first conference.

The most important event of this period was the 8th World Congress of Comparative Education Societies held in Prague in 1992. The choice of Prague as the venue of the World Congress not only received the sponsorship of President Václav Havel, but was also meaningful for the theme on Education, Democracy and Development. The theme and location were intended to demonstrate the reopened communication among educationalists from all over the world that resulted from the awakening of the post-socialist countries of Central and Eastern Europe on their path to democracy. Pařízek led the organising committee, and Kotásek, Singule, Průcha, Walterová and other leading Czech comparativists participated. The staff of the Faculty of Education of Charles University helped with logistics and the programme.

The Congress brought together 600 scholars from 60 countries, and received 400 papers. Congress sessions considered the extensive socio-political changes which posed new challenges. Discussions focused on the challenges of transforming educational systems in a changing global context and identified parallels among diverse national systems. The Congress proceedings were not published in their entirety, but a selection of papers was edited by WCCES Secretary General Raymond Ryba. It was published in 1993 in a special issue of the *International Review of Education* (Vol.39, No.6), and reprinted as a book four years later (Ryba 1997). Authors included Wolfgang Mitter (Germany), Jiří Kotásek (Czechoslovakia), Gábor Halász (Hungary), Torsten Husén (Sweden), Stephen Heyneman (World Bank), Paul N'da (Côte d'Ivoire), Cândido Gomes (Brazil), Mark Bray and Lee Wing On (Hong Kong), and Roberta Bramwell and Kathleen Foreman (Canada). Kotásek's contribution, concentrating on changes in Czechoslovakia, explained the social, political and economic climate underlying educational dilemmas and visions after the collapse of the communist regime. He described the new democracy as a laboratory of social and educational reform, and underlined the significance of comparative education for educational policy.

Another positive impact of the Congress was that the Czech education community became more critically aware of its own system. The book *Education in a Changing Society: Czechoslovakia* (Průcha & Walterová 1992) elicited insightful discussions from the Congress participants and led to the publication of a critical reflection on Czech comparative education (Průcha & Walterová 1993). Among the other streams of work stimulated by from the Congress were single studies or collections of more complex analyses of educational systems as sets of juxtaposed studies. The comparison, still implicit, was based on description but did include analytical and critical perspectives (e.g. Váňová 1994; Ježková 1996; Ježková & Walterová 1997). A further stream included comparative cross-national and supra-national studies on educational trends, and also addressed current problems in Czech education. The first study of this kind was *Changes in Education in International Context* (Průcha 1992). Others included Walterová (1994, 1996), and Pol and Rabušicová (1996). The *Dictionary of Education* (Průcha et al. 1995) was also based on the comparative principle, introducing new interpretations and concepts from an international context.

During this initial period of growth, doubts concerning the further development of comparative education arose. Various factors led to a short-term crisis in the mid-1990s. Certain politicians and academics were still resistant to comparative education. They desired a restoration of the domestic *status quo ante,* the line going back to the 'golden age' of democracy and national education before World War II. Moreover, the gulf between the desired and actual capacity to develop comparative education as a systematic and regular academic field was wide, in part because of the lack of foreign language skills. The global context was changing rapidly, and Czech comparative education was not able to internalise the entire process. Likewise, the national process of educational transition was demanding. Leading researchers became engaged in educational transition, projecting and monitoring reform efforts. In this context, the institutional foundation and infrastructure were underdeveloped. The only comparative research centre in IEPR was damaged during institutional reconstruction. The comparative education community was diffused, and the activities of the Comparative Education Section of the CPS were reduced to a formal umbrella of uncoordinated and *ad hoc* events. Material and technical problems as well as financial limitations reduced participation in international events and projects.

During the second half of the 1990s, however, new strengths emerged. They partly arose from examination of patterns in developed democratic countries, together with critical evaluation of the domestic situation based on both global comparison and careful observation of neighbouring post-communist countries. Also important were forces related to accession to the European Union, for which the authorities expressed official interest in 1993 though it was only ultimately achieved in 2004. One event with this orientation was the conference entitled 'Educational Reforms in Central and Eastern Europe: Process and Results' held in Prague in 1995. It was joined by about 60 participants from every region of Europe, and was a counterpart of the broad programme of the Council of Europe.

After the Social Democratic Party came to power in 1998, comparative education was accepted as a principle of studies on education and programmes of educational development. The strategy, which included comparison in critical analyses, evaluations and projects on education, could be understood as a new phenomenon of educational policy declaring the support of education for a knowledge society. This development culminated in the White Book, a key document of Czech educational policy entitled *National Programme of Development of Education in the Czech Republic* (2001), published in Czech and

English. It was influenced by various sources, including:

- ideas from general social theories of post-industrial society, particularly the concept of the knowledge society;
- global acceptance of a changing paradigm of education, from the former dominant model of education as a transmitter of culture and stratified social structure to lifelong and lifewide education as a factor of a social prosperity and individual development;
- documents of international organisations on educational policy, particularly the UNESCO Delors Report (1996) and its concept of the four pillars of lifelong education;
- membership in the Organisation for Economic Co-operation and Development (OECD) and Council of Europe, which permitted participation in conferences on education and international projects;
- support for overcoming language problems by new bilingual dictionaries (Průcha et al. 1995; Mareš & Gavora 1999).

The formulation of the White Book was led by Jiří Kotásek, and stimulated broad public interest in comparative education. Publishers such as Portal, Paido, and Fortuna, issued numerous translated titles by internationally known authors as well as Czech versions of important international documents. A comprehensive book by Průcha (2002) introduced the scientific basis of comparative education, and explained theories and uses of comparative methodology for evaluating Czech education. It became a basic source of information for school administrators and teachers, as well as a textbook for students of education and the social sciences. The educational community at various forums, such as the National Teacher Congress in Brno in 2000, expressed the need to study the international context as an important source of inspiration for the long-term programme of Czech educational development.

Another important factor was participation in projects of the International Association for the Evaluation of Educational Achievement (IEA). In the first half of the 1990s, the studies were only slightly known by the public and had little impact on educational policy; but more vital discussion started after the reports were published in Czech. The studies in which the Czech Republic participated included the Third International Mathematics and Science Study (TIMSS), the Progress in Reading Literacy Study (PIRLS), and the IEA civic education study. OECD studies included ones on adult literacy and the Programme for International Student Assessment (PISA). Starting with small groups of researchers, academics and statisticians, these projects have over time involved politicians, practitioners, administrators and students.

Revitalising the CPS and its Comparative Education Section

During the decade and a half after 1989, the CPS organised 12 thematic conferences contributing to comparative education. They focused on Tradition and Perspectives of Education in the Contemporary World (1992), Moral Illnesses of Youth and their Prevention (1997), Education and Children's Rights on the Threshold of the Millennium (1999), and Education in the Context of Social Change (2004). Special volumes from the conferences were published.

The CPS Secretariat was based at the Faculty of Education at Masaryk University in Brno. Every President of the society between 1990 and the time of writing came from this faculty: Bohumír Blížkovský (1990-94), Zdenka Veselá (1994-98), and Vlastimil Švec (since 1998). The organisational role of the society in comparative education was rather modest until 2004, being mostly a formal umbrella for activities initiated by the informal comparative education community. The 2001 conference in Prague on 'Problems of Comparative Education' was one example. The conference was organised by the Prague group of the society, concentrated at the Faculty of Education of Charles University. Over 70 participants from central Europe discussed study programmes of comparative education, theoretical matters, and innovations in education in certain countries (Prokop 2003). The conference included Pařízek's last keynote address before his death.

The diffusion of the comparative education community and the danger of fragmentation sparked the revitalisation of the Comparative Education Section of the CPS. A significant impulse came from the WCCES, reinforced by the author's participation in the 12th World Congress of Comparative Education Societies in Cuba in 2004. Reports on the Congress and WCCES activities were published in the Czech journal *Pedagogika* (Walterová 2005a) and *The New Educational Review* (Walterová 2005b). In February 2005 the CPS held its annual conference entitled 'Changes in Education' in Prague (Prokop & Rybičková 2005). Participants supported the initiative to revitalise the Comparative Education Section, and the general assembly confirmed the effort. A paper by Walterová (2005c) entitled 'Changing Roles and Paradigms of Comparative Education' analysed the international context and development of comparative education, noted the role of the WCCES, and reported on key ideas for the Comparative Education Section.

The members of the Comparative Education Section noted the need to tap the research potential of its members and their preferred forms of activities. These could include a common forum for discussion, organisation of regular seminars, establishment of a database of comparative projects, and a website for information exchange. The content and orientation of comparative education courses in teacher study programmes was also noted to require attention.

In terms of institution-building, the Comparative Education Section foresaw closer collaboration through joint activities with the Czech Pedagogical Society, the Czech Association of Educational Research, and other informal comparative groups. With the Comparative Education Section establishing its seat at the Institute for Educational Research and Development (IERD) at the Faculty of Education of Charles University in Prague, members of the Institute could coordinate activities and offer seminars, round tables, or reviews useful for the section. The Institute could provide logistical and technical support as well as communication and information via the internet.

Conclusion

Comparative education in the Czech Republic has a long history. However, a diffusion of the comparative education community and a tendency of fragmentation and isolation have weakened the status of the field. Comparative education is taught in some universities, but it is not a degree specialisation. Comparative research and events are not concentrated at or coordinated by a specific institution. Research topics in the field education are mostly derived from projects focused on problems in national education or initiated by international projects. Comparative education is conceived more as a research method or methodological principle than a special field of study.

A revival of Czech comparative education since the 1990s is evident from the number of publications, projects and events described above. Developments have been influenced by social conditions and political forces. The reform process in education is challenging, and international comparison is widely seen as a useful instrument to assist in the process. Participation in international discussion through various networks stimulates educational progress locally as well as globally. The membership of the Czech Comparative Education Section in the WCCES is greatly valued, and is seen as an opportunity to contribute to the global discourse.

Acknowledgments

Particular thanks are due to Jiří Kotásek who shared his private archives, as well as to the CES-CPS Secretary, Marta Rybičková who made available the pertinent information for the period 1990-2004.

References

Delors, Jacques (Chairman) (1996): *Learning – The Treasure Within: Report to UNESCO of the International Commission on Education for the Twenty-first Century.* Paris: UNESCO.

Faure, Edgar (Chairman) (1972): *Learning to Be: The World of Education Today and Tomorrow.* Paris: UNESCO.

Ježková, Věra (ed.) (1996): *Education Systems Abroad.* Prague: Faculty of Education, Charles University Press. [in Czech]

Ježková, Věra (1997): 'Utilisation of Information in Czech Educational Research', in *Czech Educational Research in the Contemporary Social Conditions.* Brno: CERM Academic Publishers, pp.42-46. [in Czech]

Ježková, Věra & Walterová, Eliška (1997): *Education in the Countries of the European Union.* Prague: Faculty of Education, Charles University Press. [in Czech]

Kotásek, Jiří (1970): 'Current Trends and Problems in Teacher Education', in Yates, A. (ed.) *Current Problems of Teacher Education: Report of a Meeting of International Experts.* Hamburg: UNESCO Institute for Education, pp.119-132.

Kotásek, Jiří (1972): 'L'idée d'éducation permanente de la reforme actuelle des systèmes éducatifs et de la formation des maîtres', in *L'école et l'éducation permanente: quatre études.* Paris: UNESCO, pp.183-246.

Mareš, Jiří & Gavora, Peter (1999): *English-Czech Education Dictionary.* Prague: Portal.

Ministry of Education, Youth and Sports (2001): *National Programme of Development of*

Education in the Czech Republic. Prague: Government Printer.

Pařízek, Vlastimil (1967): *Pedagogical Problems of Educational Systems: Comparative Studies.* Prague: Academia. [in Czech]

Pol, Milan & Rabušicová, Milada (1996): *Educational Management: School Councils in International Perspective.* Brno: Paido. [in Czech]

Prokop, Jiří (ed.) (2003): *Problems of Comparative Education.* Prague: Karolinum. [in Czech]

Prokop, Jiří & Rybičková, Marta (eds.) (2005): *Changes in Education.* Prague: Czech Pedagogical Society, Faculty of Education, Charles University Press.

Průcha, Jan (ed.) (1992): *Educational Changes in International Context.* Prague: Karolinum. [in Czech]

Průcha, Jan (2002): *Education and Schooling in the World: Basis for International Comparisons of Educational Systems.* Revised 2nd edition. Prague: Portal. [in Czech]

Průcha, Jan & Walterová, Eliška (1992): *Education in a Changing Society: Czechoslovakia.* Prague: H+H Publishers.

Průcha, Jan & Walterová, Eliška (1993): 'Comparative and International Education: Analytic Evaluation of the Situation in Czechoslovakia'. *Pedagogika,* Vol.43, No.1, pp.45-54. [in Czech]

Průcha, Jan; Walterová, Eliška & Mareš, Jiří (1995): *Dictionary of Education.* Prague: Portal. [in Czech]

Richta, Radovan (ed.) (1969): *Civilisation at the Crossroad.* Prague: International Arts & Science Press, Inc.

Ryba, Raymond (ed.) (1997): *Education, Democracy and Development: An International Perspective.* Dordrecht: Kluwer Academic Publishers.

Rýdl, Karel (1993): *Views on Danish Schooling, Alias Travelling in Educational Paradise.* Prague: ISV Publisher. [in Czech]

Schriewer, Jürgen & Keiner, Edwin (1992): 'Communication Patterns and Intellectual Traditions in Educational Sciences: France and Germany'. *Comparative Education Review,* Vol.36, No.1, pp.25-51.

Singule, František (1966): *Educational Streams of 20th Century in Capitalist Countries.* Prague: State Educational Publisher. [in Czech]

Singule, František (1969): 'The Fourth Congress of the Comparative Education Society in Europe'. *Pedagogika,* No.5, pp.779-785. [in Czech]

Váňová, Miroslava (ed.) (1994): *Education Systems in Developed Countries.* Prague: Karolinum. [in Czech]

Vašutová, Jaroslava (1990a): *Higher Education in the USA.* Prague: Edition of Faculty of Education. [in Czech]

Vašutová, Jaroslava (1990b): *Higher Education in Sweden.* Prague: Edition of the Faculty of Education. [in Czech]

Walterová, Eliška (1994): *Curriculum: Changes and Trends in International Contexts.* Brno: Masaryk University Press. [in Czech]

Walterová, Eliška (1996): *Secondary School Leaving Examinations Abroad.* Prague: Institute for Information in Education. [in Czech]

Walterová, Eliška (2005a): 'The 12th World Congress of Comparative Education Societies'. *Pedagogika,* Vol.55, No.2, pp.172-175. [in Czech]

Walterová, Eliška (2005b): 'Education and Social Justice: 12th Congress of the World Council of Comparative Education Societies.' *The New Educational Review,* Vol.5, No.1, pp.263-268.

Walterová, Eliška (2005c): 'Changing Roles and Paradigms of Comparative Education', in Prokop, Jiří & Rybičková, Marta (eds.) *Changes in Education.* Prague: Czech Pedagogical Society, Faculty of Education, Charles University Press, pp.186-192.

24

The Bulgarian Comparative
Education Society (BCES)

Nikolay POPOV

The Bulgarian Comparative Education Society (BCES) was founded in Sofia in October 1991, and joined the World Council of Comparative Education Societies (WCCES) in March 1992. This chapter examines the preconditions, origin and development of the BCES. It also discusses the political, socio-cultural, economic and other challenges to comparative education in Bulgaria during different periods of history.

The Periods Leading up to the Formation of the BCES

The foundation of the BCES may be seen as part of the long process of development of comparative education as a science, academic discipline and policy tool. For this perspective, it is useful to review developments in the 19th and 20th centuries.

From 1878 to 1918

Following the Russian-Turkish War of 1877-78, Bulgaria overturned the Turkish yoke which had lasted for five centuries, and the builders of modern Bulgaria began to lay the foundations of a new education system. The newly-liberated country looked towards more developed ones for ideas on laws and structures. Comparative education studies were a natural instrument for addressing various problems. In the words of Aleksiev (1912, p.9):

> The school had to serve the newly established public groups and institutions, to serve for uplifting the cultural level of the Bulgarian people, helping it to acquire the knowledge it needed to become a member, equal in rights, of the family of the European cultured nations.... There was no time for considerations and experiments. What could best be done was to follow the example of the cultured nations. Our first policy-makers imitated the school systems of Russia, Austria and Germany. But that imitation was not slavish: those copies were immediately adjusted to the Bulgarian conditions.

The first Bulgarian university, which today is Saint Kliment Ohridsky University of Sofia, was opened in Sofia in 1888. Some courses on foreign education appeared in the early 1900s, and most Bulgarian comparativists of that time were university professors. Favourable circumstances contributed to the development of the field. They included a swift increase in the number of foreign education journals received in Bulgaria, study trips for Bulgarian scholars to other countries, and participation of Bulgarian administrators and scholars in international conferences. About 120 comparative education articles and reports were published during this period, mostly in the *School Review, Education,* the *Education Magazine,* and *Democratic Review.* Books with a comparative education included Illiev's *Bourgeois and Proletarian Pedagogy* (1911) and Aleksiev's *Our School Policy* (1912). The countries examined most frequently were France and Germany. After them came England, the USA, Russia, Austria, Belgium and other European countries. Particular focus was given to secondary education because during that period there were frequent attempts (in 1880, 1885, 1891, 1898 and 1909) at secondary education reform. Studies on teacher training were also significant. The principal interest was in teachers' pedagogical and scientific training, especially in Germany.

The first Bulgarian professor in education and the most prominent comparativist of that time was Peter Noykov (1868-1921). His contribution covered three main fields: case studies, the theory of comparison, and lecture courses on foreign education and school organisation. Noykov made research visits to Germany, France and England, and was the first Bulgarian scholar to work on the theory of educational comparison. He developed what he called 'a general method of studying characteristics of a given national education'. This method had three phases: categorisation, comparison and generalisation. With his lecture courses on German education, English education and school organisation and management at the University of Sofia in 1908-09, Noykov prepared the ground for comparative education as a university field of study.

Other important comparativists during the period included:

- Luca Dorosiev, who published studies of education in England, Italy, Spain, Serbia, the USA, France and Guatemala from the 1890s to the 1920s;
- Ivan Georgov, who wrote short but detailed materials on education around the world and was especially interested in Swiss education; and
- Nikola Lazarov, who studied education in Romania, Germany and France and published an important study entitled 'Trade Education in Advanced Countries' (Lazarov 1906).

Comparative education studies were not only a necessity but also perhaps the only auspicious means for building modern education after the Liberation. Description prevailed over analysis, but a tendency for deep analytical consideration was established. The period 1878 to 1918, and especially the years 1900 to 1914, could be considered as a transitional phase to the differentiation of comparative education as a science and a university discipline.

From 1919 to 1944

In the post-war years, 1919-23, comparative education activities stagnated. This was for several reasons. From 1912 till 1918 Bulgaria took part in three wars: the Balkan War (1912), the Inter-Allied War (1913), and the First World War (1914-18). Bulgaria lost the latter two wars, and was a broken country in 1919. The post-war governments operated in unstable political and social circumstances, and the Ministry of Education had to focus on restoring the normal functions of schools.

By 1923, structures had become more stable. Trade grew, and better conditions for the development of education were created. The world economic crisis of 1929-33 barely concerned Bulgaria, and from the mid-1920s to 1944 Bulgaria was one of the most developed countries in Central and Eastern Europe. The state invested considerable funds in education, partly because highly qualified specialists were much needed in administration, agriculture, banking and other sectors. Foreign education experiences were considered very relevant in the search to satisfy needs. The Bulgarian Ministry of Education maintained close contact with the UNESCO International Bureau of Education (IBE) in Geneva, Switzerland following its establishment in 1925, and the IBE yearbooks were received regularly.

Much interflow also developed in the scholarly community. Bulgarians undertook research visits to centres of comparative education such as Columbia University Teachers College, the University of London Institute of Education, the Zentralinstitut für Erziehung und Unterricht in Berlin, and the Institut International de Coopération Intellectuelle in Paris. In addition, many foreign scholars came to Bulgaria. For example, Paul Monroe and William Russell from the USA visited in the 1920s and 1930s. The process of differentiation of comparative education was assisted by the fact that many comparative sciences – comparative theory of literature, comparative linguistics, comparative law, comparative anthropology, etc. – had been introduced in Bulgarian universities.

Over 220 comparative education articles and reports were published during this period. They included three important books: Piryov's *New Education in the New World* (1933), Gavovski's *Education in the Far East* (1937), and Piryov's *Entire Education* (1941). Germany featured in over half the studies, with considerable interest also focusing on the USA, England, France, the USSR, Switzerland, Italy, Denmark, Austria, and Poland. Focus on secondary education remained strong because of reforms in 1921, 1924 and 1934. The studies on teacher training continued to increase, and other strong foci included education reforms, admission and graduation procedures, school administration, school hygiene, school inspection, and education budgets.

Christo Negentzov (1881-1953) was the first Bulgarian scholar to introduce comparative education as a university discipline. He wrote over 20 articles on education in China, Switzerland, the USA, Denmark, Sweden and Norway, and made systematic use of comparison as a basic research method (see e.g. Negentzov 1926). In 1925, Negentzov launched a course at Sofia University on general theory of school organisation. The course began with a history of education in the 19th century, and then turned to a detailed comparison of school organisation in many European countries and the USA.

In this period, Gencho Piryov (1901-2001) was the author with the largest number of comparative education publications: over 35 articles and two books. During the 1930s, Piryov wrote articles on all levels of the education systems in England, Italy, Japan, Poland and the USA. In some articles, Piryov compared education in countries from Europe, Asia and North and South America. Piryov was the first scholar in Bulgaria to use the term comparative education, and spoke about it as a distinguished science.

During the period 1919 to 1944, the analytical character of comparative education studies was much stronger than previously. Description and comparison of data continued to be the basis of research, but many studies used comparative analysis as the main research method. Prognoses were also developed, and much attention was paid to the historical, economic, cultural and social conditions determining the development of education systems. Studies addressed many themes, including democracy in education, freedom of teaching, the social prestige of teachers, and social equity. Interdisciplinary approaches were common, and comparative education was developed as a university subject. It also began to be considered as a science needed for academic life, school practice and policy making. During the period 1919-44, and especially during the second half of the 1920s and the 1930s, comparative education in Bulgaria was established as a differentiated science.

From 1944 to 1989

During the period of the communist regime, from 1944 to 1989, comparative education was strongly dependent on Marxist-Leninist ideology. The second half of the 1940s and the 1950s were the darkest years. The slightest interest in education in Western countries was considered a provocation and potentially even a crime. The worldwide perspective of Bulgarian comparative education established before 1944 was reduced to study of the 'leading' Soviet educational experiences and other socialist countries. Negentzov left Sofia University, and Piryov switched his interests to psychology. All education research was controlled, centralised and unified, and Bulgarian comparative education was left desolate.

In the early 1960s it was realised that the disconnection of Bulgarian education from Western Europe had caused an information vacuum. The ideological curtain gradually started to open, but researchers still had to examine foreign education theories and practice from a class viewpoint and apply the Marxist methodological approach. The Institute of Education in Sofia was the only research centre to conduct comparative education studies.

In 1962, Nayden Chakarov began a lecture course on comparative education to students in Sofia University. Although it was not the first academic course in Bulgaria to consider foreign education in a comparative perspective, it was the first to be entitled comparative education. The course continued to exist in the 1970s and 1980s. It had the narrow field of vision of that time, but it was one of the few windows open to the world of education. Master's and doctoral theses in comparative education were written at Bulgarian universities on educational policy, structures and curricula.

Although few in number, some projects were performed under the auspices of the Ministry of Education. In the early 1980s some new trends appeared: to breaking the neck of the ideological monism; to a deeper understanding of education in Western countries; to establishing reliable approaches to comparative studies.

While the development of Bulgarian comparative education from the Bulgarian revival till 1944 has been studied thoroughly (Popov 1990, 1994), work on the 1944 to 1989 period has been less detailed. Nevertheless, it would appear that the number of published items was larger than in the previous period. Materials on education in the Soviet Union and other socialist countries dominated, and scholars were expected to criticise the education systems of capitalist countries. Marxist methods and approaches were the only research instruments, and publications were closely censored.

Two important books published during that period were Chakarov's *Problems of Comparative Pedagogy* (1969), and Chakarov and Bishkov's *Comparative Pedagogy* (1986). The 1969 work was the first Bulgarian book in the field, and was also one of the first books on comparative education published in the socialist countries. Chakarov tried to discuss in detail the basic problems of comparative pedagogy from a dialectical-materialistic viewpoint. He considered the theoretical and methodological aspects of that science, and showed the significance, main tasks and role of comparative pedagogy. The problem of education as a subject of comparative study and of the methods of its research occupied a considerable part of the book. Chakarov tried to explain the reasons for the differences in education of different countries. The principles of school organisation were examined in the light of their practical value. A compilation of the comparative characteristics of typical capitalist and typical socialist educational systems was done as a stage towards a study of concrete educational systems. Although having the negative ideological features of all education books of that time, *Problems of Comparative Pedagogy* was a very important and even progressive work.

Comparative Pedagogy was the second book in this field in Bulgaria. Its authors tried to analyse all aspects of comparative pedagogy in selected socialist and capitalist education systems, and included focus on the history and methodology of comparative pedagogy. Unfortunately, the book included a large critical review of contemporary bourgeois education theories examined from a Marxist viewpoint. While in the 1960s such an approach was obligatory, in the mid-1980s it was no longer necessary. This feature decreased the value of the book in the development of comparative education in Bulgaria.

New Beginnings and the Formation of the BCES

End of the Communist Regime

In 1989 the communist regime in Bulgaria cracked, and all life began to change. The following years, in education as much as other sectors, were filled with hope, contradiction and disillusion.

With the end of the regime, party prejudices in education and research were removed. Comparative educators gained the freedom to decide what, why and how to study. However, they faced severe financial constraints. Education research during the 1990s could be described in three words: freedom, perplexity and penury. Research contacts with countries all over the world could be established, and a very strong trend to internationalisation was evident. Academic mobility greatly increased, and hundreds of thousands of Bulgarian youths went abroad to study. Also, many foreign educational and cultural offices were established in Bulgaria. The USA and most European countries had centres to provide information on education in their countries.

In 1997, comparative education was made an obligatory field of study in all university teacher training programmes. This increased the number of lecturers and researchers, and extended the students' interests in the history, methodology and practice of comparative education. In turn, the expansion gave students better possibilities for writing bachelor's, master's and doctoral theses.

Characteristics and Activities of the BCES

The BCES is registered in Sofia City Court as a non-governmental organisation. Any changes to the Statutes must first be passed by the BCES General Assembly and then approved by a judge and registered at the court.

The BCES is an elitist society. It is open to the Bulgarian education community, but the entry criteria are strict. Applicants should have at least a master's degree in education or a related subject, and preferably a doctorate. Applicants should also have research experience in the field of comparative education and recognised publications. Articles and conference papers are by themselves not adequate: authorship or co-authorship of books is necessary. Further, to become a BCES member the candidate should receive at least 50 per cent of the votes of the society's members.

The BCES members are university professors, high-ranking officials in the Ministry of Education and Science, and school teachers. At the time of writing all members were Bulgarian citizens, but the BCES had decided to open its membership to distinguished foreign scholars. The Statutes permit the BCES to involve people outside its membership in various activities. The BCES actively uses that possibility, and involves students, researchers, teachers and others in the society's projects, conferences, seminars and other events.

The Statutes determine that the managing bodies of the society are the General Assembly and the Management Board. The General Assembly consists of all members of the society, and is responsible for passing and amending the Statutes, adopting other internal acts, electing members of the Management Board, taking decisions on admission of new members, deciding on membership fees, accepting the President's annual report, and approving the society's programme.

In turn, the Management Board is the executive body of the society and elects the President of the Board who is also President of the society. The Board also organises the society's activities, prepares reports on the society's activities, and decides on organisational, financial, research and other matters. The members of the Management Board and the President are each elected for five-year terms of office. There is no limit of the number of terms for a person to be elected as member of the Management Board or as President. Between the foundation of the BCES in 1991 and the time of writing the President has been Nikolay Popov.

According to the Statutes, the overall objectives of the BCES are to:

- gather together efforts of its members towards studying historical, methodological and practical aspects of comparative education as a science, towards its development as an academic discipline, and towards studying foreign educational theories and practices;
- establish cooperation and keep contacts with scholars, research organisations, institutions, and other related societies in Bulgaria and abroad; and
- organise, coordinate and support research in the field of comparative education performed by its members.

The society achieves its objectives by organising national and international seminars, conferences, congresses and other forums; conducting research projects; organising, coordinating and managing discussions on education in Bulgaria and abroad; maintaining a comparative education library and data-base; and applying to foundations and other donors for financing of research projects. The BCES has also provided Bulgarian policy-makers with information on educational reforms, innovations and trends in countries around the world. Projects include collection, translation and studying of ABC and other elementary literacy books used in Grade 1 of primary school in different countries. Particular focus has been given to the member countries of European Union.

In 2002, the BCES launched what became a series of international conferences on comparative education in teacher training. The conferences aim to develop links with colleagues who teach comparative education in teacher education programmes around the world. They have examined different approaches to comparative education as a science, research method and academic discipline. The first conference was held in November 2002, the second in October 2003, the third in April 2005, and the fourth in May 2006. The BCES decided to hold its fifth conference in August 2007, just prior to the 13th World Congress of Comparative Education Societies in Sarajevo, Bosnia and Herzegovina. In that way, the BCES aimed both to benefit from and to contribute to the global event, utilising the fact that many international scholars were planning to come to the region and attracting some scholars who might not otherwise have come. The motto of these conferences is "Our way of being an integral part of the international comparative education community".

The third Bulgarian book in the field, entitled *Comparative Education* and written by Georgi Bishkov and Nikolay Popov, was published in 1994. This book was the first in Bulgaria to examine the historical, methodological and practical aspects of the science in a systematic and balanced way. The book began with the history of comparative education, before turning to theory and methods and then describing and comparing education systems in countries from all regions of the world. The second edition of the book appeared in 1999, and in 2006 the authors decided to prepare a third edition.

Other books have also been written by these and other authors. One focused on 20 education systems in Europe, comparing goals, systems of management and finance, structures, and teacher training (Popov & Bishkov 1997). Two other books took global perspectives (Popov 2001, 2002a). A detailed comparison of elementary reading books in nine Slavonic countries was undertaken by Popov and Mihova (2003). This study presented a clear systematic research strategy of how the legal bases, formats, structures, contents, and other features of the reading books could be examined, juxtaposed, compared, generated, and explained. A subsequent work was *The Contemporary Education System in Bulgaria* (Popov 2004). It had a national focus on Bulgaria's education system, but examined it in a comparative context.

Because of foreign currency restrictions and the small size of the society, the BCES encountered challenges in making cash payments of annual dues to the WCCES. The WCCES By-Laws allowed for contributions in kind in place of cash, and during the 1990s the BCES translated the WCCES Statutes and By-Laws into French. This arrangement went further in 2004 with the translation from English to Bulgarian of the book from the 11th World Congress in Korea (Bray 2005). Most of the translation was undertaken by students under the supervision of Nikolay Popov and Marinela Mihova, and the work was thus a training activity as well as a service to the field. The WCCES provided finance to print the book, using income from sales of the English version. The volume thus disseminates international perspectives on the field and information on the WCCES itself through the Bulgarian language.

Other books in English were published for each of the conferences on 'Comparative Education in Teacher Training' (Popov 2002b, 2003; Popov & Penkova 2005; Popov et al. 2006). The volumes brought together the work of Bulgarian and international scholars, with the latter including Karen Biraimah, Marco Todeschini, Yang Shen-Keng, Mark Bray, Reinhard Golz, Masami Matoba, Charl Wolhuter, Eliška Walterová, Mark Ginsburg, and Marta Luz Sisson de Castro.

Conclusion

The BCES is a small but active society which is playing a significant role. The BCES values its membership of the WCCES, which is one channel through which the society can have a global voice. Financial constraints usually prevent the BCES from sending representatives to the meetings of the WCCES Executive Committee, but the internet provides a channel through which the BCES is able to make its voice heard, including in matters of voting and policy.

Through the centuries, and especially in its modern history, Bulgaria has had few years of free development. The education system has had limited possibilities for normal functioning, and comparative education has always been a window to the world of others. Bulgaria has been a member state of the European Union since 1 January 2007 and new perspectives are given to the development of this country. In the contemporary era, Bulgarian comparative education has to meet the following challenges:

- *as a university discipline*: not only to offer deep knowledge on foreign education systems, but also to teach students how really to do comparisons;
- *as a problem-solving tool*: to observe, describe and analyse reform processes and their results around the world, to compare them to Bulgaria's needs, efforts, achievements and mistakes, and to offer solutions;
- *as a research field*: to assist in carrying out theoretical and empirical studies, and to seek new research instruments.

In all these domains, the BCES is proud to play a role. And in turn the BCES is proud to be a member of the WCCES.

References

Aleksiev, Nikola (1912): *Our School Policy*. Sofia: [in Bulgarian]

Bishkov, Georgi & Popov, Nikolay (1994): *Comparative Education*. 1st edition, Sofia: Sofia University Press [2nd edition 1999; 3rd edition in printing]. [in Bulgarian]

Bray, Mark (ed.) (2005): *Comparative Education: Continuing Traditions, New Challenges and New Paradigms*. Sofia: Bureau for Educational Services. [in Bulgarian]

Chakarov, Nayden (1969): *Problems of Comparative Pedagogy*. Sofia: Narodna Prosveta. [in Bulgarian]

Chakarov, Nayden & Bishkov, Georgi (1986): *Comparative Pedagogy*. Sofia: Sofia University Press. [in Bulgarian]

Gavovski, Sava (1937): *Education in the Far East*. [in Bulgarian]

Illiev, Bratovan (1911): *Bourgeois and Proletarian Pedagogy*. [in Bulgarian]

Lazarov, Nikola (1906): Trade Education in Advanced Countries. *School Review*, Vol.11, No.8, pp.811-822. [in Bulgarian]

Negentzov, Christo (1926): Schooling in Germany and the United States. *Teacher's Thought*, Vol.7, No.2, pp.90-112. [in Bulgarian]

Piryov, Gencho (1933): *New Education in the New World*. [in Bulgarian]

Piryov, Gencho (1941): *Entire Education*. [in Bulgarian]

Popov, Nikolay (1990): *Development of Bulgarian Comparative Education from the Time of the Bulgarian Revival till 1944*. PhD dissertation, Sofia University & The Bulgarian Higher Testimonial Committee. [in Bulgarian]

Popov, Nikolay (1994): Primary Education in Europe. *Primary Education*, Vol.34, No.1, pp.48-61. [in Bulgarian]

Popov, Nikolay (2001): *Primary Education: Comparison of Structural Aspects in 90 Countries*. Sofia: Sofia University Press. [in Bulgarian]

Popov, Nikolay (2002a): *The World Comparison: A Challenge to Comparative Education*. Sofia: Bureau for Educational Services. [in Bulgarian]

Popov, Nikolay (ed.) (2002b): *Comparative Education in Teacher Training*. Sofia: Bureau for Educational Services.

Popov, Nikolay (ed.) (2003): *Comparative Education in Teacher Training*. Volume 2. Sofia: Bureau for Educational Services.

Popov, Nikolay (2004): *The Contemporary Education System in Bulgaria*. Sofia: Bureau for Educational Services. [in Bulgarian]

Popov, Nikolay & Bishkov, Georgi (1997): *Educational Systems in Europe*. Sofia: Sofia

University Press. [in Bulgarian]

Popov, Nikolay & Mihova, Marinela (2003): *ABC Books in Slavonic Countries: A Comparative Study*. Sofia: Bureau for Educational Services. [in Bulgarian]

Popov, Nikolay & Penkova, Rossitsa (eds.) (2005): *Comparative Education in Teacher Training*. Volume 3. Sofia: Bureau for Educational Services.

Popov, Nikolay; Wolhuter, Charl; Heller, Craig & Kysilka, Marcella (eds.) (2006): *Comparative Education and Teacher Training*. Volume 4. Sofia: Bureau for Educational Services.

25

The Polish Comparative Education Society (PCES)

Józef KUŹMA

Comparative studies of education in Poland date back to the 1930s. However, only in the 1960s did comparative education develop as a field of academic research; and for political reasons, strong cooperation with comparative education centres in Europe and worldwide was possible only after 1990. This chapter begins with an overview of the development of the field before turning to the specifics of the Polish Comparative Education Society (PCES) which was founded in 1991.

Comparative Education in Poland

Among the milestones in the Polish literature on comparative education is the 1936 monograph by Chałasiński entitled *School Systems in the American Society*. Its author recommended incorporating the sociological analysis of educational processes. His later work *Society and School Systems in the United States* (Chałasiński 1966) is an application of this.

After World War II, special attention was paid to comparative analysis of education systems in the former socialist countries. Of particular interest are the monographs by Pęcherski (1959) on the USSR, Dąbrowska-Zembrzuska (1963) on Czechoslovakia; Pęcherski (1970) on Bulgaria, and Kuźma (1993) on Poland, Ukraine, Bulgaria, Slovakia and East Germany. Other books focused on specific countries, including ones in capitalist Europe. Examples are Kotłowski (1960) on education in Great Britain, Nawroczyński (1961) on France, Mońka-Stanikowa (1963, 1970, 1976) on Belgium, Switzerland and other Western countries, and Dowjat et al. (1971) on France, the Federal Republic of Germany and Sweden.

Another major group of studies included global analyses of education systems. Pioneering work was done by Hessen who, having completed comprehensive comparative studies, produced major books entitled *School and Democracy at the Breakthrough* (1938) and *Structure and Contents of the Present-day School* (1959). Hessen argued that fundamental problems in education lay in implementing the principles of social justice, whereby every human being should have a right to education and societal advancement according to personal capabilities. Although the major works and renowned books on methodology by such authors as Marc-Antoine Jullien, Pedro Rosselló, and Isaac Kandel were never translated into Polish, most scholars were acquainted with them.

The educational sociologists and specialists in pedagogy who employed the methodology of comparative education included Józef Chałasiński, Bogdan Suchodolski, Bogdan Nawroczyński, Sergiusz Hessen, Czesław Kupisiewicz and Ryszard Pachociński. Florian Znaniecki was a particularly prominent figure who co-authored a classic multi-volume book entitled *The Polish Peasant in the Europe and America* (Thomas & Znaniecki 1976).

In general terms, the subject matter of comparative education was defined by Nawroczyński (1972, p.9) as encompassing "educational facts, chiefly school systems, education and teaching methods, influences and results, theories of teaching and learning, and the conditions that affect all these processes". Most comparative education scholars in Poland have been concerned about the practical applications of their studies. For example, Suchodolski (1972) sought strong connections with educational policy. He felt that formulation of the main concepts of comparative education as a tool of educational policy should give comparative education the status of an academic subject separate from other pedagogic studies.

Polish academics have also displayed growing interest in global transformations, focusing on environmental hazards and other social threats. For example, Kupisiewicz (1978, 1982, 1985) asserted that observation and rigorous analysis of the relationships between education and society in several countries allowed the forecasting of major changes in education systems. Kupisiewicz concluded that despite constant reforms, contemporary educational institutions were not able to cope adequately with broader societal requirements. He suggested that schools would remain necessary, but that they must be entirely different from and superior to the dominant models (Kupisiewicz 1985, pp.245-246). Related views were presented by Potulicka (2001), who focused on Michael Fullan's paradigms of education changes and Per Dalin's concepts of development of school organisations. Potulicka also compared changes in the education systems of Israel, Anglo-Saxon countries and Scandinavian countries. Other studies incorporating sociological studies include Melosik (1994).

Further publications included quasi-encyclopaedic studies focused on selected aspects of education in individual countries. In these works, information and facts predominated while comparative analysis was of minor importance. Works in this category include Pachociński's *Teacher Training Abroad* (1992), *Teacher Training in European Union Countries* (1994), *Comparative Pedagogy* (1995), and *Strategy of Education Reform in the World* (2003). Another noteworthy study was by Rabczuk (1994) on education in the member countries of the European Union.

Also relevant is work on *Teachers in the Future Schools* (Kuźma 2001) and *Science of Schooling* (Kuźma, 2005). These works argue that the theoretical and practical aspects of school activities should be treated as a separate branch of science. They suggest that the name 'scholiology' – derived from the Greek word *scholion* (school) and *logos* (science, concept, word) – be used to refer to research on schools, understood as public institutions, organisational systems, teaching functions and syllabuses.

The Polish Comparative Education Society

The Polish Comparative Education Society (PCES) was founded in 1991 in Warsaw as a group of 48 members. In 2003, a regional division with 12 members was established in Cracow. In 2006, the society had about 60 members. The founder, Ryszard Pachociński, was the President until Eugenia Potulicka took over from him in 2005. The PCES was admitted to the World Council of Comparative Education Societies (WCCES) in 1992. At that time, it also began close cooperation with the Comparative Education Society in Europe (CESE).

Several open meetings of PCES members are held each year to disseminate the latest achievements in comparative education in Poland, Europe and worldwide. These events make an excellent opportunity to make known the recent publications by Polish and foreign authors. The first PCES congress was held in 2002 at the Opole University. The PCES is still a new organisation, searching for its own identity and research areas, as well as directions and methods of research work.

At the university and teachers' academies in Poland, during the 1990s educators became aware of the need to include comparative pedagogy in the curricula of the teacher education programmes. Comparative pedagogy became obligatory and is included in the basic syllabus standards, covering at least 45 hours of lectures, practical classes, laboratories or seminars. This subject is also included in the syllabus for European studies at Polish universities. Ryszard Pachociński, Józef Kuźma and other professors made great efforts to organise bachelor's and master's degree programmes for students wishing to take a major in comparative pedagogy. To date these efforts have not met with success since they have not received the support of authorities at any Polish university. However, full-time and part-time courses in comparative pedagogy are anticipated at some state-owned or private universities.

New Research Trends and Challenges

Comparative education should play a significant role in the era of globalisation as it is a universal field of knowledge, covering a growing number of countries on several continents with different political systems and levels of development. Poland, a post-socialist state, is now undergoing major economic and social transformations in which two opposing tendencies are apparent in education. The first tendency is towards supporting of the national educational systems based on traditions and patriotism, propagation of the national heritage and culture, going back to traditional Christian values. The other tendency, known as liberal, favours European integration, international contacts, supranational education, and research systems based on universal and European human values. This tendency has strong ties with the United States for mobility schemes, joint research, and cultural projects particularly in the field of mass culture.

Following the Bologna Treaty in 1999, more and more countries seem to adopt liberal policies, particularly the countries that recently joined the European Union, including Poland. This trend is clearly revealed in the subjects of research programmes and syllabus design. Many research programmes undertaken at specialised research centres are concerned with the processes of pro-European education, which are also the subject matter of the growing number of MA and PhD dissertations. Examples of this new trend in research areas are two PhD dissertations at the University of Cracow:

- Adam Ryk (2002): 'Values and Life Perspectives of the Young People in Poland and Italy: A Comparative Study'; and
- Ewa Pająk (2003): 'Educational activity of the American Peace Corps in the Eastern and Central European Countries'.

The results of these studies suggest that the generation of young Polish, as a consequence of rapid societal transformations, has to confront new challenges and values. Axiological pluralism, new possibilities confronting the family, educational and explorative aspirations, imply changes in the range of awareness, revaluation of ideas, changes in systems and hierarchy of values. Especially in the question of attitudes towards moral values, we can observe among the Polish youth an ensuing moral atmosphere fashioned after liberal democratic European societies.

Conclusion

During the decade from the mid-1990s several new publications in the field of comparative education were translated into Polish. However, original empirical studies by Polish authors utilising comparative methods remained rather scarce. This is changing as the country opens and integrates with the regional and global economies.

All in all, it seems that we are witnessing the formation of a new democratic order, based on free competition, universal human and Christian values, multiculturalism and tolerance. Those in favour of the new order are not mainly the young generations of Poles, who did not know the nightmare of the World War II and do not remember the dramatic period of martial law in Poland during the 1980s. The PCES is a small society which to some extent owes its origin to the opening of Polish society and which is evolving with the changing circumstances. The field of comparative pedagogy has been recognised as essential in Poland's teachers colleges, and considerable scope exists for consolidation and deepening of comparative education research.

References

Chałasiński, Józef (1936): *Szkoła w społeczeństwie amerykańskim* [*School Systems in the American Society*]. Warszawa: Naukowe Towarzystwo Pedagogiczne.

Chałasiński Józef (1966): *Społeczeństwo i systemy szkolne w Stanach Zjednoczonych* [*Society and School Systems in the United States*]. Warszawa: Państwowe Wydawnictwo Naukowe.

Dąbrowska-Zembrzuska, Eugenia (1963): *System edukacji w Czechosłowacji* [*The Education System in Czechoslovakia*]. Wrocław: Ossolineum.

Dowjat, Tadeusz; Pęcherski, Mieczyslaw & Wróbel, Tadeusz (1971): *Oświata i szkolnictwo we Francji, Niemieckiej Republice Federalnej i Szwecji* [*Education and School Systems in France, Federal Republic of Germany and Sweden*]. Warszawa: Państwowe Wydawnictwo Naukowe.

Hessen, Sergiusz (1938): *Szkoła i demokracja na przełomie* [*School and Democracy at the Breakthrough*]. Warszawa: Nasza Księgarnia.

Hessen, Sergiusz (1959): *Struktura i treść szkoły współczesnej* [*Structure and Contents of the Present-day School*]. Wrocław: Ossolineum.

Kotłowski, Karol (1960): *Szkoła angielska po drugiej wojnie światowej* [*The Education System in Great Britain after World War II*]. Warszawa: Państwowe Zakłady Wydawnictw Szkolnych.

Kupisiewicz, Czesław (1978): *Przemiany edukacyjne w świecie na tle raportów oświatowych* [*Education Changes in the World in the Light of Reports*]. Warszawa: Wiedza Powszechna.

Kupisiewicz, Czesław (1982): *Szkolnictwo w procesie przebudowy* [*Education in the Period of Transformation*]. Warszawa: Wydawnictwa Szkolne i Pedagogiczne.

Kupisiewicz, Czesław (1985): *Paradygmaty i wizje reform oświatowych* [*Paradigms and Vision of Education Reform*]. Warszawa: Państwowe Wydawnictwo Naukowe.

Kuźma, Józef (1993): *Optymalizacja systemu pedagogicznego kształcenia, dokształcenia i doskonalenia nauczycieli* [*Optimisation of the System of Teacher Education and self-education*]. Warszawa: Państwowe Wydawnictwo Naukowe.

Kuźma, Józef (2001): *Nauczyciele przyszłej szkoły* [*Teacher of the Future School*]. Kraków: Wydawnictwo Naukowe Akademii Pedagogicznej w Krakowie.

Kuźma, Kózef (2004): 'Comparative Studies of Teacher Education Systems in Selected Post-socialist Countries'. Paper presented at the 12th World Congress of Comparative Education Societies, Havana, Cuba.

Kuźma, Józef (2005): *Nauka o szkole: Studium monograficzne – Zarys koncepcji* [*Science of Schooling: Monographic Study – Outline of Conception*]. Kraków: Oficyna Wydawnicza Impuls.

Melosik, Zbyszko (1994): *Współczesne amerykańskie spory edukacyjne: Między socjologią edukacji a pedagogiką postmodernistyczną* [*Controversies in the American Education Systems: Between Education Sociology and Post Modernist Pedagogy*]. Poznań: Wydawnictwo Naukowe UAM.

Mońka-Stanikowa, Anna (1963): *Szkolnictwo w Belgii współczesnej* [*Education in Present-day Belgium*]. Warszawa: Państwowy Zakład Wydawnictw Szkolnych.

Mońka-Stanikowa, Anna (1970): *Szkolnictwo szwajcarskie w świetle nowoczesnych tendencji oświatowych* [*Education in Switzerland in the Light of Modern Tendencies*]. Warszawa: Państwowe Wydawnictwo Naukowe.

Mońka-Stanikowa, Anna (1976): *Szkoła średnia w krajach zachodnich* [*Secondary School in the Western Countries*]. Warszawa: Wydawnictwa Szkolne i Pedagogiczne.

Nawroczyński, Bogdan (1961): *O szkolnictwie francuskim* [*The School System in France*]. Warszawa: Państwowe Wydawnictwo Naukowe.

Nawroczyński, Bogdan R. (1972): 'Przedmiot i metoda pedagogiki porównawczej' ['Subject Matter and Method of Comparative Pedagogy'. *Studia Pedagogiczne*, Vol.26.

Pachociński, Ryszard (1992): *Kształcenie nauczycieli za granicą* [*Teacher Education Abroad*]. Warszawa: Wydawnictwo Instytutu Badań Edukacyjnych.

Pachociński, Ryszard (1994): *Edukacja nauczycieli w krajach Unii Europejskiej* [*Teacher Training in the European Union Countries*]. Warszawa: Instytut Badań Edukacyjnych.

Pachociński, Ryszard (1995): *Pedagogika porównawcza* [*Comparative Pedagogy*]. Białystok: Trans Humana.

Pachociński, Ryszard (2003): *Strategie reform oświatowych na świecie* [*Strategy of Education Reform in the World*]. Warszawa: Instytut Badań Edukacyjnych.

Pęcherski, Mieczysław (1959): *Reforma szkolnictwa w ZSRR* [*School Reform in the USSR*]. Warszawa: Państwowe Zakłady Wydawnictw Szkolnych.

Pęcherski, Mieczysław (1970): *Szkolnictwo i oświata w Bułgarii* [*The School System in Bulgaria*]. Warszawa: Państwowe Wydawnictwo Naukowe.

Potulicka, Eugenia (2001): *Szkice z teorii i praktyki zmiany oświatowej* [*Sketches in Theory of Education Changes*]. Poznań: Eruditus.

Rabczuk, Wiktor (1994): *Polityka edukacyjna Unii Europejskiej na tle przemian w szkolnictwie krajów członkowskich* [*Education Policy of the European Union on the Background Transformation in the School Systems of Member Countries*]. Warszawa: Instutut Badań Edukacyjnych.

Suchodolski, Bogdan (1972): 'Pedagogika porównawcza i polityka oświatowa'. *Studia Pedagogiczne*, Vol.26.

Thomas, William J. & Znaniecki, Florian (1976): *Chłop polski w Europie i Ameryce Warszawa, Ludowa Spółdzielnia Wydawnicza* [Polish edition]; *The Polish Peasant in Europe and America* [English edition]. Chicago: Chicago University Press.

26

The Southern African Comparative and History of Education Society (SACHES)

Crain SOUDIEN

The history of the Southern African Comparative and History of Education Society (SACHES) shows that professional and scholarly associations may be important windows on the societies in which they are located. SACHES emerged against, and in some ways in response to, the complex colonial and racial dynamics of Southern Africa; and in its development, SACHES reflected some of the challenges that the field of comparative education commonly encounters. This chapter describes the formation and development of SACHES, locating its history within the larger social and academic politics of South Africa and the broader Southern African region.

The Development of Comparative Education in South Africa
Although SACHES serves the whole of the Southern African region, it has been dominated by developments in South Africa. Accordingly, the chapter begins by recounting some historical features in that country.

Emergence of the Field
As a result of South Africa's colonial history and its relationship with Europe, comparative education as a formal field of study entered the academy at a later stage than in the metropolitan countries. Although both educational borrowing and more self-conscious comparison have been important components of the country's educational history, comparative education itself only became a field of study in the second half of the 20th century. Further, only in the mid-1960s – at least a decade and a half after comparative education had been institutionalised in Europe and the United States – was it introduced into universities and colleges in South Africa.

The period of the entry of the field was fraught with difficulty because central to the plans of the then apartheid state was the intention to use education for the purposes of racial separation. Key elements of these plans included the Extension of University Education Act in 1959 (Anderson 2002, p.22). This Act mandated the exclusion from 'white' universities of people of colour, both students and faculty, and instituted the establishment of 10 'ethnic' universities, including the Universities of Zululand (for people classified as Zulu), the Western Cape (for people classified as coloured), Durban-Westville (for people classified as Indian), the University of the North (for people classified as Tswana), and the University of Transkei (for people classified as Xhosa). The apartheid state expected the higher education community to provide the intellectual ballast for its policies, and to ensure their production and reproduction. The Afrikaans component of this community, while not entirely trusted by the state, enjoyed a favoured relationship with it and was required to play the role of its intellectual handmaiden.

The place of comparative education in this environment was controversial. The apartheid state did not trust educationists in general, and some comparative educationists in particular. It created, as a result, its own cadre of experts or quasi 'academic-practitioners', ignoring the experiences and knowledge base of academics at universities. This development had two consequences: some scholars found themselves deliberately ignored, while others, such as those who enjoyed some recognition and who went out of their way to demonstrate their loyalty to the apartheid state, were drawn into its inner circle. The posture of the Afrikaans universities, and their approach to comparative education with respect to the political authority of the apartheid state, was compliant and even complicit with its apartheid philosophy. Their approach was a convenient way to avoid critical sociological, economic and political issues facing South African education under apartheid. As noted by Herman (1993, p.22), "academics in education faculties at Afrikaans-medium universities have to a large extent been seen to acquiesce with Apartheid structures".

While the Afrikaans universities began to close ranks, a process intensified by the hostility of the historically English-speaking white universities which were more liberal and more ambiguous in their attitude towards apartheid, a debate took place within this community about the place of comparative education in the arena of Fundamental Pedagogics. This concept was based on phenomenology, and attempted to articulate education as a distinct discipline. Some Afrikaner scholars sought to shoehorn comparative education into Fundamental Pedagogics, but others resisted attempts to appropriate the field into the government's racist ideology. In the camp of the former were Potgieter (1972, p.8) and Van Zyl (1968, pp.43-45), who attempted to reconfigure comparative education as a part-discipline of Fundamental Pedagogics. Others within the Afrikaans community were less inclined to seek this alignment for comparative education, and worked within the more conventional political science and sociological frameworks. For example, Dekker and Van Schalkwyk (1989), who wrote a popular comparative education text entitled *Modern Education Systems*, worked in the traditions set by the European and North American scholars such as Nicholas Hans, Isaac Kandel and Friedrich Schneider.

The situation at the new historically-black universities at the time of the entry of comparative education into the domain of higher education was similar. Dominated by Afrikaans faculty members, they tended to take their lead from the intellectual shifts in the universities in which their professors had studied. As a consequence, comparative education in these institutions was little different in character to that in the Afrikaans universities.

Given their historical relationships with the United Kingdom and, contradictorily their financial and political dependence on the apartheid state, English-speaking white universities were in a similarly complex position. While much was made in these institutions of the right to academic freedom, their general orientation to the state tended towards pragmatism (Michau 1982, p.68). This was particularly evident in the approaches taken towards comparative education. In the few institutions where the subject was introduced, such as the Universities of the Witwatersrand and Cape Town, a range of approaches developed. The texts available, and the fact that many academics received their training with doyens in the field such as Edmund King and Brian Holmes, ensured that the kinds of discourses that were dominant in the United States and United Kingdom were reproduced in these institutions. However, significant elements of Marxist and neo-Marxist analyses were taught alongside systems-theory approaches.

Resistance to the Apartheid State

The differences in approach to comparative education were exacerbated as political conditions in South Africa deteriorated during the mid-1970s. The shifts in discourse coalitions coincided with the heterodoxy of the time (Bergh & Soudien 2006); and an eruption of new political and sociological movements expressed itself in the emergence of the black consciousness movement and a resurgence of radical and working-class activism around the country. The 1976 Soweto student uprising catalysed a range of student, civic, labour and political movements. Attempting to comprehend these developments, the social sciences underwent a major radicalisation, culminating in a break in the English-speaking universities with their traditional pragmatism, a new caution amongst Afrikaner academics, and a powerful upsurge of militancy at the historically black universities.

Indicative of this change was Herman's (1986) inaugural address as Professor and Head of the Department of Comparative Education at the University of the Western Cape, which urged comparative education to break out of its North-South paralysis and to focus its attention on the questions of social development. Similar movements were evident in the liberal English-speaking white universities where the issues of the Third World assumed greater prominence (Bergh & Soudien 2006). The Afrikaans universities could not stand aloof from these developments. While generally they remained faithful to the ideology of Christian National Education, faculty members, particularly those who in the earlier period had expressed their discomfort with the new Afrikaner dogma, began looking for new ways to teach comparative education (Bergh & Soudien 2006). As a consequence, old alliances and loyalties loosened, and a dramatic rupture appeared between the Afrikaans and historically black universities. New coalitions were strengthened after apartheid was abolished and when the democratic government came to power in 1994.

The realignments that took shape in this period were critical in reconfiguring the comparative education landscape. The urgency in debates, research and teaching that marked the field in the 1980s gave way to a different kind of social engagement. While certain Afrikaner academics began to turn their backs on and even denied their membership of older discourse coalitions, it was the turn of the liberals to confront the complexities of their new relationship with the democratic state. From having been critics, the liberals and radicals were called upon to assist in building the new order. The challenges of this request precipitated a turn away from the kind of comparative education that had been practised in the 1980s: theorising had to be replaced by planning and development. The impact on the field was immense, with the name 'comparative education' all but disappearing from titles of courses. Moreover, after Herman's retirement in 2004, only one chair of comparative education, at the University of the North-West, remained in the entire country. Comparative education as a taught course no longer existed in the major English-speaking universities and in leading black universities such as the University of the Western Cape, though it remained in some Afrikaans universities such as the University of South Africa and the University of the North-West. The University of Zululand also retained a Department of Comparative Education, but did not have a chair to lead it. Significantly, the focus in these universities, as had explicitly become the case elsewhere, had turned to issues of development (Maarman & Wolhuter 2006).

The South African Comparative Education Literature

The field *per se* has been the object of study since at least the early 1970s, when scholars in the mainly Afrikaans Fundamental Pedagogics tradition sought to locate comparative education within it (Potgieter 1972). Wessels (1974) moved the discussion somewhat to look at relationships with broader debates; and subsequent overviews were included in publications by Stone (1974, 1981), Barnard (1981, 1984), Bondesio and Berkhout (1987), Berkhout and Bondesio (1992), and Vos and Brits (1987, 1990). Other notable works included Ruperti (1970), Steinberg (1982, 1987), Herman (1986, 1993) and Pretorius (1992). In 1982, the 'Interchange' section of the journal *Perspectives in Education* was devoted to the field of comparative education at the Universities of South Africa (Stone 1982), Zululand (Vos 1982), Cape Town (Steinberg 1982), Natal (Michau 1982), and the Orange Free State (Vermaak 1982).

Also significant is the work during the late 1990s of a group of comparativists under the guidance of Anne-Marie Bergh and colleagues at the University of South Africa who investigated approaches to teaching in comparative education. Some of this work was presented in the 10th World Congress of Comparative Education Societies, held in Cape Town in 1998. Subsequent reviews of the field include Herman (2003), Bergh and Soudien (2006), Wolhuter (2006), and Weeks et al. (2006). The field of comparative education has to some extent depended on policy work in the national government's Education Department and other state agencies. Intensive comparative studies have been commissioned in such areas as education performance, systemic forms, and approaches to funding and governance.

The Birth and Development of SACHES

SACHES was established in 1991 at the annual conference of the Kenton Education Association (KEA), a general education society with which SACHES has retained close links and overlapping membership. The organisation, guided by its founders Harold Herman, Peter Kallaway, David Gilmour and Crain Soudien, came into being as both a comparative and a history of education society. This coalition of fields reflected the academic interests of the founding group, though within the society comparative education developed more vigorously than history of education.

The SACHES founders felt the need for a society that would devote itself to the issues of comparison and history because, especially with respect to the former, none of the existing societies in the region paid particular attention to these themes. KEA, the leading English-speaking education association, focused on curriculum and sociology of education. The Afrikaner education society, the Education Association of South Africa (EASA) did regularly include comparative education in its sessions, but it did not enjoy the kind of credibility that would have easily encouraged liberal and radical scholars of comparative education to seek refuge within it. The Southern African Society of Education (SASE), which served academics working within historically black universities and colleges, also lacked a significant interest in comparative education. While none of these three organisations was racially exclusive at the time of the formation of SACHES, they tended to operate with, respectively, a predominantly English-speaking white, an Afrikaans-speaking white, and a black membership.

Against this backdrop, SACHES emerged as a society that sought not only to focus on comparative education but simultaneously to emphasise an inclusive racial and geographic agenda. Unlike the other societies, with the exception of SASE which had members in the wider region, it specifically sought to build membership in the immediate region. Efforts were particularly focused on Namibia, Botswana, Zimbabwe, Zambia, Malawi, Mozambique, Swaziland, Uganda and Lesotho, and participation was also attracted from Kenya and Tanzania. In the context of a traditional South African reserve towards the idea of being African, SACHES deliberately projected itself as an African association. Given the historic divide between South Africa and the rest of the continent, this was very significant.

The association started with 35 members, with Harold Herman as its first President, Peter Kallaway the Vice-President, Nick Taylor the Secretary, and David Gilmour the Treasurer. In time, Crain Soudien replaced Nick Taylor; and this executive, based in the Western Cape, developed as the organisation's founding leadership. Important initiatives that would give the organisation its character developed out of the work of this executive and a small group of key members such as Anne-Marie Bergh and Petro van Niekerk at the University of South Africa in Pretoria. The first initiative was to seek membership of the World Council of Comparative Education Societies (WCCES), and the second was to establish the *Southern African Review of Education.*

Obtaining acceptance by the WCCES at the meeting of its Executive Committee in Prague in 1992 was a challenge, and required considerable diplomatic and behind-the-scenes work. SACHES was forced to confront South Africa's racial history, even as the country was attempting to divest itself of that baggage, and even as SACHES sought to position itself as the one society that self-consciously addressed the issues of the country and region's divided racial history. Although SACHES had come into being as a deliberately inclusive organisation, this fact was not apparent to, or accepted by, key individuals inside the WCCES who raised questions about SACHES' links with South Africa's apartheid past. The process of establishing the organisation's credentials as an open and inclusive organisation, awkward as it was both in the WCCES and SACHES, emphasised for all concerned how central the issues of race and difference, and the importance of working through them, were to the organisation. Having gained acceptance into the WCCES in the course of 1992, the organisation came to be known for promoting inclusion both within the region and in relation to the questions of the marginalisation of less developed countries – precisely the opposite picture projected on it during its first official engagements with the WCCES.

The establishment of the *Southern African Review of Education* as a peer-reviewed journal was also an important initiative. The journal was preceded by conference proceedings edited by Herman and Bergh, and formally emerged under the editorship of members led by Kallaway at the University of the Western Cape in 1995. The journal later joined with an important journal devoted to alternative education in the region, *Education with Production*. This was the vehicle of the eponymous movement in the region under the leadership of the renowned educationist Patrick van Rensburg, who was also elected as the society's first Honorary Fellow. The journal has developed into an important vehicle, and under the guidance of Aslam Fataar at the University of the Western Cape secured accredited status with the South African Department of Education. After Kallaway, the editorial leadership was taken over by Sheldon Weeks and colleagues at the University of Botswana. Linda Chisholm took over the editorship in 2005, by which time the journal had moved from an annual edition to two issues each year. At the end of 2006, plans were laid for the journal to be registered as an on-line publication.

While SACHES was attempting to secure admission into the WCCES, it inaugurated the tradition of holding its annual conferences on a rotational basis in the region. Because the bulk of its membership came from South Africa, it was agreed that its annual meetings would take place alongside the KEA meeting inside of South Africa every second year, and in the alternate years in one of the countries in the region. During the initial decade and a half, meetings were held in Zambia, Botswana (twice), Namibia, and Tanzania. The 2001 meeting in Botswana was particularly important because SACHES assisted in bringing together all the major research associations in the region, including the Botswana, Lesotho and Swaziland Education Association in a single conference.

The highlight of SACHES' history was winning the bid to host the 10th Congress of the WCCES. This event took place in Cape Town in 1998 under the leadership of the Western Cape Executive, chaired by Kallaway who became President after Herman had served a pair of two-year terms, and co-ordinated by

Crain Soudien. The congress was a great success, and continues to be remembered for the quality of its organisation and level of scholarship. Over 800 delegates from 60 countries attended, and Africa was well represented with scholars from Egypt, Ethiopia, Nigeria, Ghana, Kenya and elsewhere. The event secured support from the Royal Netherlands government, the British Council and the Association for the Development of Education in Africa (ADEA), which assisted in bringing not only delegates from the continent but also ministers, permanent secretaries and other senior officials. The mix of scholars and policy makers gave the meeting a sense of urgency and weight. Important initiatives came out of the congress, including the establishment of a fund for the support of comparative education scholarship in the region. SACHES membership after this event stood at approximately 100 paid-up scholars from across the region.

After the excitement of 1998, SACHES went into a period of stasis. Sheldon Weeks became the President at the Biennial General Meeting in Cape Town with Molapi Sebatane from Lesotho as his deputy. The leadership of the organisation moved to the north and was distributed among the Universities of Botswana, Pretoria, South Africa and Witwatersrand. At its 2002 Biennial Meeting, Brigitte Smit, from the University of Pretoria, became the President. She served for one term before handing over to Thobeka Mda in 2005.

Particularly challenging has been holding the membership intact and drawing in new members. Despite the intense efforts of its leadership, including Weeks' editorship of the society's electronic newsletter, the contradictions of South Africa's relative privilege in relation to the region, and the consequent access of its scholars to greater levels of support from their universities, configured and projected the role of South Africans in the organisation in complex ways. The difficult issues of South African dominance in the context of the country's racial problems, despite being the subject of regular discussion at meetings, remained difficult to solve. The leadership has been anxious to avoid becoming a patronage agency offering largesse to the region in the form of, for example, travel bursaries and stipends, but has recognised that its members do not all have equal access to resources. In this challenge, the organisation is confronted with the essence of the development conundrum confronting the region as a whole.

As SACHES approaches the end of its second decade, it remains very conscious of the issues which provide it with its reason for existence. Struggling to maintain its membership, the leadership decided to host a discussion in its journal and its meetings on questions of future direction and role. These included the challenges of being a relevant scholarly society in a time and space that were not especially conducive for its development. The 2006 annual meeting was small, but members debated with intensity the state of the field, its relevance and its future. The presidential address (Mda 2006) raised many questions about the ways in which the organisation ought to assert itself in relation to the opportunities in the region to put comparative expertise to good use. Importantly, while the difficulty of sustaining the organisation presented itself as a threat, the opportunity (which might not be proportionate in its potential) for thinking through difficult questions made itself available in a way which could only be for the longer-term good of the society and the region.

References

Anderson, Gregory M. (2002): *Building a People's University in South Africa.* New York: Peter Lang.

Barnard, Stephanus S. (1981): *Vergelykende Opvoedkunde vir Onderwysstudente.* Second edition, Durban: Butterworths.

Barnard, Stephanus S. (1984): *Inleiding tot die Vergelykende Opvoedkunde* Durban: Butterworths.

Bergh, Anne-Marie & Soudien, Crain (2006): 'The Institutionalisation of Comparative Education Discourses in South Africa in the 20th Century. *Southern African Review of Education* with *Education with Production*, Vol.12, No.2, pp.35-60.

Berkhout, Susara J. & Bondesio, Michael J. (eds.) (1992): *Onderwysstelselkunde: Perspektiewe.* Pretoria: Van Schaik.

Bondesio, Michael J. & Berkhout, Susara. J. (1987): *Onderwysstelselkunde.* Pretoria: University of Pretoria.

Dekker, Elise I. and Van Schalkwyk, Ockert J. (1989): *Modern Education Systems.* First edition, Durban: Butterworths.

Herman, Harold (1986): 'Crisis in Schooling and Society: The Role of Comparative, International and Development Education'. Inaugural address as Professor and Head of the Department of Comparative Education at the University of the Western Cape, 13 November.

Herman, Harold (1993): 'Comparative Education: Recent International Trends and Suggestions for New Approaches in a Changing South Africa', in Kros, C.J. & Herman, Harold (eds.), *Educational Change in Southern Africa: Proceedings of the 1992 Annual Conference of the Southern African Comparative and History of Education Society.* Belleville: SACHES.

Herman, Harold. (2003): 'SACHES – Respice! Prospice!'. *Southern African Review of Education* with *Education with Production*, Vol.8, pp.17-22.

Maarman, Rouaan & Wolhuter, Charl (2006): 'Thematic and Infrastructural Overview of Comparative Education and History of Education at South African Universities', in Wolhuter, Charl (ed.), *Aurora Australis: Comparative Education and History of Education at Universities in Southern Africa.* Potchefstroom: North-West University, pp.41-49.

Mda, Thobeka (2006): Presidential Address to the 2006 SACHES Annual Meeting.

Michau, Maureen (1982): '"The Common and the Diverse" and Comparative Education'. *Perspectives in Education*, Vol.6, pp.67-71.

Potgieter, Frederik J. (1972): *Inleiding tot die Vergelykende Pedagogiek.* Johannesburg: Perskor.

Pretorius, Fanie (1992): 'Comparative Education: Perspectives in a Changing South Africa'. *Prospects: Quarterly Review of Education*, Vol.22, No.1, pp.102-111.

Ruperti, Ruth (1970): 'Vergelykende Opvoedkunde: 'n uitdaging (1)'. *Onderwysblad*, Vol.1, pp.215-226.

Steinberg, Bernard (1982): 'Comparative Education in South Africa: Towards an Effective Rationale'. *Perspectives in Education*, Vol.6, pp.56-60.

Steinberg, Bernard (1987): 'Comparative Education in South Africa: An Irrelevant Academic Exercise?', in Young, Douglas & Burns, Robert (eds.), *Education at the Crossroads: Papers to Mark 75 years of Teacher Education at the University of*

Cape Town, 1911-1986. Rondebosch: University of Cape Town.

Stone, Henry (1974): *Struktuur en Motief van die Onderwysstelsel: 'n Studie in die Vergelykende Opvoedkunde*. Cape Town: SACUM.

Stone, Henry (1981): Gemeenskaplikheid en Diversiteit: 'n Profiel van die Vergelykende Opvoedkunde. Johannesburg: McGraw-Hill.

Stone, Henry (1982): 'The Common and the Diverse'. *Perspectives in Education*, Vol.6, pp.47-52.

Van Zyl, Pieter (1968): 'The Structure of Pedagogy and its Part Disciplines'. Unpublished Paper, Pedagogic Studies, University of Pretoria.

Vermaak, Dudley (1982): 'The Implications of the Common and Diverse Approach for Education System Planning'. *Perspectives in Education*, Vol.6, pp.61-66.

Vos, A.J. (1982): 'The Nature and Value of Comparative Education'. *Perspectives in Education*, Vol.6, pp.53-55.

Vos, A.J. & Brits, V.M. (1987): *Comparative and International Education for Student Teachers*. Second edition, Durban: Butterworths.

Vos, A.J. & Brits, V.M. (1990): *Comparative Education and National Education Systems*. Durban: Butterworths.

Wessels, Susara J. (1974): *Doelstellingsproblematiek van die Vergelykende Pedagogiek*, Pedagogiekstudies/Pedagogic Studies, No.78. Pretoria: Work Community for the Advancement of Pedagogy as a Science.

Wolhuter, Charl (ed.) (2006): *Aurora Australis: Comparative Education and History of Education at Universities in Southern Africa*. Potchefstroom: North-West University.

Weeks, Sheldon; Herman, Harold; Maarman, Rouaan & Wolhuter, Charl (2006): 'SACHES and Comparative, International and Development Education in Southern Africa: The Challenges and Future Prospects'. *Southern African Review of Education* with *Education with Production*, Vol.12, No.2, pp.5-20.

27

The Greek Comparative Education Society (GCES)

Dimitrios MATTHEOU

Since the early national period in the late 1820s, Greece has been open to the outside world. During the first part of the 19th century, many intellectuals, statesmen and merchants who had lived and worked abroad returned to the new nation state. Many merchants gave economic support to the floundering state, and brought their cosmopolitanism to the traditional and rather backward Greek society. Intellectuals, who had been influenced by the European Enlightenment and had made a name for themselves abroad, brought ideas and inspiration that contributed to the development of the national institutional infrastructure. Ordinary people too, especially displaced farmers who had travelled abroad to seek their fortunes in the communities of the Greek Diaspora, provided new experiences and diverse cultural outlooks (Tsoukalas 1975; Svoronos 1978).

The frailty of the new nation state made it dependent on the great European powers which included England, France and Russia. The first Greek political parties were actually named after these powers, as the English, French and Russian parties (Hering 2004). The upper social classes imitated the ways of life of these societies; many university professors studied in Germany and France; and the Munich School of Art was the cradle of modern Greek painting (Markezinis 1966; Kokkinos 1971). The nascent Greek education system was built by the Bavarian regency in the 1830s in the image of the German prototype (Bouzakis 1991; Mattheou 1997, 2001).

During the 20th century, Greek society maintained its focus on developments in Europe, which included the domain of education. No major education report, reform or public debate omitted references to education trends and policies in Europe. This was especially evident in the 1958 Report on Education, the 1965 Education Reform Act, the 1976 Education Act, and the reforms in the 1980s and the 1990s (Kazamias 1995).

The reverse pattern was also evident, with various international organisations taking an interest in Greek education. For example, in the late 1960s the World Bank was an advocate of the Centres of Advanced Technical and Vocational Education (KATEE), and the Organisation for Economic Co-operation and Development (OECD) was responsible for the Mediterranean Regional Project which included

Greece (OECD 1965). The OECD also sponsored a major post-secondary education study (Kazamias & Psacharopoulos 1985) and the National Reviews in Education in 1979 and 1995 (OECD 1980, 1982, 1995).

When Greece joined the European Union (EU) in 1981, this interest took a qualitative turn. Although education in the EU is *de jure* the prerogative of member states according to the so-called 'subsidiarity principle', decision-making in Brussels has influenced public and government interest in education abroad. In the Greek case, the European Commission has become the focal point, and its educational guidelines and programmes have attracted more attention than education in such countries as France, Germany and England which had tradi-tionally influenced reform debates. The process of European integration has also created an interest in smaller European countries such as Finland, Ireland and Sweden. Finland has attracted particular attention in Greece because its successful economic performance and its high ranking in the OECD international PISA study have been attributed to the provision of high quality education.

Despite these changes, public interest in foreign systems of education has retained the primarily political character it has always had. Evidence from abroad continued to be used as the staple of the comparative argument, with least attention being paid to its contextual dimensions or to the reliability and the validity of the method used in the collection of relevant information. These factors set both the context and a role for the Greek Comparative Education Society (GCES).

Development of the GCES: Context and Protagonists

The GCES was established in 1991. European Union initiatives such as the ERASMUS and the COMENIUS programmes were already in progress, while preparation for the first Operational Program for Initial Education and Training (OPIET) – a national plan for education subsidised by the EU – was in its final stage of preparation. These initiatives underlined the value of systematic comparative study of education, and made educationists more aware of the need for a professional body in the field. On the internal front, extensive education reforms initiated during the 1980s were maturing, and these were also calling for a comparative reassessment of their progress in view of the emerging knowledge society and the world of globalisation.

In this context, one specific reform was particularly influential. In 1985, two new departments were established in each of the nine Greek universities: a Department of Preschool Education and a Department of Elementary Education. In these Departments, for the first time Comparative Education became part of the academic course offerings. A number of professors of Comparative Education were appointed, and by the mid-1990s at least 10 were in place. Soon afterwards, the first Master of Arts (MA) programme in Comparative Education in the Department of Elementary Education of the University of Athens enrolled its first students. Around the same time, at the initiative of Dimitrios Mattheou, the Centre of Comparative Education, International Education Policy and Communication was established in the University of Athens. Thus, the academic infrastructure, both human and organisational, allowed and indeed called for the creation of a society of comparativists.

The initiative for the establishment of a professional society was taken by two scholars, Andreas Kazamias of the University of Wisconsin-Madison, USA and the University of Athens, and Maria Eliou, first of the University of Ioannina and later of the University of Athens. With the help of the newly-appointed Dimitrios Mattheou at the University of Athens, Kazamias and Eliou established the GCES. Its governing body comprised Kazamias as President, Eliou as Vice-President, Mattheou as Secretary General, Christos Saitis as Treasurer and Alexis Dimaras as member. About 80 per cent of its founding members were professors in five Greek universities that specialised in comparative education and in history, sociology, political science and economics. Other prominent researchers were also included.

The composition of the founding body of the GCES was symbolic in at least three respects. First, it demonstrated the founders' intentions to develop a professional organisation of high academic standards that, in the words of Article 2 of the Constitution, would contribute to "the advancement of Comparative Education and comparative research in Greece; the study and the scientific analysis of the problems of Greek education; the articulation of alternative education policy proposals by making use of relevant international experience; and the development of cooperation with relevant foreign scientific institutions". Second, it recognised the interdisciplinary character of comparative education; and third, it made clear that all regions in the country and all qualified sectors of public life should be represented in the society.

Ideological, Epistemological and Methodological Considerations

Concern for high professional standards found formal expression in Article 5 of the Constitution, which stated that individuals applying for membership should either hold an MA degree or have substantial published work in the field of Comparative Education. In addition, applicants were required to provide recommendations from two members of the society (Article 6). Allied to the provision that quality rather than quantity should determine the society's public recognition and influence, it was asserted that high academic standards in comparative research were the only safeguard against the prevailing arbitrariness in the use of comparative evidence in public discourse. Thus it was hoped that the GCES would become the guardian and guarantor of genuine comparative educational work in the country.

Another issue that was raised at the time and has long been discussed internationally was the interdisciplinary character of comparative education and its epistemological and methodological orientations. A matter raised from the very beginning was the relationship between comparative education and pedagogy. The question was whether the new *episteme* and hence the society, should be called Syngritike Pedagogike (comparative pedagogy), as it was known in Greek universities, or Syngritike Ekpedeuse (comparative education), which was the prevalent term internationally.

The difference in nomenclature bore important conceptual and epistemo-logical connotations. Some people felt that pedagogy was a broader term than education. They maintained that it signified the aims, principles, content, organisation and methods to guide children to intellectual, moral and aesthetic maturity through not only formal schooling but also the family and the wider society. Reflecting central European traditions, especially those of German pedagogues, the cultivation of the mind and the soul was seen as an autonomous activity. It was also considered to be less dependent on, for example, the social context, in the sense that the aims of education themselves were perennial, fixed and shared by society as a whole. To their way of thinking, 'education' signified the institutional realisation of pedagogical aims, and was in this sense coextensive with schooling and instruction. It was also believed that it gave undue emphasis to the parochial and the timely rather than to the general and the timeless. On the other hand, those who preferred the term 'comparative education' considered this appellation to be broader than 'comparative pedagogy'. For example, Eliou (1984, p.13) argued: "When the latter (i.e. pedagogy) is used it should always be made clear whether it refers to 'didactics' or to the comparative study and analysis of the educational reality as it is constructed in different social, economic, political, historical and cultural contexts". This distinction was closer to the traditions of comparative education in the Anglo-Saxon world.

It was finally agreed that the term comparative education should be used in the title of the society. The field itself, in teaching and research, moved away from the traditions of Greek educationists with their emphasis on the pedagogical principles and theories of the great pedagogues of the past (e.g. Rousseau, Pestalozzi, Froebel) and their modern counterparts (e.g. the American John Dewey and the Greeks A. Delmouzos and E. Papanoutsos), with their prime concern for instruction and learning and with their preoccupation with psychology and moral philosophy. Comparative research, it was argued, should instead look more closely into the relations between education and its broader context, including the social, political, economic and cultural factors that have influenced the Greek and other systems of education. It should focus on policy making and decision taking, on the politics of reform, on the political economy of education reform episodes, and on the interplay between tradition and change. A deeper understanding and explanation of the various educational phenomena should be at the centre of this type of comparative investigation. To recapitulate, comparative education gradually acquired a more theoretical and explanatory character, adopting at the same time a critical stance on policy making, although many members of GCES have on several occasions participated in policy making committees and have held high posts in state education agencies.

Despite the general agreement on the overall orientation of the field in Greece, it cannot be said that a particular school of thought prevailed. Differences were evident in methodology, epistemology and the relations between com-parative education, history and the social sciences. In various forums and conferences organised by the GCES between 1993 and 1998, such issues were extensively debated. For example, Kazamias has long argued for comparative historical approaches and for the need to combine the historical approach in comparative education with the social scientific approach (see e.g. Kazamias 2001). He has also argued for a type of comparative education that disentangles education from political exigencies and expediencies, and for an emphasis on the humanistic foundations of the field itself. Among other things, this approach entailed the freeing of comparative education from the epistemological shackles of 'scientism' in the spirit of the liberal arts and the humanities. On the opposite side George Psacharopoulos, an economist, advocated a social scientific and applied form of comparative education. He advocated the type of comparative work that tried to find practical solutions to contemporary education problems (Psacharopoulos 1990). Defending a middle ground, Mattheou (1997) considered understanding not only as an end in itself but also as a precondition for successful policy making. By the same token, he has asserted, history keeps in store precious evidence for understanding and explaining not only the past but also contemporary education phenomena and developments. It can also help to explain the possible short-term outcomes of policy decisions, as patterns are influenced by the past through long-lasting traditions and mores. This understanding is, according to him, very valuable for the success of reform. The GCES has hosted and encouraged fruitful debates on such important matters.

Further Developments

In 2002, a new forum for debate was added. The GCES, together with the newly-established Centre of Comparative Education, International Education Policy and Communication at the University of Athens, launched a biannual journal, the *Comparative and International Education Review*. This journal was designed to publish articles and book reviews in Greek and in English. It also aimed to provide information with critical comments on major education developments in selected countries, and inform readers about the activities of the Greek and other comparative education societies. The journal immediately attracted favourable comments from the Greek academic community for its high standards.

The GCES also has inter-society linkages. It joined the World Council of Comparative Education Societies (WCCES) in 1994, and many of its members are active in the Comparative Education Society of Europe (CESE), of which Mattheou became Vice-President while also being President of the GCES. In 1996 the GCES hosted the 17th CESE Conference in Athens. The theme of the Conference was 'Education and the Structuring of the European Space: Centre-Periphery, North-South, Identity-Otherness'. Over 300 people from 33 countries took part, and a book of selected presentations was subsequently published (Kazamias & Spillane 1998).

During the period covered by this chapter, the GCES made significant contributions and underwent important developments. Its leaders worked hard on its mission, drawing lessons and insights from the external study of education for the development of education in Greece. They also focussed on conceptual domains that have had wide relevance, and have contributed to the international literature.

Acknowledgement

The author is indebted to Andreas M. Kazamias for his helpful comments on earlier versions of this chapter.

References

Bouzakis, Sifis (1991): *Modern Greek Education*. Athens: Gutenberg. (in Greek)

Eliou, Maria (1984): 'The Comparative Approach in Education Sciences', in Desesse, Maurice & Mialaret, Gaston (eds.), *Comparative Education*. Athens: Diptyho, pp.11-20.

Hering, Gunnar (2004): *Political Parties in Greece, 1821-1936*. Athens: MIET (Cultural Foundation of the National Bank of Greece). (in Greek).

Kazamias, Andreas M. (1995): 'The Curse of Sisyphus: The Tantalizing Course of Greek Education Reform', in Kazamias, Andreas M. & Kassotakis, Michael (eds.), *Greek Education: Prospects for Reconstruction and Modernization*. Athens: Seirios, pp.40-72. (in Greek)

Kazamias, Andreas M. (2001): 'Re-inventing the Historical in Comparative Education: Reflections on a *Protean Episteme* by a Contemporary Player'. *Comparative Education*, Vol.37, No.1, pp.439-449.

Kazamias, Andreas M. & Psacharopoulos, George (1985): *Education and Development in Greece: Social and Economic Study of Tertiary Education*, Athens: National Centre of Social Studies.

Kazamias, Andreas M. & Spillane, Martin G. (eds.) (1998): *Education and the Structuring of the European Space: North-South, Centre-Periphery, Identity-Otherness*. Athens: Seirios.

Kokkinos, Dimitrios (1971): *History of Modern Greece*. Athens: Melissa. (in Greek)

Markezinis, Speros (1966): *Political History of Modern Greece*. Athens: Papyros. (in Greek)

Mattheou, Dimitrios (1997): *Comparative Study of Education*. Athens: Centre for Comparative Education, International Education Policy and Communication. (in Greek)

Mattheou, Dimitrios (2001): *The University in the Era of Late Modernity: A Comparative Study of its Ideological and Institutional Transformation*. Athens: Centre for Comparative Education, International Education Policy and Communication. (in Greek)

OECD (1965): *The Mediterranean Regional Project: Greece*, Paris: Organisation for Economic Co-operation & Development.

OECD (1980): *Educational Policy and Planning: Greece*, Paris: Organisation for Economic Co-operation & Development.

OECD (1982): *Reviews of National Policies for Education: Greece*, Paris: Organisation for Economic Co-operation & Development.

OECD (1995): *Reviews of National Policies for Education: Greece*, Paris: Organisation for Economic Co-operation & Development.

Psacharopoulos, George (1990): 'Comparative Education: From Theory to Practice, or Are You A:\neo.* or B:*.ist?'. *Comparative Education Review*, Vol.34, No.3, pp.369-380.

Svoronos, Nikos (1978): *Review of Modern Greek History*. Athens: Themelio. (in Greek)

Tsoukalas, Constantinos (1975): *Dependence and Reproduction: The Social Role of Educational Mechanisms in Greece (1830-1922)*. Athens: Themelio. (in Greek)

28

The Russian Council of Comparative Education (RCCE)

Nina BOREVSKAYA

The foundation for systematic comparative research on education in Russia was laid by Konstantin Ushinsky, an outstanding scholar who published a series of analytical pedagogical surveys after his field studies abroad in the 1850s. Ushinsky declared that as long as education is closely linked with the indigenous system of values, the adoption of any other country's educational system as a whole is impossible. He also argued that the ideal educational system, even if it could be compiled from the best of each country's experience, would be less adequate than any real national school (Ushinsky 1948, p.147). In contrast to that approach, much later another prominent Russian pedagogue, Pavel Kapnist (1900, pp.4-5), stressed "the connection and some kind of continuity between all cultures" in the educational domain. Nevertheless, he rejected "blind imitation", and presented the comparative method as a tool to distinguish national characteristics and the "common achievements of the civilised world".

After the powerful social reformist movement was launched in the 1860s, interest grew in educational reforms abroad. For instance, in 1894 alone, among the publications on educational issues were 362 works on foreign schools (Wulfson 2003, p.20). One magazine, *Russian School*, introduced a special section entitled 'New Pedagogical Trends in the West'. The first monographs of analytical comparative character appeared at the beginning of the 20th century. The works of Mizhuev (e.g. 1912) focused on the economic effectiveness of European and American schools; and numerous monographs by Yanrul (e.g. 1917) highlighted the differences between the Russian and American education systems.

The chapter begins with further detail on comparative education during the Soviet period. It then turns to the field in the new (post-1991) Russia, before focusing on the specifics of the Russian Council of Comparative Education (RCCE). The chapter discusses some of the achievements and constraints of the RCCE, and concludes by noting efforts to form a body with wider participation and outreach.

Although the title of this chapter refers to the Russian Council of Comparative Education, part of its content focuses on its Soviet predecessor.

Within the Union of Soviet Socialist Republics (USSR), this body was called the Scientific Council on Comparative Pedagogics (SCCP). However, it was admitted to the World Council of Comparative Education Societies (WCCES) in 1989 under the name of Soviet Council of Comparative Education (SCCE). That body ceased to exist after the collapse of the Soviet Union, and its successor body was admitted to the WCCES in 1996 as the Russian Council of Comparative Pedagogics (RCCP). Subsequent usage within the WCCES converged on RCCE in echo of the predecessor SCCE. The title of the chapter uses this name even though it is not in standard usage within Russia itself.

Comparative Education in the USSR

Comparative education in the USSR during the 1920s was stimulated by the search for a new revolutionary educational system which could absorb the best achievements of the Western experience. Between 1924 and 1930, around 800 works on the theory and practice of education in European countries and in Japan, China, Turkey and Iran were published in the USSR (Wulfson 2003, p.28). American schooling, with its great innovative power, aroused particular interest; and John Dewey lectured in Russia and encouraged projects on progressive education. While analysing the foreign experiences, Soviet scholars often compared the situations in different countries with patterns in Russia, though they did so without using such terms as comparative studies and without any special comparative methods.

The situation changed after the 1930s following the rise of the totalitarian regime. Leninism, carefully polished by Josef Stalin, became the only epistemological base for all sciences. The ideology had to be displayed in all settings, and objective research and comparison became impossible. The scholarly pursuits of Soviet humanities were isolated from the outside world. In the 1940s and early 1950s, against a background of ideological campaigns against 'cosmopolitism', any works on foreign (especially American) school or pedagogy could be published only if the title included the cliché 'in the service of imperialistic reaction'.

Stalin's death and the following political thaw of the 1960s brought changes in the role of different sciences, including pedagogy. In 1957 a small department of 'modern school and education abroad' was organised at the Institute of Pedagogical Theory and History, which was affiliated with the Academy of Pedagogical Sciences. In the 1960s this department (later called a laboratory) changed its orientation from the mere provision of information to more analytical research, and became the leading centre in that field of studies. It focused on projects including 'The systems of education in foreign countries', and 'Theory and practice of labour education abroad'. The works of outstanding foreign comparativists such as Brian Holmes in the United Kingdom were included in the scholarly discourse. In 1955 the laboratory launched a bulletin entitled *Pedagogy and People's Education in Foreign Countries*, which in 1967 was renamed *Pedagogy and the School Abroad: Critical and Bibliographical Survey*. Thirty issues of this bulletin edited by Mariya Shabaeva and Georgii Mikaberidze were published between 1955 and 1974, and contained reviews and summaries of important foreign books. In spite of ideological restrictions, works were published on educational trends in Western countries (e.g. Nikandrov 1978), and Eastern countries (e.g. Kuhtina 1971; Tanguiane 1975).

In Russia, the term 'comparative pedagogy' has been used more commonly than 'comparative education', and it came into vogue later than in many European countries. Only in 1966 at the Moscow State Pedagogical Institute was the first laboratory (small department) of comparative pedagogics organised. The first university textbook on this topic was published in 1978 (Sokolova et al. 1978). Although critical invective prevailed over the scholarly analysis in that publication, the authors worked hard to overcome the cautious approach of most bureaucrats to the term 'comparative pedagogics'. They were supported by Zoya Malkova, who argued that the unfavourable (or even falsified) Western research on the socialist education system could not be stopped by rejecting the term. She suggested that only by improving the methodology of comparative studies and by raising its quality could Soviet scholars prove their advantages.

The collaboration of the Soviet pedagogues with foreign colleagues was enhanced during that period, but among the latter the scholars from the socialist countries predominated. In the early 1970s they organised a 'Commission of experts on the critique of bourgeois pedagogy' in which Boris Wulfson and Zoya Malkova were the Soviet representatives. The Commission existed for 20 years and had annual meetings in various socialist countries. Under its auspices, various books were published (e.g. Hofmann et al. 1983). However, in spite of the formal resurgence of the study of foreign educational systems, these studies were even further from comparative works 50 to 60 years previously because of their ideological commitments and the inaccessibility of most foreign sources. Although many books on foreign education systems were published in the 1970s and 1980s, they interpreted the data only on the basis of Marxist class ideology. This pre-supposed a critical approach to capitalism and its pedagogical concepts. The lack of egalitarian tendencies in education abroad and its ideologically unacceptable moral norms were not the only factors behind the situation. Another factor was the self-satisfaction and complacency of the Soviet leaders, lulled by the real achieve-ments of the Soviet education system and its high evaluation not only inside the country but also abroad.

In the second half of the 1980s, the political atmosphere in the USSR was characterised by new phenomena. The new leaders developed the era of perestroika (reconstruction), which advocated an ideological renaissance. They declared the goal of building 'socialism with a human face', which entailed the acceptance of universal moral values and created a new climate in the humanities and social sciences.

In 1986, a Russian translation of the UNESCO journal *Prospects* was launched in the USSR. It introduced the works of many outstanding foreign comparativists and gave an impetus to national research. Unfortunately, publication ceased in 1993 because the new Russia faced serious financial stringencies. Nevertheless, a new wave of interest in education in Asia and Africa also became evident (e.g. Borisenkov 1987; Salimova 1993).

The 1989 article by Nikolai D. Nikandrov entitled 'Comparative Pedagogy: Lessons and Hopes' sounded like a bell to renew the approach to the comparative research. The framework for comparative studies enlarged and became more objective. Scholars analysed the global tendencies in school reforms and the processes of modernisation of the school curriculum and teaching methods abroad. They came closer to scholarly investigation of such matters as the correlation between global trends and national traditions in education, and analysis of the roles of international organisations such as the World Bank and UNESCO in designing regional and global policies.

The new political climate enriched the links between Soviet comparativists and the WCCES, and opened the way for Russian scholars to take part in its congresses. Russian delegates did participate in the 1st World Congress in 1970 (Ottawa, Canada), but were not able to form sustained and substantial delegations on a regular basis. Malkova participated in the 6th World Congress in Rio de Janeiro, Brazil in 1987, where the Soviet delegate supported the invective toward educational privatisation and the technocratic approach to the quality of education advocated by the World Bank representatives. Soon after that, by the decision of the Presidium of the Academy of Pedagogical Sciences of the USSR, in April 1988 the Scientific Council on Comparative Pedagogics (SCCP) was organised. Malkova, who was by that time the Director of the Scientific Research Institute of Pedagogics, became its Chairperson, and Boris Wulfson and Valerii Pivovarov became Vice-Chairpersons. The Council was affiliated to the Academy of Pedagogical Sciences, which partly explains its name.

The SCCP had 26 members (eight of them in the Bureau) with some representatives from the pedagogical universities. In 1988 and 1990, Soviet scholars participated in conferences of the Comparative Education Society in Europe (CESE). In 1989, the SCCP, with support from the Academy of Pedagogical Sciences, decided to apply for WCCES membership. The application was approved during the 7th World Congress in Montreal, Canada in 1989, and Malkova made a presentation during a plenary session about the reconstruction of the Soviet educational system according to global humanistic trends.

Those three years of the SCCP in the Soviet period produced a good harvest. The Council discussed the problems of integration processes in European education, the quality of Candidate of Sciences theses on comparative education, and the need for publication in the field. A book entitled *Methodological Problems of Comparative Pedagogy* was published (Malkova & Wulfson 1991a), and the Council led comparative education projects in universities and academic institutions as well as in different Soviet republics. It also made an impressive contribution to development of comparative education methodology, through organisation of an international conference and enhanced the collaboration with international comparative education centres. In particular, prominent comparativists from the UK, Australia, USA and Japan participated in the book *Education in the World at the Turn of the Twenty-first Century* (Malkova & Wulfson 1991b).

With the wave of interest in comparative research and the possibility of implementing findings from lessons of comparative study in the practice of the Soviet school reforms, the SCCP together with the Presidium of the Academy of Pedagogical Sciences suggested that a journal of comparative education should be launched. However, this proposal was not realised because of the economic stringencies and the forthcoming political reforms. Yet as a result of SCCP activity, annual surveys entitled 'Education in the Modern World' were disseminated among the educational administration and university staff.

The establishment of the Council opened the way for the organisation of a Society of Comparative Pedagogics. Malkova was very enthusiastic about the project, and prepared its charter. Unlike the Council, the Society was intended to move beyond the auspices of the Academy. The vision was of an independent and more open body, which would permit both individual and collective members. The admission procedure would be by written application, and members would have to pay membership fees. The idea did not presuppose the elimination of the SCCP but rather the mutual cooperation of two organisations. However, this project was designed on the eve of the collapse of the USSR in 1991. It never got off the ground, and even the SCCP fell apart.

Comparative Education in New Russia

The collapse of the USSR brought huge change in all spheres of life, including comparative education. For some years the institutional infrastructure for the field remained in abeyance; but the new patterns also increased interest in the field and stimulated new perspectives. The transformation of the former Soviet republics into independent states presented new dimensions for investigation. Also, the demise of the one-party system and the Communist Party's dictatorship, and the development of the market economy and democratic trends, stimulated dialogue between Russia and the West. Article 57 of the 1992 Law on Education granted educational institutions the right to establish direct links with foreign partners. Under such circumstances, the interest in comparative and international studies in education increased. New university textbooks on comparative education were compiled, including ones written by Malkova and Wulfson (1996), and Dzhurinsky (1998, 2005).

The political changes also overthrew Marxism-Leninism as the main philosophical foundation for all social sciences and humanities, and encouraged pluralism in political and ideological life. However, Marxism and neo-Marxism still had their followers. In general, the state of comparative education in Russia remained ambiguous. Very few of the numerous publications on education in other countries could be attributed to the comparative field if strictly evaluated according to their theoretical levels and the potency of explicit or implicit comparisons. Among the best are those by Dzhurinsky (1993), Tseikovich & Tarasiuk (1994), Gershunsky (2003), Borisenkov et al. (2004), and Wulfson (1999, 2006).

Among the few binary studies that were published, one major theme to which the author of this chapter devoted attention was comparison of Russia with China (Borevskaya 2001; Bray & Borevskaya 2001; Borevskaya et al. 2007).

These studies reflected China's strategic role and recent technological breakthrough, and shed light on characteristics of educational modernisation in transitional societies. Other foci included Japan and other parts of East Asia (e.g. Salimova 1993; Boyarchuk 1996; Lim 2000; Mikaberidze 1998). However, in general Russia remained more Western-oriented in its comparative works. The phenomenon of East Asian education never aroused such intensive attention among scholars or practical educators as in the USA. Countries comprising the Commonwealth of Independent States (CIS) became new foci of comparative studies.

The epistemological base of comparative education in Russia, as in the humanities, looked rather eclectic. The discourse on the theory of modelling the personality and students' socialisation contained elements of neo-existentialism, neo-Freudianism and pedagogical anthropology. The few Russian specialists in comparative education theory mostly introduced the pursuits and achievements of the Western scholars to Russian audiences. Comparative education in Russia, together with the broader family of social sciences, remained in the process of designing its own theoretical epistemological base.

Even at the beginning of the 21st century, courses in comparative education were delivered by only a few pedagogical faculties. In Moscow only three of the six pedagogical universities delivered such courses, together with St. Petersburg State Pedagogical University, the Far Eastern State University, Tomsk State Pedagogical University, Rostov State Pedagogical University and Pyatigorsk State Linguistics University. Comparative education was not taught in most Russian pedagogical institutes, in part because of a shortage of appropriate personnel. The universities which did teach comparative education relied on the graduates of Moscow pedagogical institutes. One example was Tomsk, where Elena Fedotova was very active in a laboratory of comparative analysis of education. Another example was Liudmila Suprunova, who organised a similar laboratory in Pyatigorsk State Linguistics University.

The Russian Council

The Scientific Council on Problems of Comparative Pedagogics in the new Russia was created in March 1995 in place of the Soviet one. The full name was practically never used, and within Russia, the name Scientific Council on Comparative Pedagogics (SCCP) was more common. The Council was also affiliated with the Academy, which changed its name to the Russian Academy of Education (RAE). The renaissance of the Council symbolised the further opening of Russian society, and stimulated contacts with international organisations. Nikolai D. Nikandrov, who was at that time Vice-President of the RAE, headed the Council with Zoya Malkova and Boris Wulfson as Co-chairpersons. Thus the membership of the new Council had significant continuity with the old one.

According to its charter, the Council was an open scientific-social organisation which welcomed membership of scholars, university teachers, school teachers, leaders of educational departments, journalists and others who were interested in the educational development of the modern world, its regions and countries. The Council was expected to have branches in different regions of Russia, and to establish links with corresponding organisations. As noted, the Council became a member of the WCCES in 1996, registered as the Russian Council of Comparative Education (RCCE).

At the beginning, the Council had only 28 members, and this figure did not greatly change during the following decade. More than a half of the members worked at the Institute of Pedagogical Theory or were members of the RAE, and only four were from outside Moscow. This situation reflected the lack of comparative education centres in Russian universities.

The Council's activity focused on scientific discussions of the core themes and problems of comparative education, including methodology, the prospects of the field, internationalisation of higher education, different approaches to educational phenomena, the national idea and values education in Russia and elsewhere. It stimulated research on many theoretical problems such as multicultural education, learning the experience of Western European educational integration, and modernisation of comparative education courses. The Council recommended enlargement of the list of regions and countries covered by comparative researchers in Russia, a list of research topics, and a database in the field. The first small dictionary of comparative education terms was published by the Council members (Makaev & Suprunova 1998). However, some of the goals could not be achieved immediately.

Unlike other societies, the Council had no fees or commercial activities, and therefore no financial foundation. This fact limited the extent to which its members could participate in international conferences. Nikolai D. Nikandrov took part in such activity in his capacity as a President of the RAE; and, with the financial support of the WCCES, Liudmila Suprunova participated in the 11th World Congress in South Korea in 2001. Nina Borevskaya was similarly able to join the 12th congress in Cuba in 2004.

From the beginning the Council was organised from above, and hence was concentrated in Moscow. It had no local branches, and, despite intentions, did not bring together specialists from around the country. The Council waned in activity to the extent that in 2003 its work was suspended.

However, as a result of the enthusiasm of the author of this chapter, the Council was revitalised in 2005. Thus, Vladimir A. Miasnikov, Director of the Institute of Educational Theory and History, an affiliate institute of the RAE of which he is a Corresponding Member, became the Council's official Chairperson, with Nina Borevskaya and Boris Wulfson as Vice-Chairpersons. The new leaders identified goals which could give impetus to the modernisation of Russian education and the search for its national identity in the process of globalisation.

Among the main tasks of the revitalised Council were organisation of branches and the establishment of mutual links in order to coordinate research and give an impetus to explicitly comparative studies. This required regular exchange of information which, the Council observed, could be done by e-mail, through a website, and through a special page in the journal *Pedagogika*. A further suggestion was the organisation of special sections of foreign language books from private collections in pedagogical libraries. Scientific consultations for the Council members from outside Moscow could be a useful support, especially for young scholars. The Council decided to make a renewed thrust to prepare a database on comparative research in Russia. As an important step, the Council published its first bulletin in April 2006. It contained information on activities in the previous year, reports of recent international conferences, announcements about forthcoming conferences, and information on new publications in Russia and abroad.

Conclusions

Comparative education as a field of study in Russia has a long history, but has never been strong. Among the reasons have been political factors and organisational ones linked to the structure of academic leadership. However, the forces of internationalisation and the new forms of cooperation in post-Soviet educational space have contributed to significant changes. Russian participation in the Bologna declaration on higher education in Europe, and its intention to become a member of the World Trade Organisation (WTO) were among factors that made comparative research more important than before and opened wider perspectives for its future.

This chapter has sketched the development of organisational structures in the field, and the transition from the Soviet body to the Russian one. In one sense, this transition has led to a contraction of educational space, and the exclusion of scholars (e.g. in Ukraine and Kazakhstan) who could otherwise have been incorporated in the remit. In another sense, however, the transition to independence of the former Soviet republics has enhanced the scope for instructive comparative studies. The RCCE still faces challenges of moving from a narrow institutional base in Moscow to a more inclusive structure; but it has much potential, especially since the post-Soviet is characterised by extensive international contacts far beyond the old Soviet bloc.

References

Borevskaya, Nina (2001): 'Searching for Individuality: Educational Pursuits in China and Russia', in Peterson, Glen; Hayhoe, Ruth & Lu, Yongling (eds.), *Education, Culture and Identity in Twentieth-Century China*. Hong Kong: Hong Kong University Press, pp.31-53.

Borevskaya, Nina; Borisenkov, Vladimir P. & Zhu, Xiaoman (eds.) (2007): *Educational Reforms in Russia and China at the Edge of the XX-XXIst Century: Comparative Aspects*. Moscow: Nauka. [in Russian with English Appendix]

Borisenkov, Vladimir P. (1987): *People's Education and Pedagogical Thought in Free African Countries*. Moscow: Pedagogica. [in Russian]

Borisenkov, Vladimir P.; Gulalenko, Olga V. & Daniluk, Alexandr Ya. (2004): *Multicultural Education in the Space of Russia: History, Theory, and the Basis for its Design*. Moscow: Russian National Pedagogical University. [in Russian]

Boyarchuk, Julia V. (1996): *General School in Modern Japan*. Moscow: Puschino. [in Russian]

Bray, Mark & Borevskaya, Nina (2001): 'Financing Education in Transitional Societies: Lessons from Russia and China'. *Comparative Education*, Vol.37, No.3, pp.345-366.

Dzhurinsky, Aleksandr N. (1993): *The School Abroad: A Contemporary State and the Tendencies of Development*. Moscow: Prosveschenie. [in Russian]

Dzhurinsky, Aleksandr N. (1998): *Comparative Education*. Moscow: Academia. [in Russian]

Dzhurinsky, Aleksandr N. (2005): *Scientific and Methodological Problems of Educational History and of Comparative Pedagogy*. Moscow: Prometei. [in Russian]

Gershunsky, Boris S. (2003): *Russia-USA: Integration in the Educational Domain*. Moscow: Internet Education & Training Program. [in Russian]

Hofmann, Hans-Georg; Malkova, Zoya & Wulfson, Boris (eds.) (1983): *Policy of Capitalist States in the Educational Domain*. Moscow: Pedagogika. [in Russian]

Kapnist, Pavel (1900): *A Historical Survey of the Development of Middle Schools in Germany.// Classical Studies as the Necessary Foundation of Teaching in Gymnasium*. Vol. 2. Moscow. [in Russian]

Kuhtina, Tatiana (ed.) (1971): *Education and Training the National Cadres in Oriental Countries*. Moscow: Nauka. [in Russian]

Lim, Sofia Ch. (2000): *The History of Education in Japan: The End of the 19th and Beginning of the 20th Century*. Moscow: Institute of Oriental Studies, Russian Academy of Sciences. [in Russian]

Makaev, Viktor V. & Suprunova, Liudmila L. (1998): *Vocabulary of Terms on Comparative Education and the History of Educational Thought*. Pyatigorsk: Pyatigorsk State Linguistics University. [in Russian]

Malkova, Zoya & Wulfson, Boris (eds.) (1991a): *Methodological Problems of Comparative Pedagogy*. Moscow: Academy of Pedagogical Sciences. [in Russian]

Malkova, Zoya & Wulfson, Boris (eds.) (1991b): *Education in the World at the Turn of the Twenty-first Century*. Moscow: Institute of Theory and History of Pedagogy. [in Russian]

Malkova, Zoya & Wulfson, Boris (1996): *Comparative Pedagogy*. Moscow: Voronezh [in Russian]

Mikaberidze, Georgii V. (1998): 'South Korea: Educational Strategy for the 19th Century'. *Pedagogy*, No.3, pp.97-102. [in Russian]

Mizhuev, Pavel G. (1912): *Modern School in Europe and America*. Moscow: Polza. [in Russian]

Nikandrov, Nikolai D. (1978): *Modern Tertiary School in Capitalist Countries*. Moscow: Vizshaya Shkola. [in Russian]

Nikandrov, Nikolai D. (1989): 'Comparative Pedagogy: Lessons and Hopes'. *Soviet Pedagogy*, No.10, pp.37-49. [in Russian]

Salimova, Kadriya (1993): *Ascent to the Success: Moral Education in Japan – History and Modernity*. Tokyo: Shindokusho-sha. [in Russian]

Sokolova, Maria A.; Kuzmina, Elena N. & Rodionov, Mikhail L. (1978): *Comparative Pedagogy*. Moscow: Prosvescenie. [in Russian]

Tanguiane, Simeon A. (1975): *Education and the Social Progress in Developing Countries*. Moscow: Nauka. [in Russian]

Tseikovich, Konstantin & Tarasiuk, Laura (1994): *Comparative Analysis of Educational Development in Russia and the Leading Countries in the World: A Statistical Survey'*. Moscow: Goskomstat. [in Russian]

Ushinsky, Konstantin D. (1948): 'On the National Roots in Social Training', in Ushinsky, Konstantin D., *Collected Works*. Moscow and Leningrad: Pedagogika Vol.2., pp.69-166. [in Russian]

Wulfson, Boris L. (1999): *The Strategy of Educational Development in the West at the*

Turn of the 21ˢᵗ Century. Moscow: University under Russian Academy of Education. [in Russian]

Wulfson, Boris L. (2003): *Comparative Pedagogy: History and Modern Problems*. Moscow: University under Russian Academy of Education. [in Russian]

Wulfson, Boris L. (2006): *Educational Space at the Edge of the Centuries*. Moscow: Psychology-Sociology Institute. [in Russian]

Yanrul, Ekaterina N. (1917): 'Comparative Essay of School Administration System in France, Germany, England and the United States'. *The Ministry of Education Magazine*. St. Petersburg, Nos.11-12, pp.84-118. [in Russian]

29

The Comparative Education Society of Asia (CESA)

Kengo MOCHIDA

The Comparative Education Society of Asia (CESA) was founded in Hong Kong in 1995. Its establishment resulted from initiatives among comparative education-ists in Asia who had been considering the potential value of a regional body. Comparative education societies did exist in China, Japan, Korea, Hong Kong, India and Taiwan, but other parts of the region had no society. The architects of CESA felt that a regional organisation was desirable, along the lines of the Comparative Education Society in Europe (CESE).

Two streams led to the formation of CESA. First, the Japan Comparative Education Society (JCES) established a special committee to work for the formation of the regional body. Yoshio Gondo, former President of the JCES, was appointed Chairperson of the committee, and Kengo Mochida of Kyushu University was appointed Secretary. As a part of committee's activity, in July 1994 the JCES organised a meeting with the Presidents of the Chinese Comparative Education Society (CCES) and the Korean Comparative Education Society (KCES), who gave active support to the idea of an Asian society.

The first major event leading to the establishment was the International Symposium on Development and Education in Asia, held in Fukuoka, Japan, in December 1994. The symposium was organised by members of the special committee and others from the JCES. Participants included Lee Byung-jin and Park Jun-hye from South Korea, Wang Chia-tung from Taiwan, Isahak Haron and Molly Lee from Malaysia, Mark Bray from Hong Kong, Mohammad Fakry Gaffar from Indonesia, Sumon Amornviat from Thailand, Sureshchandra Shukla from India, and Dao Trong-thi from Vietnam. The programme highlighted the vigorous economic and social development of parts of Asia, and the role attributed to education in this development. It added observations about the nature of comparative study of education. The programme included a special session to discuss the feasibility of establishing the Asian society. Zhou Nanzhao, then Vice-President of the CCES, could not attend the symposium because of a visa problem, but sent a message indicating that the CCES would strongly support the establishment of an Asian society.

The symposium was a great success. A founding committee for establishing the Asian society was created, consisting mostly of invited scholars from overseas and three scholars from Japan. In the first meeting of the committee, Gondo was elected Chairperson and Mochida was elected Secretary.

Parallel to these initiatives was another stream of activity. A group named the Comparative Education Forum, consisting of scholars from China, Hong Kong, Korea, Japan and Malaysia had met in Prague in 1992 during the 8th World Congress of Comparative Education Societies. Some of these scholars subsequently met again in San Diego, USA and in Seoul, Korea, to discuss the feasibility of establishing an Asian society. Gondo, as the Chairperson of the special committee of the JCES, contacted this group, and both groups agreed to work jointly to found the Asian society. Thus, the work of the JCES special committee and that of the Forum merged to form a strong force for the establishment of CESA. The founding committee included members from both streams.

The founding committee held its second meeting in Hong Kong in 1995, in conjunction with the inaugural symposium of the Comparative Education Research Centre (CERC) at the University of Hong Kong. The committee agreed on a constitution, and CESA was officially founded on 30 May 1995. The following year CESA applied for membership of the World Council of Comparative Education Societies (WCCES), and was admitted in 1997.

Goals and Characteristics

The goals of CESA proclaimed in its constitution are:

- to promote exchange and cooperation in comparative education research among educationists in Asia;
- to promote exchange and cooperation in teaching of comparative education in Asia;
- to promote mutual understanding and friendship among educationists in Asia; and
- to enhance international dialogue and exchange among scholars interested in Asia.

Thus, CESA aims to promote not only exchange and cooperation in comparative education research and teaching but also mutual understanding and friendship. CESA is open to the wider world, since it welcomes any scholar or student interested in education in Asia. Faced by the linguistic plurality of the region, CESA operates in English as the major international language acceptable to its members.

The constitution prescribed the major activities that CESA should perform. They include holding conferences, issuing lists of members, and publishing newsletters. Within this list, holding conferences has been CESA's main activity. At the start it was hoped that CESA could have its own journal, but due to financial constraints and other factors, this wish could not be realised.

CESA's initial constitution created a Board of Directors of not more than 22 members. The composition was intended to ensure geographically balanced representation, and the number reflected the places of residence of members in the founding committee. CESA adopted the term 'place of residence' instead of 'country', to allow for Hong Kong and Taiwan to be included as separate categories. Two members from each place of residence were elected directors. The Board of Directors was mandated to consider the revisions to the constitution, to consider the places and dates of conferences, to consider relationships with the WCCES, and to consider the admission of new members to CESA. In 2005 the places of residence represented in the Board of Directors were Japan, China, Korea, Hong Kong, Taiwan, Malaysia, Singapore, Thailand, Vietnam, Indonesia and India. Asia is of course not confined to these locations, and it seemed desirable to widen the representation in the Board.

Although CESA is a regional society, the membership is not based on national societies since many countries in Asia have no national comparative education societies. Thus, membership is on an individual basis. The society does not have definite admission criteria. As noted above, any scholar or student who has interests in comparative education research and teaching can join CESA. As of August 2004, CESA had 262 members. Japan had the largest number of members, followed by Korea, Taiwan, Malaysia, Thailand, Hong Kong and Indonesia (Table 29.1). In addition to members from Asia were members from other parts of the world.

Table 29.1: CESA Number of Members by Places of Residence, 2004

Place of Residence	Number	Place of Residence	Number
Japan	138	Israel	2
Korea	21	Philippines	2
Taiwan	20	Singapore	2
Malaysia	13	Bangladesh	2
Thailand	13	Canada	2
Hong Kong	11	Egypt	1
Indonesia	10	France	1
USA	6	Italy	1
Vietnam	5	Macau	1
India	4	Mexico	1
China	3	UK	1
Germany	2	**Total**	**262**

CESA Conferences

Table 29.2 lists the conferences and their themes during CESA's initial decade. The first conference was held in Tokyo in 1996, and was followed by events in Beijing in 1998, Taipei in 2001, Bandung (Indonesia) in 2003, Bangi (Malaysia) in 2005, and Hong Kong, China in 2007. The last of these was a combined event with the annual conference of the Comparative Education Society of Hong Kong (CESHK). During this 2007 conference, Kengo Mochida was elected CESA President. The concern of the CESA leadership with the future of Asian education in the 21st century was reflected in the conference themes. CESA conferences have been good forums for Asian scholars to discuss issues in education. Over 100 scholars and students took part in each conference. The 2003 conference attracted about 300 people thanks to efforts by the organising committee to encourage many Indonesian scholars to participate. This conference was particularly significant because it moved the venue to a location which did not have its own national or sub-national comparative education society. The outreach was maintained in 2005 with the conference in Malaysia.

Table 29.2: CESA Conferences, 1996-2007

	Year	Venue	Theme
1	1996	Waseda University (Tokyo, Japan)	Asian Perspectives in Education for the 21st Century
2	1998	Beijing Normal University (Beijing, China)	Modernization of Education vs. Cultural Traditions: Prospect of Asian Education in the 21st Century
3	2001	National Taiwan Normal University (Taipei, Taiwan)	The Prospects of Asian Education for the New Century
4	2003	Indonesia University of Education (Bandung, Indonesia)	Global Challenges and the Role of Education in Asia
5	2005	Universiti Kebangsaan Malaysia (Bangi, Malaysia)	Education for World Peace: The Asian Context
6	2007	University of Hong Kong (China)	Learning from Each Other in an Asian Century

In the first four conferences, 322 presentations were made. Some characteristics can be discerned from analysis of the titles and abstracts. Among the topics chosen, higher education accounted for 18.9 per cent. Within this category, specific topics varied considerably, but study abroad, finance, massification, students' attitudes, information and communications technology, national/social development, gender, globalisation, and reforms were addressed by more than three presentations. The focus on higher education reflected major changes in this component of the systems of Asian countries.

Teachers were the focus of the next most prominent topic, accounting for 11.4 per cent of the total. Within this topic over half the presentations focused on teacher education and teacher training. A small number of presentations (5.9%) addressed theories and research in comparative education. This indicates that interest in this domain was not strong among scholars in Asia, who seem to have been more interested in educational problems and tasks.

Of the 322 presentations in the four conferences, 182 (56.5%) focused on single countries or locations (Table 29.3). This reflected the tendency of scholars to focus on their own places of residence. Studies addressing more than one country or location accounted for 47 (14.7%). Of these, 34 focused on two, six focused on three, and seven focused on four or more countries or locations. A small number of papers referred to regions, but comparison of regions was not very explicit in these studies.

Table 29.3: Papers in CESA Conferences, by Dimension of Comparisons

Geographic Focus of Comparison	No.	%	Geographic Focus of Comparison	No.	%
Single country/ location	182	*56.5*	*Two countries/locations*	34	*10.6*
Taiwan	30		Japan, China	3	
Malaysia	26		Japan, Korea	3	
Indonesia	23		Japan, Thailand	3	
China	20		Japan, Indonesia	2	
Japan	19		Japan, Myanmar	1	
Korea	13		Japan, Russia	1	
Thailand	10		Japan, Vietnam	1	
India	7		Japan, USA	1	
Hong Kong	6		Japan, England	1	
Britain, England	5		China, Korea	1	
Vietnam	4		China, Hong Kong	1	
France	3		China, Singapore	1	
Philippines	3		Taiwan, China	2	
Bangladesh	2		Taiwan, USA	2	
Russia	2		Taiwan, England	1	
Singapore	2		Korea, Australia	1	
Sri Lanka	2		Hong Kong, Macau	1	
Bhutan	1		Hong Kong, Malaysia	1	
Australia	1		Hong Kong, Singapore	1	
Germany	1		Hong Kong, Taiwan	1	
Saudi Arabia	1		Malaysia, Brunei	1	
USA	1		Malaysia, Thailand	1	
			Papua New Guinea, Thailand	1	
Three countries/ locations	6	*1.9*	Indonesia, Philippines	1	
Japan, Malaysia, USA	1		USA, Australia	1	
China, Germany, USA	1				
China, USA, Japan	1		*Four or more countries /locations*	7	*2.2*
Taiwan, China, Hong Kong	1		Hong Kong, Singapore, China, Taiwan	1	
Taiwan, China, Japan	1		China, Hong Kong, USA, Australia	1	
Vietnam, Laos, Cambodia	1		USA, Canada, Germany, Australia, Hong Kong	1	
			Britain, China, France, Germany, Japan, Russia, Sweden, USA	1	
			Britain, France, Germany, Russia, Sweden, USA, Japan, China	1	

(continued on next page)

Table 29.3 (Continued):

Geographic Focus of Comparison	No.	%	Geographic Focus of Comparison	No.	%
			Japan, Hong Kong, Korea, China, Taiwan, Singapore, Thailand, Philippines, Malaysia	1	
			Cambodia, China, Indonesia, Laos, Mongolia, Myanmar, Philippines, Thailand, Vietnam	1	
Regional	*18*	*5.6*	*Not Specified*	75	23.2
Asia	5				
East Asia	3				
Southeast Asia	3				
South Asia	2				
Asia Pacific	2				
Asia-Europe	1				
Japan, Thailand, North America, Europe	1				
Latin America, Asia, Europe	1		**Total**	**322**	**100.0**

With the dominant focus of presentations on Asian countries, it can be argued that CESA was playing a global role of balancing the centre of gravity in comparative education research. However, detailed analysis of papers revealed some problems. Although several studies had a dimension of intra-national comparisons, many did not have any element of comparison. If scholars concentrate on their own countries without any element of comparison, it would be difficult to differentiate their studies from those of other fields of education. Therefore, it is desirable for Asian comparative educationists to try to base their studies on paradigms of comparative education research in order to improve the quality of their research.

Conclusions

The establishment of CESA was evidence that comparative education research in the region had developed enough to justify such a society. In the past, Asian scholars tended to look toward Europe and North America rather than to each other for dialogue and discussion.

CESA has achieved major accomplishments during its relatively short history, but also faces challenges. One challenge arises from diversity within the region. East Asia, particularly Japan, Korea, China, Taiwan and Hong Kong, has strong traditions of comparative education research and teaching. By contrast, the field is weaker in most other parts of the region. CESA has begun to reach out to Southeast Asia, but has not yet strongly penetrated west and north Asia. That, indeed, should be a mission for CESA in the coming years and decades. CESA was established with founding members representing 11 different places of residence. Reflecting this representation, the constitution prescribes the number of directors as "not more than twenty-two ensuring geographically balanced representation". During the first decade, only members from founding countries were elected directors. It is desirable to include directors from more locations to widen and promote activities. Another indication of the geographic imbalance is seen in geographic composition of the members. Table 29.1 shows that in 2004 Japanese members accounted for over half, and no other place of residence had more than 30 members. This partly reflected economic barriers and highlighted a need for attention.

Another challenge is to manage a regional society which holds great diversity in academic and other circumstances. A regional society like CESA requires special effort by office holders, particularly the President and Secretary General. CESA operates in English, but still needs to reach out to many language groups. Like many such societies, the potential is great but much depends on the enthusiasm and persistence of the leadership. The link with the WCCES is among the valued ways in which CESA collaborates with partner societies in the global community.

30

Completing the Family Picture

Maria MANZON & Mark BRAY

This chapter is entitled 'Completing the Family Picture' for two reasons. First, in a rather literal sense, it does indeed contain pictures. These are photographs from selected points in history, to allow readers to see what various actors looked like. Second, the chapter contains summary facts on the member societies for which it was not possible to include full chapters in the book. This arrangement ensures that these societies are visible, even in the contents pages of the book. The editors hope that members of these societies will be inspired to write more complete histories of their societies at some point in the near future.

Photographs of People and Events

Because of the constraints of space, it has been possible to select only a few pictures. The ones chosen are mostly concerned with the WCCES rather than the member societies; but because the WCCES brings together all its member societies, this choice has been a mechanism to show some of their leading figures too.

The first picture is from the opening session of the 2nd World Congress of Comparative Education Societies, which was held in Geneva in 1974. It was given to one of the editors (Mark Bray) by Anne Hamori, who was Secretary General from 1972 to 1978 and who organised the Congress. She is seated in the back row, on the left-hand side. Next to her is Brian Holmes from the United Kingdom, who was at that time President of the Comparative Education Society in Europe (CESE). He became WCCES President during that Congress, holding the

Picture 1: The 2nd World Congress, Geneva, Switzerland, 1974

post until the 3rd World Congress in London in 1977. Next to him is Douglas Ray from Canada, who at that time was President of the Comparative and International Education Society of Canada (CIESC).

In the front row of the photograph, the man on the left is André Chavanne, from the Education Bureau in Geneva. In the centre is Leo Fernig. At that time, Fernig was Director of UNESCO's International Bureau of Education (IBE) in Geneva, and in that capacity was providing the resources to employ Anne Hamori as WCCES Secretary General. Subsequently, Leo Fernig himself took on the role of Secretary General from 1978 to 1982. At the right in the front row is Joseph Katz from the University of British Columbia, in Canada. As indicated in Chapter 1 of this book, Katz is regarded as the founder of the WCCES, and was its President from 1970 to 1974.

The second picture shows Masunori Hiratsuka (on the right), the third President of the WCCES (1977-80). He is standing with Takehiko Tezuka, who was the first Secretary General of the Japan Comparative Education Society (JCES). The picture was taken in July 1980 during the 4th World Congress, organised by the JCES and held at the National Women's Education Centre, Saitama, Japan.

Picture 2: The 4th World Congress, Saitama, Japan, 1980

The next picture is from the 6th World Congress in Rio de Janeiro, Brazil. Vandra Masemann (front right) had just been declared the sixth President (and first woman President) of the WCCES, and was making a speech in English which was being translated into Portuguese. On the left of the picture is Eurides Brito da Silva, founding President of the Sociedade Brasileira de Educação Comparada (SBEC), the Congress host. She was at that time Vice-President of the

Picture 3: The 6th World Congress, Rio de Janeiro, Brazil, 1987

WCCES. On the right in the background is Brian Holmes.

Picture 4 was taken during the 9th World Congress at the University of Sydney, Australia. During that Congress, David Wilson was elected WCCES President and in this photograph is seated in the centre. On the right is Harold Herman of the University of the Western Cape, South Africa. Harold Herman was the founding President of the Southern Africa Comparative and History of Education Society (SACHES). On the left is Raymond Ryba, the longest-serving Secretary General of the WCCES (1983-96). They are relaxing at the table after having negotiated the contract for the 10th World Congress, which was hosted by SACHES at the University of Cape Town, South Africa, in 1998.

Picture 4: A Planning Meeting, Sydney, Australia, 1996

Picture 5 was taken in 1997 in Mexico City, after the meeting of the WCCES Executive Committee held there in conjunction with a conference of the Comparative and International Education Society (CIES). At that time, Erwin Epstein (centre), who had been WCCES President from 1980 to 1983, was a co-opted member of the Executive Committee. He is flanked by Jürgen Schriewer and his wife, Bruni. Jürgen Schriewer, who for some years chaired the WCCES Research Standing Committee, was in that meeting representing CESE.

Picture 5: Meeting of the Executive Committee, Mexico City, 1997

The next picture shows an event similar to that in Picture 4, this time in 2000 at the University of Bologna, Italy. David Wilson (left) is in the process of signing the contract for the 11th World Congress with Yoon Kiok (centre) and Wolfgang Mitter (right). Yoon became WCCES Vice-President the following year at the 11th World Congress hosted by the Korean Comparative Education Society (KCES) in Chungbuk, South Korea. Mitter had been WCCES President from 1991 to 1996, immediately before Wilson. In 2000 he was still a member of the Executive Committee, having been co-opted in the role of Past President.

Picture 6:
Signing the Contract in Bologna, Italy, for the 11th World Congress, 2000

Another group is presented in Picture 7. Third from the left is Anne Hickling-Hudson, WCCES President from 2001 to 2004. When the picture was taken, she was working on plans for the 12th World Congress in Havana, Cuba. Standing on the left is Christine Fox, who had been President of the Australian and New Zealand Comparative and International Education Society (ANZCIES) between 1994 and 1996. At the 9th World Congress at the University of Sydney, she became WCCES Vice-President; and in 2005 she was elected WCCES Secretary General. The photograph was taken in December 2003 at the University of Wollongong, Australia, which employed Christine Fox and which in 2005 became the host for the WCCES Secretariat.

Picture 7: A Further Planning Meeting,
Wollongong, Australia, 2003

The other two persons in this photograph are Robert Arnove (second left) and Rosemary Preston (right). Arnove had been President of the CIES in 2000/01, and at the time of this photograph, he was Chairperson of the WCCES Special Projects Standing Committee. Preston had been Chair of the British Comparative and International Education Society (BCIES), and was a leading member of its successor body, the British Association for International and Comparative Education (BAICE). At the time of this photograph she was Chairperson of the WCCES Congress Standing Committee.

The next picture is more closely tied to the production of this book. Mark Bray (left) and Maria Manzon (right) are interviewing Michel Debeauvais (centre), who had been WCCES President between 1983 and 1987. The meeting was held in the library of the UNESCO Headquarters in Paris, France. Bray and Manzon were on the way from Hong Kong to Cuba to participate in the 12th World Congress.

Picture 8: Discussing Earlier Decades, Paris, France, 2004

Finally, two pictures show many members and invited observers of a pair of meetings of the WCCES Executive Committee. Picture 9 was taken in Toronto, Canada, at the time of a meeting which was held in conjunction with the CIES annual conference. Wolfgang Mitter and Suzanne Majhanovich are holding the WCCES logo which had been created for the 7th World Congress in Montreal in 1989 and had been stored in the Toronto home of Vandra Masemann. Suzanne Majhanovich later (2001-03) became President of the CIESC, and in 2006 became Chairperson of the WCCES Publications Standing Committee.

From left to right, the persons in the picture are N'Dri Assié Lumumba (USA), Mark Bray (Hong Kong), Lee Fung-Jihu (Taiwan), Marco Todeschini (Italy), Sheldon Weeks (Botswana), Lee Byung-Jin (South Korea), Lino Borroto Lopez (Cuba), Wolfgang Mitter (Germany), Jesús M. García del Portal (Cuba), David Wilson (Canada), Suzanne Majhanovich (Canada), Karen Biraimah (USA), Harold Herman (South Africa), Vandra Masemann (Canada), Margaret B. Sutherland (UK), Christine Fox (Australia), Tatsuo Yamada (Japan), Namgi Park (South Korea), Crain Soudien (South Africa), Eleonor Rico (Philippines), and Erwin Epstein (USA).

Picture 9: WCCES Executive Committee, Toronto, Canada, 1999

Picture 10, as the counterpart of Picture 9, was taken in Bangi, Malaysia, in 2005. With the goal of spreading geographic emphases, the meeting of the WCCES Executive Committee was held for the first time in conjunction with the biennial conference of the Comparative Education Society of Asia (CESA). Just before this photograph was taken, Christine Fox had been elected WCCES Secretary General. The picture also shows Giovanni Pampanini, who at that time was the President of the Mediterranean Society of Comparative Education (MESCE) and soon after became Vice-President of the WCCES; David Turner, who since 2000 had been Treasurer of the WCCES; Adila Kreso from the University of Sarajevo, who was nominated to organise the 13th World Congress in Sarajevo in 2007; and Akira Ninomiya, who was Chairperson of the WCCES Finance and Fund-Raising Standing Committee.

From left to right, the persons in the photograph are Akira Ninomiya (Japan), Yang Shen-Keng (Taiwan), Giovanni Pampanini (Italy), Kengo Mochida (Japan), Tai Hsiou-Hsia (Taiwan), Tatsuya Kusakabe [squatting] (Japan), Lee Byung-Jin (South Korea), Lee Jeong-Seon (South Korea), Christine Fox (Australia), Kwon Dong-Taik (South Korea), Mark Bray (Hong Kong), David Turner (UK), Anne Hickling-Hudson (Australia), Rosemary Preston [squatting] (UK), Adila Kreso (Bosnia and Herzegovina), Dietmar Waterkamp (Germany), Wong Suk-Ying (Hong Kong), and Maria Manzon (Hong Kong).

Picture 10: WCCES Executive Committee, Bangi, Malaysia, 2005

The Remaining Members in the WCCES Family

This part of the chapter provides summary information on the 15 societies which were members of the WCCES in 2007 and which have not been the focus of full chapters in the book. Chapters 9 to 29 presented societies in order of the year in which they were established. That is also the principle for ordering the societies here.

The Hungarian Pedagogical Society (Comparative Education Section) (HPS-CES)

The Hungarian Pedagogical Society (HPS) was established in 1891 by the founders of modern Hungarian pedagogy, and was reorganised in 1967. In 2007, it had over 2,000 members and operated in regional departments and 23 sections, among which was the Comparative Education Section (CES). The idea of an independent HPS-CES was raised in 1968, and implemented in 1970. The founder President and Secretary were Ferenc Arató and Magda Illés. Initially, the CES was supported by the National Pedagogical Library and Museum, the duties of which included supplying the Ministry of Education with international information about education. Arató was the general director of the Library, and Illés the head of the Documentary and Comparative Pedagogical Section.

In 1975 a discussion was initiated in the Hungarian journal *Pedagogical Review* on 'The Subject, Forms and Tasks of Comparative Education'. During the autumn session of the HPS-CES a proposal was made to teach comparative education as a compulsory subject at universities and teacher training colleges. In 1978, work on an 11-language pedagogical dictionary was launched in cooperation with national and international experts, and in 1980 it was presented to the Deputy Director-General of UNESCO in Geneva.

At the 11th CESE conference in Würzburg, Germany in 1983, the HPS-CES was admitted as a member of CESE; and at the plenary session of that conference, Magda Illés presented the section's 11-language pedagogical dictionary to the CESE President, Wolfgang Mitter. Since that time, the HPS-CES has had close links with the CESE, actively participating in its conferences and hosting the 1988 CESE Conference in Budapest.

After Hungary's political transition in 1989/90, the HPS underwent various transformations. The CES was reorganised in 1997 and again in 2003. András Benedek (Budapest University of Technology and Economics) became its President in 1997, with Magda Illés as Co-President and Péter Tóth as Secretary. In 2007, it had about 50 members, most of whom were scholars and policy makers. The new aims of the HPS-CES were to:

- keep in contact with international scholars and agencies (such as the World Bank and the European Union);
- contribute to the 'catching up' of Hungarian education with its new Western partners;
- operate as an interface between the new challenges and continuing traditions; and

- take special interest in neighbouring states, especially ones in which Hungarian-language communities existed.

The section's links with the WCCES date from 1984, when it was represented at the Paris World Congress by Tamás Kozma and Magda Illés. In 1994, the section was admitted as a WCCES member. In 2006, the HPS-CES and the University of Debrecen published the Hungarian version of the volume from the 11th World Congress in Chungbuk, South Korea (Bray 2003), accomplished under the direction of Péter Tóth, Trencsényi László and Tamás Kozma.

The Chinese Comparative Education Society-Taipei (CCES-T)

The body which is known in the WCCES as the Chinese Comparative Education Society-Taipei (CCES-T) was established in 1974. It was the third comparative education society to be established in the Asian region, and was admitted to the WCCES in 1990.

Sun Pang-Chen together with several distinguished Taiwanese educators took the lead to organise the society. The first preparatory committee meeting was held in October 1973 at the National Taiwan Normal University. The 18 distinguished participants included Lin Pen, Sun Kang-Tseng, Liu Chen, Sun Pang-Chen, Lei Kuo-Ting, Lin Ching-Chiang, Lian Shang-Yung, and Huang Kun-Hui. Lei Kuo-Ting was nominated Chairman of the preparatory committee, and subsequent meetings were held in January and April 1974. Finally, on 18 May 1974, the Society's General Assembly was inaugurated and the Constitution approved (Chiang 2005).

According to the Constitution, the main purpose of the CCES-T is "to study current education in the important countries, to achieve international education and academic cooperation, and to promote education at home" (CCES-T 2006). In 1982 the society launched a newsletter, which in 1997 became the Chinese-language *Journal of Comparative Education*. Between 1982 and 1997, the society published 42 issues of its newsletter, and in the decade since 1997, 15 issues of the journal. The table of contents and abstracts for most of the issues were placed on the society website (www.ced.ncnu.edu.tw/ccest).

The CCES-T has also organised annual or more frequent conferences since 1975, which have led to a steady stream of publications. One of the books published in 2000 (CCES-T 2000) was a collaborative work among scholars from Taiwan and Mainland China. The conference themes included:

- 2001: 'Prospects of Asian Education for the New Century' (3rd Conference of the Comparative Education Society of Asia);
- 2001: 'Knowledge Economy and Educational Development';
- 2002: 'Promoting Integrated Higher Education and Enhancing Higher Education's Competitiveness';
- 2002: 'A Dialogue between Educational Research and Practice';
- 2003: 'Globalisation and Educational Competitiveness: Comparative Education Perspectives';

- 2004: 'Quality Management of Higher Education and International Competitiveness';
- 2005: 'Globalisation and Localisation of Higher Education Reforms: International Reform Trends and Reflections from the Taiwanese Experience'; and
- 2006: 'Higher Education Development and Mobility of Human Talent: Analysis and Comparison of National Experiences'.

The Comparative Education Society of India (CESI)

The fourth Asian national society was the Indian society, established in 1979 (in the same year as the Chinese Comparative Education Society) and admitted to the WCCES in 1980, becoming its third Asian member. The decision to form CESI was made in the late 1970s during a meeting in Allahabad of the Indian Association of Professors of Education. It had its inaugural meeting in 1979 with a three-day workshop held at the Jawaharlal Nehru University, New Delhi, where Sureshchandra Shukla was Honorary Visiting Professor. Fifty scholars of education and international education participated. At that inaugural meeting, Shukla was elected CESI President and D.A. Dabholkar as Vice-President. Both served their respective offices for three consecutive terms (total of six years), and Dabholkar was later elected President (1985-89).

The society was registered with the government in 1982 with the following aims:

- to promote the comparative study of education and to make social scientists and others conscious of the importance of comparative education as a science and as a subject;
- to provide a forum for exchanging ideas on the national, regional and international aspects of education and further new research in their comparative aspects for improvement in the standard of teaching, policy-making and administration of education, by organising academic discussions and symposia, field-visits, excursions and conferences, and by publishing journals and monographs, reviews, pamphlets and other literature; and
- to cooperate with other societies with similar objectives in India and abroad, with official agencies and departments of the Government of India and of the United Nations (including UNESCO) and other organisations for the study of and research in comparative education and generally for the advancement of the subject.

CESI had held its second meeting in Pune (1982), and subsequent meetings in Hyderabad (1985), New Delhi (1986), Chandigarh (1987), and Jamia Millia Islamia (1989). In the 1989 meeting, Gulistan Kerawalla (University of Mumbai) was elected President, together with Malla Reddy as Vice-President, and Mohammad Miyan as General Secretary. The society then became rather inactive. After sixteen years, on 12 May 2005 CESI organised a joint-talk by Budd Hall and

Nina Dey-Gupta on 'Education in Cuba', as participants at the 12th World Congress in Cuba (2004). Finally, with the constant efforts of Nina Dey-Gupta to reunite the group, CESI had come back to life. In December 2006, CESI had around 60 members.

The Sezione Italiana della CESE (SICESE)

The national body called the Italian Section of the Comparative Education Society in Europe was established in September 1986 during the 25th anniversary congress of the Comparative Education Society in Europe (CESE) in Garda, Verona, Italy. SICESE was admitted to the WCCES in July 1987.

As explained in Chapter 10, CESE was constituted as a society of individual members, open to comparative educationists from throughout Europe and beyond. This arrangement permitted the concurrent membership of individuals in the regional CESE and the incorporation of constituted national or other groups with parallel purposes. These constituted bodies were likewise eligible for membership in the WCCES, and as such existed side by side with CESE. Organisations of British and German comparative educationists were thus formed as sections of CESE in the 1960s, and the Italians followed in the 1980s. While the British Section subsequently became independent from CESE as the British Comparative Education Society, the Italian Section remained unchanged, although it was effectively admitted to the WCCES in 1987 as a national society.

A parallel Italian society of comparativists was formed around the same time as SICESE (Todeschini 2004). Both Italian groups had applied simultaneously for membership to the WCCES in 1984, and re-applied in 1987. One group was called the Italian Comparative Education Society, and the other the Italian Section of CESE, which was the body admitted to the World Council.

The Statutes of SICESE included a formal link to the Centro Europeo dell'Educazione (CEDE), which was a think-tank under the patronage of the Italian Ministry of Education and based in Frascati. SICESE's administrative council included a CEDE representative as a member with full voting rights, as SICESE was granted the technical and financial support of CEDE (hence indirectly the Ministry) for its activities. This link had been made possible because one of SICESE's founding members, Aldo Visalberghi of the Università degli Studi di Roma La Sapienza, had been appointed Chairman of CEDE. The Journal of CEDE, *Ricerca Educativa*, hosted contributions by SICESE members, and a special issue published papers from the 1986 CESE Conference in Garda (Orizio 1988). It also assisted in the publication of proceedings of the first two SICESE congresses (Izzo & Tassinari 1994; Telmon & Borghi 1995). However, the CEDE link weakened when Visalberghi's successor as CEDE President was not likeminded in his enthusiasm for SICESE. Moreover, Italian interest in comparative education declined at the beginning of the 1990s, and this decline was felt in the dramatically reduced membership of the society.

The turn of the century witnessed a shift in SICESE's base to Bologna, under the leadership of Vittorio Telmon, of the Università di Bologna. During his term, SICESE hosted the 19th CESE Conference in Bologna (2000) on the theme

'The Emergence of the "Knowledge Society": From *Clerici Vagantes* to Internet'.

In 2001, a possibility arose in Rome for SICESE to join forces with the editorial team of *Educazione Comparata*, a small quarterly journal on comparative education set up by Antonio Augenti and indirectly supported by the Ministry of Cultural Exchanges. A new council was elected with Augenti at the helm and including some SICESE veterans and some newcomers. The council decided to rewrite the Statutes which had become obsolete after the phasing out of the CEDE as a formal unit of the Ministry of Education. However, little action was taken. In 2006, a new move to resurrect SICESE was initiated by Donatella Palomba from the Università di Roma Tor Vergata, who was a Past President of CESE (2000-04).

The Israel Comparative Education Society (ICES)

The Israel Comparative Education Society was founded in 1988, and joined the WCCES in June 1989. The ICES aims to promote research and teaching of comparative education within higher education institutions and teacher training colleges. It encourages policy makers, mainly in the Ministry of Education, to consider comparative research findings in their decision-making processes.

The ICES is part of the Israeli Association for Educational Research (IAER), and conducts its meetings in conjunction with IAER meetings. No formal membership or dues are required, but about 20 to 30 members usually participate in the IAER sessions. Publications of its members include Iram and Wahrman (2003) and Iram et al. (2006). ICES members have participated regularly in the conferences of the CIES and CESE, as well as in the congresses of the WCCES.

The Egyptian Comparative Education and Educational Administration Society (ECEEAS)

Formed as a non-governmental organisation in August 1991, the ECEEAS did not join the WCCES until March 2006. It is the only WCCES member society which combines Comparative Education and Educational Administration in its name.

Egypt had in the 1980s been a strong centre for the teaching of comparative education in the Arab world (Benhamida 1990, p.305). As explained in Chapter 8, an earlier Egyptian society, the Egyptian Group of Comparative Education (EGCE), had been admitted to the WCCES in 1984, but later appeared to have become defunct and was removed from the WCCES membership list in 2000. The establishment of the ECEEAS, with its dual foci of comparative education and educational administration, signalled a renaissance of the field in the Arabic-speaking world. Abod (2004) has written a detailed history of the ECEEAS.

According to its Constitution, the objectives of the ECEEAS are: to establish communication channels between specialists in comparative education and educational administration at the national and regional levels; to organise forums, conferences and seminars in the field of comparative education and educational administration; to issue newsletters, journals and books on comparative education and educational administration; to examine problems in the Egyptian education system and its administration as well as providing advice to specialised agencies; to study education systems and educational administration in foreign countries and learn from their experiences in developing the education system in Egypt; and to conduct studies in the fields of comparative education and educational administration and benefit from the findings of these studies in improving education in Egypt.

The Egyptian society has held annual conferences since its inception, which have included:

- 2005: 13th annual conference, 'Accreditation and Quality Assurance of Educational Institutions';
- 2006: 14th annual conference, 'Globalisation and Education'; and
- 2007: 15th annual conference, 'Preparing Educational Leaders in Egypt and the Arab World'.

Based in the Faculty of Education of Ain Shams University in Cairo, the society had around 100 members in 2006. Most were professors of education from over 15 Egyptian universities, though several were researchers from the National Center for Educational Research and Development in Cairo.

The Nordic Comparative and International Education Society (NOCIES)

The decision to establish a Nordic Comparative and International Education Society was taken by a group of Nordic scholars participating in the 14th CESE conference in Madrid in 1990. In January 1991, a meeting was held in Oslo, and a working group was established with representatives from Denmark, Finland, Norway, and Sweden (Winther-Jensen 1991). In May 1992, it held its founding General Assembly on the occasion of a Nordic comparative conference organised by the Educational Research Institute at the University of Oslo, and supported by the Programme for Education Research (NAVF). The conference gathered about 60 participants from the Nordic countries, and resulted in a publication describing the history of comparative education in Denmark, Finland and Norway (Harbo & Winther-Jensen 1993). The General Assembly decided on the name of the society and its Constitution, and appointed an Executive Committee with Thyge Winther-Jensen (University of Copenhagen) as Chairperson.

According to its Constitution, NOCIES shall promote aims similar to those of the CESE. In particular the society shall encourage the growth of comparative and international studies by promoting and improving the teaching of comparative education in institutions of higher learning; stimulating research in the field; facilitating the publication and distribution of comparative and international studies; and organising conferences and meetings for members and other educationists.

NOCIES hosted the 16th CESE conference at the University of Copenhagen in 1994, from which selected papers were published in an edited volume (Winther-Jensen 1996). In 2004, NOCIES members were the core organisers of the 21st CESE conference hosted by the Danish University of Education, Copenhagen (Sprogøe & Winther-Jensen 2006). The society has also hosted a number of smaller seminars with participants from inside and outside Scandinavia. For a period it also published a Newsletter. Members of the society have been very active in the field of comparative education, and have organised courses in comparative education at Nordic universities including the University of Copenhagen, University of Oslo, The Danish University of Education, and University of Tampere.

In 1997, NOCIES was admitted as a member society of the WCCES. In 2002, it submitted a bid to host the 12th World Congress, but the award was given to Cuba.

The Asociación de Pedagogos de Cuba (Sección de Educación Comparada) (APC-SEC)

The Asociación de Pedagogos de Cuba (Cuban Pedagogical Association – APC) was founded on 6 March 1989. A non-governmental and non-profit academic and professional organisation, the APC provides in-service professional development programmes for members through workshops and postgraduate courses. The APC has around 13,000 members from Cuba's 14 provinces and the special municipality of the Isla de la Juventud (Isle of Youth). Its Comparative Education Section (APC-SEC) was launched in 1994 with an inaugural seminar held among Cuban and American professors. This activity has been ongoing since then. The APC-SEC's activity includes supporting doctoral studies in the field of comparative education. In this respect, studies of education systems in Jamaica, Belize, Panama, Chile, Venezuela, Haiti and Cuba have been undertaken. The APC-SEC also supports the elaboration of courses on comparative education in higher education institutions, and has designed and imparted such a programme for a Peruvian university.

In July 2002, the APC-SEC was admitted to the WCCES, and in October 2004 it hosted the 12th World Congress in Havana. The Cuban Congress was a significant stimulus for the development of comparative education not only in Cuba but also in neighbouring countries in Latin America. Through the wide national network of the APC, pre-Congress events fostered a scholarly interest in comparative education research, attracting over 600 Cuban educators. It also provided a cultural space for Congress participants to learn about worldwide experiences in education (Martín Sabina 2006). In February 2007, the APC-SEC organised a workshop on comparative education during the Congreso Internacional Pedagogía. The section has around 90 members, including school teachers and academics.

The Association française pour le développement de l'éducation comparée et des échanges (AFDECE)

In English, the title of AFDECE may be translated as the French Association for the Development of Comparative Education and Exchanges. AFDECE was founded in August 1998, and at that time was called ADECE: Association pour le développement des échanges et de la comparaison en éducation, which may be translated as Association for the Development of Exchanges and Comparison in Education. ADECE changed its name to AFDECE in 2004, and was also admitted to the WCCES in that year.

The AFDECE Statutes state that the association aims to play an active part in the development of comparative education and in beneficial exchanges between primary schools, secondary schools, and universities in France. The Statutes also declare an aim to serve as a meeting place for theories and practices, academics and teachers, and administrative officers and pedagogues. AFDECE further endeavours to provide biographical and practical information to those who are interested in the problems of comparative education and exchanges, offering an international forum relevant to the field. Between 1999 and 2005, AFDECE published 24 issues of its electronic newsletter, *Le Courrier de l'AFDECE*. It also organised colloquia including:

- 1999, Versailles, France: 'Educational Exchanges and Comparative Education';
- 2000, Montpellier, France: 'International Exchanges and Scholastic Achievement for All';
- 2002, Strasbourg, France: 'Building a European Identity: Otherness, Education, Exchanges';
- 2003, Geneva, Switzerland: 'Migrant Populations and the Right to Education: Urban Prospects';
- 2005, Potsdam, Germany: 'The School Compared: National Cultures of School Evaluation'.

AFDECE has also organised various seminars, and has had a steady stream of publications in its *Collection éducation comparée* published by L'Harmattan in Paris (e.g. Groux & Tutiaux-Guillon 2000; Etienne & Groux 2002; Groux 2002; Ulma 2005). The AFDECE website (www.afdece.com) provides further information. The association commenced with approximately 50 members, and has grown to several hundred. Most members are university professors, while others are officials in the French Ministry of Education, school teachers, graduate students, and consultants.

The Sociedad Argentina de Estudios Comparados en Educación (SAECE)

SAECE was established in August 2001, during its Inaugural Assembly which was attended by 70 university professors and researchers from different regions of Argentina. It was admitted to the WCCES in May 2005.

The aims of the society are: to promote and disseminate the development of comparative studies in the area of education and culture; share relevant academic work with all levels of the educational community and various sectors of society; develop a spirit of cooperation, cordiality and solidarity among its members to further intellectual and academic advancement; give preferential attention to the preparation of specialists and academics in higher education and other levels of the education system; organise events, congresses, seminars, courses; promote the publication of bulletins, journals and books related to the academic and professional areas of the society; and establish links with other public and private educational institutions, both nationally and internationally.

SAECE has been an active catalyst of comparative education in South America. Together with the Spanish society (Sociedad Española de Educación Comparada), it was a co-founder of the Asociación Iberoamericana de Sociedades de Educación Comparada (AISEC), a grouping of comparative education societies in the Ibero-American region. SAECE held its 1st Argentinean Congress of Comparative Studies in Education in 2005, followed by a second conference in 2006. In June 2007, it hosted the 1st Latin American Meeting on Comparative Education in Buenos Aires.

The Comparative Education Society of the Philippines (CESP)

The Philippine society is a small group of scholars who share an interest in the field of comparative education. In the late 1990s, Josephine Campanano of St. Paul University, Tuguegarao wrote to the WCCES expressing interest in its membership. Eleonor Rico, based at the University of Pittsburgh, USA, was a regular participant at CIES meetings and was regularly invited as an observer to the WCCES meetings. In 1999, they gathered a group of interested scholars. Subsequently, Roberto Borromeo, Chair of Educational Leadership at De La Salle University, Manila, joined forces; and in 2001, they formed the CESP. In March 2002 their application for the admission to the WCCES was approved.

The founding members of the CESP set as the society's aim the promotion of comparative education by assisting their respective universities in the Philippines to offer courses in comparative education. Motivated by the desire to improve the lives of the country's poverty-stricken population, they have stressed the value of comparative education in mobilising research competence to aid the government's pursuit of educational equity and efficiency.

The Sociedad Mexicana de Educación Comparada (SOMEC)

The Mexican Society of Comparative Education was established in November 2003. It was admitted to the WCCES in 2004 during the 12th World Congress hosted by its Spanish-speaking neighbour, Cuba, thereby strengthening the voice of the Spanish-speaking scholarly community.

Marco Aurelio Navarro (2005a), the society's founding President, traced the origins of SOMEC to the active and assiduous participation of Mexican academics in conferences of the US-based Comparative and International Education Society (CIES), during which they were invited by World Council executives to form their own national society. Carlos Ornelas, Armando Alcántara, Medardo Tapia, Ernesto Treviño, Germán Treviño and Marco Aurelio Navarro comprised the core group who laid the foundations of the society. A first exploratory meeting was held in June 2003, with about 25 Mexican scholars who expressed support for the initiative and resolved to become a duly constituted civil association eligible for WCCES membership.

SOMEC held its inaugural assembly during November 2003 in Guadalajara, Jalisco, during the 7th Congreso Nacional de Investigación Educativa (National Congress of Educational Research). In that meeting, SOMEC welcomed its founding members who totalled almost 40. The assembly approved the society's objectives as laid out in its Constitution, echoing the aims of the WCCES. In May 2004, during the 2nd International Congress on Teaching held at the Unidad Académica Reynosa-Aztlán, Universidad Autónoma de Tamaulipas (UAT), SOMEC had its first official forum with a presentation of showcase studies of comparative education research. This was later published as a book entitled *La Educación Comparada en México: Un Campo en Construcción* (Navarro 2005b).

SOMEC is open to Mexican academics, researchers and postgraduate students who are conducting studies related to the field of comparative education. The society website (http://colaboracion.uat.edu.mx/rectoria/subacademica/somec/default.aspx) based at the UAT contains society news, an e-mail list of its members, and a site for membership registration.

In June 2005, SOMEC organised an international congress on 'Challenges and Prospects of the University', held in Tampico, Tamaulipas. Among the keynote speakers were leading figures from the comparative education societies of Argentina, Australia, Hong Kong, and the United States. In the same year, a SOMEC delegation joined the 2nd Worldwide Forum of Comparative Education held in Beijing Normal University, China. In addition, Mario Lorenzo Martínez, a distinguished SOMEC member, translated into Spanish the edited volume of the 11th World Congress in Chungbuk, South Korea (Bray 2003) and arranged for its publication by Porrua in Mexico City.

The Mediterranean Society of Comparative Education (MESCE)

During the 1990s, a group of scholars of comparative education of the Mediterranean area met on various occasions during the biennial CESE conferences and in Sicily, Italy. The first meeting was held in Ragusa, Sicily, in 1992, and was followed by two meetings in Catania in 1996 and 1999. Proceedings from these events were published (Pampanini 1993, 1997, 2000).

In 2003, Giovanni Pampanini, who became the founding President of the Mediterranean Society of Comparative Education (MESCE), made a series of travels around the Mediterranean (Lisbon, Rabat, Malta, Tunis, Cairo, Paris, Frankfurt, Sarajevo, Thessaloniki, Sofia, Istanbul, Ankara, Cyprus, Beirut and Damascus) to gather a community of scholars in the field of comparative education. These meetings nurtured the desire to make a serious contribution to reciprocal understanding and peace in the Mediterranean area, and inspired the society's foundation. Finally, on 1 March 2004, MESCE was established at an inaugural conference in Catania, Italy, under the patronage of the University and the Province of Catania. The conference theme was 'Comparative Education in the Mediterranean Area: Problems and Prospects'. A few days later, MESCE was admitted to the WCCES.

MESCE aspired to play a wider leadership role, and in 2004 proposed to host the 13th World Congress of Comparative Education Societies. This bid was successful, and preparations proceeded for the event to be held in Sarajevo, Bosnia and Herzegovina, in September 2007. The chief organiser was Adila Kreso of the University of Sarajevo, who became MESCE President in 2005.

The official languages of the MESCE conferences are Arabic, French, and English. The society has a significant membership in the Arabic-speaking countries that border on the Mediterranean.

The Council on Comparative Education of Kazakhstan (CCEK)

The CCEK was established in 2005 as a non-governmental organisation in accordance with the law of the Republic of Kazakhstan. Its admission to the WCCES in March 2006 signalled a focal point of comparative activity in Central Asia. Unlike other WCCES members which commonly have the term 'Society' or 'Association' in their name, the CCEK is one of the two bodies that use the term 'Council'. Kulamergen Mussin, Vice-President of the CCEK, underscored that the rationale for naming the CCEK as a Council lies in its aim to becoming a doctoral degree-approving institution. In Kazakhstan, this authority is vested only in academic councils, not in academic societies or associations (Mussin 2007).

Askarbek Kussainov, founding President of the CCEK and President of the Academy of Pedagogical Sciences of Kazakhstan, and Kulamergen Mussin, holder of the UNESCO Chair on Pedagogical Sciences and Teacher Training in the Kazakh National Pedagogical University named after Abai, were the leaders in the formation of the CCEK. They gathered academics and practitioners from Kazakh universities in Karaganda, Almaty and Astana, who were working in the newly emerging field of comparative education.

Mussin (2007) cited the strong presence of UNESCO in Kazakhstan, mainly through its UNESCO Chair Programme, as a catalyst for comparative work and international collaboration on educational programmes and projects. Prior to forming the Council, CCEK members had been taking an active part in UNESCO events such as the First World Forum of UNESCO Chairholders (2002, Paris, France), the Round Table of UNESCO Chairholders 'Education in the Interests of the Sustainable Future' (2002, Kazan, Russian Federation), and the UNESCO International Conference on 'Teaching and Learning for Intercultural Understanding, Human Rights and Culture of Peace' (2003, Jyvaskyla, Finland).

The CCEK has been an active participant in the international meetings of the WCCES since its joining the family in 2006. A strong delegation of Kazakhs was present in comparative education conferences in Hawaii, USA, and Granada, Spain, in 2006, as well as in Hong Kong, China, in 2007.

The Turkish Comparative Education Society (TCES)

The youngest member of the family is the TCES. Formed in March 2006, the society was admitted to the WCCES during the July 2006 Executive Committee meeting in Granada, Spain. The main driving force that brought the national society into being was the desire to form part of an international research and scholarly community. Fatma Gök, founding President of the TCES, cited the pivotal role of the 12th World Congress at Havana, Cuba in 2004, where 18 Turkish scholars mainly from Ankara and Istanbul participated, and which cemented the decision to establish the society (Gök 2007). The TCES also traces its roots to the involvement of some its founding members in the activities of the CIES and later in MESCE.

The main aims of the TCES are to:

- promote teaching and research in the field of comparative education and facilitating related publication in order to disseminate ideas and information;
- promote understanding of cross-cultural, interdisciplinary and international studies contributing to the interpretation of developments in the field of education in their broad and interrelated political, economic, and social context;
- promote international understanding and educational cooperation in the academic field;
- encourage educational and cultural exchanges; and
- study the educational policy-making processes in order to facilitate economic and social development and transformation.

In 2007, the TCES had around 50 members. The society had organised sub-committees to oversee its activities, which included publishing an electronic journal and hosting annual conferences to elicit a nationwide interest on issues about Turkish education and world development.

Conclusion

This chapter has presented the WCCES family picture in March 2007. Taken together with the preceding 29 chapters of personal memoirs and institutional histories in this book, these accounts have illustrated the hopes and challenges, the lofty ambitions and the down-to-earth struggles of comparativists all over the world. They have shown that the World Council is a global body that embraces a diversity of educational traditions and politics, and is at the same time a family with its elders, its loving (and at times rival) siblings, and its strong and weak members. Just as a family is kept perennially young with the coming of new members, it is hoped that these histories will encourage the future generations to extend the family to new frontiers. It is also hoped that the younger generations will, with the wisdom and experience of their venerable predecessors, rise to greater heights by standing on the shoulders of their elders.

This family picture has also shown that the WCCES family and its outreach are the result of the collective efforts of countless persons, known and unknown, who share the common goal of "promoting education for international understanding in the interests of peace, intercultural co-operation, mutual respect among peoples and observance of human rights" (WCCES 1996). The goal remains lofty and *uncommon* as does its achievement, but the histories in this book have shown that the interest to attain it is strikingly *common*.

Acknowledgments

The completion of this family picture has been made possible thanks to the generous collaboration of many persons. Special thanks are due to the member society representatives for contributing information: Elvira Martín Sabina (APC-SEC), Dominique Groux (AFDECE), Nina Dey-Gupta (CESI), Eleonor Rico (CESP), Kulamergen Mussin (CCEK), Nagwa Megahed (ECEEAS), András Benedek, Magda Illés, Péter Tóth and Tamás Kozma (HPS-CES), Yaacov Iram (ICES), Thyge Winther-Jensen and Lennart Wikander (NOCIES), Norberto Fernández Lamarra and Cristian Perez Centcno (SAECE), Marco Aurelio Navarro (SOMEC), and Fatma Gök (TCES). We also express appreciation for the help of Volker Masemann (Toronto), Kitty Chow and Samsom Liu (The University of Hong Kong) in scanning the photos.

References

Abod, AbdelGhany (2004): *Comparative Education at the Beginnings of the Century: Ideology, Education, and the Third Millennium*. Cairo: Dar ElFeker ElAraby. [in Arabic]

Benhamida, Khemais (1990): 'The Arab States', in Halls, W.D. (ed.), *Comparative Education: Contemporary Issues and Trends*. Paris: UNESCO, and London: Jessica Kingsley, pp.291-317.

Bray, Mark (ed.) (2003): *Comparative Education: Continuing Traditions, New Challenges, and New Paradigms*. Special double issue of *International Review of Education*, Vol.49, Nos.1-2. Republished 2003 as book with same title, Dordrecht: Kluwer Academic Publishers.

Chiang, Tien-Hui (2005): 'The Historical Records of Chinese Comparative Education Society-Taipei'. Paper presented at the 5th Biennial Conference of the Comparative Education Society of Asia, Universiti Kebangsaan Malaysia, 30-31 May.

Chinese Comparative Education Society-Taipei (CCES-T) (2000): *Comparative Education Theory and Practice*. Taipei: Taiwan Bookstore Press. [in Chinese]

Chinese Comparative Education Society-Taipei (CCES-T) (2006): Constitution of the Chinese Comparative Education Society-Taipei. www.ced.ncnu.edu.tw/ccest/constitutionsE/constitutionsE.htm.

Etienne, Richard & Groux, Dominique (eds.) (2002): *Échanges éducatifs internationaux: difficultés et réussites*. Coll. éducation comparée. Paris: L'Harmattan.

Gök, Fatma (2007). Interview by Maria Manzon, 10 January. Hong Kong, China.

Groux, Dominique & Tutiaux-Guillon, Nicole (eds.) (2000): *Les échanges internationaux et la comparaison en éducation*. Coll. éducation comparée. Paris: L'Harmattan.

Groux, Dominique (ed.) (2002): *Pour une éducation à l'altérité*. Coll. éducation comparée. Paris: L'Harmattan.

Harbo, Torstein & Winther-Jensen, Thyge (eds.) (1993): *Vi og de andre*. Oslo: Ad Notam Gyldendal.

Iram, Yaacov (ed.) & Wahrman, Hillel (asst. ed.) (2003): *Education of Minorities and Peace Education in Pluralistic Societies*. Westport, CT: Greenwood Press.

Iram, Yaacov (ed.); Wahrman, Hillel & Gross, Zehavit (assoc. eds.) (2006): *Education towards a Culture of Peace*. Greenwich, CT: Information Age Publishing.

Izzo, Domenico & Tassinari, Gastone (eds.) (1994): *L'Autonomia delle Scuole in Europa: Realtà e Prospettive*. Roma: Armando.

Martín Sabina, Elvira (2006): 'Twelfth Congress of the World Council of Comparative Education Societies (WCCES), Havana, Cuba'. *International Review of Education*, Vol.52, No.1, pp.1-7.

Mussin, Kulamergen (2007): Interview by Maria Manzon, 11 January. Macao, China.

Navarro, Marco Aurelio (2005a): President's Report for 2003-2005. SOMEC, 1 November.

Navarro, Marco Aurelio (2005b) (ed.): *La Educación Comparada en México: Un Campo en Construcción*. México: Editorial SOMEC-Universidad Autónoma de Tamaulipas.

Orizio, Battista (ed.) (1988): *L'Educazione Comparata Oggi – Comparative Education Today – L'Éducation comparée aujourd'hui: Atti della Conferenza di Garda*. Conferenza straordinaria per il 25° anniversario della CESE 1961-1986, Garda (Verona), 3-6 ottobre 1986. Frascati: Centro Europeo dell'Educazione.

Pampanini, Giovanni (ed.) (1993): *Prospettive Euro-arabe di Educazione Interculturale: Per una Cooperazione nel Mediterraneo*. Catania: Cooperativa Universitaria Editrice Catanese di Magistero.

Pampanini, Giovanni (ed.) (1997): *L'Educazione degli Adulti nel Confronto Mediterraneo: Problemi e Prospettive*. Catania: Latessa.

Pampanini, Giovanni (ed.) (2000): *'Un Mare di Opportunità': Cultura e Educazione nel Mediterraneo del III Millennio*. Roma: Armando.

Sprogøe, Jonas & Winther-Jensen, Thyge (eds.) (2006): *Identity, Education and Citizenship: Multiple Interrelations*. Frankfurt am Main: Peter Lang.

Telmon, Vittorio & Borghi, Loris (eds.) (1995): *Valori Formativi e Culture Diverse: L'Interazione Educativa in Prospettiva Transnazionale*. Roma: Armando.

Todeschini, Marco (2004): 'The Comparative Approach to Education in Italy'. Unpublished manuscript.

Ulma, Dominique (ed.) (2005): *L'Europe: objet d'enseignement?* Coll. éducation comparée. Paris: L'Harmattan.

WCCES (1996): 'Statutes'. World Council of Comparative Education Societies.

Winther-Jensen, Thyge (1991): 'Nordic Comparative and International Education Society'. *CESE Newsletter*. October.

Winther-Jensen, Thyge (ed.) (1996): *Challenges to European Education: Cultural Values, National Identities and Global Responsibilities*. Frankfurt am Main: Peter Lang.

31

Comparing the Comparers: Patterns, Themes and Interpretations

Maria MANZON & Mark BRAY

The histories in this book are set within their wider contexts, partly echoing works on disciplinary histories and sociology of the social sciences such as Graham et al. (1983) and Wagner et al. (1991). Taking the comparative education societies and the umbrella global body as the units of analysis, this book demonstrates that professional and scholarly associations are windows on the wider communities that they serve. At the same time, broader forces in political, academic and other domains shape the sizes, structures and activities of these societies.

This chapter examines relationships between the broader environment and the professional bodies. Using insights from the preceding chapters, the chapter identifies some patterns and themes from the main body of the book, and in a sense compares the comparers. It begins with conceptual literature on disciplinary institutionalisation and scholarly networking before turning to the specifics of the comparative education societies. It includes comments on society formation and names, which are themselves linked to the ways in which the societies have been founded, positioned themselves and recruited members. The chapter again emphasises the diversity of patterns within the common framework.

Disciplinary Institutionalisation and Scholarly Networking

Some Concepts from the Analytical Literatures

While in the academic arena comparative education is widely, albeit not universally, considered to be a field of study rather than a discipline, some conceptual understanding of the nature and purpose of disciplinary institutionalisation is useful. Becher and Trowler (2001) highlighted the importance of epistemology and phenomenology in drawing disciplinary boundaries. Using the metaphor of academic tribes and territories, Becher and Trowler denoted on the one hand the distinctive cultures within academic communities (tribes), and on the other hand the ideas with which academics work (territories). They defined disciplinary epistemology as "the 'actual' form and focus of knowledge within a discipline", and the phenomenology of that knowledge as "the ideas and understandings that practitioners have about their discipline (and others)" (p.23). Becher and Trowler argued that epistemology and phenomenology were inseparably intertwined. They conceived of an academic discipline as the result of a mutually dependent interplay between the structural force of the epistemological character of disciplines that conditions culture and the capacity of individuals and groups as agents of autonomous action, including interpretive acts (2001, pp.23-24). Wagner and Wittrock (1991a, p.3) described the disciplinary institutionalisation in the social sciences as the "creation of a separate sphere of scientific activity". They added that institutionalisation:

- does not necessarily occur in academic forms alone;
- does not always, or even often, occur on the basis of having an un-equivocal theoretical or methodological baggage; and
- does not entail complete stability over time or place, but exhibits regional and intellectual variety and transformations.

Emerging disciplines usually endeavour to distinguish themselves from amateur or lay explanations of the reality studied, as well as from older, neighbouring disciplines. In the social sciences, and indeed in other domains, development has commonly been diachronic, exhibiting highly dissimilar and uneven levels in different geographic locations (Wagner & Wittrock 1991b, pp.349-350; see also Lambert 2003). Institutionalisation of a discipline is not necessarily limited to its formal recognition and location within the academic structure of a department or faculty. Institutionalisation also includes the development of links with different arenas, for example through practical engagements in research and consultancies.

Various scholars have identified the formation of scholarly societies as a dimension of disciplinary institutionalisation (e.g. Coser 1965; Manicas 1990). Clark (1987, p.233) observed that disciplinary associations in higher education have helped "tighten the hold of specialisation upon academic life, a device that would serve externally as a carrying mechanism for a discipline at large, a way of furthering specialties without regard to institutional boundaries". He added (p.238) that scholarly associations mirror the ongoing contest between centrifugal and centripetal academic forces, paving the way for further subdivisions along subject-matter lines. He offered three metaphors in which multidisciplinary associations may operate (p.241):

- *umbrella associations* refer to large amalgams of organisations, including global bodies which are constituted by national member societies;
- *spider-web groupings* weave themselves around larger national associations by holding their annual meetings in the same city, presenting their own programmes right before, right after, or during the meetings of the major group; and
- *pyramid networks* include smaller regional associations within indi-

vidual disciplines, which feed loosely into national associations that, in turn, offer the institutional building blocks plus the members for international associations.

Clark remarked that "in a confusing manner only partially caught in any one metaphor, associations structure the metainstitutional life of the academic profession" (1987, p.241), and that "voluntary associating is a good way to have structure follow knowledge" (p.253).

Communication networks among researchers were discussed in a book edited by McGinn (1996). In that volume, Lauglo (1996) posited that networks have a 'natural history', wherein persons with shared interests group together. As the group grows, Lauglo observed, a newsletter is commonly published, a forum may be organised, and the network is formalised as an association. Watson's (1996) chapter on professional associations and academic networks conceived three levels of networking: (1) personal/academic links through professional associations; (2) institutional developments; and (3) political pressure groups. The first level, which is relevant to this chapter, is represented in Figure 31.1.

Figure 31.1: Academic Networking

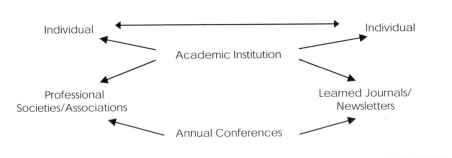

Source: Watson (1996, p.130).

Fields of study are unlike disciplines, which usually take institutional shape in university departments and faculties. According to Klein (1990), a field's presence and importance are largely determined by its relative visibility, which may take at least two forms. One is the overt form of interdisciplinary institutions, such as a single umbrella organisation or interdisciplinary graduate programmes. The other embraces less overt forms for interdisciplinary dialogue such as study groups, symposia, conferences, publications, and institutes. This observation has particular resonance in interdisciplinary fields such as comparative education. Having evolved from multiple disciplinary lineages, the interdisciplines lack a common epistemological core. In this respect, academic networks play a pivotal role in fields of study, since they "give shape and substance to the links between knowledge forms and knowledge communities" (Becher & Trowler 2001, p.104).

Applications to Comparative Education

Equipped with these conceptual lenses, we position the rationale for using comparative education societies as the principal unit of analysis in this book. Comparative education, being an interdisciplinary field, is interstitial (Epstein 1981, p.270). Having evolved from multiple disciplinary lineages in different parts of the world, comparative education has no common epistemological core. Scholarly networks such as the comparative education societies play a pivotal role since they provide the links between academic tribes and territories.

Cowen (1990, p.333) defined comparative education infrastructures as the dedicated networks specifically engaged in "the definition, creation and reorganization, and transmission of 'comparative education' as a field of knowledge". Among the social actors and agencies dedicated to 'producing comparative educations' are scholarly networks, governments, professional societies, university centres, the specialist journals, publishing and teaching activities. Cowen observed (p.322) that:

> lack of clarity over what is the epistemological core and institutional centre of comparative education means that the networks of connection between the bits and pieces of comparative education take on extra importance. Changes in networks (of new centres, journals and societies) are one measure of what comparative education is, and one indication of the definition, demand, and supply of comparative education on a world basis.

He continued by posing a series of questions that help to identify some of the issues raised in the institutional histories contained in this book. Reflecting on how comparative education had been shifting ground from the historically metropolitan centres to the non-metropolitan peripheries, and on the formation of new professional societies, among Cowen's (1990, p.322) questions were:

> Are the best international and comparative Societies essentially national institutions? What is the point and purpose of the supranational professional Societies? What is the international interplay of 'comparative education(s)'? And what are the educational politics of our self-construction?

To conclude his chapter, Cowen mapped out a research agenda (p.343):

> [Do] we know what is the critical mass of interested persons [in comparative education]; are they nowadays specialists in comparative education, or do they normally share only the experience of having studied overseas? Are they copying foreign models of professional societies, or has their experience made them alert to the need to resist, or at least understand very thoroughly the nature of foreign educational influence? ... [We] may hope that comparative education will institutionalize itself world-wide but we are not too clear about either the practicalities or the purposes which are the most efficient in achieving that goal. Nor are we very clear about the political and epistemological price tags which may come with that diffusion.

The academic societies of comparative education are specialist organisations dedicated to the advocacy and transmission of comparative education as a field of knowledge and enquiry. Nevertheless, in this book the comparative education societies are not analysed in isolation from the other producers of comparative education. Moreover, the scholarly networks are themselves socially constructed. The knowledge communities which comprise comparative education are embedded in and shaped by their social contexts of multiple cultural, political, economic and epistemological factors at the global and local levels. Figure 31.2 indicates some of the relationships in operation.

Figure 31.2: Social Contextualisation of Comparative Education Societies

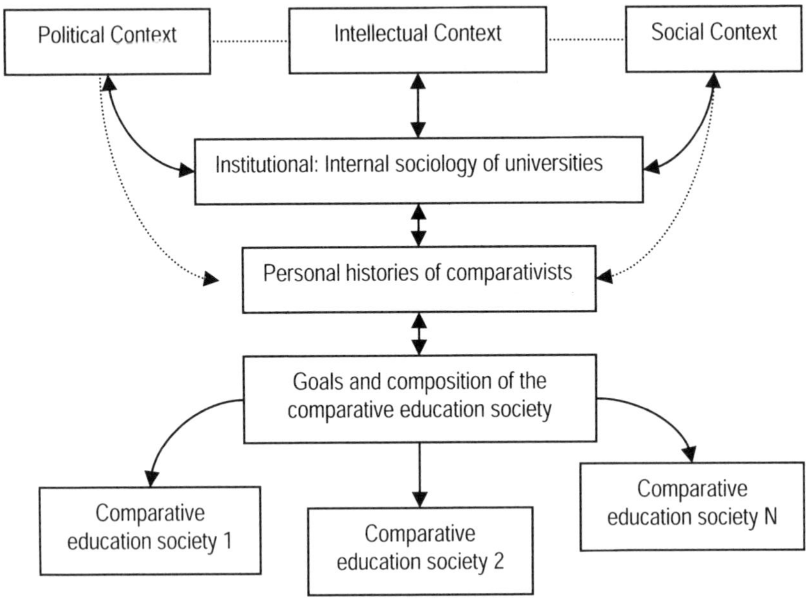

The Founding of Comparative Education Societies

The processes leading to the birth of societies as reported in this book can initially be described as follows:

- the societal demand phase (contextual dimension),
- demarcation of a new academic territory (epistemological dimension), and
- the growth of an academic tribe (sociological dimension).

Although these phases have not always occurred in the same sequence and with the same distinctiveness in all parts of the world, the examples in this book broadly exhibit these common patterns. The tripartite paradigm can be applied by extension to the entire life cycle of a society, i.e. not only to its birth but also to its growth, decline and possible demise. Thus, the contraction of societal demand can lead to the demise of a society.

The contextual dimension encompasses macro-level factors which set a favourable environment for comparative work and create a societal demand for the work of comparativists. In the 1950s and 1960s, the first comparative education societies were founded within a discourse of international under-standing, Cold War competition in education, national modernisation, and development in the post-World War II era. Similar discourses were evident in later decades in Eastern Europe and in other regions emerging from isolation, decolonisation and crises. Among the macro-level catalysts were government foreign policies which encouraged examination of educational models in other countries for policy improvement at home. Availability of funds for external study visits and international collaboration opened a new field of work, and attracted entrants to meet the demand for new knowledge. Comparative education as a new sub-field of knowledge with its distinctive purposes, methods and specialist literatures had been in existence before this period. The young shoots were institutionalised through courses on comparative education, some of which were compulsory, in universities and/or teachers' colleges. However, the new societal demand after World War II translated into a new phase in the development of the sub-field, marked by the formation of its scholarly societies.

Viewed from a sociological perspective, the new academic territory was inhabited by individuals who congregated with like-minded colleagues and formed local and later international scholarly networks. In this process, the entrepreneurial and charismatic leaders played a pivotal role in founding new societies and in encouraging other communities to follow. The new academic group was sensitive to its external environment and the changing characteristics of the societies, and their work reflected dynamic interplays of local and global factors.

Catalysts of Society Formation

Table 0.3 in the Introduction to this book indicated the decades during which the 36 WCCES member societies existing in 2007 were established. That table can usefully be elaborated upon. First it is pertinent to note the factors supporting the formation of the two oldest societies: the Comparative Education Society (CES) in the United States, which later became the Comparative and International Education Society (CIES), and the Comparative Education Society in Europe (CESE). Then it is instructive to observe ways in which these two societies, together with the umbrella WCCES, stimulated the formation of other societies. The generations of comparative education societies which came after these pioneers exhibited common patterns of lineage and discourse surrounding their establishment. Applying a simple form of social network analysis on the historical narratives in this book, one can see certain personalities and societies as having played a pivotal role in the histories of others (Schriewer 2005; see also Roldán Vera & Schupp 2006). Several genealogies can thus be identified (Figure 31.3).

Figure 31.3: Preliminary Genealogies of Comparative Education Societies

CIES (1956)	CESE (1961)	WCCES (1970)
JCES (1965)	British Section (1966)	SEEC (1974)
CIESC (1967)	German Section	SBEC (1983)
CESHK (1989)	(1966)	RCCE (1988)
CESA (1995)	CES-CSPS (1964)	APC-SEC (1994)
CESP (2001)	HPS-CES (1970)	CESA (1995)
SOMEC (2003)	AFEC (1973)	CESP (2001)
TCES (2006)	NGVO (1973)	SOMEC (2003)
	SEEC (1974)	TCES (2006)
	Italian Section (1986)	
	NOCIES (1992)	
	MESCE (2004)	

Note: The dates beside the society names refer to the foundation dates of the societies, not the initial contact with the 'catalyst' bodies.

In Chapter 9 of this book, Sherman Swing traced the beginnings of the CES (later CIES) to the scholarly community that had been gathering annually for the New York conferences organised by William Brickman. The purpose of these conferences, and the formation of the professional society, was to gain academic and professional recognition for the field, disassociating it from "junketlike tours abroad" and the resultant courses run by amateurs (Brickman 1977, p.398). More pragmatically, the creation of a formal body allowed the CES leadership to secure group rates for the study tours. These moves took place within the context of a favourable government policy and societal demand for teachers of comparative education, although also of some measure of societal mistrust of further connections with the Soviet Union.

Five years after the birth of the CES, CESE was formed as a European regional society. As Mitter recounted in Chapter 10, the founding members included distinguished European scholars together with institutional representation from UNESCO's International Bureau of Education (IBE) and the UNESCO Institute for Education (UIE). CESE's Statutes were drafted by a North American rather than a European: Joseph Katz, who modelled them after the CES Statutes. Katz was to become a pivotal figure in the field, as President of the CES, as founder of the Comparative and International Education Society of Canada (CIESC), then as founder of the WCCES.

The genealogy of the societies that were established after the CIES and CESE reveals some further instructive patterns. As recounted by Majhanovich and Zhang (Chapter 14), the CIESC began partly as a 'reaction' to the CES. Founder members considered forming a regional chapter or affiliate of the CES, but preferred an independent body. The CIESC was born in 1967 as the second North American national society.

The Japan Comparative Education Society (JCES) also owed part of its origin to developments in the USA. Ninomiya (Chapter 11) noted the influence of the New York conferences organised by Brickman, and some of the professors who formed the core group of the nascent JCES had studied comparative education in the United States or United Kingdom. Japan in the 1950s witnessed the institutionalisation of comparative education with a dual face: as an aid to teacher training courses in the national universities, and as an instrument of policy advice for the government.

In Europe, the German and British societies began as sections of CESE in 1966, tracing their roots to the 1961 founding conference of CESE at the University of London Institute of Education (see Waterkamp, Chapter 12; Sutherland, Watson & Crossley, Chapter 13). The German section had a parallel national body, and existed as the Commission for Comparative Education within the German Society for Education. The British section of CESE was not simultaneously part of another organisation, and became an independent national body (BCES) in 1979. The Italian section of CESE was established in 1986, and was admitted to the WCCES in 1987 as a quasi-national body.

Several other bodies also trace their roots to the CIES or CESE. Among the societies that have explicitly cited the role of the CIES as a catalyst or as a venue for their foundational meetings are those of Hong Kong, Asia, the Philippines, Mexico, and Turkey. In Europe, CESE's regional congresses provided a stimulus for the Dutch-speaking society (NGVO), and for the Nordic and Mediterranean societies.

The WCCES also played a major role in the creation and encouragement of several societies. The chapters on the Spanish and Cuban societies indicated that representation as a national body in the world body was a motivation to get themselves organised as a society. Thus, the Spanish society was formed explicitly with the intention of "being represented in the WCCES" (Tusquets 1971, p.377) and gaining stable links with other comparative education societies (García Garrido 2005). Similarly, the Cuban section (APC-SEC) was formed upon the encouragement of Erwin H. Epstein with a view to seeking admission to the WCCES. As Epstein (2004) explained: "Without the World Council, there would not have been sufficient motivation for them to come together as a group ... to project an international identity, to be part of the global picture".

The WCCES also catalysed society formation through the personal net-working of its officers, particularly the President and Secretary General. Its World Congresses and its Executive Committee meetings during the large CESE and later CIES conferences provided opportunities for the WCCES to exercise its networking and advocacy functions. The excitement and confluence of interna-tional scholars in World Congresses encouraged the revitalisation of smaller or weaker societies so that they could once more be living members of the global body. Examples from this book include the Brazilian society, which acknowl-edged the strong impulse it received from WCCES President Michel Debeauvais and Secretary General Raymond Ryba in organising its society and in the preparations for the 1987 World Congress in Rio de Janeiro. The Russian Council pointed to the participation of several Russian scholars in the 1987 Congress as decisive in their foundation as the Soviet Council of Comparative Pedagogics, and the Cuban Congress in the formation of a newly reorganised Russian body.

Mochida's chapter on CESA recalled that several Asian scholars started to think seriously about forming their own regional society during the 1992 World Congress in Prague. And SOMEC, which began from a core group of Mexican scholars who assiduously participated in CIES meetings, took shape as a national society with the encouragement of World Council President Mark Bray, who invited them to WCCES meetings.

Other societies have acknowledged the moral support received from WCCES officers in encouraging and, in some cases, revitalising their work. This has occurred through e-mail and other forms of communication in addition to meetings during international conferences. Among the bodies in which such support has been important are the Comparative Education Society of India (CESI), the Comparative Education Section of the Czech Pedagogical Society (CES-CPS), and the Comparative Education Society of the Philippines (CESP). The hosting by member societies of the World Congresses had, in the words of Masemann and Epstein (Chapter 1), "long-term effects on comparativists in the host country". Preparation for the 2004 Congress in Havana was particularly instructive in the way it introduced comparative education to university educators and postgraduate students all over Cuba (Hickling-Hudson, Chapter 7). It was also effective in germinating the seed of comparative education in other parts of Latin America, marked by the admission of the Mexican and the Argentinean societies in 2004 and 2005.

Advocacy of society formation has been particularly challenging in places where the institutional framework was weak. Hickling-Hudson (Chapter 7) posited that

> if a country has no comparative education subjects in its university system, it is unlikely that a new society can be established and maintained. It would take the work of one or more committed and influential comparative education scholars in the particular country to provide the leadership that would contribute to a successful society.... It is a voluntary task and a big demand on people's time, often not supported or rewarded by universities, so in some settings there is little motivation for academics to devote much time to it.

This is partly confirmed in the accounts in this book. However, the history of the Association francophone d'éducation comparée (AFEC) provides a different slant. Unlike its counterpart societies which were built on a core group of academics engaged in teaching comparative education, the Francophone society was born on French soil (though its scope extended to all Francophone countries) where comparative education and educational studies did not enjoy a strong status. Thus, AFEC was not founded on a strong academic base in teacher training or university studies. It addressed itself to educational administrators, together with educational researchers, and focused on sharing of experience and provision of information. Another body was formed in France in 1998, the Association française pour le développement de l'éducation comparée et des échanges (AFDECE), despite this rather narrow and fragile institutional context for comparative education. This scenario was echoed in other societies where the academic institutionalisation of comparative education was tenuous. The Mexican society (SOMEC), for example, was born in 2003 with no institutional base in teaching and research. As its founding President, Marco Aurelio Navarro described it (2005, p.15), in Mexico, comparative education was "still a field in construction".

Before turning to other genealogical groupings, it is interesting to observe that while CESE, a regional society in a diverse but relatively small continent, spawned several national, regional and language-based societies, a movement in the opposite direction was witnessed in Asia. The Asian regional society, CESA, was formed only in 1995, long after several Asian national societies had been created. These societies formed the backbone for the initial years, with the initial formation of CESA being achieved in Hong Kong and the first three biennial conferences being held in Japan, mainland China and Taiwan. Only in 2003 did CESA hold its first conference in a country which did not have its own comparative education society. This event was in Indonesia, and was followed in 2005 by Malaysia. However, in 2007 the CESA conference again moved to Hong Kong, and the society announced that the 2009 event would be in Korea. It can be surmised that the diversity and breadth of the Asian region, and perhaps the difficulty for comparative education to take root in various Asian countries, gave reason to create an Asian society as a home for Asian scholars dispersed throughout the region with no national society to which they could belong. The centre of gravity appeared to remain with the established strongholds, but they were prepared to contribute to the wider arena. The creation in 2005 of the Thailand Comparative and International Education Society (see Chapter 8) was in part due to CESA's social networking.

A fourth genealogical grouping salient in the 1990s embraced societies in the post-Soviet socialist countries: Bulgaria, Czechoslovakia, Poland and Russia. A common thread among these bodies was the work of international organisations such as UNESCO, which facilitated international scholarly collaboration and comparative work. The end of the Cold War with the dissolution of the Soviet Union in 1991 led to the independence of new nation-states, a phenomenon mirrored in the flourishing of national professional societies of comparative education from that region. As Masemann foretold in 1994 (p.947): "With the fragmentation of power blocs, there will be a proliferation of national societies". Masemann also correctly predicted some geomorphic shifts in the opposite direction. The Southern African Comparative and History of Education Society (SACHES) projected itself as a regional African association, striving to overcome the historic divide between South Africa and the rest of the continent (Soudien, Chapter 26). A similar discourse of regionalisation, though in a very different context, occurred in Europe. The Mediterranean Society of Comparative Education (MESCE) was born in 2004 with the explicit aim of fostering mutual understanding and peace through education in a region which embraced North Africa and Southern Europe.

Inhibitors of Society Growth

Cases of weak, dormant and dead societies exhibit a pathology characterised by a disruptive structural context such as the contraction of societal demand and/or the lack of individual leadership. The experience of the CES-CPS (formerly the Czech and Slovak Pedagogical Society – CSPS) illustrates this point. Formed in 1964, the society and its sections became dormant for two decades after the Soviet invasion of the country in 1968 and the inception of Communist rule. That period witnessed the censure of leading CSPS members after their public criticism of the prevailing ideology (see Walterová, Chapter 23).

This disruptive political context which muted comparative and international work had parallels in Bulgaria, China, East Germany, Hungary, Poland and Russia. As Popov noted with respect to Bulgaria (Chapter 24), during the period 1944-89, the "slightest interest in education in Western countries was considered a provocation and potentially even a crime". In China, the study of foreign education was discouraged in the mid-1980s, in the context of a campaign against spiritual pollution (Gu & Gui, Chapter 20).

A related but different pattern was reported by Sisson de Castro in Brazil (Chapter 21). The Sociedade Brasileira de Educação Comparada (SBEC) was formed in 1983 within a strong nationalist political environment and a highly politicised academic community. As explained in the chapter, "everything had to be black or white, leftist or rightist". The SBEC was considered rightist, which "created unnecessary resistance". Within this context, comparative education – with its practice of policy borrowing from other nations – was seen as an instrument of American imperialism and colonisation (Nogueira 2004; Verhine 2004). Comparative education was removed from the postgraduate programmes of Brazilian universities in the mid-1990s. Thus, despite the successful hosting of the World Congress in Rio de Janeiro in 1987, the SBEC's radius of action was undermined by factors beyond its control.

A different set of cases exhibits the role of institutional factors which constrained the growth of societies. A first typology relates to the contraction of institutional space for academic comparative education in teacher training colleges and universities. The decline in the teaching of the foundation courses including comparative education, and the discontinuation of graduate programmes in comparative and international education in some places, caused comparativists to redefine themselves academically, and was felt in the shortage of core specialists in society membership. This was among the experiences in Australia, Italy, Korea and, initially, Spain. Nevertheless, the dynamism and advocacy of the younger societies created a place for academic comparative education in teacher training universities, e.g. in Bulgaria.

Another typology, still under the category of institutional factors, relates to the competition from other professional societies which encroached on societies' territories and recruited from the same pools of members. This process was compounded by the fact that the vocational prospects of academic comparative education were not strong. Although Sutherland's comment in Chapter 16 was in the context of AFEC, her observation is applicable to other contexts where the role and relevance of comparative education was no longer clear. In the case of the SACHES, the scenario was made even more challenging by its complex racial dynamics and unequal access to resources. Soudien noted in Chapter 26 that "the organisation is confronted with the essence of the development conundrum confronting the region as a whole".

A third group illustrating the role of institutional factors relates to the competition from other professional societies in adjacent disciplinary domains (e.g. JCES and the Japan International Education Society), or overlapping linguistic or geographic territories (e.g. AFEC with respect to Canadian Francophone members; CESE with respect to members from European national societies). Limitations on funding for participation in international conferences discouraged membership of more than one society. As a result, many individuals opted for membership in their national bodies rather than wider organisations. While some bodies addressed competition by way of merger and consolidation, e.g. in the United Kingdom and Germany, others preferred to keep their independence and continued to struggle for survival in a competitive environment.

Finally, at the level of the individual, the obvious role of human agency or lack of it was decisive, particularly in weak societies. Some chapters in this volume cite the withdrawal of institutional support hinging upon the leader of the professional society (e.g. in Italy), or discontinuities in society leadership (e.g. in India and Southern Africa), or financial and at times language constraints inhibiting attendance at international meetings with other comparative education societies.

The Names of the Societies

Table 0.2 in the Introduction listed the 36 WCCES member societies in 2007, and Table 0.4 classified the societies by geography and type. All had some variant of Comparative Education in their names. Six societies included the related field of international education in their names, one linked comparative education with educational administration (Egypt), another linked it with history of education (Southern Africa), and a third included intercultural education with comparative and international education (Germany). Further, among the 36 WCCES members:

- 26 were Societies,
- three were Associations (AFDECE, AFEC, BAICE),
- two were Councils (Russia and Kazakhstan),
- four were specialised Comparative Education Sections in their respective national educational societies (Czech Republic, Cuba, Germany, and Hungary), and
- one (SICESE) operated as a quasi-national body but in constitutional terms was a section of a regional comparative education society.

The distinction between Societies and Associations was not of great significance. In French, the word Association is more commonly used than Society (*Société*) for academic bodies, with Society being in widespread use in the commercial sector. It was chiefly for that reason that the French translation of World Council of Comparative Education Societies, which was originally *Conseil mondial des sociétés d'éducation comparée* (CMSEC) was changed during the

1980s to *Conseil mondial des associations d'éducation comparée* (CMAEC). In the United Kingdom, the word Association had been used in the London Association of Comparative Educationists (LACE), which was formed under the leadership of Brian Holmes during the late 1970s but died during the 1980s. When the British Comparative and International Education Society (BCIES) merged with the British Association of Teachers and Researchers in Overseas Education (BATROE) to form the British Association for International and Comparative Education (BAICE), the new body used the word Association partly because it took the first two letters from BATROE and partly because the letters formed a good acronym.

In other cases, more important principles underlay the naming. For example, the Kazakh body chose to call itself a Council rather than a Society or an Association because its members desired the body to have authority to grant doctoral degrees. In Kazakhstan, such power was given only to academic councils, and not to academic societies or associations. Similar factors related to the Russian Council.

Also significant have been changes over time, which have reflected changes in the nature and mission of some bodies. Three categories of changes deserve more extended comment, namely a shift from comparative education to comparative *and* international education; a shift from comparative pedagogy to comparative education; and a shift from foreign to comparative education.

From Comparative to Comparative *and International* Education

The six WCCES member societies that had International Education in their names in 2007 were:

- the Comparative and International Education Society (CIES),
- the Sektion International und Interkulturell Vergleichende Erziehungswissenschaft in der Deutschen Gesellschaft für Erziehungswissenschaft (SIIVEDGE),
- the British Association for International and Comparative Education (BAICE),
- the Comparative and International Education Society of Canada (CIESC),
- the Australian and New Zealand Comparative and International Education Society (ANZCIES), and
- the Nordic Comparative and International Education Society (NOCIES).

As indicated in Chapter 14, in the CIESC "the international component of the society was acknowledged from the very outset". The only other member society that had, from the beginning, 'CIES' in its name was the Nordic society, established in 1992. The historical evolution of the names of the four older bodies – American, German, British, and Australian – reveals interesting patterns. They are discussed below in chronological order of the year in which they underwent the name change.

The CES existed for 12 years from 1956 without International in its name, and made the change a year after the founding of the CIESC. The society witnessed a changed composition with a constituency of members engaged in the applied field of international education, as distinguished from academics concerned with the theoretical and explanatory focus of comparative education. Paradoxically, by the time the CES changed its name to CIES, its 'international education' nature, characterised by its organisation of international study trips, had become less salient. The name change was motivated more by a practical circumstance: the membership thought the society would attract funding if it added International to its name. Thus, the name change was less a matter of academic dominance but of pragmatic convenience.

The British case tells a different story. The society in that country started as the British Section of CESE in 1966. It gradually diverged from its CESE parent, taking a more international and development orientation, and in 1979 became an independent national society called the British Comparative Education Society (BCES). Like its US counterpart, the British society witnessed a bifurcation of research interests between comparativists and those engaged in international education. As Sutherland, Watson and Crossley explained in Chapter 13:

> Two distinct but parallel fields of study were thus emerging.... [C]omparative education emphasised theory, methodology, and research in industrialised countries, while those involved in the study of education and development emphasised the improvement of educational planning, policy and practice in the developing world.

To reflect better the dual nature of its societal constituency, in 1983 the BCES became the BCIES. Fourteen years later, in response to a changed educational environment, it merged to create BAICE, but retained both International and Comparative in its title. This societal metamorphosis reflected broader patterns of transformation in academic and international affairs (Manzon & Bray 2006). As noted, comparative education societies are socially contextualised and are nested in wider environments that determine the shape of the academic territory, and in their turn, of the communities of academics who inhabit it.

The British phenomenon of separation and then consolidation in response to wider interactions was echoed in Germany. First was the German Section of CESE, formed in 1966 with a parallel membership as a commission of comparative education in the Deutschen Gesellschaft für Erziehungswissenschaft (DGfE – German Society for Education). This created the Kommission für Vergleichende Erziehungswissenschaft in der Deutschen Gesellschaft für Erziehungswissenschaft (KVEDGE). In 1978, a Commission for Education with the Third World was formed alongside the comparative education body in the DGfE, echoing the emergence of an international education community in the United States and Great Britain. An Intercultural Education Unit was also formed within the DGfE in 1992, reflecting the growing research interest in migration and its impact on education in German universities. In 1998, these three bodies were consolidated into one umbrella section, called the Section for International and

Intercultural Comparative Education (SIIVE), also known as SIIVEDGE. These transformations were catalysed by changing research interests and opportunities prevalent during the period. The initial fragmentation and splintering of research fields, as embodied in the proliferation of commissions and units, was later reversed with consolidation into one Section. Waterkamp explains in Chapter 12 that this was due to a paradigm shift adopting a 'One World' approach to comparative and international studies.

ANZCIES offers another interesting case. It began in 1973 as the Australian Comparative Education Society (ACES). Within a decade, it underwent three name changes: in 1975, it became the Australian and International Comparative Education Society (AICES); then the Australian Comparative and International Education Society (ACIES) in 1976; and finally in 1983, it became bi-national (and regional) as the Australian and New Zealand Comparative and International Education Society (ANZCIES). In the 1990s, ANZCIES witnessed further questioning about its identity, with "calls to move away from comparative to a focus on cultural analysis" (Fox, Chapter 17). As Fox added, "the naming of the society reflects the ongoing debate about its aims and purposes".

The debate about names and aims of societies (and of the field) remained vigorous. The above examples have demonstrated that the evolution in nomenclatures of the societies mirrors a parallel evolution in the field's object of study, its research interests, which is embodied sociologically in the population density of the academics who inhabit the territory. These academics in turn respond to wider forces in their habitats (international politics, institutional politics, funding policy, intellectual shifts, migration, etc.) which influence the shape and boundaries of their territory.

Table 31.1: Emergence of 'International Education' in Society Names

1950s	1960s	1970s	1980s	1990s
	CIESC (1967)			
CES (1956)	→CIES (1968)			
	British Section of →BCES (1979) CESE (1966)		→BCIES (1983)	→BAICE (1997)
	KVEDGE [Germany] (1966)	→	→	→ SIIVEDGE (1998)
		ACES [Australia] (1973); AICES (1975); ACIES(1976) →	ANZCIES (1983)	
				NOCIES (1992)

Mapped on a timeline (Table 31.1), patterns of chronological proximity emerge. Applying the typology of the diffusion of innovations (Rogers 2003), the North Americans took the lead in the late 1960s. The Canadian society was the innovator, and the US society an early adopter. The Australian and British societies followed, and it was perhaps not insignificant that all four societies served Anglophone countries (or that Joseph Katz argued in all four cases in favour of the wider nomenclature). The spread to Germany and the Nordic countries brought diversification, but may also have reflected the growing dominance of English, and its accompanying values, as the language of international academic discourse. It also reflected the strengthening work of the governments in these countries in international aid.

Elsewhere, the Spanish society in 1984 considered modelling its name after the CIES, but the proposal was not implemented (Naya & Ferrer, Chapter 19). Similarly, the Japan Comparative Education Society, whose host country was actively engaged in international development assistance, considered adding International to its name in the mid-1990s. The move was stalled by awareness that renaming the society would cause confusion and overlap with an existing society called Japan International Education Society (see Chapter 11). Scholars in neighbouring China also wanted to incorporate 'international education' in their institutions. In 1995, under the leadership of Gu Mingyuan, the Institute of Comparative Education in Beijing Normal University was renamed the Institute of International and Comparative Education (see Chapter 20). Perhaps surprisingly, China's national professional society retained its name, Chinese Comparative Education Society. Gu (2005) reasoned that there was no need, just as the WCCES did not change its name. Yet the Thailand Comparative and International Education Society, which was formed in 2005 and which was encouraged to apply for WCCES membership (see Chapter 8), seemed to be part of the trend of formally pairing International Education with Comparative Education. At the same time, the fact that none of the other 30 WCCES constituent societies had the word International in their titles demonstrated that international education was not universally paired with comparative education – and indeed it was not universally recognised as a strong field in its own right in tandem with comparative education (Manzon & Bray 2006, p.72). Another explanation may be that the some communities had their own separate societies, such as the International Society for Educational Planning.

A further qualification is that although all the WCCES societies had Comparative Education in their names, there was some divergence between the work done by the avowed members of these societies and the academic field they professed to support. The comparative characteristic was not universally exhibited in the work of the societies which bore this label. As several chapters have observed, much research done within the field was not strictly comparative. Much had only single units/sites of analysis, and fitted more easily under the label of foreign education or education abroad. The name Comparative Education was commonly used, but also commonly abused.

From Comparative Pedagogy to Comparative Education

The marked historical transition in the usage of the terms 'comparative pedagogy' and 'comparative education' is illustrated by several societies in Europe. For example, although the German professional society did not use 'comparative pedagogy' in its name, the designation of the field witnessed a shift. As Waterkamp explained in Chapter 12:

> 'Pädagogik' [Pedagogy] indicates a collection of knowledge that is not only of interest to scholars and possibly politicians, but also to teachers and other practitioners. Like other educational disciplines which use the term 'Päda-gogik', comparative pedagogy aims to remain a practical science. By contrast, the term 'Vergleichende Erziehungswissenschaft' [Comparative Education] announces an orientation to disciplinary and interdisciplinary scientific dis-courses.

Waterkamp noted that up to the 1960s, in a Germany divided by the Cold War both East and West Germans used the older terminology 'comparative pedagogy' (Vergleichende Pädagogik). But later, partly under the influence of Berger's (1976) textbook, *Vergleichende Erziehungswissenschaft*, many West Germans changed to the expression 'comparative education' and argued for the redefinition of pedagogy as a 'science of education'.

The East-West German divide in the designation of the field reflected in microcosm a wider global bi-polarity during the Cold War period. The terms 'pedagogy' and 'comparative pedagogy' prevailed in the Soviet Union and Eastern Europe (see chapters on Bulgaria, Czech Republic, Russia and Poland, and accounts on Hungary and Kazakhstan in Chapter 30), as well as in Spain, Cuba and Greece. Comparative pedagogy was reflected in the names of the:

- Sociedad Española de Pedagogía Comparada (SEPC),
- Russian Council of Comparative Pedagogics (RCCP),
- Comparative Education Section of the Czech Pedagogical Society (CES-CPS),
- Hungarian Pedagogical Society, Comparative Education Section (HPS-CES), and
- Asociación de Pedagogos de Cuba, Sección de Educación Comparada (APC-SEC).

In Spain, the original name of the field was Pedagogía Comparada [Comparative Pedagogy]. Consequently, its institutional infrastructures including its professional society used this term. As early as 1980 there was a move within the SEPC to rename itself the Sociedad Española de Educación Comparada (SEEC), echoing debates in other European scholarly circles (see e.g. Martínez 2003). This name was finally introduced in 1994. The final push for change came from the ever-wider usage of 'comparative education' in Spanish publications, as well as the government policy directive making comparative education a com-pulsory subject in education degree courses (see Chapter 19).

The case of the Russian Council of Comparative Education (RCCE) offers two aspects for comment. First, the original professional society formed in 1988 within the Soviet Union was called the Scientific Council on Comparative Pedagogics (SCCP). This was admitted to the WCCES in 1989 under the English-language name Soviet Council of Comparative Education (SCCE), but ceased to exist after the collapse of the Soviet Union. Its successor body, the Russian Council of Comparative Pedagogics (RCCP), was admitted to the WCCES in 1996, but subsequent English-language usage within the WCCES converged on RCCE in echo of the predecessor SCCE, even though this name was not in standard usage within Russia itself. This second 'name change' shows the preference for Comparative Education in the English-language version of the name, and seems to have reflected the dominant international discourse rather than the local (national) one.

From Foreign Education to Comparative Education

The German and Chinese cases offer further interesting points for reflection on the use of foreign education in contrast to comparative education. In the late 1950s, institutions in the German Democratic Republic [East Germany] made a distinction between foreign countries and West Germany, since West Germany was not considered a foreign country. However, the term 'comparative education' was not used at that time since most work was descriptive or consisted of translated articles of foreign authors. From 1963 to 1974, a Department for Comparative Education existed in East Berlin, and comparative work between East and West flourished. This phase came to a close in 1974, and the term Comparative Education was replaced by Education Abroad, since comparisons were once more viewed by the authorities as ideologically risky. Only in 1990 did comparisons become visible again, though initially under the name Comparative Pedagogy rather than Comparative Education.

China offers a related story. The professional society in China initially started as a Foreign Education Research Sub-commission of the Chinese Society of Education (CSE), which was China's largest learned society in the field of education. In 1983, the sub-commission's name was changed from Foreign Education to Comparative Education. As Gu and Gui explain in Chapter 20, the name change reflected a change of understanding about the nature of comparative education as a sub-discipline of educational science, and a desire to provide reference for educational reform at home by identifying general laws in the development of education through comparative analyses. This new understanding of the nature and purpose of comparative education took place against the backdrop of China's Open Door Policy, which aimed to accelerate national development by importing knowledge from all pertinent locations. A partial offshoot of these new thrusts was the renaming of several institutes of foreign education as institutes of comparative education. However, as Gu and Gui note, in practice much of the work done in China would have continued to fit more easily under the old label than the new one.

Positioning, Membership and Publications

Among the questions asked by Cowen and listed above was: "What is the critical mass of interested persons in comparative education?'. The answer appears to vary in different locations and at different points in time. It is related to the positioning of professional societies within their national or regional scientific communities, and to the activities which societies aspire to undertake.

Positioning the Comparative Education Societies

The chapters in this book provide examples of each category in Clark's (1987) classification of disciplinary associations as the umbrella bodies, spider-web groupings which weave themselves around larger associations, and pyramidal networks within individual disciplines which feed into national associations. Applying this typology to the professional groupings of comparative educators, the WCCES is an umbrella organisation comprising national member societies. CESE could be described as a pyramidal structure comprising national sections which have their counterpart groupings in the respective home countries. The spider-web

Table 31.2 Comparative Education Societies in National Settings

Society (Year Founded)	Affiliate of (duration)
AFEC (1973) and AFDECE (1998)	Centre international d'études pédagogiques
APC-SEC (1994)	Asociación de Pedagogos de Cuba
BAICE (1966 as British Section of CESE)	United Kingdom Forum for International Education and Training (1991-) and joint conference with British Educational Research Association (2003-)
CCES (1979)	Chinese Society of Education
CES/CIES (1956)	Joint meetings with the National Society of College Teachers of Education, the American Association of Colleges of Teacher Education, and the Association of Student Teaching (1956-70)
CES-CSPS (1964; became CES-CPS 1990)	Czechoslovak Pedagogical Society and Czechoslovak Academy of Sciences (1964-70); Czech Pedagogical Society (1990-)
CIESC (1967)	Canadian Society for the Study of Education (1972-), joint meetings at the Conference of Learned Societies (1967-) and the Congress of Humanities and Social Sciences (1998-).
HPS-CES (1970)	Hungarian Pedagogical Society; National Pedagogical Library and Museum
ICES (1988)	Israeli Association for Educational Research
KCES (1968)	Korean Society for the Study of Education (1970-)
RCCE (1988 as SCCP; 1995 as RCCP)	USSR Academy of Pedagogical Sciences (1988-89); Russian Academy of Education (1995-)
SACHES (1991)	Kenton Education Association
SBEC (1983)	Associação Nacional de Política e Administração da Educação
SIIVEDGE (1966)	Deutschen Gesellschaft für Erziehungswissenschaft

associations are more numerous. Table 31.2 lists the societies which are (or have been) affiliated or linked with national scientific societies, and notes evolutions over time. These transformations reflect wider epistemological and pragmatic forces which have centrifugal or centripetal effects.

The CIES (then CES) was initially identified with teacher education and until 1970 had held its meetings in Chicago jointly with professional societies in that field (e.g. National Society of College Teachers of Education). Sherman Swing noted in Chapter 9 that by 1965, "there was talk of autonomous meetings or of meetings in which the intellectual focus was oriented more toward philosophy and the social sciences than toward teacher education". In 1969, the CIES decided to hold its independent meetings. The decision may have been motivated by the simple reason of wanting to meet at a venue other than Chicago. It can however be surmised that, against the backdrop of changes in the intellectual orientation of comparative education in the US, it signalled a veering away from teacher education towards the social sciences and philosophy.

The Canadian society (CIESC) began as an independent body in 1967, but held joint meetings at the Conference of Learned Societies. Then in 1972 the CIESC became one of five founding associations to form an umbrella organisation, the Canadian Society for the Study of Education. Moreover, the Canadian society had from the beginning allied itself with associations of higher education and adult education as well as teacher education and educational research.

A third case is that of the British society (BAICE), which began as the British Section of CESE in 1966 and underwent several subsequent trans-formations. In 1991, it became a member of a British umbrella organisation, the United Kingdom Forum for International Education and Training (UKFIET), which brought together under one roof the then British Comparative and International Education Society (BCIES) with several other bodies. This consoli-dation was brought about by a changed institutional and epistemological environ-ment entailing a reconceptualisation of the field in the United Kingdom.

The WCCES member societies which are constituted as sections of their own national pedagogical societies include the Cuban, Czech and Hungarian bodies. The membership in the sections as a proportion of the total national body has varied. For example, in 2007 the comparative education section in Cuba had 90 members out of 13,000 in the APC, while the section in Hungary had 50 members out of 2,000 in the HPS.

In terms of the links that the comparative education societies had with their respective governments, the CIES cited the role of the US Office of Education in its foundation. The Japan society's Secretariat was housed in the National Insti-tute of Educational Research, where Masunori Hiratsuka, the JCES founding President, had been employed. Under a similar arrangement, SICESE had for several years enjoyed strong links with the Centro Europeo dell'Educazione, which was a think-tank under the patronage of the Italian Ministry of Education. The Hungarian Pedagogical Society was supported by Hungary's Ministry of Education and the National Library.

As for institutional links with international organisations, one supranational body commonly cited by comparative education societies in this book as having been a catalyst or a support for their work was UNESCO, including its institutes and most notably the IBE and UIE. Other supportive supranational bodies have included the World Bank, the Organisation for Economic Co-operation and Development, the Council of Europe, and the European Union.

Membership and Inclusiveness

Crane (1972) pointed to the role of scientific communities in the growth and diffusion of knowledge. She identified two important groups in the social organisation of research areas: first, groups of collaborators with direct ties; and second, a communication network or 'invisible college' of productive scientists linking separate groups of collaborators within a research area. Crane described networks as being open or closed, admitting the existence of a large outer circle of professional acquaintances or, by contrast, limited to a small inner circle of specialists. Most WCCES member societies were fairly open groupings. Some were extremely open with no clear admission criteria (e.g. CESA), and/or did not charge membership fees (e.g. RCCE, NGVO). For these bodies it suffices for potential members to have an interest in comparative education or its related fields such as international education, development education or cross-cultural studies. By contrast, other societies were closed or fairly elitist networks (e.g. BCES, GCES), requiring members to have at least a Master's degree plus research experience in comparative education and publications. The SEEC began as a heterogeneous group of academics from different disciplinary areas, but after comparative education became a compulsory subject in Spanish universities in 1994, the society gradually changed its membership profile and in 2007 had 140 specialists in its ranks. Most societies have mixed profiles of members from teacher training colleges, university departments of education, international organisations, research institutes, and, sometimes, government bodies.

Most societies admit individual members only, but a few also have institutional members (e.g. CIES, CESE, CCES). In the Chinese society (CCES), all scholars working in a research centre or department of comparative education that is an institutional member of the CCES can consider themselves to be CCES members. Indeed, the CCES has very few individual members, and most of the people in that category are overseas students (see Chapter 20). The WCCES itself goes one step further: it admits only duly-constituted professional societies, including specialist sections of national educational associations as member societies which have equal rights of voice and vote. Epstein records in Chapter 2 that throughout the 1980s the WCCES heard advocacy of bicameral structure with one part representing comparative education societies and the other composed of individuals from countries without a society to represent them. However, this proposal was subsequently formally voted down.

The WCCES member societies have also exhibited diversity in organisational leadership. While some societies have explicitly addressed the democratic nature of the election of officers and have had clear policies on term limits (e.g. CIES), others have been less stringent. Some societies have reported Presidents having tenures of 14 years or more (e.g. BCES, KCES, JCES, CCES, PCES).

Similar remarks apply to the locations of conferences. Organisers have to be mindful of the economics of operations, and tend therefore to hold events in centres of population which are transportation hubs. This observation applies to national societies as much as to regional and language-based bodies. Among the regional societies, CESE, SACHES and CESA have made strong efforts to hold conferences in different countries of their regions, though have also been mindful that some voices and locations have been represented more strongly than others.

Society Publications

Journals are important vehicles for disciplinary institutionalisation and knowledge legitimation. Altbach (1994) noted an implicit hierarchy among journals, with the top level occupied by specialist international journals, followed by interdisciplinary international journals, and then the regional/national journals. Some comparative education societies run journals, although not all belong to the first category. Moreover, other scholarly journals focusing on comparative education exist outside the sphere of the professional societies. Masemann (1994, p.947) observed that some comparative education societies published significant journals and conference proceedings. The decade that followed Masemann's remarks brought huge developments, to some extent supported by new technologies (Wilson 2003; Naya 2005).

Among the 36 WCCES member societies existing in 2007, only 13 were operating society-sponsored journals (Table 31.3). This low number to some extent reflected the difficulties of sustaining journals, which require not only a constant flow of adequate-quality submissions but also considerable labour for refereeing, editing, page-setting, distribution, etc.. Some journals had histories extending for several decades, but others were recent initiatives which were yet to stand the test of time. With the striking exception of the *Comparative Education Review* (USA) which was launched a year after its society sponsor was established, most journals had a fairly long gestation period. Seven journals came into being within 10 years from the births of their societies; but three were only within 20 years, one (SEEC) was after 21 years, and one (ANZCIES) was after 24 years.

Not included in Table 31.3 are endeavours which have not been sustained. For example, Sutherland records in Chapter 16 that in 2001 AFEC launched a journal entitled *Politiques d'éducation et de formation: Analyses et comparaisons internationales*. The journal was jointly operated with the Institut européen d'éducation et de politique sociale (IEEPS) and the Institut européen pour la promotion et l'innovation de la culture dans l'éducation (EPICE). It was published by De Boeck in Brussels, Belgium, and appeared three times a year. However, after three years (nine issues), AFEC dropped out. The journal continued for two more issues with just IEEPS and EPICE, but then ceased publication altogether. The experience showed the demands of operating journals and the complexities of collaboration with other organisations.

Partly with awareness of such challenges, some societies have focused more on books and proceedings than journals. For example, Mitter refers in Chapter 10 to several of the books published following CESE conferences; and Chapter 30 refers to the series of books sponsored by AFDECE in its *Collection éducation comparée.* The Chinese Comparative Education Society-Taipei (CCES-T) publishes both a journal and periodic books.

Table 31.3: Journals of WCCES Member Societies, 2007

Society Name (year established)	Society Journal	Year Journal Commenced	Language(s) of Journal
CES/CIES (1956)	*Comparative Education Review*	1957	English
BAICE (1966)	*Compare: A Journal of Comparative Education*	1970	English
KCES (1968)	*Korean Journal of Comparative Education* (formerly *World Culture and Education*)	1971	Korean
CIESC (1967)	*Canadian and International Education*	1972	English, French
JCES (1965)	*Comparative Education* (formerly *The Bulletin of Japan Comparative Education Society*)	1975	Japanese
CCES (1979)	*Comparative Education Review* (formerly *Foreign Education Conditions*)	1991	Chinese (simplified characters)
SEEC (1974)	*Revista Española de Educación Comparada*	1995	Spanish, French, English
SACHES (1991)	*Southern African Review of Education*	1995	English
CCES-T (1974)	*Journal of Comparative Education* (launched 1982 as a newsletter)	1997	Chinese (traditional characters)
CESHK (1989)	*Comparative Education Bulletin* (launched 1993 as a newsletter)	1998	English; Chinese (traditional characters)
GCES (1991)	*Comparative and International Education Review*	2002	Greek, English
CESA (1995)	*Compare: Journal of the Comparative Education Society of Asia*	2006	English
ANZCIES (1973)	*The International Education Journal: Comparative Perspectives*	2007	English

Another dimension of Table 31.3 deserving comment is the language of publication. Among the 13 journals, nine were at least partly in English, reflecting the growing global dominance of that language. The journals from Korea, Japan, and mainland China and Taiwan were exclusively in the official languages of those jurisdictions (i.e. Korean, Japanese and Chinese). Canada has two official languages – English and French – and published its journal in both those languages; and a similar remark applied to Hong Kong where the official languages are English and Chinese. However, the Greek journal published in English as well as Greek even though English was not an official language of Greece; and the Spanish journal published a few articles in English and French even though those are not official languages in Spain. The SACHES and CESA journals were exclusively in English even though they served multiple countries with multiple official languages.

Common Patterns, Uncommon Themes

This concluding chapter has shown both commonality and diversity among the comparative education societies. It has shown that the society can itself be an instructive unit for analysis to understand the changes in demand and supply of comparative education on a world basis and the factors which determine them. The societies both reflect and interact with their wider contexts, and, as Cowen (1990) pointed out, are socially contextualised.

Parts of the literature on disciplinary institutionalisation and scholarly networking help to explain the patterns set out in this book. Becher and Trowler used the metaphor of tribes and territories to describe processes in disciplinary formation. Although speaking of the social sciences, Wagner and Wittrock's (1991b, pp.349-350) description of disciplinary development as diachronic and exhibiting highly dissimilar and uneven levels in different geographic locations is echoed in the field of comparative education. This field of study sought to create its own identity, and the formation of both the individual societies and the world body assisted in this process. Yet, in the field of comparative education, as in other domains, the process has not been straightforward.

The uneven process of development of the field is partly explained by its socially constructed nature. This chapter has noted the diverse ways in which global and local forces shaped the contours of comparative education societies, ranging from the national, regional and language-based groupings to the global confederation of the WCCES. With reference to the analytical framework in Figure 31.2, the histories in this book demonstrated the interplay of the political, epistemological and sociological factors at the macro, meso and micro levels. They pointed to the different pathways that led to the formation of comparative education*s* in the plural, which, by analogy, are partially embodied by the comparative education societ*ies*. These comparative education societies in turn comprise the WCCES confederation; and, as the historical demography of the WCCES shows, its global forums are "the most visible points where the national and international modalities of comparative education intersect" (Cowen 1990, p.339). In and through the World Council and its Congresses, the dialectic of the national and the international comparative educations is played out over time. This dialectic remits to forces which are outside the field of comparative education but which shape and act on the different comparative education*s* which comprise it. Cowen elucidated this point. He took the World Congress as a unit of analysis, but could also have referred to the World Council (1990, p.342):

> The World Congress itself has mirrored in microcosm some of the eco-
> nomic power, and networks of political influence of the world outside of
> comparative education. Some of the strains of that external divided world
> are likely to become more visible in the politics of the Council....[T]he
> World Council and the World Congress of Comparative Education Socie-
> ties is that part of our professional infrastructure where the national and the
> international elements in our professional identity meet most visibly.

The epistemological and political tensions have also been felt at the level of
the societies. Even the largest and strongest society, the CIES, has had to grapple
with ambiguities in its mission and mandate. The CIES has chosen to be an
inclusive body, a policy which has assisted in its growth but raised challenges
about its internal coherence. Other societies are elitist and therefore necessarily
smaller, but they also confront ambiguities in mode of operation. These and other
examples discussed in this chapter epitomize the political and epistemological
price tags which have come with the worldwide diffusion of comparative
education (Cowen 1990, p.343).

Borrowing the terminology of Clark (1987), the scholarly bodies have been
classified into the umbrella association (i.e. the WCCES), a set of spider-web
groupings, and a set of pyramid networks. The chapter has also noted aspects of
genealogy in the field, and evolutions in names. Concerning the last of these, a
common colloquial question in diverse settings is: 'What's in a name?'. In this
case, the reply might be "a lot". Paraphrasing Michael Sadler's description of a
national system of education (original 1900, reprinted 1964, p.310), it can be said
that a professional society is "a living thing, the outcome of forgotten struggles
and 'of battles long ago'", and that it "has in it some of the secret workings of
national life". An exploration of the historical evolution of society names
uncovers the living nature of scholarly societies and their 'battles of long ago'.
Nomenclatures designate the nature of the realities they represent. While society
names depict the reality of the academic groups they stand for, names of
disciplines and fields encapsulate the essence of the academic field that they see as
their domain. Knowledge and its social organisation are both dynamic processes,
and the names of both societies and the field as a whole can be expected to
continue to evolve.

This chapter and the book as a whole have highlighted the social networking
role of scholarly societies, fostering friendship and scholarly exchange. These
networks "stabilise the discipline across international frontiers" (Schriewer 2005);
and if they are successful, they attract young scholars and thus new blood. In this
respect, the WCCES has played the unique role of, in Aristotelian terms, a *final
cause* (that for the sake of which a thing is done), serving as an incentive for a
society to be organised *in order to* become a constituent society of the world body.
Its World Congresses have also been, despite the political and epistemological
tensions, a fertile seedbed for fostering an environment of scholarly camaraderie and
of awakening a sense of national, linguistic or regional identity that in due course

becomes incarnated in a comparative education society. It could also be surmised that the operation of a visible global body might attract new entrants or persuade sceptical onlookers about the benefits of joining the field of comparative education.

Yet these positive signs of life do not necessarily augur well for the field of comparative education. An optimistic reading of the growth in the number of societies needs to be tempered with the realisation that there is diversity in size, inner cohesion, scholarly expertise, and status within their respective national and regional scientific communities. Patterns are thus complex and open to multiple interpretations.

The Introduction to this book explained the reason for the choice of title. It noted that Joseph Katz (1970, p.5) had written in the preface to the Proceedings of the 1st World Congress of Comparative Education Societies that:

> The Congress itself is evidence that people will work together to achieve not only common but uncommon goals as well.

The book has echoed this observation, noting ways in which scholars have worked together in the global arena as well as in regional, national and local settings, and in this sense, has shown the international interplay of comparative educations (Cowen 1990, p.322). Many of them have had common goals, including the advancement of conceptual understanding. At the same time, they have had uncommon goals in the sense of distinctiveness arising from a special mission. This includes promotion of international and intercultural understanding, and improvement of both policy and practice in the education of future generations, as well as the highly idealistic goals of its founders.

The book as a whole, and this chapter in particular, has also stressed the diversity in characteristics and modes of operation of comparative education societies. Some are large and pluralistic while others are small and elitist; some have deep roots while others are younger creations; some have strong governance structures while others are less robust. One of the elements that brings them together is membership of the World Council. Within the organisational space provided by this global body are many currents and counter-currents; but the WCCES has clearly played a useful role and has contributed to the discourse of the field.

Kazamias (2001) called for the re-invention of the historical dimension in comparative education, arguing that this, among other benefits, would help to humanise the field (p.439). This work on the histories of comparative education societies is a major response to that call, and the editors hope that it will be a catalyst for further historical research. Histories, by their nature, are backward-looking documents which describe the patterns of the past and present interpretations of those patterns. But histories can also be guides to the future. This book has charted uncertainties as well as more positive dimensions; and the present chapter, in particular, has highlighted some circumstances in which organisational structures as well as fields of study can get overtaken by broader circumstances. It also shows reasons why the field of comparative education has grown vigorously in certain parts of the world and during particular periods of time. Further, it illustrates some of the factors which can make participation in the field and in its organisational structures a very rewarding experience. Both the common and the uncommon goals will continue to provide much vibrancy to the field at multiple levels during the decades to come.

References

Altbach, Philip G. (1994): 'International Knowledge Networks', in Husén, Torsten & Postlethwaite, T. Neville (eds.), *The International Encyclopedia of Education*, 2nd edition. Oxford: Pergamon Press, pp.2993-2998.

Becher, Tony & Trowler, Paul R. (2001): *Academic Tribes and Territories: Intellectual Enquiry and the Cultures of Disciplines*, 2nd edition. Buckingham: The Society for Research into Higher Education and Open University Press.

Berger, Walter (1976): *Die Vergleichende Erziehungswissenschaft: Einführung – Forschungsskizzen – Methoden*. Wien: Jugend und Volk Verlag.

Brickman, William W. (1977): 'Comparative and International Education Society: An Historical Analysis'. *Comparative Education Review*, Vol.21, Nos.2/3, pp.396-404.

Clark, Burton R. (1987): *The Academic Life: Small Worlds, Different Worlds*. Princeton: The Carnegie Foundation for the Advancement of Teaching.

Coser, Lewis (1965): *Men of Ideas*. New York: Free Press of Glencoe.

Cowen, Robert (1990): 'The National and International Impact of Comparative Education Infrastructures', in Halls, W.D. (ed.), *Comparative Education: Contemporary Issues and Trends*. Paris: UNESCO and London: Jessica Kingsley, pp.321-352.

Crane, Diana (1972): *Invisible Colleges: Diffusion of Knowledge in Scientific Communities*. Chicago: University of Chicago Press.

Epstein, Erwin H. (1981): 'Toward the Internationalization of Comparative Education: A Report on the World Council of Comparative Education Societies'. *Comparative Education Review*, Vol.25, No.2, pp.261-271.

Epstein, Erwin H. (2004): Interview by Maria Manzon, Havana, Cuba, 25 October.

García Garrido, José Luis (2005): Personal communication with Maria Manzon, 13 March.

Graham, Loren; Lepenies, Wolf & Weingart, Peter (1983): *Functions and Uses of Disciplinary Histories*. Dordrecht: D. Reidel Publishing Company.

Gu, Mingyuan (2005): Interview by Maria Manzon, Beijing Normal University, Beijing, China, 23 August.

Katz, Joseph (1970): 'The Purpose, Plan and Program for the World Congress of Comparative Education Societies', in *Proceedings of the First World Congress of Comparative Education Societies*, Vol.2. Ottawa: Secretariat, World Council for Comparative Education, pp.4-5.

Kazamias, Andreas M. (2001): 'Re-inventing the Historical in Comparative Education: Reflections on a *Protean Episteme* by a Contemporary Player'. *Comparative Education*, Vol.37, No.4, pp.439-449.

Klein, Julie Thompson (1990): *Interdisciplinarity: History, Theory, and Practice*. Detroit: Wayne State University Press.

Lambert, Peter (2003): 'The Professionalization and Institutionalization of History', in Berger, Stefan; Feldner, Heiko & Passmore, Kevin (eds.), *Writing History: Theory and Practice*. London: Arnold, pp.42-60.

Lauglo, Jon (1996): 'Evolution of Networks: Evolution from Networks', in McGinn, Noel (ed.), *Crossing Lines: Research and Policy Networks for Developing Country Education*. Westport: Praeger, pp.7-10.

Manicas, Peter T. (1990): 'The Social Science Disciplines: The American Model', in

Wagner, Peter; Wittrock, Björn and Whitley, Richard (eds.), *Discourses on Society: The Shaping of the Social Science Disciplines.* Dordrecht: Kluwer Academic Publishers, pp.45-72.

Manzon, Maria & Bray, Mark (2006): 'The CIES and the WCCES: Leadership, Ambiguities and Synergies'. *Current Issues in Comparative Education*, Vol.8, No.2, pp.69-83.

Martínez, María Jesús (2003): *Educación Comparada: Nuevos Retos, Renovados Desafíos.* Madrid: La Muralla.

Masemann, Vandra (1994): 'Comparative Education Societies', in Husén, Torsten & Postlethwaite, T. Neville (eds.), *The International Encyclopedia of Education.* 2nd. Oxford: Pergamon Press, pp.942-948.

McGinn, Noel F. (ed.) (1996): *Crossing Lines: Research and Policy Networks for Developing Country Education.* Westport: Praeger.

Navarro, Marco Aurelio (2005) (ed.): *La Educación Comparada en México: Un Campo en Construcción.* México: Editorial SOMEC-Universidad Autónoma de Tamaulipas.

Naya, Luis M. (2005): 'La Educación Comparada en los Nuevos Espacios Virtuales (1995-2004)'. *Revista Española de Educación Comparada*, No.11, pp.241-272.

Nogueira, Sonia (2004): Interview by Maria Manzon, Havana, Cuba, 29 October.

Rogers, Everett M. (2003): *Diffusion of Innovations*, 5th edition. New York: Free Press.

Roldán Vera, Eugenia & Schupp, Thomas (2006): 'Network Analysis in Comparative Social Sciences'. *Comparative Education*, Vol.42, No.3, pp.405-429.

Sadler, Michael (1964 reprint [original 1900]): 'How Far Can We Learn Anything of Practical Value from the Study of Foreign Systems of Education?'. *Comparative Education Review*, Vol.7, No.3, pp.307-314.

Schriewer, Jürgen (2005): Interview by Maria Manzon, Beijing, China, 23 August.

Tusquets, Juan (1971): 'La Personalidad, el Pensamiento y la Obra de P. Rosselló'. *Perspectivas Pedagógicas*, No.27, pp.333-381.

Verhine, Robert (2004): Interview by Maria Manzon, Havana, Cuba, 27 October.

Wagner, Peter & Wittrock, Björn (1991a): 'Analyzing Social Science: On the Possibility of a Sociology of the Social Sciences', in Wagner, Peter; Wittrock, Björn & Whitley, Richard (eds.), *Discourses on Society: The Shaping of the Social Science Disciplines.* Dordrecht: Kluwer Academic Publishers, pp.3-22.

Wagner, Peter & Wittrock, Björn (1991b): 'States, Institutions, and Discourses: A Comparative Perspective on the Structuration of the Social Sciences', in Wagner, Peter; Wittrock, Björn & Whitley, Richard (eds.), *Discourses on Society: The Shaping of the Social Science Disciplines.* Dordrecht: Kluwer Academic Publishers, pp.331-357.

Wagner, Peter; Wittrock, Björn & Whitley, Richard (eds.) (1991): *Discourses on Society: The Shaping of the Social Science Disciplines.* Dordrecht: Kluwer Academic Publishers.

Watson, Keith (1996): 'Professional Associations and Academic Networks: Some Observations for the United Kingdom', in McGinn, Noel (ed.), *Crossing Lines: Research and Policy Networks for Developing Country Education.* Westport: Praeger, pp.129-133.

Wilson, David N. (2003): 'The Future of Comparative and International Education in a Globalised World', in Bray, Mark (ed.), *Comparative Education: Continuing Traditions, New Challenges and New Paradigms.* Dordrecht: Kluwer Academic Publishers, pp.14-33.

Notes on the Authors

Nina BOREVSKAYA received her PhD from the Moscow State University and her postdoctoral degree in history at the Institute of Far Eastern Studies (IFES) of the Russian Academy of Sciences (Moscow, Russia). She was a recipient of the IREX Fellowship award at State University of New York at Buffalo, USA (1994-95). She is a leading scholar at the IFES. Her primary research interests involve educational policy, sociology and economics of education, educational history in China as well as comparative education. She is a Vice-President of the Russian Council of Comparative Education (RCCE) and was a member of the Research Standing Committee (2003-06) of the World Council of Comparative Education Societies (WCCES). *Correspondence*: Institute of Far Eastern Studies, Russian Academy of Sciences, Nakhimovsky Prosp. 32, Moscow 117218, Russia. E-mail: borevskaya@ifes-ras.ru.

Mark BRAY is Director of UNESCO's International Institute for Educational Planning (IIEP). Prior to taking that post in March 2006, he held various posts at the University of Hong Kong, including Director of the Comparative Education Research Centre (CERC). He was Assistant Secretary General of the World Council of Comparative Education Societies (WCCES) from 1994 to 2000, and then became Secretary General (2000-05). He was WCCES President from 2004 to 2007. He is also a past President of the Comparative Education Society of Hong Kong (1998-2000), and has served on the Boards of Directors of the Comparative and International Education Society (CIES) and the Comparative Education Society of Asia (CESA). *Correspondence*: UNESCO International Institute for Educational Planning, 7-9 rue Eugène Delacroix, 75116 Paris, France. E-mail: m.bray@iiep. unesco.org.

Sylvia van de BUNT-KOKHUIS is Associate Professor of Human Resources Management at the Haagse Hogeschool in The Hague, Netherlands, and lecturer of Business Studies at the Faculty of Economics of the Vrije Universiteit at Amsterdam. She is Visiting Professor at Middlesex University in London, and President of the Nederlandstalig Genootschap voor Vergelijkende Studie van Opvoeding en Onderwijs (NGVO). She is member of the Supervisory Board of Kennisnet ICT op School, and the Advisory Board of the Dutch Knowledge Centre for Commissarissen (NKCC). She has over two decades of consultancy experience for companies, the European Commission and universities on issues such as corporate culture, e-learning and human resource management. She has authored two books and over 50 articles in international journals. *Correspondence*: Vrije Universiteit, FEWEB, room 3A-40, De Boelelaan 1105, 1081 HV Amsterdam, The Netherlands, E-mail: sbunt@feweb.vu.nl.

Michael CROSSLEY is Professor of Comparative and International Education at the University of Bristol, UK. He is Director of the Education in Small States Research Group, and Co-director of the Research Centre for International and Comparative Studies. He is the Editor of *Comparative Education*, and was Chair of the British Association for International and Comparative Education (BAICE) from 2002 to 2004. He is a member of the Editorial Board for *Compare* and the *International Journal of Educational Development*, and a founding Series Editor for the *Bristol Papers in Education: Comparative and International Studies*. In 2005 he was elected as an Academician by the UK Academy of Learned Societies for the Social Sciences. *Correspondence*: Research Centre for International and Comparative Studies, University of Bristol, Graduate School of Education, 35 Berkeley Square, Bristol BS8 1JA, UK. E-mail: m.crossley@bristol.ac.uk.

Michel DEBEAUVAIS co-founded the Institute of Economic and Social Development (IEDES, Sorbonne, France) in 1958, where he conducted research and teaching in the field of educational planning, human resources development and comparative education. He was also co-founder of the University of Vincennes (Paris VIII) in 1968, and of several professional societies: the Association des enseignants et chercheurs en sciences de l'éducation (AECSE, 1968), the Association francophone d'éducation comparée (AFEC, 1973), and the Groupe d'études sur l'éducation en Afrique (GRETAF, 1991). He was Director of UNESCO's International Institute for Educational Planning (IIEP, 1977-82). He was President of the World Council of Comparative Education Societies (WCCES, 1983-87), served as a co-opted member (1988-96), and was WCCES delegate to UNESCO and to the NGO-EFA working group at UNESCO (1989-98). *Correspondence*: 11 rue Pierre Demours, 75017 Paris, France. E-mail: michel.debeauvais@wanadoo.fr.

Erwin H. EPSTEIN is Professor of Cultural and Educational Policy Studies and Director of the Center for Comparative Education at Loyola University of Chicago, USA. He was President of the World Council of Comparative Education Societies (WCCES) from 1980 to 1983 and of the Comparative and International Education Society (CIES) in 1982/83, and was Editor of the *Comparative Education Review* from 1988 to 1998. He is the CIES Historian-Elect as of 2007. He served for several years as Chair of the WCCES Constitution Committee, and was responsible for major revisions in the Statutes and By-Laws. His research interests focus on comparative theory, history of comparative education, democratisation, and the impact of education in socio-culturally marginalised communities. *Correspondence*: Center for Comparative Education, Loyola University of Chicago, 820 N. Michigan Avenue, Chicago, Illinois 60611, USA. E-mail: eepstein@luc.edu.

Gregory P. FAIRBROTHER is an Assistant Professor at the Hong Kong Institute of Education. He is Vice-President of the Comparative Education Society of Hong Kong (CESHK), and was previously a member of the management committee of the Comparative Education Research Centre at the University of Hong Kong. He has taught at the secondary and tertiary level in Hong Kong and mainland China, and served as Student Advisor and Associate Director of the Hong Kong office of the Institute of International Education. His primary areas of research include citizenship education, political socialisation, education policy, and student political attitudes in Hong Kong and mainland China. *Correspondence*: Department of Mathematics, Science, Social Sciences & Technology, The Hong Kong Institute of Education, 10 Lo Ping Road, Tai Po, Hong Kong, China. E-mail: gfairbro@ied.edu.hk.

Ferran FERRER is Professor of Comparative Education in the Autonomous University of Barcelona, Spain. He has written books and articles in Spanish and international journals. He has also collaborated with international organisations. He is the past President of the Sociedad Española de Educación Comparada (SEEC), and is Professeur invité at the University of Fribourg. *Correspondence*: Departament de Pedagogia Sistemàtica i Social, Facultat de Ciències de l'Educació, Edifici G-6, Universitat Autònoma de Barcelona, 08193 Cerdanyola del Vallès, Spain. E-mail: Ferran.Ferrer@uab.es.

Christine FOX is a senior academic at the Faculty of Education, Wollongong University, Australia, and past President of the Australian and New Zealand Comparative and International Education Society (1994-96; 2000-02). In 1996, she was elected Vice-President of the World Council of Comparative Education Societies and in 2005, its seventh Secretary General. Her academic work has revolved around leadership in teacher education, intercultural learning, qualitative research, and postcolonial theory. She has worked for long periods in the Americas and the UK, and has extensive consultancy experience in the Asia-Pacific region for AusAID, the Asian Development Bank, the World Bank, and the Swedish International Development Cooperation Agency. *Correspondence*: Faculty of Education, University of Wollongong, NSW 2522, Australia. E-mail: cfox@uow.edu.au.

GU Mingyuan is President of the Chinese Society of Education, Honorary President of the Chinese Comparative Education Society (CCES), and Professor of Beijing Normal University, China. He has written extensively in the field of comparative education, with particular emphasis on aspects of cultural tradition and modernisation of education and on theory and methodology. *Correspondence:* Institute of International and Comparative Education, School of Education, Beijing Normal University, 19 Xinjiekouwai Dajie, Beijing 100875, China. E-mail: mygu@sina.com.

GUI Qin is a Professor at Capital Normal University, Beijing, China, where she has taught since 1994. She was the fourth candidate to earn a doctorate in Beijing Normal University in the field of comparative education under the supervision of Gu Mingyuan. She worked as a postdoctoral fellow from 1997 to 1999 in the Comparative Education Research Centre at the University of Hong Kong, and was a Visiting Professor in 2004/05 in Humboldt University of Berlin. *Correspondence*: College of Education, Capital Normal University, 83 Xisanhuan North Road, Beijing 100089, China. E-mail: guiqin@hotmail.com.

Anne HICKLING-HUDSON has studied and taught in the Caribbean, Britain, Hong Kong, Australia and the USA, and teaches socio-cultural and international education at the Queensland University of Technology (QUT), Australia. She was President of the World Council of Comparative Education Societies from 2001 to 2004. She is a past President of the Australian and New Zealand Comparative and International Education Society (1997-98), an elected Board member of the Comparative and International Education Society (1998-2001), and a founding member of the Australian Association of Caribbean Studies. She has been a pioneer in applying postcolonial theory to the comparative analysis of educational policy and national development, teacher education and the intercultural curriculum. She is also leading a cross-cultural research study on how educators are helping to counter the crisis of HIV/AIDS. *Correspondence*: School of Cultural and Language Studies in Education, Queensland University of Technology, Kelvin Grove, Queensland 4059, Australia. E-mail: a.hudson@qut.edu.au.

Józef KUŻMA is Professor of Humanities at Cracow Pedagogical University, Poland. He completed his Masters at the Agricultural University in Sankt Petersburg (1958), and his pedagogical studies in Warsaw (1963). He is author of a theory of the school and creator of the term 'scholiology'. He has published over 200 works, mainly monographs and scientific articles. He was Dean of the Faculty of Pedagogics and Rural Culture at Podlaska Academy, and the Faculty of Pedagogics at Cracow Pedagogical University. He is an active member of the Polish Comparative Education Society (PCES). *Correspondence*: ul. Brazownicza 2a/2, 30-142 Cracow, Poland. E-mail: jozkuz@neostrada.pl.

KWON Dong-Taik is an Assistant Professor in the Korea National University of Education, South Korea. He served as Secretary of the 11th World Congress of Comparative Education Societies held in Chungbuk, Korea, in 2001. In 2004, he worked as a postdoctoral fellow in the Comparative Education Research Centre at the University of Hong Kong. His teaching and research have focused on elementary education, educational leadership and organisation. *Correspondence*: Department of Education, Korea National University of Education, San 7, Darak-ri, Gangnae-myeon, Cheongwon-gun, Chungbuk 363-791, South Korea. E-mail: kdt@knue.ac.kr.

LEE Byung-Jin is Emeritus Professor in the Korea National University of Education, South Korea. He was a founding member of the Comparative Education Society of Asia (CESA) and has served as its President. He has also been President of the Korean Comparative Education Society (KCES) for several terms. His primary areas of research are elementary education, educational leadership, and teacher education. *Correspondence*: Department of Education, Korea National University of Education, San 7, Darak-ri, Gangnae-myeon, Cheongwon-gun, Chungbuk 363-791, South Korea. E-mail: leebj@knue.ac.kr.

Suzanne MAJHANOVICH is Professor of Education and Languages in the Faculty of Education at the University of Western Ontario, Canada, where she teaches courses on theories of education, language policies, and issues in language acquisition and second-language teaching and learning. Her research interests include educational restructuring, decentralisation, and privatisation, as well as implications of language policies on minority language groups. She is a former President of the Comparative and International Education Society of Canada (CIESC), and Editor of the society's journal *Canadian and International Education*. She is also the Chair of the World Council of Comparative Education Societies (WCCES) Publications Standing Committee. *Correspondence*: Faculty of Education, The University of Western Ontario, 1137 Western Road, London, Ontario, Canada N6G 1G7. E-mail: smajhano@uwo.ca.

Maria MANZON is a doctoral student in comparative education at the Faculty of Education of the University of Hong Kong. She is a member of the management committee of the Comparative Education Research Centre (CERC) at the University of Hong Kong, and was Assistant Secretary General of the World Council of Comparative Education Societies (WCCES) in 2005. She initially studied in the Philippines and in Italy, and then graduated with distinction from the MEd programme in Comparative Education at the University of Hong Kong. She has published on theory and methodology in comparative education, and on home-school partnerships. *Correspondence*: Comparative Education Research Centre, Faculty of Education, The University of Hong Kong, Pokfulam Road, Hong Kong, China. E-mail: mimanzon@hku.hk.

Vandra MASEMANN is an anthropologist who has worked in the fields of comparative education, multicultural and anti-racist education, and international and global education. She has devoted much of her career to advocating the uses of ethnographic and other qualitative methods in comparative education. She has taught at the University of Toronto, the University of Wisconsin-Madison, the University of Pittsburgh, the State University of New York at Buffalo, and the Florida State University, and is presently Adjunct Associate Professor at the Ontario Institute for Studies in Education at the University of Toronto. She was President of the World Council of Comparative Education Societies (1987-91) and its Secretary General (1996-2000). She was also President of the Comparative and International Education Society (1990-91), and the Comparative and International Education Society of Canada (1985-87). *Correspondence*: Comparative and International Education Centre, Room 7-107, OISE/UT, 252 Bloor Street West, Toronto, Ontario, Canada M5S 1V6. E-mail: masemann@interlog.com.

Dimitrios MATTHEOU is Professor of Comparative and International Education, and Director of the University of Athens Center of Comparative Education, International Education Policy and Communication. He is President of the Greek Comparative Education Society (GCES) and Vice-President of the Comparative Education Society in Europe (CESE). He is Editor of the Journal *Comparative and International Education Review*. He is author and editor of several books in Greek. He has also published extensively in academic journals and in volumes in Greek and in English, some of which have been translated into French, Spanish, German and Portuguese. *Cor-*

respondence: 20 Ippokratous Str., 106 80 Athens, Greece. E-mail: dmatthe
@cc.uoa.gr.

Wolfgang MITTER is Emeritus Professor of Education at the German Institute for
International Educational Research (DIPF) and Johann Wolfgang Goethe-
University of Frankfurt am Main, Germany. He was Head of Department
(1972-98) and Director (1978-81; 1988-95) of the DIPF. He was Chairman
of the Kommission für Vergleichende Erziehungswissenschaft in der
Deutschen Gesellschaft für Erziehungswissenschaft (1970-72; 1987-89),
and President of the Comparative Education Society in Europe (1981-85),
the World Council of Comparative Education Societies (1991-96), and the
World Association for Educational Research (1997-2000). He is a member
of the Academia Europaea and the Russian Academy of Education. He has
led research projects on comparative topics, particularly on education in
Eastern and Central Europe, and has published extensively on theoretical
aspects of comparative education, politics of education and history of education. *Correspondence*: DIPF, Schloss-Strasse 29, D-60486 Frankfurt am
Main, Germany. E-mail: mitter@dipf.de.

Kengo MOCHIDA is Professor of Comparative Education in Kyushu University,
Japan. He is President of the Japan Comparative Education Society (JCES)
and of the Comparative Education Society of Asia (CESA). He has been
Secretary General of the CESA from 1995 until 2000. His research in
comparative education has focused on secondary education reform in
England. *Correspondence:* School of Education, Kyushu University,
6-19-1, Hakozaki, Higashi-ku, 821-8581 Japan. E-mail: kengoedu@
mbox.nc.kyushu-u.ac.jp

Luis M. NAYA is Senior Lecturer in Comparative Education at the University of
the Basque Country (EHU-UPV). He was Secretary of the Sociedad
Española de Educación Comparada (SEEC) from 2002 to 2006, is the
Webmaster of the SEEC, and was the President of the 10th National
Congress of the SEEC held in San Sebastian, Spain in September 2006. His
research focuses on the use of ICTs, minority languages and the rights of
children. *Correspondence*: Department of Theory and History of Education,
Universidad del País Vasco/Euskal Herriko Unibertsitatea, Avda de Tolosa,
70. P.B. 1249, 20018 Donostia/San Sebastián, Spain. E-mail: luisma.naya@
ehu.es.

Akira NINOMIYA is Professor of Comparative and International Education and
Vice-President for International Relations at Hiroshima University, Japan.
In 1997, he was Director of the Center for the Study of International Co-
operation in Education of the same university, after which he became a
visiting professor at Seton Hall University, New Jersey, USA (1997-2004).
He has been Chair of the Finance and Fund-Raising Standing Committee
(2003-06) of the World Council of Comparative Education Societies
(WCCES). He is also a Board Member of the Japan Comparative Education
Society (JCES), the Japan Educational Research Society, the Japan Society
for Education for International Understanding, and the Japan Society for
Educational Systems. His book publications have focused on comparative

and international education and moral education in Japan, the USA and other contexts. *Correspondence*: Kagamiyama 1-1-1, Higashi-Hiroshima, 739-8524 Hiroshima, Japan. E-mail: animiya@hiroshima-u.ac.jp.

Nikolay POPOV is Professor of Comparative Education at Sofia University, Bulgaria. He is author of 15 books and 90 articles in the field of comparative education. In 1986 he obtained his Master's degrees in Education and Philosophy from Sofia University, and in 1990 his first doctorate degree. He founded the Bulgarian Comparative Education Society (BCES) in 1991, and since then has been its President. In 2002, he obtained his second doctorate in education sciences. Throughout his research career, he has undertaken studies on the history and methodology of comparative education, administration and finance of education systems worldwide, primary and secondary school curricula, school structures, higher education, and national education policies and reforms. *Correspondence*: Sofia University, Faculty of Primary and Preschool Education, Blvd Shipchenski prohod 69 A, 1574 Sofia, Bulgaria. E-mail: nikolaip@bgcell.net.

Elizabeth Sherman SWING is an Honorary Fellow of the US-based Comparative and International Education Society (CIES) and is CIES Historian (1999-2008). She is also Professor Emerita of Education at Saint Joseph's University, Philadelphia, USA. In 1990 she was named *Ridder in de Kroonorde* (Knight in the Order of the Crown) for research on the Belgian language controversy. *Correspondence*: 3500 West Chester Pike, J 303, Newtown Square, PA 19073, USA. E-mail: eswing1@verizon.net.

Marta Luz SISSON DE CASTRO is Professor of Education at the Pontificia Universidade Católica do Rio Grande do Sul, Graduate School of Education, Brazil. She is also a researcher of the National Council for Scientific and Technological Development, Brazil. She obtained a Master's degree in Human Development from the University of Maryland (1976), and a doctorate from Boston University (1987). She then undertook postdoctoral work (1988-89) at Indiana University, as a Capes-Fulbright scholar. Her main research area is in educational administration. She was Vice-President for the South Region of the ANPAE (National Association of Policies and Education Administration) in Brazil, and is the President of the Sociedade Brasileira de Educação Comparada (SBEC). *Correspondence*: Pós- Graduação em Educação, Pontificia Universidade Católica do Rio Grande do Sul, Av. Ipiranga 6681 – CEP 90619-900 Porto Alegre RS, Brazil. E-mail: msisson@pucrs.br.

Crain SOUDIEN is Professor in and Director of the School of Education at the University of Cape Town, South Africa, and teaches in the fields of Sociology and History of Education. He has published over 80 articles, reviews, and chapters in the areas of race, culture, educational policy, comparative education, educational change, public history and popular culture. He was educated at the University of Cape Town, South Africa and holds a PhD from the State University of New York at Buffalo, USA. He is a founder member of the Southern African Comparative and History of Education Society (SACHES) and a past Vice-President of the World Council of

Comparative Education Societies (WCCES). *Correspondence*: Humanities Graduate School Building, University of Cape Town, Private Bag X3, Rondebosch 7701, South Africa. E-mail: Crain.Soudien@uct.ac.za.

Margaret B. SUTHERLAND is Professor Emeritus of Education, University of Leeds, UK. She is an honorary member of the British Association for International and Comparative Education (BAICE), the Comparative Education Society in Europe (CESE), and the Association francophone d'éducation comparée (AFEC). She is a past President of AFEC (1991-93) and was Chair (1968-70) and President (1976) of the British Section of the CESE. She has also served on various committees of the World Council of Comparative Education Societies (WCCES) and was a co-opted member (1999-2002) of its Executive Committee. *Correspondence*: 46 The Scores, St. Andrews KY 16 9AS, Scotland, UK. E-mail: mb.sutherland@virgin.net.

Henk VAN DAELE was Professor at the Department of Comparative Education and History of Education at the Universiteit Gent, Belgium and part-time professor of comparative education at the Vrije Universiteit Brussels until his retirement in 1995. During 1995/96 he was a visiting professor at the College of Europe in Bruges, Belgium. He has published extensively on the history of education and comparative education. He was Secretary-Treasurer (1977-88) and President (1988-92) of the Comparative Education Society in Europe (CESE), President (1990-95) of the Dutch-speaking Society of Comparative Education (NGVO), and Vice-President (1994-2000) of the Association francophone d'éducation comparée (AFEC). He was also a member of the Belgian National Commission of UNESCO. Since 1999, Van daele has been a male-breast-cancer survivor. On this topic he published a book. He is an active member of several cancer advocacy groups. *Correspondence*: Amerikalei 13 bus 17, B-2000 Antwerpen, Belgium. E-mail: henk.vandaele@pandora.be.

Eliška WALTEROVÁ is Associate Professor of Education and Director of the Institute for Educational Research and Development of the Faculty of Education at Charles University in Prague, Czech Republic. Her research focuses on European studies in education, education reforms, education policies, curriculum development and methodology. *Correspondence*: Institute for Educational Research and Development, Charles University, Faculty of Education, Myslíkova 7, 110 00 Prague 1, Czech Republic. E-mail: ewa@uvrv.pedf.cuni.cz.

Dietmar WATERKAMP has been Professor of Comparative Education at the University of Technology at Dresden, Germany since 1993. He obtained his PhD and Habilitation at Ruhr-University in Bochum. He has been teaching as a visiting professor in Regensburg and Greifswald. From 2002 to 2005, he was President of the Sektion International und Interkulturell Vergleichende Erziehungswissenschaft in der Deutschen Gesellschaft für Erziehungswissenschaft (SIIVEDGE), and made contributions to the Comparative Education Society in Europe (CESE) and the World Council of Comparative Education Societies (WCCES). His publications started with analyses of the East German education system and later focused on comparative topics. In 2006 he published a textbook on comparative education. *Correspondence*: Technische Universitaet Dresden. Fakultaet Erziehungs-wissenschaften. D-01062 Dresden, Germany. E-mail: Dietmar. Waterkamp@ tu-dresden.de.

Keith WATSON is Emeritus Professor of Comparative and International Education at the University of Reading, UK, where he was Director of the Centre for International Studies in Education Management and Training (1990-2001). He previously served with the British Council for 11 years in different international posts. He was Editor-in-Chief of the *International Journal of Educational Development* (1990-2006); Chair of the UK Forum for International Education and Training (1992-99); and was a founder member of the Oxford International Conferences on Education and Development. He was the last President of the British Comparative and International Education Society (1996-97), having previously been Secretary (1975-80), Vice-Chairman (1980-82), and Chairman (1982-84). *Correspondence*: Institute of Education, University of Reading, Bulmershe Court, Reading RG6 1HY, UK. E-mail: j.k.p.watson@reading.ac.uk.

David N. WILSON was President of the World Council of Comparative Education Societies (WCCES) from 1996 to 2001. Prior to that, he was Chair of the Finance Standing Committee. He was also President of the Comparative and International Society of Canada (CIESC) and of the Comparative and International Education Society (CIES). During an early part of his career, he attended the 1st World Congress of Comparative Education Societies in Ottawa, Canada (1970). For several decades he taught at the Ontario Institute for Studies in Education (OISE) in Toronto, Canada. He also had extensive consultancy experience for organisations such as the Asian Development Bank, UNESCO and the World Bank. He died in 2006 aged 68.

WONG Suk-Ying received her PhD from Stanford University, USA, and was a recipient of the National Academy of Education Spencer Fellowship award. She is Associate Professor of Sociology at the Chinese University of Hong Kong. Her primary research interests involve the sociology of curriculum and comparative institutions. Her research projects include a comparative study on the role of social studies education in the construction of modern citizenship and national identity formation. She is past President of the Comparative Education Society of Hong Kong (CESHK) and past Co-President of the Comparative Education Society of Asia (CESA). *Correspondence*: Department of Sociology, The Chinese University of Hong Kong, Sino Building, Shatin, Hong Kong, China. E-mail: sukyingwong@ cuhk.edu.hk

ZHANG Lanlin graduated in 2005 from the doctoral program at the Faculty of Education of the University of Western Ontario, in London, Canada. His research interests include international education, cross cultural language education, English as a Second Language theory, and Chinese culture. *Correspondence*: 11-532 Platt's Lane, London, Ontario, Canada N6G 3A8. E-mail: llzhangg@yahoo.com.

Index

as a subject, 77, 81, 190, 204, 219,
271-2, 279, 324, 344
centres, 10, 50, 217-8, 223, 247, 270,
278, 302, 305, 339
courses/programmes, 71, 161, 175,
178, 180, 228-9, 246-7, 252, 265,
271, 280, 294, 305, 328, 341, 346
discipline, 96, 100, 102, 117, 130,
148, 176, 181, 197, 228, 233, 236,
238, 268-70, 274, 276, 285, 353,
360
field of study, 78, 126, 137, 148,
159, 224, 248, 254, 266, 269, 273,
284, 306, 336, 359
institutes, 130, 229
institutionalisation of, 247, 343-5
interdisciplinary character of, 3, 113,
123, 144, 152, 259, 271, 295, 339
research, 69-70, 122, 143, 158, 186,
198, 238, 247, 281, 310-1, 314,
328, 331
shape, 141, 159, 247, 286, 340, 359
teaching of, 79, 81, 95-6, 117, 130-1,
172, 184, 190, 220, 240, 310,
326-7
textbook, 78, 144, 184, 227-8, 232-3,
264, 301, 303, 352
theory of, 78, 108-9, 126, 184, 237-
8, 304
Comparative Education Research Centre (CERC), 67, 76, 235, 251-2, 310
CERCular (CERC's newsletter), 76,
235
comparative education societies
language-based, 1, 7, 15, 27, 85, 117,
345, 357
national, 1, 4, 6, 15, 43, 57, 66, 118-
9, 159, 190-201, 311, 324-5, 330,
332, 342, 344-5, 347, 349, 357
regional, 1, 4, 14-5, 85, 148, 311,
315, 342, 344-5, 357
sub-national, 1, 7, 26-7, 312
Comparative Education Society (CES),
13, 116, 131, 170, 200, 202, 341
Comparative Education Society in
Europe (CESE), 4-5, 8, 10, 13, 15,
18, 25-6, 29, 31, 33, 42, 50, 52-3, 55,
72-6, 85, 88-9, 109, 116-27, 142,
149-50, 155, 162, 167, 172, 195-6,
200, 210-1, 213, 215-6, 218, 235,
259-60, 280, 297, 302, 309, 316, 318,

322, 325-7, 331, 341-3, 345, 347,
349-50, 354-8
British Section of, 19, 117, 155-6,
158-61, 164-6, 190, 325, 342-3,
349-50, 354-5
Italian Section of, 4, 45, 325-6, 342-
3, 347, 355
German Section of, 150, 342-3, 349
Sections of, 19, 117, 125, 325, 343,
354
Comparative Education Society of Asia
(CESA), 5, 66, 85, 89, 183, 185-7,
236, 253, 309-15, 321, 323, 342,
344-5, 356-9
Comparative Education Society of
Hong Kong (CESHK), 5, 89, 245-55,
311, 342, 358
Comparative Education Society of India (CESI), 5, 22, 24, 26, 65, 79,
324-5, 334, 344
Congo, Republic of, 98
Constitution (society's), 20-1, 63, 75,
85, 110, 119, 156, 164-5, 172, 205-6,
245, 256, 310-1, 315 *see also*
WCCES
consultants, 163, 329
Council of Europe, 53, 60, 118, 263-4,
356
Council on Comparative Education of
Kazakhstan (CCEK), 5, 84, 88, 332,
334
countries
capitalist, 144, 149, 272
developed, 183, 261, 270
developing, 2, 15, 31, 34-5, 71-2, 81,
144-5, 148-50, 160-1, 163, 172,
174, 201, 258
Eastern European, 144
English-speaking/Anglophone, 78,
89, 351
European, 25, 118, 130, 141, 196,
257, 259, 269, 271, 273, 281, 294,
300-1
former socialist, 278
French-speaking/Francophone, 77,
80, 195-6, 344
industrialised, 2, 150, 160, 349
less developed, 136-7, 233, 289
post-communist, 263
post-socialist, 262, 278, 280, 345
Slavonic, 275

CERC Studies in Comparative Education 19

Comparative Education Research
Approaches and Methods

Edited by
Mark Bray
Bob Adamson
Mark Mason

Publishers: Comparative Education Research Centre and Springer
ISBN: 978-962-8093-53-3
Date: 2007; 444 pages
Price: HK$250 / US$38

Approaches and methods in comparative education research are of obvious importance, but do not always receive adequate attention. This book contributes new insights within the longstanding traditions of the field.

A particular feature is the focus on different units of analysis. Individual chapters compare places, systems, times, cultures, values, policies, curricula and other units. These chapters are contextualised within broader analytical frameworks which identify the purposes and strengths of the field. The book includes a focus on intra-national as well as cross-national comparisons, and highlights the value of approaching themes from different angles. The book will be of great value not only to producers of comparative education research but also to consumers who wish to understand more thoroughly the parameters and value of the field.

The editors: *Mark Bray* is Director of the UNESCO International Institute for Educational Planning, in Paris; *Bob Adamson* is Associate Professor in the Hong Kong Institute of Education; and *Mark Mason* is Associate Professor in the Faculty of Education at the University of Hong Kong. They have all been Presidents of the Comparative Education Society of Hong Kong (CESHK), and Directors of the Comparative Education Research Centre (CERC) at the University of Hong Kong. They have also written extensively in the field of comparative education with reference to multiple domains and cultures.

More details: www.hku.hk/cerc/Publications/publications.htm

CERC Studies in Comparative Education 20

Changing Education
Leadership, Innovation and Development in a Globalizing Asia Pacific

Edited by
Peter D. Hershock
Mark Mason
John Hawkins

Publishers: Comparative Education Research Centre and Springer
ISBN: 978-962-8093-54-0
Date: 2007; 348 pages
Price: HK$200 / US$32

This book responds to the growing unease of educators and non-educators alike about the inadequacy of most current educational systems and programs to meet sufficiently the demands of fast changing societies. These systems and programs evolved and were developed in and for societies that have long been transformed, and yet no parallel transformation has taken place in the education systems they spawned. In the last twenty years or so, other sectors of society, such as transportation and communications systems, have radically changed the way they operate, but education has remained essentially the same. There is no doubt: education needs to change.

To those ready to accept this challenge, this book represents a welcome guide. Unlike most books on educational policy, this volume does not focus on improving existing educational systems but on changing them altogether. Its focus is not on doing things better, but on doing better things; not on doing things right, but on doing the right things to prepare students for a fast changing interdependent world.

Peter D. Hershock is an Educational Specialist and Coordinator of the Asian Studies Development Program at the East-West Center in Honolulu, Hawaii. He is trained in both Western and Asian philosophy, with a specialization in Buddhist philosophy.

Mark Mason is Associate Professor in Philosophy and Educational Studies in the Faculty of Education at the University of Hong Kong, where he is also Director of the Comparative Education Research Centre (CERC).

John N. Hawkins is a Professor in the Graduate School of Education and Information Studies at the University of California, Los Angeles. He is Director of the Center for International and Development Education at UCLA, where he served for twelve years as Dean of International Studies.

More details: www.hku.hk/cerc/Publications/publications.htm